*Reforming Memory: Essays on South African Church and Theological History*

Published by AFRICAN SUN MeDIA under the SUN MeDIA imprint.

All rights reserved.

Copyright © 2017 AFRCAN SUN MeDIA and Robert Vosloo

No part of this book May be reproduced or transmitted in any form or by any electronic, photographic or mechanical means, including photocopying and recording on record, tape or laser disk, on microfilm, via the Internet, by e-mail, or by any other information storage and retrieval system, without prior written permission by the publisher.

Views expressed in this publication do not necessarily reflect those of the publisher.

First edition 2017
ISBN 978-1-928314-36-3
ISBN 978-1-928314-37-0 (e-book)
DOI: 10.18820/9781928314370

Set in Bembo 11/14
Cover design and typesetting by AFRICAN SUN MeDIA.
Cover image: D.H. Herberger, History and Chronos, ca. 1750, Wiblingen Monastery, Ulm, Germany.
Photo: Atelier Juliane Zitzlsperger.

SUN MeDIA is an imprint of AFRICAN SUN MeDIA. Academic and prescribed works are published under this imprint in print and electronic format. This publication May be ordered directly from www.sun-e-shop.co.za.

Produced by AFRICAN SUN MeDIA.

www.africansunmedia.co.za
africansunmedia.snapplify.com (e-books)
www.sun-e-shop.co.za

Volume XII in the Beyers Naudé Centre Series on Public Theology

# REFORMING MEMORY

## ESSAYS ON SOUTH AFRICAN CHURCH AND THEOLOGICAL HISTORY

Robert Vosloo

*For Dion Forster, Nico Koopman, Nadia Marais, Retief Müller,
Mary-Anne Plaatjies-Van Huffel, Wilma Riekert, and Dirkie Smit;*

*colleagues in recent years in the Department of Systematic Theology and
Ecclesiology at the Faculty of Theology, Stellenbosch University;*

*with much appreciation and gratitude for our collegiality and friendship,
and for making our work of doing theology together so joyful*

The same events are found to signify glory for some, humiliation for others. To their celebration, on the one hand, corresponds their execration, on the other. It is in this way that real and symbolic wounds are stored in the archives of collective memory.

Paul Ricoeur, Memory, *History, Forgetting*, p. 82.


Self-styled 'Traditionalists' often forget that the nature of tradition is not that of a humanly manufactured mechanical or architectural structure with a constant outline and form, but rather that of a plant, pulsing with life and continually changing shape while keeping the same ultimate identity.

Diarmand MacCoulloch, *A History of Christianity*, pp. 7-8.


Waar die stryd die afgelope veertig jaar hoofsaaklik om die deurbreking van die volkskerkkarakter van die NG Kerk gegaan het, sal dit in die volgende dekades waarskynlik om die uitbouing van die eenheid van die NG familie van kerke gaan, sowel as om die bewaring van die gereformeerde karakter van hierdie kerke en hulle profetiese roeping in die samelewing.

[While the struggle of the past forty years was mainly to challenge the way in which the Dutch Reformed Church was a *volkskerk*, the following decades will probably involve the development of unity within the Dutch Reformed family of churches, as well as the conservation of the Reformed character of these churches and their prophetic role in society].

Willie Jonker, *Selfs die kerk kan verander [Even the Church can Change]*, p. 221.

# CONTENTS

INTRODUCTION . . . . . . . . . . . . . . . . . . . . . . . . . . . . . . . . . . . . . . . . . . ix

## PART 1 – IN SEARCH OF A RESPONSIBLE HISTORICAL HERMENEUTIC

1  On forgetting: Historical injustice and the art of forgetting . . . . . . . . . . . .  3
2  On history: The writing of history as remedy or poison? . . . . . . . . . . . . . 15
3  On remembering: Memory, history, and justice . . . . . . . . . . . . . . . . . . . 25
4  On the archive: Archiving otherwise . . . . . . . . . . . . . . . . . . . . . . . . . . . 37
5  On tradition: Reforming tradition? . . . . . . . . . . . . . . . . . . . . . . . . . . . . 51
6  On doing Church history: Five theses . . . . . . . . . . . . . . . . . . . . . . . . . . 65
7  On commemorating: Remembering the Reformation after 500 years . . . 77

## PART 2 – REVISITING SOME EPISODES IN THE HISTORY OF THE DUTCH REFORMED CHURCH (1916-1960)

8  On poverty: The Dutch Reformed Church and 'the poor white problem' . . . . . . . . . . . . . . . . . . . . . . . . . . . . . . . . . . . . . . . . . . . 91
9  On urbanisation: The Dutch Reformed Church and the city . . . . . . . . . 105
10 On division: The Dutch Reformed Church and some responses to the Second World War . . . . . . . . . . . . . . . . . . . . . . . . . . . . . . . . . . 115
11 On reading Scripture: The Dutch Reformed Church and the biblical justification of apartheid . . . . . . . . . . . . . . . . . . . . . . . . . . . . . 127
12 On ecumenism: The Dutch Reformed Church, Beyers Naudé and the ghost of Cottesloe . . . . . . . . . . . . . . . . . . . . . . . . . . . . . . . . . . . . 139

## PART 3 – ENGAGING REFORMED THEOLOGIANS

13 On Calvin's theological heritage in South Africa: Engaging an ambivalent, contested and promising legacy . . . . . . . . . . . . . . . . . . . . 155
14 On the displaced Calvin: 'Refugee reality' as a lens to examine Calvin's life, theology and legacy . . . . . . . . . . . . . . . . . . . . . . . . . . . . 175

| 15 | On Calvin and the mirror of the stranger: 'Refugee reality' and the gift of recognition | 189 |
| 16 | On Beyers Naudé: Revisiting a legacy of hospitality and truth-telling | 201 |
| 17 | On Dirkie Smit: Take, read ... interpret, confess | 209 |
| 18 | For John de Gruchy: Democracy is coming to the RSA | 225 |

## PART 4 – REVISITING REFORMED PRACTICES AND CONFESSIONAL DOCUMENTS

| 19 | On the Lord's Supper: The 'welcome table', exclusion and the Reformed tradition | 239 |
| 20 | On theological education: Calvin, the Academy of Geneva and 150 years of theology at Stellenbosch | 255 |
| 21 | On the Heidelberg Catechism: Remembering a 16th-century Reformed confession in South Africa today | 267 |
| 22 | On the Belhar Confession: Remarks on the reception of a 20th century confessional document in the Dutch Reformed Church | 277 |

# INTRODUCTION

*Reforming Memory* – as the title suggests – combines an interest in the notion of "memory" with an interest in (South African) Reformed theology and history. The title, one might add, has a double meaning in the sense that the book is based on the belief that, although we should acknowledge the fragility of memory (also as a way to access the past), we should affirm the remarkable ability of memory to reform and transform our identity. It provides the resources for us to face the present and re-imagine the future. But memory does not merely have the power to form or reform identity. Our memories and ways of remembering are often marked by trauma and violence. We are also scarred by the way we recollect the past, and we often wound others through the way in which we narrate or construct the past. Memory therefore does not merely have a reforming capacity; it is itself in need of reformation and transformation. Memory too is in need of healing and redemption; it too is in need of being touched by grace.

The 22 essays collected in this book were all written after I had been appointed as a lecturer in the Department of Systematic Theology and Ecclesiology at the Faculty of Theology, Stellenbosch University in 2005. My teaching duties at this ecumenical faculty with Reformed roots from the outset included courses on the 16th-century Reformations as well as on South African church and theological history. Especially in the class on South African church history, it soon became evident that students from the different partner churches (including from churches that shared the same Reformed heritage) had very different intellectual and emotional responses to figures, events, doctrines and documents from the past. It was clear that, even though there was a common history, this shared history was also a deeply divided and ambivalent history. The same figures were heroes for some and villains for others; the same events were seen by some as high points worth remembering and commemorating, while for others they pointed to painful realities that one should rather forget; and the same documents and doctrines were interpreted by some as irrelevant or dangerous, while others saw them as liberating and life-giving. Yet this process of grappling together with a shared and divisive past also brought home the insight that the histories (and maybe also the futures) of the respected churches and faith traditions are inextricably interwoven. Hence the continuous and urgent need arises to ask the question: What does a responsible recollection and representation of our shared – but also ambivalent and devisive – past entail?

It is this question that lies at the heart of the essays collected in the first section under the heading "In search of a responsible historical hermeneutic". The basic assumption is that the sources and documents through which we have access to the past (including for Reformed historiography) are not self-evident and do not speak for themselves. They are in need of interpretation, and our interpretations and appropriations are determined by the place from where we read and write, hear and speak. Hence hermeneutics is not only extremely important for our reading of Scripture or contemporary texts, but also for our engagement with the past. In this regard, a book by the French philosopher Paul Ricoeur entitled *Memory,*

## INTRODUCTION

*History, Forgetting* became especially formative for my thinking on memory and historical methodology.[1] The influence of Ricoeur's work will be evident throughout *Reforming Memory*. The first three essays, respectively on "forgetting", "history" and "memory", will deal in fact with the notions referred to in the title of Ricoeur's book, albeit in reverse order.

This is followed by essays that engage with concepts such as "the archive", "tradition" and "commemoration". The essay on "the archive", which draws on the thinking of Jacques Derrida, suggests – as do several of the other essays – that remembering, archiving and interpreting are not merely interconnected, but must also not be separated from notions of justice and a vision of the future. Hence the need for an ethics of memory, an ethic that is "other-wise" and future-oriented. The historical hermeneutic, furthermore, that is argued for throughout these essays, and especially in the essay "Reforming tradition", requires an understanding of tradition as a "living tradition", to use the phrase of the moral philosopher Alasdair MacIntyre. Applied to the Reformed tradition, this means that Reformed identity is not something static or fixed, a mere repetition of timeless truths from the past, but rather that it is fundamentally determined by a continuous and creative process of risking new articulations to express the deep-seated convictions that lie at the heart of the tradition. Wallace Alston and Michael Welker express this idea well in the Editorial Introduction to the book *Reformed Theology: Identity and Ecumenicity*: "It is characteristic of Reformed theology to be in a constant search for Reformed identity and to define this identity time and time again".[2] This process, moreover, is not arbitrary; rather, it is situated "in response to the word of God and in the midst of the challenges of the world".[3] The final essay in the first section of the book deals with "commemoration", partly in conversation with the work of Tzvetan Todorov. This essay reminds us of the fact that commemorations are not immune to the abuses of memory, and with this emphasis in mind the essay attends to some challenges for the 500th anniversary of the Protestant Reformation(s), also in the light of the way in which the Reformation was commemorated by the Dutch Reformed Church in South Africa in the past.

The second part of *Reforming Memory*, revisits more specifically some episodes in the history of the Dutch Reformed Church in the 20th century, roughly between 1916 and 1960. In 1916 an important conference on "the poor white question" was held in Cradock and this was followed by further conferences and inquiries, culminating in the Carnegie report of 1932, with national and church conferences following in its wake. The first article in this section takes a closer look at the Dutch Reformed Church's role in this regard, and indicates how "the poor white question" was tightly connected with what was described as "the native question". The so-called "native question" was also intertwined with the way in which the Dutch Reformed Church responded to the challenges of white urbanisation in the 1940s, or so the next essay argues. Another challenge for the Dutch Reformed Church in the 1940s, addressed in another essay, was the divisions among some of its members as a result of the fact that some supported South Africa's participation in the Second

---

1 See Ricoeur, P, *Memory, History, Forgetting* (Chicago: University of Chicago Press), 2004.
2 Alston, W M and Welker, M (eds.), *Reformed Theology: Identity and Ecumenicity* (Grand Rapids: Eerdmans, 2003), x.
3 Alston and Welker, *Reformed Theology*, x.

World War, while others saw it as a betrayal to support Britain in the light of the memories of the Anglo-Boer War. During the 1940s theologians from Reformed churches also put forward arguments for the biblical justification for the policy and practice of apartheid. In the essay that takes a closer look at these arguments, as well as at the voices critical of such an endeavor, an attempt is made to chart and interpret the biblical justification of apartheid and the critique of it by looking at some representative figures and texts. The question of the historical hermeneutic at work in this regard receives special attention. The final essay in this section revisits an event that continues to function as a "site of memory" in Reformed church circles, namely the Cottesloe consultation that took place in December 1960 and that was convened by the World Council of Churches as a direct result of the Sharpeville massacre earlier that year. Special attention is given to the role of Beyers Naudé, an influential Reformed pastor who subsequently played a pivotal role in the church struggle against apartheid.

The third section of this book engages with specific Reformed theologians. The first three essays focus on the 16th-century Protestant Reformer John Calvin. In 2009 the 500th anniversary of Calvin's birth was celebrated worldwide. In South Africa too several publications, conferences and commemorative events celebrated Calvin's life and work. The first essay attends to Calvin's (contested) reception and legacy in South Africa, and points to the promise of his thought for a theological response to some of the challenges still facing us today, such as polarisation, migration and economic inequality. This is followed by an essay that looks at the fact that Calvin was himself a refugee who ministered mostly to other refugees. The question is asked whether this fact can offer us a lens to understand his theology anew. The next, and related, essay looks at Calvin's thought-provoking idea that the stranger and even the enemy carry with them a mirror that reminds us that we share a common humanity, that we are "of the same flesh", and that all humans have an inalienable dignity because we are created in the image of God. The next three articles engage with three figures associated with the Reformed tradition who have been influential in different ways in my own theological journey, namely Beyers Naudé, Dirkie Smit and John de Gruchy. The essay on Dirkie Smit was originally written in Afrikaans and was part of a journal publication that celebrated his 55th birthday. This essay – presented here in English translation – deals with the hermeneutical commitments that in my view undergird his remarkable theological oeuvre. The essay dedicated to John de Gruchy focuses in part on De Gruchy's vital distinction between a democratic system and a democratic vision, and makes some comments on political theology drawing on insights from De Gruchy's (as well as Derrida's) thinking.

The final section of this book, "Remembering Reformed practices and documents", opens with two essays that deal respectively with the Lord's Supper and theological education, two practices that are associated with what constitutes the core of Reformed identity. The essay on the Lord's Supper asks what it means to see the Lord's Supper as a feast of unconditional hospitality, also given histories of Eucharistic exclusion on the grounds of race and class. And: How can one affirm this radical hospitality while at the same time protecting the integrity of the meal as a disciplined practice? The essay on theological education was written with a view to the celebration of 150 years of theological education at Stellenbosch (in 2009). The essay makes some remarks about theological education in the light of the founding history of the theological seminary at Stellenbosch as well as of the Academy of Geneva, founded by Calvin in 1559, with Theodore Beza as the first rector. The last two essays deal respectively with two important confession documents in Reformed memory, namely the Heidelberg Catechism (1563) and the Belhar Confession (1982, 1986). In 2013 the 450th anniversary of the Heidelberg Catechism was commemorated, and the essay presented here addresses the question (which was also the theme of an international conference at Stellenbosch): "What does it mean to remember the Heidelberg Catechism in South Africa today?" The final essay looks at the reception of the Belhar Confession in the Dutch Reformed Church. The Belhar Confession, which emerged out of the theological struggles in apartheid South Africa in the 1980s, was accepted as a draft confession in 1982 and officially adopted as the fourth confession in 1986 by the then Dutch Reformed Mission Church. This essay traces some of the official responses by the Dutch Reformed Church to the Belhar Confession, and concludes with some perspectives on this history of reception (or non-reception) of this influencial Reformed confession.

The essays collected here are all published with the permission of the original publishers. The first footnote in each article indicates where the essay was first presented and published. These essays have in most cases been revised only slightly, mainly to avoid repetition or to enhance clarity. All the translations from Afrikaans are my own, unless stated otherwise.

In this Introduction it is appropriate to acknowledge the assistance of several people. A word of thanks to Edwin Hees, who edited the first draft of this book and whose pertinent questions and perceptive remarks added much value to this text. I am also indebted to Marlene Schoeman and the other staff at the Dutch Reformed Church Archives in Stellenbosch, who went out of their way to help me find certain documents. I also owe a word of thanks to Marnus Havenga for translating one of the essays and for re-formatting several of the other essays. And a special word of thanks to Emily Vosloo and Wikus van Zyl from AFRICAN SUN MeDIA for publishing the book.

Given the fact that these essays where written over a period of more than a decade, my debt and gratitude to my wife and colleague, Julie Claassens, as well as to Jana, Roux and Suzanne, is great. I remember our many honest, explorative, animated and often humorous family conversations during this time with great fondness.

This book would not be possible without the positive working environment I experienced at the Faculty of Theology at Stellenbosch University. I gratefully dedicate this book to the colleagues of recent years in the discipline group of Systematic Theology and Ecclesiology for their role in making this book possible.

# PART 1 –
# IN SEARCH OF A RESPONSIBLE HISTORICAL HERMENEUTIC

# 1. ON FORGETTING: HISTORICAL INJUSTICE AND THE ART OF FORGETTING[1]

## 1. THE ART OF MEMORY

Around 500 BCE in Greece, or so the story goes, a celebration was held to honour a boxer named Skopas. The poet Simonides of Keos was asked to deliver an ode to commemorate the athlete's victory. Skopas was not pleased with Simonides' speech, though, since he only devoted one third of the speech to praising him, while the other two thirds celebrated the twin divinities Castor and Pollux. Skopas therefore felt that Simonides deserved only one third of the honorarium. After delivering his song of praise, Simonides was unexpectedly called outside by a messenger, who said that two young men were waiting for him there. At the moment when Simonides left the banquet hall, the roof of the building suddenly collapsed and the host and all his guests were killed and buried in the rubble.

The Latin rhetoricians Cicero and Quintilian offer a continuation of this story by noting that after the catastrophe the relatives tried to identify their loved ones, but without any success, as the corpses had been disfigured beyond recognition. Simonides, however, was able to reconstruct the building in his mind and remembered the places where everybody sat. Because of Simonides' pictorial memory he was able to identify the victims on the basis of their location in the banquet hall. Hence the name of Simonides is often associated – together with this founding myth that links memory to 'places' (Greek *topoi*, Latin *loci*) – with the so-called art of memory (the *ars memoriae*). As Harald Weinrich, on whose account of the story I draw here, has noted in his impressive book *Lethe: The Art and Critique of Forgetting*: "In the ancient and medieval art of memory … memory is fundamentally spatialized".[2]

This 'art of memory' has captivated people throughout the ages and we have fascinating descriptions of how it functioned from, for instance, the time of the ancient Greeks until the Renaissance. Francis Yates's book *The Art of Memory* is a classic work in this regard, and it traces how a memory system (that linked memory to 'places') passed from the Greeks and the Romans into the European tradition, and particularly how it took form during the Renaissance in the thought of Giordano Bruno.[3] And a recent bestselling book by Joshua Foer entitled *Moonwalking with Einstein: The Art and Science of Remembering Everything* offers a modern-day

---

1 This essay was originally published (in a slightly different form) under the title "On Historical Injustice and the Art of Forgetting" in the *Oral History Journal of South Africa* 2/2, 2014: 72-84. Versions of this essay were read at the Joint Conference of Academic Societies in the Fields of Religion and Theology held from 18-22 June 2012 in Pietermartizburg, as well as at the Summer School conference of the Humboldt University that took place in June 2013 in Berlin.
2 Weinrich, H, *Lethe: The Art and Critique of Forgetting* (Ithaca: Cornell University Press, 2004), 10.
3 Yates, FA, *The Art of Memory* (London: Pimlico, 1992). Cf. Samuel, R, *Theatres of Memory Volume 1: Past and Present Contemporary Culture* (London: Verso, 1994), vii-xi.

investigation into our capacity to remember.[4] We also find vestiges of the spatialised art of memory in Augustine's famous engagement with memory in Book X of *The Confessions*.[5] Augustine writes, for instance, about the "vast mansions of memory, where are treasured innumerable images", as well as about the ability of memory to bring things to the surface when they are summoned: "The huge repository of the memory, with its secret and unimaginable caverns, welcomes and keeps all these things, to be recalled and brought out for use when needed".[6] Therefore Augustine marvels: "This faculty of memory is a great one, O my God, exceedingly great, a vast, infinite recess. Who can plumb its depth?"[7] Augustine even marvels at the fact that one can remember that one has forgotten something.[8]

In Augustine, therefore, something of the spirit of the ancient art of memory is recognisable, albeit that he develops his views on memory in theological language. In this essay I would like to focus not so much on the art of memory (the *ars memoriae*), but rather ask heuristically with scholars such as Harald Weinrich and the French philosopher Paul Ricoeur whether we can or should also speak of an art of forgetting (an *ars oblivionis*).[9] At the outset of such an undertaking I want to emphasise the importance of not placing this question, and the discursive world that it opens up, merely on an abstract level where it is dislocated from specific historical and social contexts. Therefore this essay will consider the question of whether it is responsible to introduce and/or cultivate the language of forgetting against the backdrop of the more specific discourses on what a responsible engagement with South Africa's colonial and apartheid past entails.

Any attempt to create space for positive claims regarding the art of forgetting should also take into account the moral and religious significance of memory. In writings originating from contexts permeated with memories of historical injustice, the call, and more specifically the duty, to remember and the implied need to fight against forgetting are rightfully emphasised.

The plea for an 'art of forgetting' should also take into account that memory is a powerful religious concept, and religions like Judaism and Christianity are often described as "memory religions" in light of the way these religions are "bound by

---

4   Foer, J, *Moonwalking with Einstein: The Art and Science of Remembering Everything* (London: Allen Lane, 2011).
5   Saint Augustine, *The Confessions* (New York: New City Press, 1997), 237-283.
6   Augustine, *The Confessions*, 244, 245.
7   Augustine, *The Confessions*, 246.
8   Cf. Weinrich, *Lethe*, 23.
9   Weinrich also calls attention to an anecdote, recounted by Cicero, of a meeting between Simonides and Themistocles in which the former offered to teach the latter the art of memory so that he might be able to remember everything. According to one version of the story, Themistocles replied "that he was not interested in the art of memory (*ars memoriae*) but rather was in interested in the art of forgetting (*ars oblivionis*)". See Weinrich, *Lethe*, 11.

rituals of commemorations".[10] In his classic book *Zakhor: Jewish History and Jewish Memory* Yosef Yerushalmi summarises the centrality of memory for Judaism:

> (A)ncient Israel knows what God has done in history. And if that is so, then memory has become crucial to its faith and, ultimately, to its very existence. Only in Israel and nowhere else is the injunction to remember felt as a religious imperative to an entire people. Its reverberations are everywhere, but they reach a crescendo in the Deuteronomic history and the prophets. 'Remember the days of old, consider the years of ages past' (Deut. 32:7). 'Remember these things, O Jacob, for you, O Israel, are My servant; I have fashioned you, you are My servant; O Israel, never forget Me' (Is. 44:21). 'Remember what Amalek did to you' (Deut. 25:17). 'O My people remember now what Balak king of Moab plotted against you' (Micah 6:5). And with hammering insistence: Remember that you were a slave in Egypt ...[11]

Or in the words of the Holocaust survivor and Nobel Peace Prize winner Elie Wiesel: "Remember ... No other Biblical Commandment is as persistent. Jews live and grow under the sign of memory ... To be Jewish is to remember – to claim our right to memory as well as our duty to keep it alive".[12]

Given Christianity's Jewish roots it is not surprising that the concept of memory also lies at the heart of the Christian tradition. In Luke 22: 19 we read that Jesus took a loaf of bread, broke it and gave it to the apostles, saying in the context of this Passover meal on the night that he was betrayed: "This is my body, which is given for you. Do this in remembrance of me". Throughout the ages Christians have celebrated the Lord's Supper as a meal of remembrance, recounting and performing the passion of their risen and living Lord. Memory is thus a central theological notion in Christianity, and Christianity too can rightly be described as a memory religion, as is evident in its forms of worship.[13]

Given the fact that memory is such a central ethical and religious concept, one might justly ask whether we can speak – also with theological integrity – of an art or even a duty of forgetting. One reason why it is nevertheless important to consider this question in our discourse has to do with the fact that some scholars have called attention to a growing emphasis in memory studies on the notion of forgetting. Anne Whitehead, for instance, mentions how the proliferation of scenes of public repentance, forgiveness, apology, or confession, as well as the institution of a number of Truth Commissions, has led to a growing public interest in restorative

---

10   Signer, A (ed.), *Memory and History in Christianity and Judaism* (Notre Dame: University of Notre Dame Press, 2001), ix.
11   Yerushalmi, Y H, *Zakhor, Jewish History and Jewish Memory* (Seattle: University of Washington Press, 1982 [1996]), 9, 10.
12   Wiesel, E, *From the Kingdom of Memory: Reminiscences* (New York: Summit Books, 1990), 9, 10.
13   Cf. Markschies, C and Wolf, H (eds), *Erinnerungsorte des Christentums* (München: Verlag C.H. Beck, 2010). The editorial introduction to this elaborate work observes: "Erinnerung is nicht irgendeine periphere theologische Kategorie des Christentums. Im Gegenteil: Gedächtnis ist ein theologischer Zentralbegriff ... Das Christentum ist eine Gedächtnisgemeinschaft par excellence und ist das inbesondere im christlichen Gottesdienst" (15).

justice and the need to promote healing and reconciliation in post-conflict contexts. These developments "suggest that a discursive shift is beginning to take place from memory to forgetting".[14] Given the possibility of such a discursive shift, the need for a responsible discourse on forgetting – also in South African contexts – seems to be of paramount importance. With this in mind, this essay first considers some possible arguments for giving greater prominence to the notion of forgetting in our memory discourse. This is followed by a section that reiterates the 'critique of forgetting', drawing also on some examples from 20th -century South African political and church history. In the final section I consider, in conversation with the work of Paul Ricoeur, whether we should view the relationship between an art of memory and an art of forgetting as symmetrical or asymmetrical.

## 2. THE ART OF FORGETTING?

Given the powerful moral and theological claims that can be made as part of an ode to memory, the odds seem to be against any attempt to speak responsibly of an 'art of forgetting'.[15] Yet there is also something like a cultural history of forgetting, as outlined by Harald Weinrich in *Lethe: The Art and Critique of Forgetting*. For the Greeks Lethe was the goddess opposed to Mnemosyne, the goddess of memory and mother of the muses. But above all Lethe is the name of an underworld river that confers forgetfulness on the souls of the dead. In these soft-flowing waters "the hard contours of the remembrance of reality are dissolved and, so to speak, *liquidated*".[16] Forgetting, symbolised by Lethe, the meandering stream of forgetfulness, is the subject of Weinrich's book and in the genealogy that he offers – which draws on a wide array of poets, writers and scholars – the close proximity of the concepts of memory and forgetting is clear from the outset.

In some sense one can say that the plea for memory is only possible because of the reality of forgetting. Forgetting is inevitable and therefore memory and forgetting are tightly interwoven. The novelist Milan Kundera even writes: "Remembering is not the negative of forgetting. Remembering is a form of forgetting".[17] And in his impressive and extensive study, *Memory, History, Forgetting*, the French philosopher Paul Ricoeur not only discusses the intricate relationship between memory and history, but also places this discussion within the broader context of the need for hermeneutical reflection on our vulnerable historical condition, a condition that

---

14   Whitehead, A, *Memory* (London: Routledge, 2009), 154.
15   For the sake of greater conceptual clarity, I can mention that this essay uses the concept of 'the art of forgetting' not merely in its narrow sense as a strict corollary to 'an art of memory' understood as a memory technique. The notion of an *ars memoriae* is often situated within the context of memorialisation (or what some scholars call artificial memory). We train our memories through techniques (such as linking memory to 'places') to remember things. This 'art of memory' suggests something like voluntary control over our memory, but memory (as a multifaceted concept) is of course about more that this kind of technique. In this essay I will, moreover, often use the notion of an 'art of memory' more broadly that in just this technical sense. The notion of an 'art of forgetting' too is used in a wider metaphorical sense as shorthand for a responsible integration of the notion of forgetting into our discourse on memory.
16   Weinrich, *Lethe*, 6.
17   Kundera, M, *Testaments Betrayed* (London: HarperCollins, 1995), 128.

includes the reality of forgetting.[18] Because we are 'timeful' beings, we forget. This is part of what Ricoeur calls elsewhere "the sorrow of finitude".[19] With the passage of time and the reality of aging, our memories fade or become distorted. Forgetting therefore challenges the reliability of memory,[20] albeit that the significant role of memory (and history) should not be disregarded in the light of the vulnerability of our historical condition. The important point is that the phenomenon of forgetting is part and parcel of any engagement with the equivocal and slippery notion of memory, and that "memory defines itself, at least in the first instance, as a struggle against forgetting".[21] But one can also further ask, Ricoeur continues, whether forgetting is in every aspect the enemy of memory, and whether memory must not enter into some kind of negotiation process with forgetting, "groping to find the right measure in its balance with forgetting".[22]

If we do not view forgetting merely as the enemy of memory, can and should we make a plea for a positive affirmation of the notion of forgetting in our moral and theological discourse? And if so, in what way can we speak of an art of forgetting alongside an art of memory? Can we even speak of a duty to forget in a similar way that we speak of a duty to remember?

Several arguments, I propose, can be put forward in defence of 'an art of forgetting'. A first possible response against a total demonisation of forgetting could be to call attention to the fact that our lives would be unbearable if we were to remember everything. We know the stories of persons who have lost their memory and how they had to painfully reconstruct everything, or of people who remembered selectively, like the book dealer from Milan who only remembered what he read in books in Umberto Eco's wonderful novel *The Mysterious Flame of Queen Loana*.[23] But the literary imagination has also produced works such as Jorge Luis Borges's enigmatic short story "Funes the Memorious" (*"Funes el memorioso"*). Funes's problem was not that he forgot things, but rather that he did not forget anything; his memory was infallible, storing everything. Hence Funes's remark: "My memory, sir, is like a garbage heap".[24] It was therefore very difficult for him to sleep, given all the memories in his head. Towards the end of the story we read the following about Funes: "With no effort, he had learned English, French, Portuguese and Latin. I suspect, however, that he was not very capable of thought. To think is to forget differences, generalize, make abstractions. In the teeming world of Funes, there were only details, almost immediate in their presence".[25]

---

18    Ricoeur, P, *Memory, History, Forgetting* (Chicago: University of Chicago Press, 2004).
19    Ricoeur, P, *Freedom and Nature: The Voluntary and the Involuntary* (Evanston: Northwestern University Press, 1966), 447-448. Cf. also Ricoeur, *Memory, History, Forgetting*, 440.
20    Ricoeur writes: "Forgetting is the challenge par excellence put to memory's aim of reliability". Ricoeur, *Memory, History, Forgetting*, 414. However, Ricoeur also notes that "many memories, perhaps among the most precious, childhood memories, have not been definitely erased but simply rendered inaccessible, unavailable, which makes us say that one forgets less than one thinks or fears" (416).
21    Ricoeur, *Memory, History, Forgetting*, 413.
22    Ricoeur, *Memory, History, Forgetting*, 413.
23    Eco, U, *The Mysterious Flame of Queen Loana* (London: Secker & Warburg, 2005).
24    Borges, J L, *Labyrinths: Selected Stories and Other Writings* (Harmondsworth: Penguin, 1962), 92.
25    Borges, *Labyrinths*, 94.

To remember everything would indeed make life unbearable and one can rightly argue that there is some grace in forgetting. Therefore one can argue that forgetting is not only unavoidable but also, in some sense at least, desirable.

In his famous essay "On the uses and disadvantages of history for life" (1874) Friedrich Nietzsche too considers the extreme example of a man who did not possess the power of forgetting. Such a man, argues Nietzsche, would lose himself in the stream of becoming and will not be able to act. Therefore Nietzsche remarks: "Forgetting is essential to action of any kind, just as not only light but also darkness too is essential for the life of anything organic".[26] In this essay Nietzsche targets the historicism of his day and makes a claim for the value of living "unhistorically", i.e. unburdened by the pressures of the past: "Man ... braces himself against the great and ever greater pressure of the past: it pushes him down or bends him sideways, it encumbers his step as a dark, invisible burden".[27] For Nietzsche it is possible to live almost without memory (he uses the example of grazing cattle in this regard), but that it is impossible to live without forgetting. Therefore his claim: "*there is a degree of sleeplessness, of rumination, of historical sense, which is harmful and ultimately fatal to the living thing, whether this living thing be a man or a people or a culture*".[28] For Nietzsche the unhistorical and the historical are necessary in equal measure to ensure the health (and happiness) of an individual, a people and a culture. A first possible argument in favour of forgetting thus relates to the fact that too much memory of the past will make life unbearable, and that it will have an unhealthy impact on our life and happiness.

A second possible argument in defence of a more positive assessment of forgetting relates to some abuses of memory in the light of experiences of trauma. Much has been written on the relationship between memory and trauma, and on the need to work through what Ricoeur has called blocked or wounded memory.[29] Through a healthy therapeutic engagement with our memories, we can experience some healing of our memories. In addition, one can also argue that memory protects victims from further violence. In his book *The End of Memory: Remembering Rightly in a Violent World* Miroslav Volf quotes the following remark by Elie Wiesel: "memory of evil will serve as a shield against evil, ... the memory of death will serve as a shield against death". By exposing evil (through memory) one can deter its perpetration. But Volf also highlights that even this protective function of memory can become problematic:

> As victims seek to protect themselves they are not immune to becoming perpetrators ... The memory of their own persecution makes them see dangers lurking even where there are none; it leads them to exaggerate dangers that do exist and overreact with excessive violence or inappropriate preventive measures so as to ensure their own safety.

---

26 Nietzsche, F, *Untimely Meditations* (Cambridge: Cambridge University Press, 1983), 62.
27 Nietzsche, *Untimely Meditations*, 61.
28 Nietzsche, *Untimely Meditations*, 62.
29 Cf. Ricoeur, *Memory, History, Forgetting*, 69-80. For some important perspectives on the relationship between memory and trauma engaging South African contexts, see also the essays collected in Goboda-Madikizela, P and Van der Merwe, C, *Memory, Narrative and Forgiveness: Perspectives on the Unfinished Journeys of the Past* (Newcastle upon Tyne: Cambridge Scholars Press, 2009).

> Victims will often *become* perpetrators *on account of* their memories. It is *because they remember* past victimization that they feel justified in committing present violence … So easily does the protective shield of memory morph into the sword of violence.[30]

The memories of trauma and pain, one can therefore say, are not always on the side of peace and protection, but can also motivate aggressive and violent acts of retaliation and release new oppressive forces. Some may argue that this possibility points towards the need for some form of forgetting to counter destructive memory.

A third possible argument in defence of forgetting relates specifically to the abuses of memory that have created manipulative forms of commemoration and memorialisation, leading some theorists to bemoan that fact that we are not only suffering from too little memory but also from too much memory. In the Preface to *Memory, History, Forgetting* Ricoeur noted that one of his reasons for writing the book had to do with the fact that he was troubled "by the unsettling spectacle offered by an excess of memory here, and an excess of forgetting elsewhere, to say nothing of the influence of commemorations and abuses of memory – and of forgetting".[31] And indeed it seems to be the case that we are suffering in our modern world from either too much memory or too little memory. Maybe we can say more accurately that the problem is not simply that there is too much memory, "but that there is too much memory of the wrong sort".[32] Memory is not only selective, but it is often manipulated in the light of projects of identity construction and power consolidation or accumulation, often without the necessary sensitivity to ideological distortions. Memorials and commemorations are also often highly contested events and spaces. It can be argued that these expressions of memory fuel polarisation and should therefore have been minimised. In addition, the argument can also be put forward that our current context of a capitalistic consumer-driven culture is more conducive to amnesia than memory. As Paul Connerton has argued persuasively in his book *How Modernity Forgets*:

> The increased scale of human settlement, the production of speed, and the repeated intentional destruction of the built environment, generated a diffuse yet all-encompassing and powerful cultural amnesia and they are in their turn generated by the capitalist process of production. Modernity … produces cultural amnesia not by accident but intrinsically and necessarily. Forgetting is built into the capitalist process of production itself, incorporated in the bodily experience of life-spaces.[33]

The cultural air that we breathe, one can say, strengthens habits of forgetting, and perhaps, some might say, it is better to embrace this reality in order to prosper in our fast-paced consumerist society, and not allow habits of memory to slow us

---

30 Volf, M, *The End of Memory: Remembering Rightly in a Violent World* (Grand Rapids: Eerdmans, 2006), 32, 33.
31 Ricoeur, *Memory, History, Forgetting*, xv.
32 Bluhstein, J, *The Moral Demands of Memory* (Cambridge: Cambridge University Press, 2008), 17.
33 Connerton, P, *How Modernity Forgets* (Cambridge: Cambridge University Press, 2009), 125.

down and leave us less relevant and effective in the present world with its specific demands and opportunities.

One can also argue, fourthly, that it is possible to construct a theological argument as part of the plea for a more affirmative attitude towards forgetting. What about 'forgive and forget'? Don't we read in the Bible, in Jeremiah 31: 34, that the Lord declares: "For I will forgive their wickedness and will remember their sins no more"? And one can indeed recall many examples from the Jewish and Christian tradition that seem to affirm that complete forgiveness involves some sense of forgetting.[34] It should be noted, though, that attempts to draw on the Jewish and Christian tradition to make some sort of link between forgiveness and forgetting is not unproblematic and that the statement 'forgive and forget' is often contested.[35]

## 3. THE CRITIQUE OF FORGETTING

It is possible, therefore, to make an argument (even a moral and theological argument) for the notion of forgetting in our discourse about a responsible engagement with the past. However, these attempts will, and – in my view – should, always be heard against the backdrop of the voices that critique the language of forgetting.

I have already referred to the strong appeal that we have a duty to remember in the light of experiences of historical injustices. Within the context of, for instance, the horror of the Holocaust or the brutality of apartheid, the language of forgetting seems to be irresponsible, unjust and dangerous. Forgetting is equated not with healing, but with death.[36] In post-apartheid South Africa there is also a proliferation of works that engage directly or indirectly with the notion of memory, often with reference to the work of the South African Truth and Reconciliation Commission.

---

34  Miroslav Volf offers a sampling from the Jewish and Christian tradition in this regard, drawing in the process on Bible texts such as Jeremiah 31:34 and Psalm 51:9, as well as statements from Gregory of Nyssa, Augustine, John Calvin, Karl Rahner and Karl Barth. See Volf, *The End of Memory*, 132-135.

35  See, for instance, L. Gregory Jones's chapter "Healing the Wounds of Memory" in Jones, L G and Musekura, C, *Forgiving as We've Been Forgiven: Community Practices for Making Peace* (Downers Grove, Illionois: IVP Books, 2010, 85-101. Cf. also the chapter "Why Time Cannot and Should not Heal the Wounds of History, but Time Has Been and Can Be Redeemed" in Hauerwas, S, *A Better Hope: Resources for a Church Confronting Capitalism, Democracy, and Postmodernity* (Grand Rapids: Brazos Press, 2000), 139-154.

36  As Elie Wiesel writes in his autobiography *All Rivers Run to the Sea*: "What does it mean to remember? … It is to revive fragments of existence, to rescue lost beings, to cast harsh light on faces and events, to drive back the sands that cover the surface of things, to combat oblivion and to reject death". Wiesel, E, *All Rivers Run to the Sea: Memoirs Volume One 1928-1969* (London: HarperCollins Publishers, 1994), 150. Elsewhere Wiesel writes in similar vein: "If there is a single theme that dominates all my writings, all my obsessions, it is that of memory – because I fear forgetfulness as much as hatred and death. To forget is, for a Jew, to deny his people – and all that it symbolizes – and also to deny himself". Wiesel, *From the Kingdom of Memory*, 9. Cf. also the chapter "Elie Wiesel: to forget is to deny" in Bigsby, C, *Remembering and Imagining the Holocaust: The Chain of Memory* (Cambridge: Cambridge University Press, 2006), 318-340.

Again the plea is often, though not always exclusively,[37] for the duty or imperative to remember the past.

The duty to remember, and even not to 'forgive and forget', also resonates in some Afrikaner literature, sermons and speeches that took shape in the aftermath of the Anglo-Boer War (or the South African War). One is reminded in this regard of the Afrikaans poet Totius's famous poem "Vergewe en Vergeet" ("Forgive and Forget").[38] Or let me quote from a sermon by Rev. C.R. Kotzé, a Dutch Reformed pastor who was wounded during the war and was a prisoner of war on St. Helena. Some of his sermons have been collected in a book entitled *Die Bybel en ons Volkstryd* (*The Bible and the Struggle of our People*). The title of one of these sermons even has a post-colonial ring to it: "God maak die nasies en die Duiwel die Empire" ("God creates the nations, but the Devil creates the Empire"). And in 1946, in the context of the growing Afrikaner nationalism, he delivered a sermon that was also broadcast on the radio, with the title "Vra na die ou paaie" ("Seek the ancient paths"), with Jeremiah 6: 16 as focus text. In this context he makes a plea for preserving memory:

> But exactly because we want to look forward, we ought sometimes to look back! The highest building must have its foundations. The tree cannot live without its roots. The nation cannot exist without its history. To forgive and forget is folly. It is pagan language. God is love and he does not forgive if there is no remorse and confession. And no people (*volk*), no Christian, dare to forget, ever … If you want to go forward in a healthy and strong way, then you must look back into history. Seek the ancient paths.[39]

In a collection of sermons of Rev. GJJ Boshoff (published in 1959) we find similar ideas. One of the sermons is on the theme "Die Afrikaner mag nooit vergeet nie!" ("The Afrikaner must never forget"). This sermon was preached on 10 October 1957 at a concentration camp cemetery during the unveiling of a restored monument after it had been vandalised:

> At this place, we forget nothing or nobody. Not our God. Not our friend. Not our enemy … A people (*volk*) that has had concentration camps may never forget. On these graves the grass of forgetfulness never grows. Sadly, however, there are Afrikaners who want to forget so easily that they replace the grass with khaki bush.[40]

These sermons illustrate the resistance to the language of 'forgiving and forgetting' in some Afrikaner church circles. In addition, we see how the South African War and

---

37  See Roodt, D, *Om die waarheidskommissie te vergeet* (Deinfern: Praag, 2000). Towards the end of this book Dan Roodt refers to the Truth Commission as consisting of blank pages with a few of Marx's beard hairs on them.
38  See Dirkie Smit's chapter "Shared stories for the future? Theological reflections on truth and reconciliation in South Africa" in Smit, D J, *Essays in Public Theology: Collected Essays 1* (Stellenbosch: Sun Press, 2007), 325-341, here 328-330.
39  Kotzé, C R, *Die Bybel en ons Volkstryd: Preke tussen 1930 en 1946 geskryf en gelewer deur Wyle Ds. C. R. Kotzé* (Bloemfontein : SACUM Bpk, n.d. [Foreword dated 1955]), 78, 79.
40  Boshoff, GJJ, *U Volk is my Volk* (Johannesburg: Voortrekkerpers Bpk., 1959), 107, 108.

the concentrations camps functioned as "sites of memory" ("*lieux de mémoire*"),[41] and that these acts of memory became part of specific constructions of the past.

These few sermon illustrations remind us that the call to remember (and the critique of forgetting) is not just about reconstructing the past faithfully, but that it functions in a certain way to construct identity in the present. More recent discourse on memory, in the wake of the Truth of Reconciliation Commission, often calls attention to the way in which memory is negotiated and produced in South Africa.[42] On the one hand, there is a critique of forgetting (especially of forgetting the pain and suffering caused to the victims), while on the other hand, there is also a sense, in some circles at least, of the complexity and contestation involved in claiming or re-claiming memory. Verne Harris puts it well in a chapter on "Contesting Remembering and Forgetting: The Archive of South Africa's Truth and Reconciliation Commission" in his book *Archives and Justice: A South African Perspective*: "Memory is never a faithful reflection of process, of 'reality'. It is shaped, reshaped, figured, configured by the dance of imagination. So that beyond the dynamics of remembering and forgetting, a more profound characterization of struggles represented in social memory is one of narrative against narrative, story against story".[43] The important point is that we should be aware of the complex dynamics of processes of remembering and forgetting, and that we should even guard against treating memory and forgetting as binary oppositions.[44] Yet the questions still lingers: How are we to view the relationship between memory and forgetting? Is this relationship symmetrical or asymmetrical? And can we speak with integrity of a duty to forget?

## 4. TOWARDS A CULTURE OF JUST MEMORY

In the Introduction to this essay I referred to the 'art of memory' (*ars memoriae*) and asked whether one can also speak of a comparable art of forgetting (*ars oblivionis*)? If one takes the art of forgetting in its strict sense, as a type of (letha)technique, this art would have to rest, as Paul Ricoeur has noted, "on a rhetoric of extinction … the

---

41  See Nora, P, *Les lieux de mémoire* (7 volumes) (Paris: Gallimard, 1984-1992). For a translated text that gives a good description of Nora's project, see Nora, P, "Between Memory and History: *Les lieux de mémoire*", *Representations* 26 (Spring 1989): 7-24.

42  See, for instance, Nuttall, S and Coetzee, C (eds.), *Negotiating the Past: The Making of Memory in South Africa* (Cape Town: Oxford University Press, 1998); Botman, HR and Peterson, RM (eds), *To Remember and to Heal: Theological and Psychological Reflections on Truth and Reconciliation* (Cape Town: Human & Rousseau, 1996); and Diawara, M, Lategan, B and Rüsen, J, *Historical Memory in Africa: Dealing with the past, reaching for the future in an intercultural context* (New York: Berghahn Books, 2010). This last book is the result of a research project jointly sponsored by the Stellenbosch Institute for Advanced Studies (STIAS) and the Kulturwissenschaftliches Institut Nordrhein-Westfalen (KWI) with the title "Dealing with the Past, Reaching for the Future".

43  Harris, V, *Archives and Justice: A South African Perspective* (Chicago: The Society of American Archivists, 2007), 289. He writes further about the TRC archive: "This space, as with all archives, is always already one in which dynamics of remembering, forgetting, and imagining are at play. My argument is that this space should be made hospitable to contestation and that we should all be vigilant against impulses in it and around it to amnesia, erasure, secreting, and control" (291).

44  See Harris, *Archives and Justice*, 301.

contrary of making an archive".⁴⁵ But this would be a barbarous dream. Ricoeur, however, makes some space for forgetting, but for him an *ars oblivionis* (understood in a broader sense) could not constitute an order distinct from memory. "It can only arrange itself under the optative mood of a happy memory. It would simply add a gracious note to the work of memory and the work of mourning".⁴⁶ This emphasis is, in my view, very important. Put differently: an art of forgetting – if it is to find its rightful place in our discourse – *can only find its place on the other side of a critique of forgetting and in close proximity to memory*. It is therefore the argument of this essay that the language of forgetting should be used with the necessary reserve. Yet one should also be attentive to the possible harmful ideological impulses that can hide in a categorical rejection of any attempt to carve out space for a qualified defence of forgetting in all its ambiguity and complexity. Dirkie Smit, writing from a theological perspective with the Christian tradition in mind, puts it well:

> And perhaps the Christian tradition can remind societies that *'forgetting'* is an ambiguous matter. There is indeed *a Christian instruction not to forget*. The Christian church depends upon this, for many reasons. One is that we must learn from the past, so that it 'will never happen again'. Yet there is *also a Christian instruction to forget*. Forgetting can also be a moral activity. The wonder of the message of the gospel for Christians is precisely that God removes our sins from us as far as the east is removed from the west and never thinks of them. It is one thing to say: we forgive, but we cannot forget. It is another to say: we forgive, but we shall never, we may never, we never wish to, we will never forget. The Christian tradition is ultimately based on the trust that God-in-Christ does not speak to the world like that, and calls us to speak and live accordingly.⁴⁷

We should indeed affirm that forgetting can be a moral activity and that we should guard against a fanatical anti-forgetting stance that keep us captives of the past and robs memory of a future. This notwithstanding, I would nevertheless like to argue, with Ricoeur, that there is not strict symmetry between the art of memory and the art of forgetting, and that the duty to remember and the duty to forget are not comparable, since "the duty to remember is a duty to teach, whereas the duty to forget is the duty to go beyond anger and hatred".⁴⁸ The challenge is to find a way between witnessing to the past through memory and some form of forgetting that will help us reconcile with the past.⁴⁹

---

45 Ricoeur, *Memory, History, Forgetting*, 504.
46 Ricoeur, *Memory, History, Forgetting*, 505.
47 Botman and Peterson, *To Remember and to Heal*, 116.
48 Ricoeur, P, "Memory and Forgetting" in Kearney, R and Dooley, M (eds.), *Questioning Ethics: Contemporary Debates in Philosophy* (London: Routledge, 1999), 5-11.
49 Cf. Liebsch, B (eds), *Bezeugte Vergangenheit oder Versöhnendes Vergessen: Geschichtstheorie nach Paul Ricoeur* (Berlin: Akademie Verlag, 2010). See especially Liebsch's opening essay "Bezeugte Vergangenheit *versus* Versöhnendes Vergessen? Fruchtbarkeit und Fragwürdigkeit von Ricoeurs Rehabilitierung eines philosophischen Geschichtsdenkens" (23-58), as well as Inga Römer's essay "Eskapistisches Vergessen? Der Optativ des glücklichen Gedächtnisses bei Paul Ricoeur" (292-310).

Ricoeur does leave some space for forgetting, but in the process he not only affirms the inseparable tie between memory and forgetting, but also the bond between these notions and justice:

> Both memory and forgetting do, however, contribute in their respective ways to what Hannah Arendt called the continuation of action. It is necessary for the continuation of action that we retain the traces of events, that we be reconciled with the past, and that we divest ourselves of anger and hatred. Once again, justice is the horizon of both processes. Let us conclude by saying that at this point in our history we have to deal with the problem of evolving a culture of just memory.[50]

In a culture of 'just memory' the emphasis should be on the duty to remember. The rhetoric of forgetting can have harmful consequences in contexts permeated with memories of historical injustice, and it might be more prudent to opt against the use of 'forgetting' in our discourse, or when we use it, to use it with the necessary nuance and differentiation. The language of 'forgetting' cannot be used as an alibi to forget or erase the past, since the past remains in the present; it can only be used and claimed with the healing motive of lifting the weight or the burden of the past.

---

50  Kearney and Dooley, *Questioning Ethics*, 11.

# 2. ON HISTORY: THE WRITING OF HISTORY AS REMEDY OR POISON?[1]

## 1. INTRODUCTION

In his monumental work *Memory, History, Forgetting* Paul Ricoeur uses as the epigraph to one part of his book the following quotation from Herodotus' *The History*:

> I, Herodotus of Halicarnassus, am here setting forth my history [historiē], that time may not draw the colour from what man has brought into being, nor those great and wonderful deeds, manifested by both Greeks and barbarians, fail of their report, and, together with all this, the reason why they fought one another.
>
> The chroniclers [logioi] among the Persians say that it was the Phoenicians who were the cause of the falling-out …[2]

Ricoeur does not comment on this quotation directly in *Memory, History, Forgetting*, apart from asking in a footnote: "Herodotus: the 'father of history' (Cicero) or the 'father of lies' (Plutarch)?"[3] Nevertheless, the quotation from Herodotus raises important questions regarding historiography and identity, questions that Ricoeur deals with at length in his work.

Herodotus justifies his project – the setting forth of his history – in the context of the danger that time might detract from the events, drawing "the colour from what man has brought into being". But Herodotus is not only interested, or at least so it seems from this quotation, in chronicling the 'facts', but also in providing an interpretative framework for the events, providing the reason "why they fought one another". In addition, the quotation (specifically chosen by Ricoeur) suggests that historiography and identity, or even historiography and prejudice or bias, are closely intertwined. Whereas Herodotus refers to the chroniclers among the Persians pointing towards the Phoenicians as the culprits in the conflict, one cannot help but reflect on how we often frame our accounts of events in such a way that we (or our friends and benefactors) become the heroes in the tale, while at the same time we paint a darker picture of our competitors or enemies. This of course raises the much-discussed concerns about historiography and objectivity, as well as the concomitant reality of contested historical portrayals.

Ricoeur places the quotation from Herodotus' famous work as the epigraph to the second part of *Memory, History, Forgetting* – the section that deals with the

---

1  This essay was published in a longer and slightly different version as "The Writing of History as Remedy or Poison? Some Remarks on Paul Ricoeur's Reflection on Memory, Identity and 'The Historiograhical Operation'" in Jonker, L (ed.), *Texts, Contexts and Readings in Postexilic Literature: Explorations into Historiography and Identity Negotation in Hebrew Bible and Related Texts* (Tübingen: Mohr Siebeck, 2011), 11-26.
2  Ricoeur, P, *Memory, History, Forgetting* (Chicago: University of Chicago Press, 2004), 133. Ricoeur quotes from Herodotus, *The History* (Chicago: Chicago University Press, 1987), 33.
3  Ricoeur, *Memory, History, Forgetting*, 525.

epistemology of historical knowledge. In this essay I will attend more closely to Ricoeur's discussion of this particular topic, with a special focus on what he calls, following Michel de Certeau, "the historiographical operation". Ricoeur refers in this regard to three phases, which he describes respectively as the documentary phase, the explanation/understanding phase and the representative phase. Central to Ricoeur's reflection in this section, and in the book as a whole, is the problem of the representation of the past. What draws me to Ricoeur's discussion is his sensitivity to what one can describe as the vulnerability and instability inherent in attempts to represent the past. But Ricoeur does not merely challenge optimistic and even arrogant claims that pretend to give 'objective' accounts of what happened in the past, accounts that do not display the necessary epistemological and hermeneutical awareness. He is also concerned with the faithful or truthful representation of the past, thus taking seriously the continuity *and* discontinuity between history and fiction. In the process Ricoeur takes on questions addressing "the reality of the historical past", to use the title of his 1984 Aquinas lecture.[4]

In order to engage with Ricoeur's discussion of the epistemology of historical knowledge, I will briefly place his discussion on 'the historiographical operation' within the context of the broader argument of *Memory, History, Forgetting*. And before outlining the different stages of the 'historiographical operation', I will draw attention to the way in which Ricoeur introduces his discussion of the epistemology of history by revisiting Plato's famous attack on writing in the *Phaedrus*. Hence the question of whether the writing of history is a remedy or a poison in the light of the vulnerability of memory. In the final section of the essay I point – in the light of the engagement with Ricoeur – to the need for what can be called a responsible historical hermeneutic, also for church and theological historiography in South Africa.

## 2. THE REPRESENTATION OF THE PAST AS FRAGILE QUEST

Just before the table of contents in *Memory, History, Forgetting* there is a picture of a Baroque bronze sculpture from the Wiblingen monastery in Ulm, Germany (for an image of the sculpture, see the front cover of *Reforming Memory*). Ricoeur interprets this sculpture in an adjacent note:

> It is the dual figure of history. In the foreground, Kronos, the winged god. An old man with wreathed brow: his left hand grips a large book, his right hand attempts to tear out a page. Behind and above, stands history itself. The gaze is grave and searching; one foot topples a horn of plenty from which spills the cascade of gold and silver, sign of instability; the left hand checks the act of the god, while the right hand displays history's instruments: the book, the inkpot, and the stylus.

The picture of this enigmatic sculpture and the accompanying commentary offer a fitting announcement of Ricoeur's intention in *Memory, History, Forgetting* to grapple with questions relating to the importance of – and difficulties associated with – the quest for the representation of the past. Kronos as an old man represents the fleeing

---

4  Cf. Ricoeur, P, *The Reality of the Historical Past (The Aquinas Lecture)* (Milwaukee: Marquette University Press, 1984).

of time into the past. One is reminded of Herodotus' concern "that time may not draw the colour from what man has brought into being". History, the other figure in the sculpture, holds the instruments for conquering time. With the passing of time, the past moves into oblivion and becomes, on a fundamental level, inaccessible to us. Nevertheless, we try to gain access to the past and interpret it, which is made possible by the fact that traces remain in memory. Through the writing, recording and reading of history, we try to represent – to make present again – the past by attending to these traces.

It is between the fallible power of memory and the force of forgetfulness that Ricoeur places his philosophy of history in his aptly titled book, *Memory, History Forgetting*. Although this book resists easy summary, the broad argument of the book is presented in three clearly defined parts. It is tempting to see these three parts as three separate books, but as Charles Reagan observes: "(T)he genius of the book is the structure, the interconnections, that Ricoeur weaves among the philosophical paradoxes of memory, the aporias of forgetting, and the mediating role of history".[5]

The first part of the book is, as the title suggests, devoted to a discussion of memory. Ricoeur's *phenomenology* of memory begins with an analysis of the object of memory (*le souvenir*) and passes through the search for a given memory (*anamnesis*, recollection); the discussion then moves to memory as it is exercised (reflective memory), with reference to the use and abuse of memory. This section also includes a discussion of individual and collective memory. The second part of the book can be viewed as an *epistemology* of history. Here Ricoeur discusses the three phases of the historical operation: the stage of testimony and the archives (the documentary phase); the phase of explanation and understanding; and the historian's representation of the past on an enscripted level (the representative phase). Throughout this discussion Ricoeur is interested in the historian's intention to produce a truthful reconstruction of the past. The third part of the book is framed within a *hermeneutics* of the historical condition. In this section Ricoeur argues for a critical philosophy of history that is "attentive to the limits of historical knowledge that a certain hubris of historical science transgresses time and time again".[6] In addition, this section contains a meditation on forgetting. The epilogue of the book deals with what Ricoeur terms "difficult forgiveness".[7] Although *Memory, History, Forgetting* has – apart from the epilogue – three clearly distinguishable sections, Ricoeur emphasises that the sections do not constitute three separate books, but can be seen instead as three masts with interlocking but distinct sails that belong to the same ship setting off on a single itinerary. There is a common concern that "flows through the phenomenology of memory, the epistemology of history, and the hermeneutics of the social condition: the problematic of the representation of the past".[8]

---

5  Reagan, C, "Reflections on Paul Ricoeur's *Memory, history, forgetting*", *Philosophy Today* 49, 3/ 5 (2005): 309.
6  Ricoeur, *Memory, History, Forgetting*, xvi.
7  See Ricoeur, *Memory, History, Forgetting*, 457-506.
8  Ricoeur, *Memory, History, Forgetting*, xvi.

## 3. THE EPISTEMOLOGY OF HISTORICAL KNOWLEDGE

### a. Historiography: remedy or poison?

Ricoeur's phenomenological sketch of memory highlights the vulnerability and fragility of memory, and points – implicitly at least – to the need for an ethics of memory and, one could add, an ethics of history/ historiography. In acknowledging the fragility of memory, one ought to reiterate Ricoeur's assertion that memory, individual and collective, is our primary resource for the representation of the past. Historiography can only take the long route through memory, since memory is the matrix of history. Moreover, history also has a certain 'autonomy' that aims at strengthening or challenging individual and collective memory. It is in this context that Ricoeur places his epistemology of historical knowledge (the second part of *Memory, History, Forgetting*).

Ricoeur introduces his discussion of the epistemology of history by revisiting Plato's famous attack on writing in the *Phaedrus*. What draws Ricoeur to the Platonic myth dedicated to the invention of writing is the fact that the myth views the gift of writing as an antidote to memory. Ricoeur views this "as the paradigm for every dream of substituting history for memory".[9] Ricoeur is interested (as is Jacques Derrida) "in the insurmountable ambiguity attached to the *pharmakon* that the god offers the king".[10] In the Platonic myth the god Theuth tells the Egyptian king that he has discovered a potion (*pharmakon*) that, once its formula has been learned, will make the Egyptians wiser and will improve their memory. This *pharmakon* is the writing (*grammata*) that comes from the father of writing. The king then gives the god the privilege of engendering the art, but he retains the right to judge its benefit or harm. How does the king respond in the end to the god's offer? Ricoeur recounts the king's response:

> In fact, it will introduce forgetfulness into the soul who learns it: they will not practice using their memory [*mnēmēs*] because they will put their trust in writing [*graphēs*] ... You have not discovered a potion [*pharmakon*] for remembering, but for reminding [*hupomnēseōs*]; you provided your students with the appearance of wisdom, not with its reality.[11]

But the myth also points to another kind of discourse, namely that of 'true memory': "It is a discourse that is written down, with knowledge, in the soul of the listener; it can defend itself, and it knows for whom it should speak and for whom it should remain silent".[12] Both these discourses are written down, but it is in the soul that the true discourse is written. Ricoeur comments: "Here, despite the kinship among these *logoi*, lies the gap between a living memory and a dead deposit".[13]

Ricoeur reads this myth against the backdrop of the relationship between living memory and written history, seeking a prudent rehabilitation of writing in which

---

9   Ricoeur, *Memory, History, Forgetting*, 138.
10  Ricoeur, *Memory, History, Forgetting*, 141.
11  Ricoeur, *Memory, History, Forgetting*, 142.
12  Cf. Ricoeur, *Memory, History, Forgetting*, 143.
13  Ricoeur, *Memory, History, Forgetting*, 143.

an educated memory illuminated by historiography overlaps with a scholarly history capable of reanimating a fading memory. Therefore Ricoeur is not only sceptical of attempts to deny history for the sake of memory, but also challenges attempts to portray history as a hindrance to memory. Ricoeur's epistemological historical inquiry is therefore accompanied by the haunting question of whether the *pharmakon* of history-writing is remedy or poison. Although Ricoeur wisely leaves open the question of whether historiography is remedy or poison, his sensitivity to the problem serves, in my view, as a rightful reminder against over-confident claims in the name of a form of historiography that promise a total shield against the vulnerability of memory and testimony. At that same time, however, Ricoeur wants to affirm that the representation of the past does require some form of trust in what he calls "the historiographical operation".

## b. The historiographical operation

In the light of Ricoeur's engagement with the question of whether historiography is remedy or poison, we can now turn to a brief summary of Ricoeur's discussion of what he calls, following Michel de Certeau, the historiographical operation.[14] When one reflects on Ricoeur's discussion on the three phases of the historiographical operation, one should state that these three phases are not seen by him as three distinct chronological stages, but as "methodological moments, interwoven with one another".[15]

### i.     The documentary phase

The first phase of the historiographical operation (the documentary phase) ranges from the reports by eyewitnesses to the constituting of archives, and aims at establishing documentary proof. But these documents in the archives are themselves derived from the testimony of memories. Hence Ricoeur observes that:

> we must not forget that everything starts, not from the archives, but from testimony, and that, whatever may be our lack of confidence in principle in such testimony, we have nothing better than testimony, in the final analysis, to assure ourselves that something did happen in the past, which someone attests having witnessed in person, and that the

---

14  Ricoeur acknowledges that his use of the term "historiographical operation" has been influenced by Michel de Certeau's contribution to the project edited by Jacques le Goff and Pierre Nora under the title *Faire de l'histoire*. See Ricoeur, *Memory, History, Forgetting*, 136. For a revised version of De Certeau's essay, see De Certeau, M, *The Writing of History* (New York: Columbia University Press, 1988), 56-113. We also need to mention that Ricoeur does not narrow the concept of "historiography" to refer only to the writing phase of the operation (as the literal meaning of the word suggests). He states: "Writing, in effect is the threshold of language that historical knowing has already crossed, in distancing itself from memory to undertake the threefold adventure of archival research, explanation and representation. History is writing from one end to another. And in this regard, archives constitute the first writing that confronts history, before it completes itself in the literary mode of 'scripturality'". Ricoeur, *Memory, History, Forgetting*, 138.
15  Ricoeur, *Memory, History, Forgetting*, 137.

principal, and at times our only, recourse, when we lack other types of documentation, remains the confrontation among testimonies.[16]

Thus history starts with testimony, and testimonies are collected, preserved and consulted in the archive. In passing through the archives, testimonies enter the critical zone in which competing testimonies are evaluated. Crucial questions with regard to the trustworthiness of testimonies are posed, balancing both confidence and suspicion. Hence testimony opens an epistemological process "that departs from declared memory, passes through the archive and documents, and finds its fulfilment in documentary proof".[17] The archive is the institutional – and also social – space where the traces of the past are collected, conserved and classified with the aim of being consulted by qualified personnel who seek to establish documentary proof. However, the change in status from spoken testimony to archived material constitutes the first historical mutation. This implies the need for a critical engagement with the very notion of the archive. Hence Ricoeur affirms Pierre Nora's exclamation: "Archive as much as you like, something will always be left out".[18]

Ricoeur emphasises the fact that the historian does not come to the archive as a blank slate, but is armed with questions. One must therefore guard against what Marc Bloch called "epistemological naïveté", i.e. the idea that there is a first phase where the historian gathers the documents, and reads and evaluates them; and then a second separate phase where s/he writes them down. Ricoeur also quotes with approval Antoine Prost's declaration: "no observation without hypothesis, no facts without questions".[19] There is thus an interdependent relationship between facts, documents and questions; "trace, document and question thus form the tripod base of historical knowledge".[20] The possible confusion between confirmed facts and past events thus underlines the need for a vigilant epistemology.

## ii.     The phase of explanation/understanding

Towards the end of his discussion of the documentary phase, Ricoeur asks rhetorically whether documentary proof is more remedy than poison for the constitutive weakness of testimony. This question points to the need for the explanation/understanding phase,[21] since there are no documents produced or consulted without some prior questions, and no questions are generated without an explanatory project. The explanation/understanding phase can be viewed as the

---

16  Ricoeur, *Memory, History, Forgetting*, 147.
17  Ricoeur, *Memory, History, Forgetting*, 161.
18  Ricoeur, *Memory, History, Forgetting*, 169. In this context Ricoeur also asks whether the *pharmakon* of the archived document, once freed of its disgrace and allowed arrogance, has not become more a poison than a remedy.
19  Ricoeur, *Memory, History, Forgetting*, 177.
20  Ricoeur, *Memory, History, Forgetting*, 177. It must also be noted that for the historian everything can become a document (debris from archaeological excavations, parish registers, wills, price curves, etc.). Everything can be interrogated by the historian who seeks information about the past.
21  Ricoeur refers to the second phase of the historical operation as the explanation/understanding phase, because he wants to challenge the dichotomy that is often created between explanation and understanding (as famously posed by Dilthey in the 19th century).

phase that seeks to deal with the complexity of the 'because' response to the 'why?' question ('Why did things happen in a certain way?' 'Because …'). Interpretation, however, is not merely limited to this phase of the historical operation, but is present during the whole historiographical operation. Nonetheless, the explanation/understanding phase adds the new dimension of "the mode of interconnectedness of the documented facts".[22] In this regard, Ricoeur is especially interested in the question of the representation of the past. To represent the past is not to offer a copy of the past (a passive *mimesis*). It is linked to explanation/understanding that seeks to provide a model for dealing with the past. This 'modelling' is for Ricoeur the work of the scientific imagination – an action that prevents the domain of history slipping over into that of fiction. In this process there are two important guiding principles. The first has to do with the fact that historians use explanatory models that have in common their tendency to relate to human reality as a social fact. Hence, history takes its place among the social sciences. A second feature has to do with the construction of time spans (for instance, macro-historical or micro-historical scales). In this regard, Ricoeur imaginatively proposes the use of a variety of time scales in the explanatory process.[23]

### iii. The representative phase

The third phase that Ricoeur discusses in his portrayal of the historiographical operation is that of the historian's representation in written form. This is not to say that the writing of history or historiography is limited to this phase. It is one of Ricoeur's theses that writing is involved in all the respective phases. To mark the specificity of the third phase, Ricoeur prefers not to speak of historiography, but of literary or scriptural representation. Such representation must understand itself as 'standing for' (*représentance*, the German *Darstellung*). Such scriptural representation has intentionality. This intended 'something' makes history the learned heir of memory. In this process of intentional representation, narrative form plays an important role. Ricoeur also acknowledges the rhetorical aspect of staging a narrative.

In this representative phase of the historiographical operation the historian selects certain figures of style, chooses a plot and mobilises probable arguments within the framework of the narrative. In the process the writer uses rhetorical means to persuade the reader, while the reader displays certain postures in the reception of the text. Ricoeur is also interested in the confrontation between historical and fictional narrative. What is at stake for Ricoeur in his discussion of the respective

---

22   Ricoeur, *Memory, History, Forgetting*, 182.
23   In his discussion of the second phase of the historiographical operation, Ricoeur also gives a thorough review of the important moments of French historiography during the first two thirds of the 20th century. He also indicates a gradual shift from the idea of "mentalities" to that of "representation" in the vocabulary of historiography during the last third of the 20th century – a move he favours. Ricoeur refers here to the French *Annales* school (and the overarching figure of Fernand Braudel) with its privileging of the notion of "mentalités". In addition, Ricoeur considers the work of what he refers to as the three advocates of rigour (Foucault, De Certeau and Elias). With regard to the move from mentalities to representation, Ricoeur writes: "Therefore, over against the unilateral, undifferentiated, massive idea of mentality, that of representation expresses better the plurivocity, the differentiation, and the multiple temporalisation of social phenomena". Ricoeur, *Memory, History, Forgetting*, 227.

relationships between representation and narrative, representation and rhetoric, and representation and fiction, is the capacity of historical discourse to represent the past. This intentional aim, the 'standing for', of history is important as it indicates the expectation that historical knowledge constitutes attempted reconstructions of past events. This is the contract between the writer and the reader. Unlike the contract between a writer of fiction and his or her reader, the author and the reader of a historical text "agree that it will deal with situations, events, connections and characters who once really existed, that is, before the narrative of them is put together".[24] The question, though, is "whether, how and to what degree the historian satisfies the expectation and promise conveyed by this contract".[25] The claim to the truth of historical representation cannot be limited to the phase of written representation. It is the three modes of the historiographical operation together that enable the claim to truthfulness.

### 4. TOWARDS A RESPONSIBLE HISTORICAL HERMENEUTIC – ALSO FOR CHURCH AND THEOLOGICAL HISTORIOGRAPHY?

While it is not possible within the scope of this essay to give an exhaustive account of Ricoeur's rich, nuanced and extensive discussion of the threefold nature of the historiographical operation, the brief outline presented above does point to Ricoeur's commitment to affirming history's role in interpreting declared memory with the intention of truthful representation, thus attending both to the vulnerability and capability of memory as the womb of history. Although Ricoeur's plea for a responsible historical methodology does not answer the question of whether historiography is remedy or poison in a fixed or final way, I do want to argue that Ricoeur's work is extremely valuable for historiographical reflection and practice by reminding us of the importance of the necessary epistemological vigilance and hermeneutical sensitivity. The absence of these two attributes may easily result in mono-dimensional portrayals and evaluations of the past that are not able to fully address the temptations inherent in our projects of identity construction and identity maintenance.

Drawing on the work of Ricoeur, I want to make three brief remarks in this final section of the essay, outlining in the process some possible contours for a responsible historical hermeneutic that can also be of service to church and theological historiography. First, a responsible historical hermeneutic ought to be critical of the idea that the historian is value-free and dispassionate in her or his account of the past. Therefore over-confident claims regarding historical objectivity that disregard the role of the subject should be deflated. E.H. Carr's remark about this model of objectivist historiography is apt:

> This was the age of innocence, and historians walked in the Garden of Eden, without a scrap of philosophy to cover them, naked and unashamed before the god of history. Since then, we have known sin and experienced a Fall; and those who pretend to dispense with a philosophy of history are merely trying, vainly and self-consciously,

---

24  Ricoeur, *Memory, History, Forgetting*, 275.
25  Ricoeur, *Memory, History, Forgetting*, 275.

like members of a nudist colony, to recreate the Garden of Eden in their garden suburb.[26]

While one should note that there is no way around subjectivity, we should remember – as Paul Ricoeur has already argued in his early essay "Objectivity and Subjectivity in History" – that "there is good and bad subjectivity and we expect the very exercise of the historian's craft to decide between them".[27] Although the debate around objectivity in history can easily become stale, it is important to keep in mind how assumptions in this regard influenced (and are still influencing) historical and church historical practices – also in the South African context. Therefore one should remain vigilant against what the South African New Testament scholar Bernard Lategan has called "the seamless transition from source to description".[28] The 'sources' do not tell the complete story and even the best archives offer us a limited window onto the past.[29] Access to archives and primary sources does not absolve us from the task of *interpreting* the sources and placing them within meaningful interpretive frameworks and narrative configurations.[30]

A second remark on a responsible historical hermeneutic relates to the question of the faithful or truthful representation of the past. Part of the value of Ricoeur's work lies, in my view, exactly in the fact that he integrates the vulnerability and fragility of memory into the discussion on historiography, while at the same time he remains concerned with the question of the reality of the historical past, hence the need to distinguish between history and fiction. Ricoeur expresses his view clearly when he writes:

> A solid conviction animates the historian here: regardless of the selective nature of collecting, preserving, and consulting documents, and of their relation put to them by the historian, even including the ideological implications of all these manoeuvres – the recourse to documents marks a dividing line between history and fiction. Unlike the novel, the constructions of the historian are intended to be reconstructions of the past. Through documents and by means of documentary proof, the historian is constrained by *what once was*. He owes a *debt* to the

---

26  Carr, E H, *What is History?* (New York, 1962), 21. Cf. also *Clark, History, Theory, Text*, 15, 16.
27  Ricoeur, P, *History and Truth* (Evanston, Northwestern University Press, 1965), 22. For Ricoeur "subjectivity" does not merely refer to the historian's subjectivity, but also to the idea that "the *object* of history is the human *subject* itself" (40).
28  See Lategan, B C, "Nuwere ontwikkelinge op die gebied van die geskiedskrywing – 'n geleentheid vir herbesinning na 350 jaar van gereformeerdheid" in Coertzen, P (ed.), *350 Jaar Gereformeerd/ 350 Years Reformed, 1652-2002* (Bloemfontein: CLF-Drukkers, 2002), 269-276, here 271.
29  For a critical engagement with the notion of "the archive" see Derrida, J, *Archive Fever: A Freudian Impression* (Chicago: University of Chicago Press, 1996).
30  One might recall Bernard Williams's remark in his book *Truth and Truthfulness*: "With history as with some everyday narrative, every statement in it can be true and it can still tell the wrong story". Cited in Bluhstein, J, *The Moral Demands of Memory* (Cambridge: Cambridge University Press, 2008), 238.

past, a debt of *gratitude* with respect to the dead, which makes him *an insolvent debtor*.[31]

Thus one can argue that a responsible historical hermeneutic is a *vulnerable* as well as a *realistic* hermeneutic. In our evaluation of historiographical projects, this aspect should also come into play. Such an emphasis on the reality of our historical past should also be accompanied by the necessary epistemological and hermeneutical vigilance. As Richard Kearney remind us: "Narrative memory is never innocent. It is an ongoing conflict of interpretations: a battlefield of competing meanings. Every history is told from a certain perspective and in the light of a specific prejudice ... Memory is not always on the side of angels. It can as easily lead to false consciousness and ideological closure as to openness and tolerance".[32]

A final remark: the engagement with Ricoeur's work on memory and history brings to the fore the importance of the need for reflection on the question of an ethics of memory and the related concern for an ethics of history.[33] Ricoeur's sensitivity to the question of whether historiography is remedy or poison already hints at this. For Ricoeur the positivist models of a value-free historiography do not hold water. And the acknowledgment of the subjectivity of the historian and historical agents points to an ethical dimension in the historical enterprise. One aspect to consider in this regard is linked to Ricoeur's remark that events seen by one person or group as founding events or high points in their history are, viewed by another person or group, more like wounds or scars in their collective memory. This idea points to the promise of engaging in projects of shared historiography that take seriously the fact that our own histories are interwoven with the histories of others. Historiography is thus not necessarily opposed to hospitality. Furthermore, a responsible historical hermeneutic – also if such a hermeneutic is motivated by theological concerns – ought to be sensitive to the way in which representations of the past have led to exclusion and victimisation. As Ricoeur comments: "We need therefore, a kind of parallel history of, let us say, victimization, which would counter the history of success and victory. To memorise the victims of history – the sufferers, the humiliated, the forgotten – should be a task for all of us".[34]

---

31   Ricoeur, *The Reality of the Historical Past*, 1, 2.
32   Kearney, R, *On Paul Ricoeur: The Owl of Minerva* (Aldershot, Ashgate, 2004), 105.
33   See, for instance, Wyshogrod, E, *An Ethics of Remembering: History, Heterology, and the Nameless Others* (Chicago: University of Chicago Press, 1998); Margalit, A, *The Ethics of Memory* (Cambridge: Harvard University Press, 2002); Carr, D, Flynn, R T and Makkreel, R, *The Ethics of History* (Evanston: Northwestern University Press, 2004).
34   Kearney and Dooley, *Questioning Ethics*, 10, 11. For an exploration of these issues within the context of the celebration of 150 years of theological education at Stellenbosch, see Vosloo, RR, "Herinnering, tradisie, teologie: Op weg na 'n verantwoordelike historiese hermeneutiek", *NGTT* 50: 1&2 (June 2009): 280-288.

# 3. ON REMEMBERING: MEMORY, HISTORY, AND JUSTICE[1]

## 1. IN SEARCH OF CONCEPTUAL CLARITY

In the Preface to *Memory, History, Forgetting* Paul Ricoeur writes that this book grew out of some private, some professional and some public preoccupations. Under the rubric of "professional consideration" he refers to the fact that this book is a prolongation of an uninterrupted conversation with professional historians who have been "confronting the same problems regarding the ties between memory and history".[2] The ties that bind history and memory – these two ways of retrospection, of looking at or engaging the past – indeed raise some serious and challenging problems and questions. Without doubt the relationship is complex, given (among other things) the fact that both 'memory' and 'history' have multiple senses. Therefore one needs to give at least some indication of what one means when using these terms, albeit that one should also recognise their conceptual fluidity. In addition, one should affirm the boundaries and the interconnectedness between memory and history. Memory and history are not to be conflated in our discourse and practice, although they overlap in some significant ways. Geoffrey Cubitt puts it well in his book *History and Memory*:

> History and memory are proximate concepts: they inhabit a similar mental territory ... (W)e can see them as conceptual terms that have constantly interacted with each other, moving in and out of each other, circling each other warily or amorously, sometimes embracing, sometimes separating, sometimes jostling for position on the discursive terrain that is their common habitat.[3]

Given the fact the memory and history are connected concepts, and that there is often tension and even conflict between these two ways of knowing the past, it is not easy to conceptualise the relationship between memory and history.

The difficulties involved in reflecting on the ties that bind memory and history have not, however, discouraged scholars from venturing into this slippery terrain, though, and it has been said that "(f)ew topics in recent years have elicited as much interest among historians as the relationship between memory and history".[4] The

---

1   A first draft of this essay was read at a conference on "Memory and Historical Justice" in Melbourne, Australia in February 2012. The paper was subsequently published under the title "Memory, History, Justice: In Search of Conceptual Clarity" in *NGTT* 53, 2012:215-227. This article is dedicated to Prof. Vincent Brümmer in celebration of his 80th birthday. I first met Prof. Brümmer in 1992 when I attended his doctoral seminars as a student in Utrecht, and I remember vividly his emphasis on the need to be clear and coherent in one's reasoning. One can rightly say that his own impressive and influential oeuvre exemplifies the search for conceptual clarity, for the sake of love and life. The essay is presented here in a slightly revised form.
2   Ricoeur, P, *Memory, History, Forgetting* (Chicago: University of Chicago Press, 2004), xv.
3   Cubitt, G, *History and Memory* (Manchester: Manchester University Press, 2007), 4, 5.
4   Hutton, P, "Recent Scholarship on Memory and History", *The History Teacher* 33/4 (2000): 533-548, 533. Cf. Gardner, P, *Hermeneutics, History and Memory* (London: Routledge,

so-called 'turn to memory' in historical scholarship (a turn that is noticeable across academic disciplines, making memory studies "a peculiarly busy interdisciplinary arena"[5]) has emphasised the need to gain greater clarity on the close but complex relationship between memory and history. This essay seeks some conceptual clarity on this intricate interrelation between memory and history, also in conversation with some questions that arise from contexts associated with historical injustice. With this purpose in mind, the essay engages especially the later work of Paul Ricoeur, albeit that there is much to be gained from positioning Ricoeur's reflections on memory and history against the backdrop of his philosophical project as a whole.

In the Preface to *Memory, History, Forgetting* Ricoeur mentions another, more public, preoccupation that has informed this book:

> I continued to be troubled by the unsettling spectacle offered by an excess of memory here, and an excess of forgetting elsewhere, to say nothing of the influence of commemorations and abuses of memory – and of forgetting. The idea of a policy of the just allotment of memory is in this respect one of my avowed civic themes.[6]

The concern for the "just allotment of memory" is also shared by those who want to reflect responsibly on South Africa's apartheid past. Discussions on memory and history – and their interrelation – do not occur in a historical vacuum and they become especially poignant in contexts saturated with narratives of historical injustice. The work of the South African Truth and Reconciliation Commission offers a fitting example to consider in this regard. If one wants knowledge of the work of the Commission one can turn to the official report (published in seven volumes). This report is and will be, without doubt, an important and in many ways indispensable source for historians who want to embark on some or other kind of historiographical project connected to South Africa's apartheid past. There are of course many traumatic memories and painful stories not included in the official report. Furthermore, the written or recorded sources that have found their way into the 'archive' are not to be equated with the testimonies themselves or the events these testimonies point to. While the value of documents such as the official report can hardly be overstated, it is nevertheless important not to limit the work and legacy of the Truth Commission to the 'documented history', just as South Africa's apartheid history cannot be viewed only through the lens of the official Truth Commission report. For a responsible historical engagement with South Africa's apartheid past, a careful and critical interaction with documented history is extremely important. However, there are many memories not represented (or even misrepresented) in these sources. Hence the need for, and value of, oral history projects. In both documented and oral history, moreover, questions (often implicit questions) regarding the relationship between memory and history keep on coming to the fore.

One of the thought-provoking more recent reflections on the Truth and Reconciliation Commission is the book entitled *There was this Goat: Investigating*

---

    2010), 90.
5    Cf. Cubit, *History and Memory*, 4.
6    Ricoeur, *Memory, History, Forgetting*, xv.

*the Truth Commission Testimony of Notrose Nobomvu Konile* by Antjie Krog, Nosisi Mpolweni and Kopano Ratele. This book offers an illuminating engagement with the testimony of Notrose Konile, the mother of Zabonke Konile, who was killed in what came to be known as the Gugulethu Seven incident. Antjie Krog, well known for her haunting observations as reporter on the work of the Truth Commission reflected in her book *Country of My Skull* (1998), attended the hearing of Konile on 23 April 1996 and was struck by her seemingly incoherent testimony. The details do not concern us directly here, although I can mention that the title of the book is taken from a part of Notrose Konile's testimony, which was recorded as follows: "I had a very – a very scary period, there was this – this goat looking up, this one next to me said oh! having a dream like that with a goat looking at you is a very bad dream".[7] Years later Krog revisited this testimony with two colleagues from the University of the Western Cape, Nosisi Mpolweni and Kopano Ratele, who were then lecturers in the Xhosa and Psychology Departments respectively. They met regularly to discuss Konile's testimony and it became clear to them that the testimony in the official report is incomprehensible as it stands, and in order to make sense of it, you need to make use of indigenous language and knowledge systems. By tirelessly exploring the gaps and inconsistencies in Konile's testimony, and drawing on their respective disciplines, Krog, Mpolweni and Ratele indicate how a greater understanding of language and cultural contexts can challenge stereotypes and reductions. They observe: "As there were slippages in the interpretation of Mrs Konile's testimony, the valuable information with regard to her feelings and aspirations could not reach many of the Truth Commission officials and the audience. Slippages in translation can lead to misinterpretation and misrepresentation of a testifier, while intimate cultural knowledge can lead to a fuller and more just interpretation of a mother-tongue testimony that could restore the dignity of the testifier".[8]

I briefly mention this book because it offers a powerful reminder that one should guard against views that overestimate the ability of documented historical sources to represent the past. This is not to say that documents and written sources are not extremely important for historical investigation, but the inherent vulnerability of the archive should be acknowledged. But does this mean that we should rather privilege memory as a more reliable way of gaining knowledge of the past? Can one privilege memory over and above history or are these two intentions of the past, to follow Ricoeur's position, "undecidable".[9] And if so, why would this be the case?

## 2. MEMORY OR HISTORY?

Before entering into a more detailed engagement with Ricoeur's thoughts on the relationship between memory and history, it might be worthwhile to bring the

---

7   Krog, A, Mpolweni, N and, Ratele, K, *There was this goat: Investigating the Truth Commission Testimony of Notrose Nobomvu Konile* (Scottsville: University of KwaZulu-Natal Press, 2009), 13.
8   Krog, Mpolweni, and Ratele, *There was this goat*, 55.
9   Ricoeur, *Memory, History, Forgetting*, 385.

differences, overlaps and tensions between memory and history into sharper focus. David Lowenthal comments helpfully in this regard:

> Memory and history are processes of insight; each involves components of the other, and their boundaries are shadowy. Yet memory and history are normally and justifiably distinguished: memory is inescapably and prima-facie indubitable; history is contingent and empirically testable.[10]

Memory and history thus point to two distinguishable yet interconnected epistemological routes to knowing the past.[11] History is based on empirical sources in a more direct way, although memory is shaped by accounts of the past by others (that is 'history'). In a similar vein, history relies on eyewitnesses and their testimony (that is 'memory'). Despite the connections and overlaps, the world of memory appears quite different from the world of history.

Philip Gardner uses some vivid images to describe these different worlds. He links the world of memory to the brightness of day in which we move around in an assured way because we can see our surrounding (although we may make mistakes in what we believe we have seen). The world of history is different, since the sun has already set, and to navigate this dark space we need artificial light as a substitute for the sun. We must therefore look elsewhere for illumination, "to the archive, to the documents of history, without which the events that happened before our time would remain unlighted".[12] Gardner not only views the movement from history to memory in terms of the metaphor of 'light', but also views it as a question of distance and scale. Whereas history has to bridge the distance, difference and dislocation between present and past, the past and the present are already more intimately connected in the case of memory, with the agency of the individual playing a central role. In addition to describing the difference between memory and history in terms of images of light and distance, Gardner refers to the movement from history to memory as a movement from silence to sound: "In terms of sources it takes us from the document to the voice. In terms of method, it takes us from reading to listening".[13]

One might refine Gardner's description of the differences between the world of memory and the world of history, but his discussion is helpful to emphasise that we are dealing with two distinct ways of representing the past. Other features of the difference between memory and history can be added. Alan Megill, for instance, has argued that memory – however one defines it – has the character of being 'immediate' and that we do not have adequate grounds for challenging what somebody remembers, while history, on the other hand, is different since it brings evidence into play.[14] For Megill the blurring of history and memory is therefore deeply problematic, and the task of the historian "ought to be less to preserve memory

---

10 Lowenthal, D, *The Past is a Foreign Country* (Cambridge: Cambridge University Press, 1985), 187.
11 Lowenthal rightfully reminds us: "'Knowing the past,' as Kubler says, 'is as astonishing a performance as knowing the stars'; and it remains no less elusive for being well documented". Lowenthal, *The Past is a Foreign Country*, 191.
12 Gardner, *Hermeneutics, History and Memory*, 89.
13 Gardner, *Hermeneutics, History and Memory*, 90.
14 Megill, A, *Historical Knowledge, Historical Error* (Chicago: The University of Chicago Press, 2007), 22.

than to overcome it or at least to keep it confined".[15] Attempts not to conflate history and memory and to respect their boundaries are certainly helpful. But, on the other hand, it also seems problematic to cast memory and history in two opposing camps, the one being private, passive, subjective and value-related, and the other public, active, objective and fact-based. Over against these dichotomies and antinomies one can also point to the fact that Ralph Samuel has rightly argued "that memory, so far from being merely a passive receptacle or storage system, an image bank of the past, is rather an active shaping force ... and that it is dialectically related to historical thought, rather than some kind of negative other to it".[16]

In the discourse on memory and history and their relation a certain tension is often highlighted. From the side of those who privilege memory over history, 'history' is viewed as pretending to make value-free objective claims about the past that do not do justice to particular memories and identities. Those who privilege history over above memory are, in turn, sceptical of the way in which memory in their view functions in an arbitrary way without means to check its validity. In short, history seems to be vulnerable to questions of identity, while memory seems to be vulnerable to questions concerning truth claims. Gardner states the matter succinctly:

> If memory settles upon identity, it opens itself to the perils of wilful manipulation or organized forgetting. If history settles only upon its own claims to truth, it closes its eyes to its own boundedness. If history deprecates memory, it lays waste to its wellspring. If memory ignores history, it squanders its credibility.[17]

The dialectic between memory and history therefore remains, and a responsible engagement with the past is probably best served by allowing space for this tension to be creative and constructive, viewing both modes of retrospection with suspicion and trust. In conversation with Ricoeur, this essay explores further why one cannot decide which one of these two epistemological routes to the past has priority. Ricoeur's response to the memory-history problem is not to view memory and history as adversaries, but to view them as conjoined and complementary as we grapple with the past and the temporality of our own lives.[18] With this in mind, we now turn more directly to Ricoeur's thought.

## 3. RICOEUR ON MEMORY AND HISTORY

*Memory, History, Forgetting* presents Ricoeur's mature thought on memory and history, and their dialectical relationship. However, the concerns of this book are not new, since – as Ricoeur has noted in his "intellectual autobiography" – much

---

15  Megill, *Historical Knowledge*, 37. Megill therefore argues that a critical historiography, although it is informed by memory, has to stand at a distance from memory: "In short: history both needs memory and needs to go beyond memory" (40).
16  Samuel, R, *Theatres of Memory, Volume 1: Past and Present in Contemporary Culture* (London: Verso, 1994), x.
17  Gardner, *Hermeneutics, History and Memory*, 115.
18  Cf. Gardner, *Hermeneutics, History and Memory*, 97.

of his previous work is marked by a concern with "a sense of history".[19] The strong continuity between the themes that announce themselves in *Memory, History, Forgetting* and Ricoeur's earlier work should thus be noted, and it is profitable to read this book against the backdrop of his whole philosophical oeuvre. For our concerns here, Ricoeur's thought is especially valuable to preserve the necessary and creative tension between memory and history, as well as to maintain a view of both memory and history – as two distinct but interconnected modes of representing the past – with suspicion and trust. Given the focus of this essay on the dialectical relationship between memory and history, it is worthwhile to attend briefly to Ricoeur's discussion of this matter in a chapter on "History and Time" in the third section (entitled "The Historical Condition") of *Memory, History, Forgetting*.

As already mentioned, Ricoeur argues that one should not give priority to either memory or history. Therefore he considers what he views as two intersecting and competing developments. On the one hand, there is the attempt to dissolve the field of memory into history (which includes the development of a history of memory). On the other hand, there is the attempt of memory to historicise itself. Therefore Ricoeur is concerned with two questions, namely "Is Memory just a province of history? " and "Is Memory in charge of history?"[20] Ricoeur implicitly answers both questions, as could be expected, in the negative. The unending debates between the rival claims of history and memory need not, however, end in a paralysing aporia. Therefore Ricoeur writes:

> the *history of memory* and the *historicization of memory* can confront one another in an open dialectic that preserves them from the passage to the limit, from that *hubris*, that would result from, on the one hand, history's claim to reduce memory to the level of one of its objects, and on the other hand, the claim of collective memory to subjugate history by means of the abuses of memory that the commemorations imposed by political powers or by pressure groups can turn into.[21]

This quotation makes Ricoeur's intentions clear. The hubris of history (that reduces memory to one of its objects) should be countered. On the other hand, the abuses of memory – the danger of too much memory – should be kept at bay. This requires

---

19  Ricoeur observes: "(T)he question of history comes up as early as 1949 in 'Husserl and the Sense of History'; the same question also returns in other guises: the status proper to the history of philosophy, objectivity and subjectivity in history, the sense of history in general, the place of violence and non-violence in history, the sense of history and Christian eschatology, progress, ambiguity, hope, and so forth. The first collection of my articles, *History and Truth*, bears the mark of this constant concern for the 'sense of history'". See Hahn, L E, *The Philosophy of Paul Ricoeur* (Chicago: Open Court, 1995), 39. And in the third volume of *Time and Narrative*, we can add, Ricoeur deals extensively with the way in which history and fiction, when taken together, offer the response of a poetics of narrative to the aporias of time. Cf. Ricoeur, P, *Time and Narrative, Volume 3* (Chicago: The University of Chicago Press, 1998), 99-240.
20  See Ricoeur, *Memory, History, Forgetting*, 385-392. In dealing with the question "Memory, just a province of history?" Ricoeur mainly engages with an essay by Krzysztof Pomian entitled "De l'histoire, partie de la mémoire, à la mémoire, objet d'histoire", while his main conversation partner in dealing with the question "Memory, in charge of history?" is the literary critic Richard Terdiman.
21  Ricoeur, *Memory, History, Forgetting*, 392, 392.

prudent consciousness, a prudence that respects, among other things, what Ricoeur calls "the uncanniness of history".[22]

## 4. TOWARDS A RESPONSIBLE HISTORICAL HERMENEUTIC?

It is clear from the brief discussion above that Ricoeur affirms the need to maintain the dialectical relationship between memory and history. For Ricoeur memory is the matrix of history, and as such one cannot conceive of history without memory. This is not say that history is merely an extension of memory, but the stance that memory and history are antithetical should be rejected. In addition, the way in which history as a mode of responsible retrospection can police the abuse of memory ought to receive due emphasis.

In the Introduction to this essay brief reference was made to some of the challenges involved for an historical engagement with South Africa's apartheid past, and the role of the Truth and Reconciliation Commission as one response to the reality of historical injustice in South Africa. For the historian working on these themes both documented and oral sources are important and this implies the need for some understanding of the complementary and conflicting relationship between memory and history. On a methodological level the nuanced work of Ricoeur provides valuable conceptual clarity in order to address these challenges in a responsible manner. In this section of the article I would like to limit the discussion to two aspects that are especially pertinent en route to a responsible historical epistemology and hermeneutic in dealing with the past in contexts marked by conflict, violence and historical injustice, as well as by the concomitant search for reconciliation, truth and justice.

A first aspect relates to the need to emphasise the vulnerability of memory (while at the same, paradoxically, affirming the capability of memory). A second aspect relates to the importance of underlining the reality of the historical past through a careful historical or historiographical operation (while at the same time highlighting the mystery or strangeness of the past in the light of our historical condition).

### a   The vulnerability of memory

The fact that memory plays an important role in the historical process is uncontested. The value of the plea for (collective) memory – made by scholars such as Maurice Halbwachs, Yosef Yerushalmi and Pierre Nora – as a challenge to reductive understandings of historiography can hardly be overestimated. But we should also keep in mind that memory is a slippery and ambiguous notion. Even a committed advocate for the importance of memory such as Yosef Yerushalmi writes at the start of his justly acclaimed book *Zakhor: Jewish History and Jewish Memory*: "Memory is always problematic, usually deceptive, sometimes treacherous … We ourselves are

---

22   Cf. Ricoeur, *Memory, History, Forgetting*, 393. Under the heading of "The Uncanniness of History" Ricoeur adopts Freud's notion of *Unheimlichkeit* in his discussion of the influential work of Maurice Halbwachs, Yosef Hayim Yerushalmi and Pierre Nora. Ricoeur concludes his informative discussion by saying that "the 'uncanniness' of history prevails, even as it attempts to understand the reasons why it is contested by commemorative memory". Ricoeur, *Memory, History, Forgetting*, 411.

periodically aware that memory is among the most fragile and capricious of our faculties".[23] Memory is indeed at once fragile and potent. The ambivalent potential of memory – also for contexts associated with the public legitimisation of historical injustice – should be noted, for, as W. James Booth perceptively observes, "Memory has fueled merciless violent strife, and it has been at the core of reconciliation and reconstruction. It has been used to justify great crimes, and yet it is central to the pursuit of justice".[24]

Ricoeur too is deeply aware of what he refers to as the vulnerability of memory, acknowledging in the process the possible abuses of memory. According to Ricoeur, the abuses of natural memory[25] occur on three levels, namely the pathological, therapeutic level (referred to by Ricoeur as "blocked memory"), the practical level (described as "manipulated memory") and the ethico-political level (termed "obligated memory").

On the therapeutic level Ricoeur refers to the vulnerability of memory in the light of what he calls wounded or even sick memory, linking blocked memory to words like "traumatism", "wound", "scar" etc. Ricoeur's discussion here – which engages two of Freud's influential essays, namely "Erinnern, Wiederholen, Durcharbeiten" ("Remembering, Repeating, and Working-Through") and "Trauer und Melancholie" ("Mourning and Melancholia") – is worth considering in the important discourse that brings memory into conversation with notions such as "trauma", "narrative" and "forgiveness". In lives and communities scarred by violence and injustice, the presence of blocked memory can indeed be something that needs to be worked through, hence the call by many for "the healing of memories".[26] Ricoeur makes a further important remark about "symbolic wounds" that requires serious consideration, especially in post-conflict situations: "What we celebrate under the title of founding events are, essentially, acts of violence legitimated after the fact by a precarious state of right. What was glory for some was humiliation for others.

---

23  Yerushalmi, Y H, *Zakhor: Jewish History and Jewish Memory* (Seattle: University of Washington Press, 1982), 5.
24  Booth, W J, *Communities of Memory: On Witness, Identity, and Justice* (Ithaca: Cornell University Press, 2006), ix.
25  Ricoeur also refers in his phenomenology of memory – before turning to natural memory – to the abuses of what he calls "artificial memory". See *Memory, History, Forgetting*, 58-68.
26  For perspectives on memory and trauma engaging South African contexts, see the essays by an interdisciplinary team of scholars in Goboda-Madikizela, P and Van der Merwe, C, *Memory, Narrative and Forgiveness: Perspectives on the Unfinished Journeys of the Past* (Newcastle upon Tyne: Cambridge Scholars Press, 2009). As the Preface notes, this collection "explores the relation between trauma and memory, and the complex, interconnected issues of trauma and narrative (testimonial and literary). It examines transgenerational trauma, memory as the basis for dialogue and reconciliation in divided societies, memorialisation and the changing role of memory in the aftermath of mass trauma, mourning and the potential of forgiveness to heal the enduring effects of mass trauma" (xi). For a valuable earlier collection of essays that includes some theological and ethical perspectives, see Botman, HR and Peterson, RM (eds.), *To Remember and to Heal: Theological and Psychological Reflections on Truth and Reconciliation* (Cape Town: Human & Rousseau, 1996).

In this way, symbolic wounds calling for healing are stored in the archives of the collective memory".[27]

Ricoeur places on the practical level – the level of manipulated or instrumentalised memory – the important problem of memory and (personal and collective) identity. He is especially interested in the way in which memory is mobilised in the service of the quest and demand for identity. As he writes elsewhere, "the diseases of memory are basically diseases of identity".[28] The fragility or vulnerability of memory is therefore interconnected with the fragility of identity.

In addition to the abuses of blocked and manipulated memory, Ricoeur discusses possible abuses on an ethico-political level as he engages the emotional topic of the alleged "duty to remember". For Ricoeur it may even be that this duty to remember "constitutes, at one and the same time, the epitome of good use and of abuse in the exercise of memory".[29] In this context Ricoeur brings the notion of justice into play: "The duty of memory is the duty to do justice, through memory, to an other than the self".[30] Here, as in Ricoeur's project as a whole, some clear ethical concerns present themselves.

Moreover, we should note that Ricoeur does not approach memory merely from the viewpoint of its deficiencies, but also in the light of its capacities.[31] For our reference to the past we have no other resource than memory itself. Consequently, Ricoeur emphasises that our acknowledgement of the unreliability of memory must be interwoven with the admission that memory is our one and only resource to signify the past character of what we declare we remember. The deficiencies of memory should thus not be viewed from the outset as pathological and dysfunctional, "but as the shadowy underside of the bright region of memory".[32] As Ricoeur states: "To put it bluntly, we have nothing better than memory to signify that something has taken place, has occurred, has happened *before* we declare that we remember it".[33] This implies, in our view, that any reflection on the relationship between memory and history should not minimise the tension brought to the relationship by a strong

---

27  Ricoeur, *Memory, History, Forgetting*, 79.
28  Ricoeur, P, "Memory and Forgetting" in Kearney, R and Dooley, M (eds.), *Questioning Ethics: Contemporary Debates in Philosophy* (London: Routledge, 1999), 7.
29  Ricoeur, *Memory, History, Forgetting*, 87.
30  Ricoeur, *Memory, History, Forgetting*, 89.
31  The themes of fallibility and capability are important for Ricoeur's philosophical project. See, for instance, his earlier work *Fallible Man* (Chicago: Regnery, 1965). In an interview with Sorin Antohi, Ricoeur refers to a move in his philosophical anthropology from fallibility to capability: "In the intermediate book between *Memory, History, Forgetting* and *Time and Narrative*, namely, *Oneself as Another*, the central concept is man as he is able and capable. What man *can* do: I *can* speak, I *can* narrate, I *can* act, I *can* feel responsible ... therefore my last book on memory, history and forgetting is related not to fallible man but to capable man, this is to say that man is capable of making memory and making history". Ricoeur, P and Antohi, S, "Memory, history, forgiveness: A dialogue between Paul Ricoeur and Sorin Antohi", *Janus Head* 8/1 (2005): 17). See also Mechteld Jansen's chapter on "Fragiliteit: Breekbaarheid en Kwetsbaarheid" in Jansen, M M, *Talen naar God: Wegwijzers by Paul Ricoeur* (Dronten: Uitgeverij Narratio, 2002), 222-273.
32  Ricoeur, *Memory, History, Forgetting*, 21.
33  Ricoeur, *Memory, History, Forgetting*, 21.

emphasis on memory as an essential category in the attempt to offer a reliable representation of the past.

## b. The reality of the historical past

One can say that Ricoeur views memory with both suspicion and trust. The abuses of memory are clearly acknowledged, but the deficiencies of memory are not a reason to view memory as a mere province of history or to take refuge in the dream of historical objectivity. The objectivist historical mentality with its over-confident claims regarding value-free, dispassionate and 'objective' accounts of the past, on the basis of an inflated confidence in the power of primary sources to provide access to the past, should be resisted. While one must rightly challenge a certain form of objectivist historiography, since there is no way around subjectivity, we should remember too that "there is good and bad subjectivity and we expect the very exercise of the historian's craft to decide between them".[34] Although the debate around objectivity in history can easily become tiresome, it is important to keep in mind that the 'sources' do not tell the complete story and even the best archives offer us a limited window onto the past. Sources require interpretation and it is important to place the sources within the narrative frameworks that give them meaning.

Although Ricoeur affirms the role of narrative in both historical-scholarly and literary representations of the past, the difference between history and fiction should be respected. This implies, among other things, that critical history (via a coherent and responsible epistemology) has a role to play alongside, and sometimes in conflict with, memory. While memory is the matrix of history, it is not the master of history. The 'autonomy' of history should be acknowledged. At the same time the affirmation that history seeks to represent the 'reality' of the past should not lead to the type of over-confidence that does not duly respect the mystery or the uncanniness of the past. The messy and recalcitrant nature of the past ought to challenge any attempt that presumes to equate our historical representations with what occurred in the past. The strangeness of the past should keep haunting history, with historians even underlining this strangeness on a more conscious level (also as they engage contexts marked and scarred by historical injustice). In this regard a remark in the book *There was this goat* comes to mind. Grappling with the irregular and marginalised testimony of Mrs Konile before the South African Truth and Reconciliation Commission, the authors comment: "These 'strange' testimonies underline the importance of refraining from 'un-strange-ing' the strange – to allow it to be strange – but within its original logical and coherent context. Accommodation of 'strangeness' would keep the spaces of tolerance open for many people emerging from contexts of conflict and estrangement".[35]

---

34  Ricoeur, P, *History and Truth* (Evanston, Northwestern University Press, 1965), 22. For Ricoeur "subjectivity" does not merely refer to the historian's subjectivity, but also to the idea that "the *object* of history is the human *subject* itself" (40).

35  Krog, Mpolweni, and Ratele, *There was this goat*, 100.

## 5. CONCLUSION: THE RECEPTION OF MEMORY TAUGHT BY HISTORY, AND THE WITNESS TO JUSTICE

An analysis of Ricoeur's discussion of the relationship between memory and history clearly reveals that he does not want to privilege any one of these modes of retrospection, but that he wants to affirm their dialectical relationship. Memory is not a province of history, and history is not merely historicised memory. The persuasive power of *Memory, History, Forgetting* lies in part in the way in which Ricoeur is able to maintain this tension within the context of the threats posed by our 'being-in-time'-ness and forgetting. For any responsible historiographical project, Ricoeur's engagement with these themes holds much promise. The question can be asked, though, whether the relevance of Ricoeur's treatment of memory, history and forgetting extends beyond the writing of history.

With this question in mind, a lecture Ricoeur presented in English under the title "Memory, history, oblivion" in March 2003 at a conference on "Haunting Memories? History in Europe after Authoritarianism" at the Central European University in Budapest makes for interesting reading. In this lecture Ricoeur engages critically with his own focus in *Memory, History, Forgetting* on the *writing* of history (in line with the lexicon definition of historiography). In Ricoeur's words:

> What I am proposing today is a shift in the prevailing standpoint, a shift from writing to reading, or, to put it in broader terms, from the literary elaboration of the historical work to its reception, either private or public, along the lines of a hermeneutics of reception. This shift would give an opportunity to extract from their linear treatment in the book some problems which clearly concern the reception of history rather than the writing of history and to emphasize them. The issues at stake clearly concern memory, no longer as a mere matrix of history, but as the *reappropriation of* the historical past by a memory taught by history and often wounded by history.[36]

Ricoeur then elaborates on what he views as the most interesting consequences of this shift concerning the relationship between memory and history. This relationship is now treated not in a linear but in a circular way, with memory now appearing twice in the course of the analysis, first as the matrix of history (from the standpoint of history-writing), and later as the channel of the reappropriation of the historical past. This is not to disregard the linear account in *Memory, History, Forgetting*, since without this movement no reappropriation of the past is possible. However, Ricoeur points to the importance of memory as the reception of the historical past.

This focus on memory as the reception of the historical past has some important implications. In closing I would like to point to the fact that, among other things, it reminds us that questions regarding the relationship between memory and history cannot be separated from certain ethical concerns, hence the need for an ethics of memory and of history.[37] Some important questions therefore present themselves,

---

36 Ricoeur, P, "Memory, history, oblivion", 1-2. See www.fondsricoeur.fr [accessed on 20 May 2017].
37 See, for instance, Wyshogrod, E, *An Ethics of Remembering: History, Heterology, and the Nameless Others* (Chicago: University of Chicago Press, 1998); Margalit, A, *The Ethics of*

such as: Whose memories of the past are remembered and privileged? Are those recalling the memories or witnesses of the past today engaging those memories through history (i.e. through a responsible historical epistemology and hermeneutic)? Are those witnesses today who are receiving or reappropriating memories from the past themselves witnessing for justice? With whom – and in which communities and as part of what tradition – are we grappling with our interwoven and often contested constructions of the past?

In our Introduction to the essay we referred to Krog, Molweni and Ratele's investigation of the testimony of Notrose Nobomvu Konile, who through her seemingly incoherent testimony occupied a specific space in documented history (with her name not included in the index of the Truth Commission's website and misspelt in the official transcriptions). Yet they witness to her memory by trying "to understand this unmentioned, incorrectly ID-ed, misspelt, incoherently testifying, translated and carelessly transcribed woman".[38] This reminds us that we should be sensitive to the way in which representations of the past have led to exclusion and victimisation. In our continual reflection on the relationship between memory and history, we are therefore continually challenged to narrate the historical past otherwise. In this process we can also remember the words of Isak Dinesen that Hannah Arendt uses at the beginning of the chapter on "Action" in *The Human Condition* (and that Ricoeur is also fond of quoting): "All sorrows can be borne if you put them into a story or tell a story about them".[39]

---

*Memory* (Cambridge: Harvard University Press, 2002); Carr, D, Flynn, R T, and Makkreel, R, *The Ethics of History* (Evanston: Northwestern University Press, 2004).

38  Krog, Mpolweni, and Ratele, *There was this goat*, 4.

39  Arendt, H, *The Human Condition* (Chicago: The University of Chicago Press, 1958). Cf. Ricoeur, "Memory, history, oblivion", 9.

# 4. ON THE ARCHIVE: ARCHIVING OTHERWISE[1]

## 1. MEMORY, HISTORY AND THE ARCHIVE

In book X of Augustine's *The Confessions* one finds his famous and influential discussion of memory. Augustine's reflections on memory point to the fact that he is deeply under the impression of the vastness of memory. He writes about "the fields and vast mansions of memory", "the huge depository of memory", "the treasure-house of memory", "the immense spaces of my memory" and "the measureless plains and vaults and caves of my memory". As he passionately exclaims: "This faculty of memory is a great one, O my God, exceedingly great, a vast, infinite recess. Who can plumb its depth?"[2]

While it is not the aim of this essay to discuss Augustine's account of memory,[3] his exclamation with regard to the vastness of memory raises important and challenging questions for (church) historians. How do we deal with the treasure house of individual and collective memory? What part of the (Christian) past do we remember and privilege in our recollection through speech, writing and embodiment? Although the distinction between memory and history, or between remembrance and historiography, needs to be respected and treated with nuance,[4] one could certainly argue that the task of the church historian or historical theologian consists of "remembering the Christian past".[5]

Despite the vastness and mysterious nature of memory, as well as the limitations and complexities inherent in the historical task, the historian is nevertheless committed to the act of remembering and collecting, recalling and archiving. In this regard, the historian does not only use the archive but also contributes to the archive. The notion of the archive is therefore closely associated with the historical task. The complexity and elusiveness of this concept requires intensive methodological reflection. On a basic level, the archive is viewed as a place where documents are stored

---

1 This essay was first published under the title "Archiving Otherwise: Some Remarks on Memory and Historical Responsibility" in *Studia Historiae Ecclesiasticae* XXXI/ 2, 2005:379-399.
2 Saint Augustine, *The Confessions* (New York: Vintage Books, 1998), 206.
3 With regard to the sizable list of literature in this regard, see Wills, G, *Saint Augustine's Memory* (New York: Viking, 2002) and Teske, R, "Augustine's philosophy of memory", in Stump, E and Kretzmann, N, *The Cambridge Companion to Augustine* (Cambridge: Cambridge University Press, 2001), 148-158.
4 Some scholars refer to history and memory as two contradictory ways of dealing with the past, while others view history as a special case of social and cultural memory.
5 This phrase is taken from Robert Wilken's book, *Remembering the Christian Past* (Grand Rapids: Eerdmans, 1995). In the last chapter of this book, dealing with memory and Christian intellectual life, Wilken writes: "The Christian intellectual tradition, then, is inescapably historical. Without memory, our intellectual life is impoverished, barren, ephemeral, subject to the whims of the moment ... there can be no Christian life without reference to the writings of the prophets and evangelists, the doctrines of the church fathers, the conceptual niceties of the scholastics, the language of the liturgy, the songs of the poets and hymn writers, the exploits of the martyrs, and the holy tales of the saints" (179, 180).

meticulously, thus constituting a space of memory. But the archive can also be used as a broader metaphor or concept that relates to the body of knowledge produced about the past. It is inevitable that the historian, who shares in the production of knowledge about the past through archiving, privileges certain persons, texts, stories or events while neglecting and suppressing others. This essay argues that the processes of remembering, archiving and historiography are intrinsically connected and cannot be separated from questions about ethical responsibility underlying the historical task.

The nature and task of historiography are topics that regularly feature in church historical discourses.[6] This essay seeks to contribute to this ongoing discussion on historiography, memory and archiving by introducing an influential book by Jacques Derrida entitled *Archive Fever: A Freudian Impression* (originally published in French as *Mal d'Archive: une impression freudienne*).[7] *Archive Fever* was first delivered in London as a lecture at an international colloquium on the theme "Memory: The Questions of Archives". At this meeting, held under the auspices of the Sociéty Internationale d'Histoire de la Psychiatrie et de la Psychanalyse, the Freud Museum and the Courtauld Institute of Art, Derrida dealt in a creative and thought-provoking way with the concept of the archive.

Derrida's *Archive Fever* offers some important perspectives that challenge our thinking about archiving, memory and the historical task. This book has stimulated intensive conversation among archivists, philosophers, historians and social scientists about the archive and the related questions of memory and historiography.[8] In this essay

---

6 These questions have been discussed extensively among South African church historians as well, also in *Studia Historiae Ecclesiasticae* (the journal of the Church Historical Society of Southern Africa). For bibliographical references to the many articles on historiography in this journal (up to 2001), see Denis, P, "Three Decades of Church History in Studia Historiae Ecclesiasticae", *Studia Historicae Ecclesiasticae* XXVII/ I (2001): 217-246. See also Gundani, PH, "Christian Historiography and the African Woman: a Critical Examination of the place of Felicity, Walatta Pietros and Kimpa Vita in African Christian Historiography", *Studia Historiae Ecclesiasticae* XXX/1 (2004): 75-89; Duncan, G, "Historiography and Ideology in the (Mission) History of Christianity", *Studia Historiae Ecclesiasticae* XXX/1 (2005): 51-69; and Plaatjies, M and Landman, C, "Vroue in die teologiese antropologie van die Afrikaanse gereformeerde tradisie", *Studia Historiae Ecclesiasticae* XXX1 (2005): 203-222. The plea is also often made for an ecumenical perspective on church historiography. In this regard, see, for instance, Kalu, OU (ed.), *African Church Historiography: An Ecumenical Perspective* (Bern: Evangelische Arbeitsstelle Oekumene Schweiz, 1998) and Wengert, TJ and Brockwell, CW (eds), *Telling the Churches' Stories: Ecumenical Perspectives on Writing Christian History* (Grand Rapids: Eerdmans, 1995).
7 Derrida, J, *Archive Fever: A Freudian Impression* (Chicago: University of Chicago Press, 1996); Derrida, J, *Mal d'Archive: une impression freudienne* (Paris: Éditions Galilée, 1995).
8 See, for instance, Marlene Manoff's overview article "Theories of the Archive from Across the Disciplines", *Libraries and the Academy* 4/1 (2004): 9-25. Manoff refers to the British journal *History of the Human Sciences*, which devoted two special issues to the concept of the archive in 1989 and 1999. In fifteen articles scholars from a wide array of disciplines reflected on the meaning and role of archives by pondering questions such as the role of archives in the formation and development of national and democratic consciousness, the role of archives in totalitarian societies as a weapon in ethnic struggles, the contribution of the archival metaphor to anthropology, classics, history, literature and the visual arts, and the role of the archival metaphor in our conceptualisation of

I will focus on Derrida's probing reflections on the word 'archive', as well as two other aspects of this intricate text, namely his discussion of the possibility of the destruction of the archive through the death drive, and his argument about the archive and openness towards the future. After a brief discussion of these themes, the rest of the essay will offer some further reflections on the act of archiving, remembering and historical responsibility.

## 2. DERRIDA AND THE ARCHIVE

### a. Archiving the word 'archive'

Derrida begins *Archive Fever* with a reflection on the word 'archive', and particularly with the archive of this familiar word. He calls attention to the fact that *arkhē* at once names the commencement and the commandment. Therefore it apparently combines two principles, namely the principle according to nature or history (there where things commence) and the principle according to the law or the nomological principle (there where men and gods command). Derrida summarises this double meaning well when he writes: "In a way, the term indeed refers … to the *arkhē* in the physical, historical, or ontological sense, which is to say the original, the first, the principal, the primitive, in short to the commencement. But even more, and even earlier, 'archive' refers to the *arkhē* in the nomological sense, to the *arkhē* of the commandment".[9] Derrida further notes that the concept of the archive shelters within itself the memory of this double meaning of *arkhē*, but it also shelters itself from this memory, which means: it forgets it.

Derrida does not merely signify the word 'archive' in terms of *arkhē*, but also in terms of the Greek word *arkheion*. An *arkheion* is "initially a house, a domicile, and address, the residence of the superior magistrates, the *archons*, those who commanded".[10] It was at this place of recognised authority that official documents were filed. The *archons* are not only responsible for the physical safety of what is deposited, but they are also accorded the hermeneutical right and competence to interpret the archives. These documents (which are not always just discursive writings) speak the law, and as such they need both a guardian and a place. The archive requires the law and domiciliation. The archive is thus not merely to be equated with living memory. It also has to do with consigning, with inscribing a trace of the past in some external

---

digital collections and the internet. She refers to the fact that ten of these fifteen articles built on, or cited, Derrida's *Archive Fever* (10). See also the extensive project "Refiguring the Archive" hosted by the Graduate School for the Humanities and Social Sciences of the University of the Witwatersrand (in conjunction with other archival institutions) in 1998. Derrida, who spoke at one of these meetings, had a major influence on this project that aimed at creating space for post-positivist critique of the archive in South Africa. See also the book that resulted from this project: Hamilton, C *et al*. (eds), *Refiguring the Archive* (Cape Town: David Philips, 2002). In this book questions about the archive are often brought into conversation with the work of the Truth and Reconciliation Commission. For a discussion of the question of memory and reconciliation, see also Vosloo, RR, "Reconciliation as the Embodiment of Memory and Hope", *Journal of Theology for Southern Africa* 109 (2001): 25-40.

9    Derrida, *Archive Fever*, 2.
10   Derrida, *Archive Fever*, 2.

space. This ;placing; is important, since there is no archive without the exteriority of place, without an outside. In this regard, Derrida uses the term topo-nomology to refer to this combination of localisation and the law.

The archive as place or dwelling marks the institutional passage from the private to the public sphere according to a particular privileged topology. At work is a certain *archontic* principle (linked to the position and power of the *archons*, the masters of the house and keepers of the law). This archontic principle relates to the power to unify, identify and classify, as well as to the power of consignation. Consignation is not only the act of assigning residence or putting things in reserve. It also refers to the gathering together of signs in such a way that there is a system or synchrony in which the elements articulate the unity of an ideal configuration.

Something of the reasoning behind Derrida's argument in *Archive Fever* relates to the interrogation, or deconstruction, of this archontic principle, the inherent archic or patriarchic principle of power at work within the concept of the archive. One can say that Derrida implies that the archive is not the *arkhē* but the trace or vestige of the origin. Evil reigns when there is confusion between the archive and the origin. As John D. Caputo rightly observes in his book *The Prayer and Tears of Jacques Derrida: Religion without Religion*: "The illness, the disorder, the crisis, the evil (*le mal*) that besets a culture that depends on archives ... is for Derrida always a *mal d'archive*, always a function of the disorder in the relations between the *arche* and the archive, a failure to remember the distance between the original and the trace".[11]

In his archiving of the word 'archive', Derrida thus challenges attempts to compound the *arkhē* and the archive. He also aims to interrupt discourse on the archive by exposing the way in which the concept of the archive is inescapably linked to archontic power. This reminds us that archives are monuments to the way in which power is reconfigured. It does not merely store and include, but also testifies to a narrative of exclusion. There is an intimate relationship between the archive and the *archons*, between archiving and a certain archontic principle. Discourses about memory, historiography and archiving that are not sensitive to these configurations need to be ruptured and interrupted.

### b. The possibility of the destruction of the archive

Derrida's *Archive Fever* is subtitled *A Freudian impression*. We have already noted that this book stemmed from a lecture given at the Freud Museum in London. Derrida mentions in a footnote that he was conscious of the fact that Yosef Hayim Yerushalmi, a famous Jewish historian, would attend this lecture on memory and psychoanalysis.[12] In a sense *Archive Fever* is a conscious dialogue with him, responding especially to Yerushalmi's book *Freud's Moses: Judaism Terminable and Interminable*. While all of the details of Derrida's engagement with Yerushalmi (and with Freud) do not directly concern us here (although we will return to Derrida's

---

11 Caputo, J D, *The Prayer and Tears of Jacques Derrida: Religion without Religion* (Bloomington: Indiana University Press, 1997), 264.
12 Derrida refers to the fact that Yerushalmi was to have been at his lecture, but was sick and could not attend. Someone else read his contribution the next day. See Derrida, *Archive Fever*, 2, as well as Hamilton *et al.*, *Refiguring the Archive*, 38, 40.

interaction with Yerushalmi in the next section), it is important to attend to the way in which Derrida utilises the Freudian notion of the death drive in his argument on the nature of the archive.

The death drive, writes Derrida, has the silent vocation to destroy the archive. It is an aggression and a destruction that incites forgetfulness, amnesia and the annihilation of memory. It aims, furthermore, not only at the destruction of memory as spontaneous experience, but also at the effacement of the archive as place of consignation. The death drive's calling is "to burn the archive and to incite amnesia … aiming to ruin the archive as accumulation and capitalization of memory on some substrate and in an exterior place".[13] It destroys every archival desire. As Derrida argued during a visit to South Africa, it is the possibility of "burning into ashes the very trace of the past".[14] There is thus a battle between the death drive, which is archive destroying, and the archive-conserving drive.

Derrida comments on the fact that a certain limitation is imposed on the archive drive (or the conservation drive) in the light of radical finitude. But the passion for the archive arises not merely because we know that traces can be lost by accident or because space or time is finite, but because something in us, something in the psychic apparatus, is driven to destroy the trace. Without the aggression and destructive nature of the threatening death drive, there is no archive fever, no passion for the archive.

Derrida's remarks on the conflict between the archive drive and the death drive remind us that memory and the archive are vulnerable. Memories can be suppressed. Documents can be lost. Archives can be destroyed. There is a drive to destroy the trace of the past in such a way that there are no reminders left, not even ashes. This reality incites a passion for memory and archiving, but it also confronts one with the reality of forces that aim to destroy these processes, challenging naïve and romanticised notions of remembering and archiving. The story of memory, historiography and archiving is therefore also a story of selective remembering and (conscious or unconscious) forgetting.

False assumptions about the so-called neutrality of the archive also sustain naïve notions of archiving. The archive is not only a place for storing and conserving an archivable content of the past. The technical structure of the archive also determines the structure of the archivable content: "The archivization produces as much as it records the event".[15]

Derrida also speculates about the impact of telephonic credit cards, portable tape recorders, computers, printers, faxes, televisions, teleconferences and above all email, on the psychoanalytic archive. Indeed it seems as if the new technology posits important challenges for thinking about the archive and archiving today. While Derrida affirms the indisputable importance of classical modes of archiving, he also points to the importance of not closing our eyes to the boundless upheaval underway in archival technology, something that must also be accompanied by

---

13  Derrida, *Archive Fever*, 12.
14  Hamilton, C et al., *Refiguring the Archive*, 42.
15  Derrida, *Archive Fever*, 12. Derrida adds the provocative remark: "This is also our political experience of the so-called news media" (17).

## c. The archive and openness towards the future

It is stating the obvious that the concept of the archive has everything to do with the past. Derrida admits that the notion of the archive refers to the signs of consigned memory and recalls faithfulness to tradition. But he also states: "As much and more than a thing of the past, before such a thing, the archive should *call into question* the coming of the future".[17] The archive is thus not merely a question of the past: "It is a question of the future, the question of the future itself, the question of a response, of a promise and of a responsibility for tomorrow".[18]

In his discussion on the archive as a question of the future, Derrida returns to a notion that he has utilised before in his work, namely the notion of messianicity.[19] In the concept of the archive a spectral messianicity is at work that ties the archive (like religion, history and science do) to a very singular experience of the promise. One should note that messianicity for Derrida is not to be equated with what he calls messianism. It is not reducible to the Messiah figure in Jewish, Christian or Islam traditions. For Derrida the relationship to the messianic is simply the relationship to the future. It is the openness to the idea that anything might happen or anyone may arrive. With regard to the archive, this means that it is always possible to re-interpret and re(con)figure the archive. The archive can never be closed. It is exactly this future-orientation of the archive that, according to Derrida, confronts us with ethical and political responsibility.

Derrida illuminates this messianic hypothesis in conversation with Yerushalmi's fictional monologue with Freud in a chapter towards the end of his book. Derrida refers in this discussion to Yerushalmi's distinction between Judaism and Jewishness. Judaism (as religion, culture and tradition) can be finite and "terminable", but Jewishness is interminable. Yerushalmi would give up everything in Judaism except its Jewishness. This "Jewishness" is not primarily about religion, belief in God or tradition, but is about the constitutional reference to the past and the unique relation to the future. This is also the belief that Yerushalmi wants Freud to affirm, or countersign, in their fictional conversation. It is especially with regard to this question of the future, with regard to the notion of hope and hopelessness, where Freud is, according to Yerushalmi, most "un-Jewish".

Derrida is prepared to subscribe to Yerushalmi's affirmation of the future to come. But there is a speck of anxiety in Derrida's mind about Yerushalmi's thoughts on Jewishness and the openness to the future, and especially about the specific nature of this hope. Derrida turns to Yerushalmi's discussion of memory in *Zakhor: Jewish*

---

16 Derrida, *Archive Fever*, 18.
17 Derrida, *Archive Fever*, 34, 35.
18 Derrida, *Archive Fever*, 36.
19 For Derrida's discussion of "the messianic", see especially his articles "Faith and Knowledge" and "The Force of Law", both included in Derrida, J, *Acts of Religion* (New York: Routledge, 2002), and his book *Specters of Marx* (New York: Routledge, 1993). See also Caputo, *The Prayer and Tears of Jacques Derrida*, 117-159.

*History and Jewish Memory* to explain this uneasiness. Derrida recalls Yerushalmi's statement from this book that "only in Israel and nowhere else is the injunction to remember felt as a religious imperative to an entire people".[20] It is as if God has inscribed one thing into the memory of a single people and of an entire people, namely the injunction: in the future, remember to remember the future. Derrida trembles before this claim of uniqueness. He comments: "Because if it is just to remember the future … it is no less just to remember the others, the other others and others in oneself, and that the others can say the same thing – in another way".[21]

Derrida wants to deconstruct the language of the "One" and of the "Unique". Hence Derrida's statement: "The gathering into itself of the One is never without violence, nor is the self-affirmation of the Unique, the law of the archontic, the law of consignation which orders the archive".[22] The moment there is the One and the Unique, there is murder, wounding and trauma. The One protects itself from the other in a movement of jealous violence. The One forgets to remember itself to itself. It claims for itself uniqueness and privilege. Derrida wants to guard against what he sees as Yerushalmi's attempt to make Israel a privileged archive. Although affirming the messianic, the openness to the future, as well as memory and repetition, Derrida wants, at the same time, to say 'no' to the death drive. This 'no' is, as Caputo notes, a 'no' to "the archival, partriarchival, nationalist, racist, sexist tendencies that irrupt whenever a house (*arkheion*) is filled with *archons*".[23]

## 3. RECONFIGURING ARCHIVAL PASSION

Derrida's *Archive Fever* serves as reminder of the need to remember the past, to burn with a passion for the past, while at the same time remembering the future that is to come. This means that the archive is not closed, but always marked by openness to the future. The rest of this essay probes this notion further by (de)positing three theses, or passions, with regard to memory, historiography and the archive.

### a. A passion for the past

In his autobiography Elie Wiesel, the holocaust-survivor and winner of the Nobel Prize for peace, writes:

> Memory is a power no less powerful and pervasive than love. What does it mean to remember? It is to live in more than one world, to prevent the past from fading and to call upon the future to illuminate it.

---

20 Derrida, *Archive Fever*, 76.
21 Derrida, *Archive Fever*, 77. In a dialogue with Elizabeth Roudinesco, Derrida reiterates his understanding and critique of Yerushalmi's position: "Yerushalmi seems ready to abandon Judaism. Not out of infidelity to Judaism, but out of fidelity to Jewishness, which, from his point of view, is marked by two fundamental vocations: the experience of the promise (the future) and the injunction of memory (the past). This was troubling to me … Every culture, every non-Jewish community would claim these two fundamental traits". See Derrida, J and Roudinesco, E, *For What Tomorrow…: A Dialogue* (Stanford: Stanford University Press, 2004), 188-189.
22 Derrida, *Archive Fever*, 77, 78.
23 Caputo, *The Prayer and Tears of Jacques Derrida*, 272.

> To remember is to revive fragments of existence, to rescue lost beings, to cast harsh light on faces and events, to drive back the sands of time that covers the surface of things, to combat oblivion and reject death.[24]

Together with memory, or as part thereof, archives and archiving are important sources and practices to challenge oblivion and death. This seems especially important in times when our historical consciousness is threatened by totalising forces that thrive on abstraction and mythologising. Often this mindset is accompanied by the strategy of either romanticising or demonising the past. Both these strategies, ironically, serve to enhance a climate of amnesia. Historical complexity and ambiguity are ignored in favour of simplistic schemes. In the process the past is domesticated and hence loses the ability to speak in a convincing and challenging manner to the present. The past becomes mute. Responsible remembering, historiography and archiving aim at dealing with the past in such a way that the past retains the power to illuminate the present and the future.

In *Archive Fever* Derrida also confirms the importance of the role of the archive and archiving. His deconstruction of the archive, one must note, is not aimed at a destruction of the archive. Derrida comments that while nothing is less reliable and clear than the concept archived in the word 'archive', we are nevertheless in need of archives. To have archive fever can also be something more than suffering from a sickness. Derrida writes: "It is to burn with a passion. It is never to rest, interminably, for searching for the archive right where it slips away. It is to run after the archive, even if there is too much of it, right where something in it anarchives itself. It is to have a compulsive, repetitive, and nostalgic desire for the archive, an irrepressible desire to return to the origin, a homesickness, a nostalgia for the return to the most archaic place of absolute commencement".[25]

One could argue that such a desire for the archive is connected with a passion for (re)collecting, gathering, writing down, recording and storing. This passion for the past is important in the fight against the wilful denial of many horrific episodes in the history of humankind and the erasure of the stories of the vulnerable and the victimised. These 'revisionist' histories, like those that deny the existence of extermination camps, must be challenged. What is needed are communities and institutions that sustain faithful memory, and consequently historians to archive the past and keep memories alive – something what Paul Ricoeur refers to as faithful testimony. This notion of faithful testimony serves as a helpful expression of the pathos of the archivist and the historian. It is an attempt to try and reconstruct the best story that one can.

In an interesting interview with Richard Kearney, included in the book *Questioning Ethics: Contemporary Debates in Philosophy*, Ricoeur emphasises the fact that a sense of what 'really happened' must keep concerning us. Questions of historical representation and reference to the past are complex indeed, but for ethical as well as epistemological reasons the truth claim must not be eliminated. Therefore historical memory needs to be supplemented by documentary and archival evidence. In this

---

24  Wiesel, E, *All Rivers Run to the Sea: Memoirs 1, 1928-1969* (London: Harper Collins, 1996), 150.
25  Derrida, *Archive Fever*, 91.

interview Kearney rightly raises the question of whether testimonies cannot also be manipulated and distorted in order to serve particular interests. Ricoeur responds: "The fundamental objective of the good historian is to enlarge the sphere of archives, that is, the conscientious historian must open up the archive by retrieving the traces which the dominant ideological forces attempted to suppress".[26] By archiving and narrating otherwise, the historian aims at giving expression to the voices of the abused and excluded. The historian does not merely oppose the manipulation and distortion of testimonies by telling the story differently, but also by providing the space for the confrontation between opposing testimonies. This idea of providing a hospitable space is vital for fostering faithful testimony. This, however, is not a romanticised space in which opposing testimonies are forced into false harmony. And the historian is by no means a neutral observer in this process, but an actor in the plot and also embedded in history.

In summary we can say that to burn with a passion for the past, a passion for the archive, is to aim for faithful testimony. Theologically speaking, one can say that the (church) historian must burn with a passion for truth, providing that we qualify the notion of truth in a way that adequately challenges positivistic assumptions. This also implies that the attempt at faithful testimony is not to be separated from a striving for justice.

### b.  A passion for justice

The faithfulness to the past, faithful testimony, is not without implications for the present (and the future). As Robert Gibbs so poignantly states in a chapter entitled "Why remember?" in his book *Why Ethics? Signs of Responsibilities*: "Remembrance is not about recalling the past or about preserving it, but is needed to disrupt the present".[27] The historian seeks to enlarge the archive, to collect, to gather, to reconsign, to narrate. But there is also the need for an awareness that the archive is embedded in a politics of power. The archive is indeed, as Derrida calls it in *Archive Fever*, the *arkheion*. Derrida reminds us of the way the archive is involved in a politics of power when he remarks in a footnote: "There is no political power without control of the archive, if not of memory. Effective democratisation can always be measured by this essential criterion: the participation in and the access to the archive, its constitution, and its interpretation".[28]

Given this interrelatedness of the archive and power, the task of the historian is also subversive, i.e. to challenge the hegemony of certain constructions of the past. The failure to interrupt and disrupt the present can easily lead to a mere affirmation of the status quo. One should note that a feverish interruption in the name of new

---

26  Kearney, R and Dooley, M (eds), *Questioning Ethics: Contemporary Debates in Philosophy* (London: Routledge, 1999), 16.
27  Gibbs, R, *Why Ethics? Signs of Responsibility* (Princeton: Princeton University Press, 2000), 354.
28  Derrida, *Archive Fever*, 4. One is well aware of the feverish control that institutional authority, such as the state and the market, exercises over archival materials. It is driven by the desire to make one's own archive authoritative and normative, and to exercise control over the archive of the other. This, writes Caputo, "lies at the basis of every feverish racism, nationalism, fundamentalism, or messianism, at the root of every 'identitarianism'". See Caputo, *The Prayer and Tears of Jacques Derrida*, 265.

ideologies could also serve the status quo and help to keep oppressive power structures in place. The historian needs to be mindful of this risk. Nevertheless, it is a real risk that the study of history will not result in a challenge to the present, but only serve as justification of the past. This may have the effect that only the stories of the victors are transmitted – a point highlighted by church historians in Africa. For instance, in his inaugural lecture as professor in Church history at the University of Stellenbosch, entitled "Kerkgeskiedskrywing in Suid-Afrika: 'n kritiese evaluasie" ("Historiography in South Africa: a Critical Evaluation"), Hannes Adonis seeks to challenge an understanding of history that privileges the victors. Towards the end of this lecture he confirms the importance of oral sources for historiography.[29] These sources help to access previously hidden experiences of people and social groups whose stories have not been incorporated into official documented history. This is the history of oppressed groups, women and the poor. Adonis sees this development to write "a history from below" as congruent with the Africa, proverb that says: "Until the lions have their historians, tales of history will always glorify the hunter".[30] It is indeed the case that the church historian's responsibility is to tell the story of the lions, albeit with the realisation that the lions are also victors when history is viewed in yet another way.

To archive otherwise, to read and write history otherwise, is to challenge the story of the victor and the way in which it has been successfully transmitted. It is to "brush history against the grain".[31] In the process we need to be mindful that the historian is most often descended from the victors and that the critique of the victors is a critique of oneself. As Robert Gibbs rightly reminds us: "My world is thus stolen from nameless others, even at the moment of my mere existence. Historiography, therefore, juxtaposes the past and present, not merely to learn something new of the present, but to interrogate my present, and to address my responsibility for others' suffering from which I have directly benefited".[32]

In her book *An Ethics of Remembering: History, Heterology, and the Nameless Others*, Edith Wyschogrod asks the crucial question whether the conveyance of history does not require a double passion: "an eros for the past and an ardor for the others in whose name there is felt an urgency to speak?".[33] To be a historian is not merely to write, photograph, film and televise. It is also binding oneself by a promise to the dead to tell the truth about the past. She writes: "The historian's responsibility is

---

29 Several church historians and theologians have reflected intensively on the importance of oral sources for the historical task (Adonis refers specifically to Oosthuizen and Claassen). One needs to be mindful also of the remark by the editors in the introduction to *Refiguring the Archive*: "The oral record is not the only alternative to public documentary archives. Literature, landscape, dance and a host of other forms offer archival possibilities capable of releasing different kinds of information of the past, shaped by different record-keeping processes". See Hamilton *et al.*, *Refiguring the Archive*, 10.
30 Adonis, H, *Kerkgeskiedenis in Suid-Afrika: 'n Kritiese evaluering*. Inaugural lecture (Stellenbosch University, 2000), 11.
31 As Gibbs writes, with reference to Walter Benjamin: "The task of historiography is to brush history against the grain, to make lost possibilities of the past register in disrupting our present". Gibbs, *Why Ethics?*, 355.
32 Gibbs, *Why Ethics*, 368.
33 Wyschogrod, E, *An Ethics of Remembering: History, Heterology, and the Nameless Others* (Chicago: University of Chicago Press, 1998), xi.

mandated by another who is absent, cannot speak for herself, one whose actual face the historian may never see, yet to whom 'giving countenance' becomes a task".[34] Wyschogrod refers in this regard to the role of what she calls the heterological historian. This is the historian who is driven by an eros for the dead and the urgency of ethics. In short, it is to burn with a passion for justice.

This sensitivity does not necessarily safeguard one against ideological constructs (it is probably not possible to give theoretical safeguards). It is, however, difficult to see how just archiving and just memory are possible without this ethical optics. Paul Ricoeur raises in this regard the question whether it should not be a task for all of us "to memorise the victims of history – the sufferers, the humiliated, the forgotten".[35] This task cannot, however, be separated from lamenting the painful injustices suffered by the victims and the bondage experienced by the oppressors. This also requires lamenting our inadequacy to remember and recall the past justly. Therefore the work of the historian is also a work of mourning.

### c. A passion for the future

As already noted, Derrida shares in his intriguing interaction with Yerushalmi the affirmation of the future to come.[36] The archive opens out to the future. It is never closed. This affirmation of the future to come is the condition of all promises, of all hope and expectation. With regard to this affirmation of the future to come, Derrida emphasises the fact that the archive is an irreducible experience of the future. As Caputo comments on Derrida's argument: "In the end the archive should be an open book, an opening to the future, the depository of a promise, it is to burn with a passion for the impossible. It is to be marked by a promise of something to come".[37]

According to Derrida, the archive should call into question the coming of the future. Derrida refers in this regard to a spectral messianicity at work that ties the archive to an experience of the promise. From a Christian perspective one can ask whether we can follow Derrida all the way on this path. Kearney rightly notes in his book *The God Who May Be: A Hermeneutics of Religion* that Derrida "is more concerned with the everyday (every moment) incoming of events than in the truth of some divine advent".[38] Derrida seems to prefer the spectral to the revealed structure of such incoming. Although Kearney makes it clear that he cannot follow Derrida in this regard, he also points to the indispensable lessons that deconstruction teaches about vigilance, patience and humility.[39]

Some historians and theologians will probably construct the archive's openness to the future in a different way than Derrida. However, *Archive Fever* reminds us that

---

34  Wyschogrod, *An Ethics of Remembering*, xii.
35  Ricoeur, P, "Memory and Forgetting", in Kearney, R and Dooley, M (eds.), *Questioning Ethics: Contemporary Debates in Philosophy* (London: Routledge, 1999), 10, 11.
36  Derrida prefers to use in French the word *l'avenir* (to-come), rather than *le future*, in order "to point towards the coming of an event rather than toward some future present". Derrida, *Archive Fever*, 68.
37  Caputo, *The Prayer and Tears of Jacques Derrida*, 278.
38  Kearney, R, *The God Who May Be: A Hermeneutics of Religion* (Bloomington: Indiana University Press, 2011), 98.
39  Kearney, *The God Who May Be*, 99.

the question of the archive is not to be separated from the question of the future. This points, among other things, to a certain *temporality* at work within the historical task. In his conversation with Yerushalmi about the future to come, Derrida recalls Walter Benjamin's famous essay "Theses on the Philosophy of History". In this essay Benjamin writes: "History is the subject of a structure whose time is not homogeneous, empty time, but time filled by the presence of the now".[40] Hence the historian establishes a conception of the presence (as the time of the now) "which is shot through with chips of Messianic time".[41] This is a temporality that sees every second of time as "the strait gate through which the Messiah might enter".[42]

While Christian and Jewish thinkers may construe differently their understanding of a temporality that critiques homogenous, empty time, there is a shared assumption regarding the importance of the incoming of the future for the understanding of the present and the past. This implies that remembering, historiography and archiving are not to be separated from taking responsibility for tomorrow and the expectation of the future to come. One can speak, therefore, not only of the presence of the past, but also of the presence of the future. As Wyschogrod writes about the historian's "ethics of remembering:" "In speaking of the dead others, the historian enters into a temporal zone that is neither past, present or future. The tense in which her promise is inscribed is that of the future-present, an impossible new time in which the future as promise cannot lose its sense of presence".[43]

## 4. CONCLUSION

Derrida's *Archive Fever* certainly invites further critique, concretisation and contextualisation. It rightfully reminds us, however, of the archive's openness towards the future as well as its archontic power in history. With regard to the latter, the complex relationship between archives and the power of the state immediately comes to mind. In the words of Achille Mbembe: "There is no state without archives – without its archives. On the other hand, the very existence of the archive constitutes a constant threat to the state".[44] The intricate relationship between the archive and power is not merely limited to state power, but also finds expression in other configurations that have a stake in the memory and reconstruction of the past. Church historical discourse is also not exempted from the subtle archontic temptations at work in the archiving process. It is therefore vital for church historians to preserve a sensitive demeanour throughout the act of writing and interpreting history.

Such sensitivity is rooted in a hermeneutic of doing church history in communion. This reiterates the importance of an ecumenical and interdisciplinary approach to church history. In addition, it points to the importance of taking into consideration those lives, groups and communities often neglected, including ordinary church members, minority groups, women and children. It implies, furthermore, resistance

---

40  Benjamin, W, *Illuminations* (New York: Schocken Books, 1969), 261.
41  Benjamin, *Illuminations*, 263.
42  Benjamin, *Illuminations*, 264. For a theological discussion of Benjamin's "Theses on the Philosophy of History", see Moltmann, J, *The Coming of God* (Minneapolis: Fortress Press, 1996), 38-41.
43  Wyschogrod, *An Ethics of Remembering*, 248.
44  Hamilton *et al.*, 23.

to hagiographical accounts of persons and communities that sanitise memory and cloud faithful testimony. Theological perspectives on church history offer important resources to challenge the hegemony of archontic power, to archive otherwise, and to remember differently.

The introduction of this essay referred to Augustine's understanding of the haunting vastness of memory. In his book *Saint Augustine's Memory*, Garry Wills challenges a static understanding of Augustine's description of memory. He writes: "This memory is dynamic, constructive, predictive, constitutive of identity, the meeting place with other humans, and the pathway to God".[45] Wills's depiction of memory can rightly also be applied to the church's historical task, reminding us of the open, dynamic and transformative nature of remembering the past.

---

45   Wills, G, *Saint Augustine's Memory* (New York: Viking, 2002), 4.

# 5. ON TRADITION: REFORMING TRADITION?[1]

## 1. THE REFORMED TRADITION AS 'LIVING TRADITION' – ALSO IN SOUTH AFRICA?

In April 2007 a group of scholars gathered in Geneva to reflect on the question of Calvin's legacy in the light of the approaching celebration in 2009 of the 500th anniversary of the Genevan Reformer's birth. On that occasion the South African Reformed theologian Dirkie Smit read a paper entitled "Views on Calvin's Ethics: Reading Calvin in the South African Context", subsequently published in *Reformed World*.[2] In this paper Smit recalls how during his student days Willie Jonker – then a newly appointed professor at the theological faculty at Stellenbosch – inspired some of them to look with new eyes at Calvin and the Reformed heritage. In the process they became acquainted with a different Calvin than the Calvin presented by apartheid theologians; in fact, in Calvin's thought they not only discovered the resources to challenge the underlying ethos of a theological justification of apartheid, but they also found an impetus for a theological response to the crises facing South Africa. In the concluding section of his interesting essay on reading Calvin in South Africa, Smit draws on Alasdair MacIntyre's description of a "living tradition" as an "historically extended, socially embodied argument, precisely in part about the goods which constitute that tradition".[3] Smit comments:

> We became very conscious that we belong, that we are socially embodied, that we have fathers and mothers, sisters and brothers, that we belonged to others, not to ourselves, to a worldwide community. We were conscious that this community extended far back into history … And we were conscious that this community through history was involved in an argument about what precisely constitutes, defines, makes this tradition what it is and us who we are. We were at the same time grateful for belonging to this community and history, and deeply critical and self-critical about the embodiment of this community in history, about its social form and its own role.[4]

Smit remarks that Jonker taught him and others to view the Reformed tradition as a living tradition, to appeal to tradition against tradition, to appeal to community

---

1 This essay emerged out of the meetings of the "Transforming traditions" research group (led by John de Gruchy). Some of the academic work of this group (including an article by De Gruchy) was published in the *Journal of Theology for Southern Africa* 139 (March 2010). For my contribution (which is republished here), see Vosloo, R, "Reforming Tradition? Remarks on Reformed Theology in South Africa, in Conversation with Alasdair MacIntyre", *Journal of Theology for Southern Africa* 139, March 2010, 18-31.
2 See Smit, DJ, "Views on Calvin's Ethics: Reading Calvin in the South African Context", *Reformed World* 57/4 (2007): 306-344. This essay has also been published under the title "Views on Calvin's ethics from a South African perspective" in Smit, DJ, *Essays on Being Reformed*, Vosloo, RR (ed.) (Stellenbosch: Sun Media, 2009), 1-34.
3 Smit, *Essays on Being Reformed*, 30. Cf. MacIntyre, A, *After Virtue: A Study in Moral Theory* (second edition) (Notre Dame: University of Notre Dame Press, 1984), 222.
4 Smit, *Essays on Being Reformed*, 30.

against community, to appeal "to our deepest identity in order to critique our actual identity".[5] In addition, Smit notes how this same logic was applied in different ways by other theologians working within the Reformed tradition in South Africa, including Allan Boesak, Lekula Ntoane, Russel Botman, Beyers Naudé, David Bosch and John de Gruchy. Drawing on the famous Reformed motto *Ecclesia reformata semper reformanda*, Smit poses some vital rhetorical questions: "Is a community that calls itself 'Reformed' not always to be reformed again, by God? Should such a Reformed church not always be engaged in 'a historically extended, socially embodied argument about the goods that constitute that tradition'? Should that not be central to the communal ethos of such a community?"[6]

For Smit it is exactly this self-critical discernment that should find embodiment in our preaching and listening, our confession and church orders, as well as our theological reflection and participation in public life. Smit closes his essay by saying that we celebrate Calvin's legacy not simply by praising him, but by standing in his living legacy, "which includes seriously discussing and debating with one another what concretely embodying gratitude for this surprising pathos of the Triune God could mean, today and in our one common world".[7]

I this essay I want to affirm Smit's plea (one often voiced by others as well) that we view the Reformed tradition as living and dynamic, especially given the ambiguous history of the Reformed tradition in South Africa – a tradition that can rightly be described as "a story of many stories".[8] In 2009 Calvin's life, work and legacy were celebrated in countless ways worldwide, also in South Africa.[9] It is with some sadness that one has to note that the Calvin celebrations in South Africa took place at a time when the reunification process between churches of the Dutch Reformed family of churches had lost momentum. Furthermore, the theologically rich Belhar Confession still faces much resistance from some church communities in South Africa. And references to the legitimacy crisis of the Reformed churches in South Africa abound. Against the backdrop of these challenges facing Reformed communities in South Africa today, I want to attend in more detail to Alasdair MacIntyre's reflection on tradition, which Smit alludes to, in an attempt to gain greater clarity on what it means for the Reformed tradition in South Africa to be 'a living tradition'. In addition, I want to argue for the need for theological discourse to re-engage critically the notion of tradition as such, since this conceptual engagement can prove valuable in understanding and addressing the challenges facing specific traditions. Hence I make a few remarks on the need for a critical engagement with the

---

5    Smit, *Essays on Being Reformed*, 31.
6    Smit, *Essays on Being Reformed*, 32.
7    Smit, *Essays on Being Reformed*, 33-34.
8    Cf. Smit, DJ, "Reformed Theology in South Africa: A Story of Many Stories", *Acta Theologica* 12/1 (1992): 88-110); Smit, DJ, "On Adventures and Misfortunes: More Stories about Reformed Theology in South Africa" in Harinck, G and Van Keulen, D (eds), *Vicissitudes of Reformed Theology in the Twentieth Century* (Studies in Reformed Theology, Vol. 9) (Zoetermeer: Meinema, 2004), 208-235; and Smit, DJ, "What does it mean to live in South Africa and to be Reformed?", *Reformed World* 58/4 (2008): 263-283. These three essays are also published in Smit, *Essays on Being Reformed*, 201-258.
9    At Stellenbosch University, for instance, a conference was held that focused on the relevance of Calvin for (South Africa) today. For the published papers of this conference, see *NGTT* 51 Supplementum (2010).

notion of tradition, before turning in more detail to MacIntyre's thought. In the final section of the essay I bring MacIntyre's views on tradition into critical conversation with questions pertaining to some theological challenges facing Reformed theology and Reformed communities in South Africa today, with a special focus on some developments within the Dutch Reformed family of churches.

## 2. RETRIEVING TRADITION, EMBRACING CHANGE

In his little book *The Vindication of Tradition* the historian and theologian Jaroslav Pelikan recalls an incident where a lecturer chided a group of students for having no sense of tradition and for supposing that the history of music begins with Bob Dylan. Then one of the students asked: "Bob who?"[10] This anecdote reiterates an experience that many people today might well want to apply to the Christian tradition, namely the experience of a growing sense of historical amnesia. And one can probably rightly argue that there is a need for a greater knowledge of, and engagement with, the Christian tradition amidst such a perceived historical vacuum. In the process, however, one should also pay attention to the resistance against retrieving the notion of tradition, while registering at the same time a possible sea change that indicates some space for a more positive reception of the emphasis on tradition.

In the *Preface* to his book published in 1981 and simply entitled *Tradition*, the Chicago sociologist Edward Shils observes that there are many books about particular traditions and about tradition in particular religions, literature, art and law, but that there is "no book about tradition which tries to see the common ground and elements of tradition and which analyses what difference tradition makes in human life".[11] Shils aims to address this gap in critical scholarship and his work indeed offers important insights for reflection on the notion of tradition. Given the influence of Enlightenment rationality and scientific knowledge, Shils argues, change and innovation have become coterminous with progress and improvement, while traditionality has become connected with ignorance and superstitions. Shils is sceptical of this scepticism towards tradition inherited from the Enlightenment and his work can be seen as an attempt to revive the notion of tradition against these impulses.

Any attempt to reclaim the notion of tradition will have to recognise, as Shils does, that the Enlightenment legacy is in many ways inhospitable to the notion of tradition. At the same time we need to acknowledge that any fossilised understanding of tradition needs to be critiqued. One should still differentiate carefully between tradition and traditionalism. Jaroslav Pelikan's oft-quoted remark remains helpful: "Tradition is the living faith of the dead, traditionalism is the dead faith of the living".[12] The Oxford historian Diarmand MacCullloch also puts it well: "Self-styled 'Traditionalists' often forget that the nature of tradition is not that of a humanly manufactured mechanical or architectural structure with a constant outline and

---

10  Pelikan, J, *The Vindication of Tradition* (New Haven: Yale University Press, 1984), 5.
11  Shils, E, *Tradition* (Chicago: University of Chicago Press, 1981), vii.
12  Pelikan, *Vindication of Tradition*, 65.

form, but rather that of a plant, pulsing with life and continually changing shape while keeping the same ultimate identity".[13]

Today, given the strong and sustained critique of Enlightenment rationality over the last few decades, there is probably a greater openness to retrieving not merely specific traditions but also the notion of tradition as such. Nevertheless, a cautionary remark is necessary: the plea for a renewed retrieval of the notion of tradition can itself be a masked form of conservatism. The neo-traditionalist can turn out to be a crypto-fundamentalist. While one can rightly argue that the idea of conservation is central to the notion of tradition, it is furthermore true – as Shils and MacIntyre, among others, have argued – that the ability to be critical of a tradition lies at the heart of a dynamic understanding of tradition.

Any attempt to reclaim the notion of tradition, also within theological discourse, must therefore challenge the way in which tradition and change are viewed as diametrically opposing categories. Put differently, the plea for re-engaging or retrieving tradition should not be separated from the plea for the transformation of traditions. This emphasis gives rise to the pivotal question: what does it mean to take the vital and enigmatic connection between tradition and transformation seriously? An important start for such an inquiry is to affirm that change, innovation and creativity are not to be contrasted uncritically with tradition.[14] The negative effects of traditionalism (understood as a static concept) make it clear that we need to have a sense of change, development and restatement as inherent to a dynamic understanding of tradition. With reference to the reception of Calvin in the Reformed tradition, Karl Barth has made this point in a forceful manner: "(T)hose who simply echo Calvin are not good Calvinists, that is, they are not really taught by Calvin. Being taught by Calvin means entering into dialogue with him … The aim, then, is a dialogue that may end with the taught saying something very different from what Calvin said but that they learned from or, better, through him".[15]

Remarks such as this by Barth, however, do not silence the voices of those proponents of a particular tradition who may view any specific attempt at a restatement, re-embodiment or transformation of their tradition as a misrepresentation. Therefore it is clear that one cannot reflect on the concept of tradition without facing the

---

13  MacCulloch, D, *A History of Christianity: The First Three Thousand Years* (London: Penguin Books, 2009), 7-8.
14  Cf. Dulles, A, "Tradition and Creativity in Theology", *First Things* 27 (1992): 20-27. Dulles opens his article by stating: "The ideas of 'tradition' and 'creativity' seem at first glance to be opposed and incompatible. Tradition says continuity; creativity says innovation and hence discontinuity. With the proper distinctions, however, it may be possible to show that the two are not only compatible but mutually supportive" (20). And Geoffrey Cubitt has rightly noted in his book *History and Memory* (Manchester: Manchester University Press, 2007): "What constitutes tradition is not so much the total absence of change – societies are never completely static and even the most traditional patterns of behaviour evolve slowly over time – as the close relationship between knowledge and repetitive practices" (179). Cf. also the remark by the Catholic moral philosopher Josef Pieper in his book translated as *Tradition: Concept and Claim* (Wilmington: ISI Books, 2008): "It is especially clear here how little real tradition is something purely static, and how false it is to confuse the concept of tradition with inertia, never mind with stagnation. In truth, the activity of the living transmission of a *traditum* is a highly dynamic business" (15).
15  Barth, K, *The Theology of John Calvin* (Grand Rapids: Eerdmans, 1995), 4.

reality of rival claims about what belongs to the heart of a specific tradition. Against traditionalism or a static understanding of tradition, one should maintain the need for tradition as a dynamic phenomenon, as 'living tradition'; but in doing so one is challenged to give some account of how the restatements and re-embodiments of the tradition show *continuity* with past statements and embodiments of the tradition in question.[16]

In reflecting on these challenges, it seems to me that the thinking of the moral philosopher Alasdair MacIntyre can provide important insights. MacIntyre's own intellectual biography reveals many transformations – from being a Marxist to being a Thomist.[17] MacIntyre's (later) views on the notion of 'tradition' are not to be detached from this biographical detail. Nevertheless, his influential and provocative views on the notion of tradition deserve thorough and critical engagement – also by those in the Reformed tradition who adhere to the adage of *semper reformanda*.[18]

## 3. ALASDAIR MACINTYRE ON TRADITION

For the purposes of this essay I want to highlight some aspects of MacIntyre's influential (and complicated) discussion of the notion of tradition that are particularly relevant as groundwork for an attempt to rethink the relevance of the Reformed tradition as a 'living tradition'. In doing so, I will draw mainly on MacIntyre's books *After Virtue* (1981), *Whose Justice? Which Rationality?* (1988) and *Three Rival Versions of Moral Enquiry* (1990), although I also view his later works such as *Dependent Rational Animals: Why Human Beings Need the Virtues* (1999), *Edith Stein: A Philosophical Prologue 1913-1922* (2006) and his more recent *God, Philosophy, Universities* (2009) as important works that reward careful reading in the light of the concerns of this essay.[19] But it

---

16  The focus on continuity raises further questions regarding the relationship between continuity and identity. In his valedictory lecture, delivered on the occasion of his retirement as professor in the philosophy of religion at the University of Utrecht, on "The identity of the Christian Tradition" (Utrecht, 16 October 1997) Vincent Brümmer writes: "(T)here are two necessary conditions for something to maintain its identity as the entirety to which the name refers: the continuity of its history as well as the fixed origin to which it is linked by this continuous history. Continuity is not enough. Without the unbroken link with the same origin, something cannot remain the same entity as it originally was" (15).

17  On MacIntyre's intellectual biography see, for instance, the chapter "A Short History of Alasdair MacIntyre" in Lutz, CS, *Tradition in the Ethics of Alasdair MacIntyre: Relativism, Thomism, and Philosophy* (Lanham: Lexington Books, 2004), 7-32, as well as Thomas D D'Andrea's "A Brief Biographical Sketch" in his comprehensive book on MacIntyre's thinking entitled *Tradition, Rationality, and Virtue: The Thought of Alasdair MacIntyre* (Aldershot: Ashgate, 2006), xvi-xix.

18  In the process of engaging MacIntyre's thinking on tradition one should take into account that the notion of tradition has multiple meanings, and that the concept of tradition is often appropriated differently in Roman Catholic and Protestant traditions. The focus in this article, however, is mainly on the way in which the idea of tradition functions on a more formal level.

19  One can also mention the value of MacIntyre's selected essays published as *Alasdair MacIntyre: The Tasks of Philosophy, Selected Essays, Volume 1* (Cambridge: Cambridge University Press, 2006) and *Alasdair MacIntyre: Ethics and Politics, Selected Essays, Volume*

is important to note, as some scholars have rightly pointed out, that MacIntyre's understanding of tradition developed and changed as his project unfolded.[20]

## a. The critique of tradition-free reasoning

In his highly influential and much-discussed book *After Virtue*, Alasdair MacIntyre critiques what he refers to as "the Enlightenment project" to ground morality in a tradition-free rationality. As MacIntyre comments in an important chapter on "The Virtues, the Unity of a Human Life and the Concept of a Tradition": "(T)he individualism of modernity could ... find no use for the notion of tradition within its own conceptual scheme except as an adversary notion".[21] MacIntyre's critique of the Enlightenment critique of tradition is closely connected to his defence of what he calls the narrative view of the self – a view that understands the self as a storied self embedded in history and communities. He writes in this regard:

> For the story of my life is always embedded in the story of those communities from which I derive my identity. I am born with a past; and to try to cut myself off from that past, in the individualist mode, is to deform my present relationships. The possession of a historical identity and the possession of a social identity coincide. Notice that rebellion against my identity is always one possible way of expressing it.[22]

The 'storied' self cannot be dislocated from a person's social and historical embeddedness. Whether one likes it or not, one is part of an inherited history and also one of the bearers of a tradition.

MacIntyre furthermore challenges any attempt to contrast tradition with rationality or reasoning. There are no tradition-free modes of reasoning. This point is made persuasively in *Whose Justice? Which Rationality?*: "What the Enlightenment made us for the most part blind to and what we now need to recover is, so I shall argue, a concept of rational enquiry as embodied in a tradition".[23] And a few pages later he writes: "So rationality itself, whether theoretical or practical, is a concept with a history; indeed, since there are a diversity of traditions of enquiry, with histories, there are, so it will turn out, rationalities, rather than rationality, just as it will turn out that there are justices rather than justice".[24] Thus rationality itself is tradition-constituted and tradition-constitutive. According to MacIntyre, there is therefore no way to engage in the conversation about justice, for instance, "except from within some one particular tradition in conversation, cooperation, and conflict with those

---

2   (Cambridge: Cambridge University Press, 2006) for understanding the development of MacIntyre's project.
20  Jean Porter, for instance, has pointed to the way in which MacIntyre's understanding of tradition evolved in the decade between the first edition of *After Virtue* and the publication of his Gifford lectures (*Three Rival Versions of Moral Inquiry*). See her essay "Tradition in the Recent Work of Alasdair MacIntyre" in Murphy, MC, *Alasdair MacIntyre* (Contemporary Philosophy in Focus) (Cambridge: Cambridge University Press, 2003), 38.
21  MacIntyre, *After Virtue*, 222.
22  MacIntyre, *After Virtue*, 221.
23  MacIntyre, A, *Whose Justice? Which Rationality?* (Notre Dame: University of Notre Dame, 1988), 7.
24  MacIntyre, *Whose Justice? Which Rationality?*, 9.

who inhabit the same tradition".[25] This critique of a tradition-free understanding of rationality (as offered by MacIntyre) is an important part of the process of retrieving tradition as a general notion, since it prepares the ground not to succumb to the tempting logic of a tradition-free rationality in the light of the contradictions and conflicts within our own traditions.

### b. Tradition as a historically extended, socially embodied argument

MacIntyre does not merely critique the contrast between tradition and rationality or reason. He also challenges attempts to contrast the stability of tradition with conflict. When a tradition is in good order, there is not an absence of conflict, but rather "when a tradition is in good order it is always partially constituted by an argument about the goods the pursuit of which gives to that tradition its particular point and purpose".[26] For instance, institutions such as universities will be partly constituted by a continuous argument as to what a university is or ought to be. Vital traditions thus embody continuities of conflict. Hence MacIntyre's oft-quoted definition of tradition: "A living tradition then is an historically extended, socially embodied argument, and an argument precisely about the goods which constitute that tradition".[27]

At least three aspects of MacIntyre's definition of a 'living tradition' are important. First, a living tradition is a *historically* extended argument extended over time; it is the pursuit of goods that extends over generations. This acknowledgment of the historical character of traditions is extremely important, since it indicates continuity (and discontinuities) over time. Our views on specific matters are not to be dislocated from historical developments. Often we view our ideas as original or creative only because we are ignorant of the way in which our outlook was formed by the thinking of those preceding us. We can only direct our inquiry now if we realise how our own thought is shaped by that of our predecessors.[28]

Second, traditions are *socially embodied* arguments. The reflection on tradition cannot be separated from reflection on communities, their narratives, practices, institutions, etc. The individual's search for his or her own good is conducted within the contexts defined by those traditions of which the individual's life is a part. Here the narrative phenomenon of embedding is crucial. The history of our own lives is embedded in and made intelligible by the larger and longer histories of a number of traditions. Also our practices (an important notion in MacIntyre's project) are embedded in a larger and longer history of the tradition that conveyed these practices to us.

---

25  MacIntyre, *Whose Justice? Which Rationality?*, 350.
26  MacIntyre, *After Virtue*, 222.
27  MacIntyre, *After Virtue*, 222.
28  In *God, Philosophy, Universities: A Selective History of the Catholic Philosophical Tradition* (Lanham: Rowman & Littlefield Publishers, 2009), MacIntyre again affirms this understanding of the historical nature of traditions when he states that one of the underlying convictions of his book "is that Catholic philosophy is best understood historically, as a continuing conversation through the centuries, in which we turn and return in dialogue with the most important voices from our past, in order to carry forward that conversation in our time" (1).

Third, traditions are socially embodied *arguments*. This implies conflict about what lies at the heart of the tradition. The fundamental agreements in the tradition are defined and redefined in terms of conflict with enemies external to the tradition, as well as with those internal to the tradition. Internal conflicts might at times destroy the fundamental agreement, so that traditions become divided. It can also happen that two independent and even antagonistic traditions might recognise possibilities for fundamental agreement and reconstitute themselves.[29]

### c. The sustainability of tradition and the relevant virtues

MacIntyre is deeply aware that traditions decay, disintegrate and disappear. Hence his questions: "What then sustains and strengthens traditions? What weakens and destroys them?"[30] For MacIntyre the key part of the answer to these questions lies in the exercise or the lack of exercise of the relevant virtues. Certain virtues – such as justice, truthfulness, courage and certain intellectual virtues – are necessary to sustain traditions, while the lack of these virtues corrupts traditions. In addition to these virtues, MacIntyre mentions what he describes as "the virtue of having an adequate sense of the traditions to which one belongs or which confront one".[31] This 'additional virtue' is not to be confused with conservative antiquarianism. Rather it is the manifestation of an adequate sense of the future possibilities which the past has made available to the present. MacIntyre writes: "Living traditions, just because they continue a not-yet completed narrative, confront a future whose determinate and determinable character, so far as it possesses any, derives from the past".[32] This does not merely mean that one possesses the knowledge of a set of maxims or generalisations pertaining to the tradition. It is rather about a "kind of capacity for judgment which the agent possesses in knowing how to select among the relevant stack of maxims and how to apply them in particular situations".[33] This remark testifies to the importance of discernment, pointing to the ability to recognise the *kairos* (or moment of truth) and to find the right ways of embodying appropriate responses.

### d. Traditions, change, and epistemological crises

Although MacIntyre emphasises the importance of the relevant virtues to sustain traditions, he is also aware of the fact that over time some features within established systems of beliefs may become evident and make it incoherent. As a tradition is confronted with new situations, and as new questions arise in the light of this, the established beliefs and practices may reveal a lack of resources to provide answers for these new questions. A crisis can also develop when two previously separated and discrete communities (with their own established beliefs, practices and institutions) come together for one or other reason, for instance, as a result of migration or

---

29 Cf. MacIntyre, *Whose Justice? Which Rationality?*, 12.
30 MacIntyre, *After Virtue*, 222.
31 MacIntyre, *After Virtue*, 223.
32 MacIntyre, *After Virtue*, 223.
33 MacIntyre, *After Virtue*, 223.

conquest. Such a development "may open up new alternative possibilities and require more than the existing means of evaluation are able to provide".[34]

The challenges resulting from the incoherence that develops within traditions over time requires the reformulation of beliefs and the remaking of practices, or both. MacIntyre sees three stages in the initial development of a tradition. During a first stage the relevant texts, beliefs and authorities have not yet been put into question. Then follows a second stage in which inadequacies and limitations have been identified, but not yet remedied. This situation can lead to a third stage in which there is a response to the inadequacies, resulting in reformulations and re-evaluations designed to remedy the inadequacies and to overcome the limitations.[35]

MacIntyre furthermore considers the kind of occurrence in the history of traditions which he describes as an "epistemological crisis".[36] How traditions respond to an epistemological crisis determines whether they attain or fail to attain intellectual maturity. What is an epistemological crisis? An epistemological crisis occurs when a tradition-constituted mode of enquiry ceases to make progress. The tradition's methods of enquiry become sterile and conflicts over rival answers to key questions cannot be settled rationally. There seem to be insufficient or no resources within the established fabric of belief to respond to the crisis, resulting in the dissolution of historically founded certitudes. Such an epistemological crisis requires inventiveness. According to MacIntyre, the invention of new concepts to address an epistemological crisis must satisfy three requirements. First, the new and conceptually enriched scheme must furnish a solution to problems previously deemed intractable. Second, an explanation must be provided of what rendered the tradition sterile and/or incoherent. Third, these tasks must be carried out in a way that exhibits fundamental continuity with the shared beliefs of the past.[37]

For MacIntyre an adequate response to an epistemological crisis in a tradition thus requires imaginative conceptual innovation. He refers in this regard to the 4th-century doctrine of the Trinity that resolved the controversies developing out of competing interpretations of scripture, as well as Aquinas's synthesis of the Aristotelian and Augustinian traditions. MacIntyre also makes a further important point regarding traditions and epistemological crises: "To have passed through an epistemological crisis successfully enables the adherents of a tradition of enquiry to rewrite its history in a more insightful way".[38] Such a history does not only provide a way of identifying continuity with the past, but also supplies the structure that underpins the justification of truth claims. Viewed from a theological perspective, this remark points to the interesting (inter-)connection between theological innovation and new projects of theological historiography.

MacIntyre further notes that every tradition, whether it recognises this fact or not, will at some stage in the future fall into a state of epistemological crisis. The

---

34  MacIntyre, *Whose Justice? Which Rationality?*, 355.
35  Cf. MacIntyre, *Whose Justice? Which Rationality?*, 355.
36  For MacIntyre's first discussion of "epistemological crises", see his important essay "Epistemological Crises, Dramatic Narrative, and the Philosophy of Science", *The Monist* 60/4 (1977): 453-472. Also published in *Alasdair MacIntyre: The Tasks of Philosophy*, 3-23.
37  MacIntyre, *Whose Justice? Which Rationality?*, 362.
38  MacIntyre, *Whose Justice? Which Rationality?*, 363.

imaginative and innovative responses to this crisis may then prove to be sterile and incoherent, resulting in the particular truth claims of the tradition no longer being sustainable. The adherents of a tradition that finds itself in such a radical crisis may then encounter the claims of a rival tradition in a new way in the process of trying to come to an understanding the beliefs and way of life of the other alien tradition. To do, so they will or will have had to learn the language of the alien tradition as a second first language. This new encounter with the alien tradition may satisfy two of the requirements MacIntyre suggests are important for a response to an epistemological crisis. The encounter may reveal the reasons why the crisis had to occur and it may also explain why the new conceptual scheme does not suffer from the same incoherence and lack of resources. But this encounter will fail to satisfy the third requirement, namely showing substantive continuity with the preceding history of the tradition in crisis. For MacIntyre such a situation "requires an acknowledgement by those who have hitherto inhabited and given their allegiance to the tradition in crisis that the alien tradition is superior in rationality and in respect of its claim to truth to their own".[39] Traditions are thus, according to MacIntyre, vindicated or not vindicated through their response to epistemological crises.

## 4. THE REFORMED TRADITION IN SOUTH AFRICA AS A LIVING AND REFORMING TRADITION?

Much more can be said on the way the concept of tradition functions in MacIntyre's project, for instance, regarding the way in which he brings the concept of tradition into conversation with questions concerning (in)commensurability and (un)translatability.[40] For the purposes of this essay, however, I want to bring aspects of MacIntyre's understanding of the idea of tradition (such as his description of a living tradition as a historically extended, socially embodied argument, as well as his discussion of the challenges that epistemological crises pose to traditions) into conversation with questions pertaining to the Reformed tradition in South Africa as a reforming tradition.[41] I want to affirm the need to view the Reformed tradition – also in South Africa – as a living tradition, as a tradition always reforming, or more precisely, as a reforming tradition always being reformed in the light of God's Word. In reflecting on the Reformed tradition in South Africa one can further argue that the theological justification of apartheid precipitated a crisis in some strands of the Reformed tradition in South Africa that is similar to what MacIntyre described

---

39   MacIntyre, *Whose Justice? Which Rationality?*, 365.
40   Cf. MacIntyre, A, *Three Rival Versions of Moral Inquiry: Encyclopaedia, Genealogy, and Tradition* (Notre Dame: University of Notre Dame Press, 1990), as well as MacIntyre, *Whose Justice? Which Rationality?*, 370388.
41   While acknowledging the value of MacIntyre's thinking on tradition, some critical questions can also be raised. MacIntyre does not explore fully how we are constituted by more than one tradition, nor how traditions are also constituted by encounters with another (rival) tradition. How does the notion of tradition relate to the notion of hospitality? Is MacIntyre's account of tradition not too agonistic? And furthermore: MacIntyre does not seem to focus much on the responsive character of traditions, on the idea that traditions developed as responses to specific persons/events. In his account, traditions just seem to have started somewhere and we are constituted by tradition. How do we engage with the idea that a living tradition points beyond itself to another reality?

as "an epistemological crisis". Some may view the diagnosis that the Reformed tradition in South Africa is experiencing an epistemological crisis as too drastic. And others may point to the fact that the theological justification of apartheid is not the only contributor to the crises and challenges facing some Reformed communities in South Africa today. Yet I think that MacIntyre's discussion offers some illuminating insights that invite further conversation. Let me make three brief remarks in this regard.

First, the deepest challenge facing Reformed theology in South Africa today is in my view not the presence of argumentative conflict per se. Conflict over what lies at the heart of the tradition is part of what it means to be a living tradition. MacIntyre reminds us that a living tradition is a historically extended, socially embodied *argument*. The maturity of the tradition is determined by the quality of the argument about the goods which constitute that tradition. The history of Reformed theology in South Africa reveals a contested legacy. This is seen, for instance, in the fact that theologians who supported apartheid and theologians who criticised the policy of racial segregation both drew on aspects of the Reformed tradition, seeing themselves as the true heirs of the tradition. It may be that the real crisis lies not in the presence of conflict or competing arguments (which some people see as a weakness in the tradition), but in the fact that the will to engage with questions at the heart of the tradition may be subsiding. The absence of the will "to critique our actual identity in light of our deepest identity"[42] (to quote Smit again), if true, indicates a serious deficiency that threatens the vitality of the Reformed tradition in South Africa to the core.

Second, MacIntyre's discussion on tradition points to the fact that in order for a tradition to survive in the aftermath of 'an epistemological crisis', inventiveness is required. But this inventiveness is not merely the inventiveness and creativity of an individual genius or talented group analysing the reasons for the crisis or providing novel solutions. Something else is also required, namely the ability to show how the 'solutions' offered are in continuity with the tradition's deepest identity. This project of providing continuity implies the need for responsible historical theological inquiry. In a climate of historical amnesia, or one in which the notion of tradition itself has become suspect, we are robbed of the resources for this kind of creative theological work. The Methodist theologian Geoffrey Wainwright has argued that the main theological innovations of the 20th century (for instance, the ecumenical and liturgical movements) were characterised by a responsible look at the past for the sake of the future.[43] And the Reformed theologian Brian Gerrish has spoken of respect for, or deference to, the past as one of the keynotes of the "Reformed habit of mind".[44] The influence of the Reformation theologians is in part based on their ability to communicate their ideas not as merely novel, but as in continuity with the tradition. These Reformers went to great lengths, for instance, to point out

---

42  Smit, *Essays on Being Reformed*, 31.
43  See Geoffrey Wainwright's article "Back to the Future" in Volf, M, Krieg, C, and Kucharz, T (eds), *The Future of Theology: Essays in Honor of Jürgen Moltmann* (Grand Rapids: Eerdmans, 1995), 29.
44  See Brain Gerrish's essay "Tradition in the Modern World: The Reformed Habit of Mind", in Welker, M and Willis, DW (eds), *Towards the Future of Reformed Theology: Tasks, Topics, Traditions* (Grand Rapids: Eerdmans, 1999).

the continuity between the Reformation and the early church. With regard to the challenges facing Reformed church communities today, one can argue that some current forms of spirituality and church life foster an anti-intellectualism and lack of historical consciousness that pose a serious threat to the sustainability of these communities *as Reformed* communities. Therefore it is of vital importance to combine a belief in the necessity of innovation and restatement of the tradition with the confidence that, through historical and theological engagement with the tradition, one can find the resources for renewal and refreshment. And one can also argue that the sort of innovation required within a tradition in crisis is often made possible by a critical and hospitable dialogue with other traditions and currents of thought. The innovative studies on Reformed theology and theologians by the South African theologian John de Gruchy, for instance, bring themes from the Reformed tradition into conversation with other currents of thought such as liberation theology and Christian humanism.[45] The question can be asked whether there are not also some other traditions and strands of thought that might prove to be exceptionally valuable as conversation partners for Reformed theology today, also in South Africa.

Third, the emphasis on the Reformed tradition as a living tradition challenges a static understanding of tradition that lapses into new forms of Reformed fundamentalism. The plea to show 'deference to the past' should not be equated with a nostalgic longing for timeless (Reformed) principles and values.[46] Often this form of Reformed fundamentalism has proved to be very tempting, especially in times of uncertainty and/or in the aftermath of trauma. One can even argue that the theological justification of apartheid was linked to this kind of reasoning. Reformed theology (as a living tradition) requires a *kairotic* or timeful engagement with reality in the light of the belief that the Triune God is present in history. The promise of Reformed theology in South Africa today is connected, then, with its ability to avoid hermeneutically suspect forms of Reformed fundamentalism as well as a faddish and uncritical move towards innovation for innovation's sake, rather seeking a responsible historical and theological engagement with the past for the sake of the present and the future.

## 5. CONCLUSION

In the conversation with MacIntyre's understanding of tradition one must remember too that in *After Virtue* he was specifically concerned with the tradition of the virtues and that he ends this book with a rather pessimistic reading of culture. Some readers

---

45 See, for instance, De Gruchy, JW, *Liberating Reformed Theology: A South African Contribution to an Ecumenical Debate* (Grand Rapids: Eerdmans, 1991) and De Gruchy, JW, *John Calvin: Christian Humanist & Evangelical Reformer* (Wellington: Lux Verbi.BM, 2009).

46 In his little book *Letters to a Young Calvinist: An Invitation to the Reformed Tradition* (Grand Rapids: Brazos Press, 2010), James KA Smith also writes against a system of timeless propositions, with reference to MacIntyre: "It seems to me very un-Reformed to prop up Reformed theology as a timeless ideal, a consummated achievement, when one of the Reformers' mantras was *semper reformanda* – always reforming. You shouldn't expect a lifetime of pursuing the truth to result in constant entrenchment into what you thought when you were twenty. Wouldn't you expect the Spirit to lead you to grow and change? Alasdair MacIntyre says that what makes a tradition a 'tradition' is precisely that we fight over what counts as part of the tradition!" (29).

have interpreted MacIntyre's views (as well as the views of theologians influenced by his work, such as Stanley Hauerwas) as sectarian. Reformed theologians will probably have a stronger public vision of the task of theology than merely pleading for smaller communities of inquiry to sustain the tradition through adverse times. However, it will be a mistake to equate such a more public theology to the belief that Reformed theology must be at the centre of power in South Africa (thus nostalgically yearning for the power configurations of the past). Edward Shils has written:

> The revival of a tradition can be effective without reconquering the center of society. The traditions which the prophets of Israel held before their audiences were the traditions which applied to the center of their society as standards which the center repeatedly disregarded. The criticism of the center was made from the periphery. It was never wholly successful but it survived for more than two and a half millennia, recurrently reanimated.[47]

Shils's comment about the persistence of the prophetic tradition reminds us that a sustainable and living tradition does not necessarily imply a numerical majority or socio-political and economic power, but is often carried by an inherent quality of conviction, often from the periphery. In the current debates in some Reformed circles on, for instance, the Belhar Confession and church reunification one must be careful about equating vitality and quality with the views of the majority. The maturity and sustainability of the tradition will depend on the way in which proponents can link their views, amidst rival interpretations, to the heart of the Reformed tradition. This implies the need to conduct the debates on a *theological* level. The question remains, though: Is there a future for a theological tradition when it turns away not only from its own historical past, but from the belief in the value of the discipline of theology as such?

---

47   Shils, *Tradition*, 286.

# 6. ON DOING CHURCH HISTORY: FIVE THESES[1]

## 1. INTRODUCTION

In order to avoid the intimidating task of reflecting on the future of Church History as an academic theological discipline, one could use as an opening gambit the remark that this discipline is not about the future but about the past, and that the past in itself is complex enough. Such a ploy would, however, not be all that convincing, since many scholars will rightly challenge an objectivistic vision of history that is abstracted from the present and the future. As the church historian Justo González observes in a chapter on the "The Future of Church History" in his book *The Changing Shape of Church History*: "No matter how much historians might claim that they are studying the past objectively, the fact is that all historians must necessarily look at the past from their own perspectives ... Furthermore, the perspective of a historian is not only a matter of the present moment, but also of the vision of the future from which history is studied and written".[2]

González continues his discussion by noting how different historiographical projects were influenced by their vision of the future. For instance, when Eusebius wrote his *Church History*, his vision of the future was mostly one in which the new order inaugurated by Constantine would continue and expand. In contrast, when Augustine wrote his *City of God* more than a century later, he did not have the same belief in the progress of the empire as Eusebius did, since Rome had fallen. The envisioned futures which underlie Eusebius' and Augustine's important works resulted in different perspectives on the relationship between Christianity and the Roman Empire. González recalls other examples as well, yet the point is clear: "the 'future' from which church history is read and written has a profound impact on the content and interpretation of that history".[3]

We are rightfully reminded by church historians like González that our vision of the future impacts on our interpretation of (church) history. A church historical engagement with the past will therefore consciously or unconsciously be determined by our own social and theological location as well as by teleological concerns, including our implicit or explicit views on the *telos* of history. With this in mind, and with apology to Martin Luther's "95 theses" and Walter Benjamin's "Theses on History", this essay offer five theses that in my view require thorough and creative engagement in order for Church History to deepen its status as a healthy academic and theological discipline.[4]

---

1 This essay was read as a paper at a conference on the theme "Theology – Quo Vadis?" at the Faculty of Theology, Stellenbosch University (10 June 2009). It was published as "Quo Vadis Church History? Some Theses on the Future of Church History as an Academic Discipline" in *Scriptura* 100, 2009: 54-64.
2 González, JL, *The Changing Shape of Church History* (St Louis: Chalice Press, 2002), 145.
3 González, *The Changing Shape of Church History*, 147.
4 In this essay I mostly use the term "Church History" to refer to the discipline. This term, however, is not uncontested. Many scholars and institutions prefer the term "History of Christianity" in order to challenge certain theological assumptions associated with "Church History", presuppositions that they view as harmful to the discipline's

## 2. FIVE THESES AS A RESPONSE TO QUESTIONS ON THE FUTURE OF CHURCH HISTORY

a. *The vitality of Church History as an academic discipline is linked to its ability to contribute towards a responsible engagement with the Christian past in a culture of historical amnesia and harmful memory.*

In his famous essay "On the uses and disadvantages of history for life" (1874) Friedrich Nietzsche powerfully challenges the historicism of the 19th century, although he did not deny the historicity of life. He acknowledges that we need history, but argues that "we need it for reasons different from those for which the idler in the garden of knowledge needs it … We need it, that is to say, for the sake of life and action, not so as to turn comfortably away from life and action".[5] Moreover, Nietzsche saw his views as "untimely", as out of step with the spirit of his times, since it is his aim to challenge the impressive historical culture of his age, arguing "that we are all suffering from a consuming fever of history and ought at least to recognise that we are suffering from it".[6] Therefore he invites the reader to meditate on the proposition that *"the unhistorical and the historical are necessary in equal measure for the health of an individual, of a people, and of a culture"*.[7] While Nietzsche's critique of an overburdened notion of history in the intellectual climate of 19th-century Germany is understandable and offers a perennial challenge, we can ask whether this historical fever that Nietzsche refers to has not been largely supplanted today by a historical amnesia. One could argue that there is a real need today to foster a stronger historical consciousness in a cultural matrix where historical forgetfulness seems to prevail. We seemingly live in a world characterised by, on the one hand, historical amnesia and an unhealthy loss of memory, while, on the other hand, processes of commemoration are often abused in the service of harmful ideologically-driven projects of identity construction. In the process our lack of engagement as well as our misguided engagement with the past invites and incites polarisation and violence. Hence the importance of reflecting on the question of *how* we remember and *how* we construct the past. In this process

---

academic integrity. The concerns of those who prefer the term "History of Christianity" need to be taken seriously, since they rightly challenge the way in which Church History has often isolated itself from the social sciences, and at times has offered sweeping theologised claims that do not respect the mystery of history. This includes large and overconfident claims concerning our ability to evaluate and judge history, as well as placing a salvation-history grid over history in a hermeneutically suspect way. On the other hand, those critical of the term "History of Christianity" have felt, also with good justification, that this term can be used in a way that conveys an anti-theological bias that will also influence the practice of the discipline. If one uses the term "Church History" one also needs to be sensitive to the porous borders with other related disciplines and sub-disciplines such as "the history of doctrine", "historical theology", "Church polity", "the history of Christian thought" and "religious history". When surveying the bountiful material in this regard, it is soon clear that there is a terminological fluidity within the broad discipline that resists easy and neat categorisation.

5 Nietzsche, F, *Untimely Meditations* (Cambridge: Cambridge University Press, 1983), 59. Nietzsche's essay was original published under the title "Vom Nutzen und Nachteil der Historie für das Leben" as the second part of his *Unzeitgemässe Betrachtungen* (Frankfurt am Main: Insel Verlag, 1981).
6 Nietzsche, *Untimely Meditations*, 60.
7 Nietzsche, *Untimely Meditations*, 63.

Church History as discipline can contribute to cultivating a passion for the past by challenging historical amnesia, as well as exemplifying a responsible engagement with the past that counters harmful memory.

Amidst a growing culture of historical amnesia, one of the tasks of Church History will continue to be the work of motivating students to consult the archive (understood in both the broader sense of collected knowledge of the past, as well as in the more specific sense of professional archives). This requires technical as well as hermeneutical skills. The training of students in this regard remains a priority and it is important that these skills be incorporated into, or remain part of, the Church History / History of Christianity curricula at seminaries and universities. Part of this type of training in Church History will certainly remain the skill to engage with primary sources. An approach to Church History that is critical of the over-optimistic methodological presuppositions regarding the noble dream of historical objectivity should not imply that we can find shortcuts around the meticulous and laborious engagement with documents and primary sources. In settings where people have access to archives, there is especially an opportunity to incite a passion for archival work by incorporating it in creative ways into the curriculum. In addition, it needs to be noted that "historians are increasingly turning to visual, oral, aural, virtual and kinaesthetic sources".[8] Reflection is therefore also needed on how to appropriate so-called 'alternative sources' into the church historical discourse. In the process, however, it remains important to counter an epistemological and hermeneutical naïveté, as if an engagement with the primary sources automatically implies responsible church historical work. Even 'original sources' do not tell the complete story and even the best archives offer us a limited window onto the past. Access to archives and primary sources does not absolve us from the task of *interpreting* the sources in the light of the narrative and rhetorical frameworks that make them intelligible.

The church historical task, moreover, does not merely entail consulting the archive in a responsible and accountable way, but also enlarging the archive with more specialised work. The vast field of Church History offers a formidable challenge in this regard. As Bradley and Muller have noted, "the broad field of church history is increasingly complex and highly fragmented".[9] No matter which periodisation of Church History one uses, different areas of Church History require different technical and language skills. It thus goes without saying that no scholar can work competently in the whole field, hence the need for specialisation. In South Africa one remains concerned about the fact that a lack of knowledge of, for instance, Latin, Greek, German and French is often a hindrance for those students interested in doing specialised scholarly work on periods such as Late Ancient, Byzantine, Medieval and Reformation Christianity. The discipline will benefit immensely if more students with these skills would do postgraduate work in Church History / History of Christianity. One can also note that students' skills in reading Dutch is

---

8 Barber, S and Peniston-Bird, CM, *History Beyond the Text: A Student's Guide to Approaching Alternative Sources* (London: Routledge, 2009), 1. This book contains chapters on alternative sources such as fine art, the cartoon, photographs, film and television, music, oral history, the internet, landscape, architecture and material culture.

9 Bradley, JE and Muller, RA, *Church History: An Introduction to Research, Reference Works, and Methods* (Grand Rapids: Eerdmans, 1995), 2.

deteriorating, leading to much of the important material related to South African Church historiography being inaccessible to many. But these difficulties ought not to discourage students who want to work in the field of Church History. Students' proficiency in South African languages offers the opportunity to work on topics inaccessible to many international scholars.

In reflecting on the future of Church History and the related disciplines within the South African contexts, one should note that the focus on South African religious, church and theological historiography remains a priority.[10] One needs to acknowledge the important contribution of the existing corpus of material, but much work still needs to be done. The important role that oral history can play in adding to the archive has often been highlighted in the discourse on South African church historiography, and the methodological and practical work already done in this area is to be commended.[11]

The challenges for Church History to consult and contribute to the archive of the Christian past remain formidable, but it is worthwhile to take on these challenges in an environment of historical amnesia and harmful memory. Such an undertaking requires a responsible historical hermeneutic that is both sympathetic and critical in its approach. Margaret Miles puts it well in her book *The Word Made Flesh*:

A history of Christian thought must narrate the triumphal story in which a small local cult within Judaism became a world religion and empire. But it must also include the failures, abuses, and violence of the Christian past. In short, it must be both sympathetic and critical. It must be sympathetic in order to present the vivid beauty of Christian resources of ideas, artworks, and practices. And it must be critical because it is not only a history of the past, but also a history for the present.[12]

b. *A constructive dialogue with the social sciences can be helpful en route to a more responsible historical hermeneutic for Church History*

In an essay "From Church History to Religious History: Strengths and Weaknesses of South African Religious Historiography" (published in 1997), Phillipe Denis makes the following observation: "In South Africa, church history is an isolated discipline, almost completely cut off from the social sciences and from secular history in particular. Its academic status can be described as weak. This situation has historical roots. In South Africa, church history has always been regarded as part of theology and is usually being taught by theologians with little or no training in

---

10  One does need to add that it will be a pity if the focus on South African church historiography is positioned against the need for work in general church history. Given the current growth in the area of Early Church / Late Antiquity studies, one can especially bemoan the neglect of this area in South African church historical circles. This fact points to the need for a quantitative and qualitative enlargement of the circle of scholars working in the discipline.

11  See, for instance, Denis, P (ed.), *Orality, Memory & the Past: Listening to Voices of Black Clergy under Colonialism and Apartheid* (Pietermaritzburg: Cluster Publications, 2000). For a valuable collection on oral history, cf. Perks, R and Thomson, A, *The Oral History Reader* (second edition) (London, Routledge, 2008).

12  Miles, Margaret, *The Word Made Flesh: A History of Christian Thought* (Oxford: Blackwell, 2005), xiv.

secular history and hardly any familiarity with the social sciences".[13] Denis's remark is representative of the critique of a number of church historians as well as scholars from other disciplines who have made a plea over the last few decades for a stronger interaction between Church History and the social sciences.[14]

The conversation with the social sciences on historiography is especially promising for the reflection on an adequate methodology for doing church and theological historiography. With this in mind, I want to highlight the New Testament scholar Bernard Lategan's critique of Reformed church historiography in his important article "Nuwere ontwikkelinge op die gebied van die geskiedskrywing – 'n geleentheid vir herbesinning na 350 jaar van gereformeerdheid" ("Recent developments in the field of historiography – an opportunity for reflection after 350 years of the Reformed faith"), published in the collection *350 Jaar Gereformeerd/350 Years Reformed*. Lategan refers to two noticeable characteristics of Reformed historiography in South Africa that reflect a hermeneutical shortcoming, namely its lack of context, as well as its mono-dimensional presentation.[15] Lategan moreover points to what he views as the surprising absence of any methodological and hermeneutical reflection on the historical task in most of the Reformed church historiographical projects. A further characteristic of this type of historiography is the seamless transition from source to description.[16] Description is thus equated with reality, displaying a lack of sensitivity to the fact that the historical material could also be arranged in other meaningful configurations. Lategan sets his critique of Reformed historiography within the context of the recent developments in historiography, with a specific focus on the

---

13   Denis, P, "From Church History to Religious History: Strengths and Weaknesses of South African Religious Historiography", *Journal of Theology for Southern Africa* 99 (November 1997: 84-93): 85.

14   See, for instance, Southey, ND, "History and Church History in South Africa: Some Reflections", *Studia Historiae Ecclesiasticae* XIV (1988): 107-123; Southey, N, "History, Church History and Historical Theology in South Africa", *Journal of Theology for Southern Africa* 68 (September 1989): 5-16; Pillay, GJ, "The relations between church history and general history: reflections on Adolf von Harnack's view", *Studia Historiae Ecclesiasticae* XX/ 2 (1992):156-168; Adonis, JC, "Kerkgeskiedskrywing in Suid-Africa: 'n Kritiese evaluasie", *NGTT* 43/ 1 & 2 (2002): 7-21.

15   Lategan, B C, "Nuwere ontwikkelinge op die gebied van die geskiedskrywing – 'n geleentheid vir herbesinning na 350 jaar van gereformeerdheid" in Coertzen, P (ed.), *350 Jaar Gereformeerd / 350 Years Reformed 1652-2002* (Bloemfontein: CLF, 2002), 270. For Lategan these two characteristics (the lack of context and the mono-dimensional approach) are closely linked. The lack of context impedes the multiplicity of meanings of specific events from becoming evident and because the potential for a multiplicity of meanings to emerge remains stifled, it unavoidably leads to a mono-dimensional understanding of the past. This hermeneutical shortcoming, Lategan argues, influences the Dutch Reformed Church's ability or inability to function in a diversified ecclesiastical setup, in a pluralistic religious environment and in a multidimensional democratic dispensation (270).

16   Lategan, "Nuwere ontwikkelinge", 271. See also his related essay "History, Historiography, and Reformed Hermeneutics at Stellenbosch" in Alston, WM and Welker, M (eds), *Reformed Theology: Identity and Ecumenicity II: Biblical Interpretation in the Reformed Tradition* (Grand Rapids: Eerdmans, 2007). Lategan writes in conversation with the work of Droysen: "The essence of historical inquiry is not its critical dimension, but its interpretive ability. The goal of history is not to understand bygone days, but to understand what remains from those times and what is still present today" (169).

emphasis of the so-called 'linguistic turn' according to which the writing of history is not merely a reconstruction of the past, but a construction.

In my view, church historical discourse in South Africa can gain much by taking note of Lategan's critique of Reformed church historiography in South Africa and his implicit plea for a greater engagement with some newer developments in the area of historiography.[17] Such an engagement can be very fruitful *en route* to a more responsible historical hermeneutic for engaging with church history. Lategan refers to the work of historians (or meta-historians) such as Kosseleck, Rüsen, Ankersmit and White. The ideas of scholars working in the field of historical theory need to be differentiated and approached critically, but they indeed hold the promise of opening up exciting avenues for the way we view the (church) historical task today. An approach to Church History that isolates the discipline from conversations with the social sciences might easily fall prey to an uncritical methodology. We need to remind ourselves that historical understanding is a hermeneutical process and that hermeneutics is not merely a relevant discipline for Biblical Studies, but that it also lies at the heart of Church History and related subjects such as the history of doctrine. The plea for ongoing hermeneutical sensitivity in Church History does not mean that the discipline is reduced to addressing methodological questions. It does mean, though, that a continuous focus on an adequate methodology, also in conversation with the social sciences, is of paramount importance for the intellectual integrity of the discipline – eschewing this task will cut the discipline off from sources that might offer possible revitalisation.

### c. As a theological discipline Church History ought to be attentive to 'history from below'

In his reflection *After Ten Years* (written from prison for his friends) the German theologian Dietrich Bonhoeffer highlights the importance of the 'the view from below': He writes: "We have for once learned to see the great events of world history from below, from the perspective of the outcast, the suspects, the maltreated, the powerless, the oppressed, the reviled – in short, from the perspective of those who suffer".[18] This emphasis on the importance of 'a view from below' has found concretisation in much of the scholarly (church) historical work done over the last few decades.

---

17  For some helpful introductions to the crucial developments in 19th- and 20th-century debates, including literature, see Breisach, E, *Historiography: Ancient, Medieval, and Modern* (2nd edition) (Chicago: University of Chicago, 1994); Clark, EA, *History, Theory, Text: Historians and the Linguistic Turn* (Cambridge: Harvard University Press, 2004); Iggers, GG, *Historiography in the Twentieth Century: From Scientific Objectivity to the Postmodern Challenge* (Middletown: Wesleyan University Press, 1999, with new epilogue 2005, expanded version of his earlier German text). Cf. also Bentley, M (ed.), *Companion to Historiography* (New York: Routledge, 2007) and Budd, A (ed.), *The Modern Historiography Reader: Western Sources* (London: Routledge, 2009). For a reflection from a more explicit theological perspective, see Tilley, TW, *History, Theology & Faith: Dissolving the Modern Problematic* (Maryknoll: Orbis Books, 1970).

18  Bonhoeffer, D, *Letters and Papers From Prison* (London: SCM, 1971), 17.

An interesting project in this regard is the seven-volume series "A People's History of Christianity" (with Denis Janz as General Editor).[19] As the Editorial Foreword makes clear, this series seeks to break new church historical ground by looking at Christianity's past from the vantage point of people's history. This approach does not view the church first and foremost as a hierarchical-institutional-bureaucratic corporation, but rather focuses on the religious lives and pious practices of the laity and the ordinary faithful. This undertaking to write a people's history, also referred to as a history from below, or grassroots history, or popular history, is not a new theme in academic historical studies. Its roots may be traced back more than a century "in conscious opposition to the elitism of conventional (some call it Rankean) historical investigation, fixated as it was on the 'great' deeds of 'great' men, and little else".[20] This approach to history is interested in those aspects which have been left out of the story, namely "the vast majority of human beings: almost all women, obviously, but then too all those who could be counted among the socially inferior, the economically distressed, the politically marginalized, the educationally deprived, or the culturally unrefined".[21]

The project to write 'a people's history' of Christianity points to the fact that in church historical discourse there was also the tendency to privilege the spiritual, intellectual or powerful elites. While it is certainly important to study mystics, theologians, pastors, priests, bishops and popes, one must also remember that no more than five percent of Christians over two millennia are included in these groups. Therefore the question whether a more balanced history of Christianity, as well as a sense of historical justice, does not require a greater engagement with the "the voiceless, the ordinary faithful who wrote no theological treatises, whose statues adorn no basilica, who negotiated no concordats, whose very names are largely lost to historical memory?"[22] One can further ask:

> What can we know about their religious consciousness, their devotional practice, their understanding of faith, their values, beliefs, feelings, habits, attitudes, their deepest fears, hopes, loves, hatreds, and so forth? And what about the troublemakers, the excluded, the heretics, those defined by conventional history as the losers? Can a face be put on any of them?[23]

One of the powerful aspects of a 'people's history' or a 'history from below' is that it amplifies voices that have often been muted or forgotten. We remember selectively and we represent the past in a way that excludes. In this process certain voices

---

19  The seven volumes in this series are: Horsley, R (ed.), *Christian Origins* (Minneapolis: Fortress Press, 2005); Burrus, V (ed.), *Late Ancient Christianity* (Minneapolis: Fortress Press, 2005); Krueger, D (ed.), *Byzantine Christianity* (Minneapolis: Fortress Press, 2006); Bornstein, DE (ed.), *Medieval Christianity* (Minneapolis: Fortress Press, 2007); Matheson, P (ed.), *Reformation Christianity* (Minneapolis: Fortress Press, 2007); Porterfield, A (ed.), *Modern Christianity to 1900* (Minneapolis: Fortress Press, 2010); Bednarowski, MF (ed.), *Twentieth Century Global Christianity* (Minneapolis: Fortress Press, 2010).
20  Janz, D R (general editor), "Foreword" in Matheson, P (ed.), *Reformation Christianity* (Minneapolis: Fortress Press, 2007), xiii.
21  Janz, "Foreword", xiii.
22  Janz, "Foreword", xiii.
23  Janz, "Foreword", xiv-xv.

are given preferential treatment, while other voices are not heard. And often it is precisely the stories of the victors, the strong, that become part of the so-called 'official history'. The voices that are omitted, on the other hand, are those of the dissidents and the victims. A focus on 'history from below' also offers access to the sources in order to challenge and deconstruct that which is sometimes described as 'official history'. Such 'official histories', which can take on all kind of forms, are often accepted uncritically and their role in creating and maintaining injustice is not always unmasked.

Writing from an American perspective, Diana Butler Bass refers to one such a version of 'official history', which she describes as the "usual story" of "'Big C' Christianity, the 'C's' being Christ, Constantine, Christendom, Calvin and Christian America". The tale runs thus:

> Jesus came to the earth to save us, but he founded the church instead. The church suffered under Roman persecution until the emperor Constantine made Christianity legal. With its new status, the Christian religion spread throughout Europe, where popes and kings formed a society called Christendom, which was run by the Catholic Church and was constantly threatened by Muslims, witches and heretics. There were wars and inquisitions. When people had had enough, they rebelled and became Protestants, their main leader being John Calvin, who was a great theologian but a killjoy. Eventually Calvin's heirs, the Puritans, left Europe to set up a Christian society in the New World. The United States of America then became the most Christian nation in the world, a beacon of faith and democracy.[24]

Bass admits that this account is a bastardisation of an old story line, but we don't need much imagination to realise that similar constructions of church history are often part of the popular imagination, also finding their way into curricula and student papers. However, we need to be vigilant concerning these 'official' constructions, since they are by no means innocent and have a powerful impact on the church and society. Careful and responsible (church) historical work, which pays attention to a wide variety of sources and excluded voices, can provide a forceful challenge to these constructions – and these new constructions must again be subjected to further scrutiny. In the process we need to take account of the fact that we cannot bracket our (church) historical work from ethical concerns.[25]

In the light of the above-mentioned remarks, it seems important to affirm the basic premise of a move towards a 'history from below' or a 'people's history'. It must be said, however, that such projects, such as the seven-volume series "People's History of Christianity" and similar undertakings, must also guard against a form of revisionism that displays an anti-intellectual and anti-theological bias. Although one can argue that theologians form just a small percentage of Christians, it is

---

24 Bass, D B, *A People's History of Christianity: The Other Side of the Story* (New York: HarperOne, 2009), 4-5.
25 For a collection that engages the ethical dimension of the historical enterprise, see Carr, DC, Flynn, TR, and Makkreel, RA, *The Ethics of History* (Evanston: Northwestern University Press, 2004).

nevertheless true that their impact often far exceeds their numbers. The 'history of the people' must not be juxtaposed uncritically with a 'history of theology'.

### d. Church History must continue to reflect on its mapping habits

In his book *The Changing Shape of Church History* Justo González argues that a radical change has taken place in the cartography of Church History. The old map in which North Atlantic-Europe and the United States formed the centre is no longer operational. He comments: "From the point of view of resources, the centers are still the United States, Canada, and Western Europe. From the point of view of vitality, missionary and evangelistic zeal, and even theological creativity, the centers have been shifting south for some time".[26] González adds that there is no single centre in the south, since exciting new theological insights are coming from Peru, South Africa and the Philippines, and that phenomenal growth is taking place in Chile, Brazil, Uganda and Korea. This new polycentric reality has consequences for Christianity: "As Christianity has become a truly universal religion, with deep roots in every culture, it is also becoming more and more contextualised, and therefore, out of its many centers come different readings of the entire history of the church. The result is frightening and exhilarating".[27]

Indeed Church History ought to reflect on its mapping habits; it needs to register "the failing map of Modernity" and take note of the changing face of World Christianity. A greater sensitivity to the polycentric reality of the church, González argues, makes it evident that it is not possible for any scholar, or even group of scholars, to function as a kind of authoritative church historical panopticon, overseeing the whole of church history.

This observation indeed points to the need for collaborative projects. Over the last few decades several such collaborative studies have appeared that were sensitive to the polycentric reality of Christianity.[28] A number of collaborative studies on African and South African Christianity have also made important contributions to the field.[29] There definitely remains a need for collaborative work on South African church and religious historiography, especially for projects that incorporate new historiographical perspectives into their approach. Church historical discourse in the future will need to take the changing cartography of Church History/ History of Christianity seriously. Collaborative projects will hopefully continue to play an important role in this regard, albeit that overview studies by single authors are also required.

---

26 González, *The Changing Shape of Church History*, 14
27 González, *The Changing Shape of Church History*, 17.
28 See, for instance, Hastings, A (ed.), *A Word History of Christianity* (Grand Rapids: Eerdmans, 1999). Peter Hinchliff, author of *The Church in South Africa* (London: SPCK, 1968), played an important role in initiating this project.
29 See in this regard, Kalu, OU (ed.), *African Christianity: An African Story* (Pretoria: University of Pretoria, 2005), with a important Introduction by Kalu on "The Shape and Flow of African Church Historiography". See also Elphick, R & Davenport, R (eds), *Christianity in South Africa: A Political, Social & Cultural History* (Berkeley: University of California Press, 1997), as well as Hofmeyr, JW and Pillay, GJ (eds.), *Perspectives on Church History* (Pretoria: HAUM Tertiary, 1991) and Hofmeyr, JW and Pillay GJ (eds.), *A History of Christianity in South Africa Vol. 1* (Pretoria: HAUM Tertiary, 1994).

A further remark on the changing cartography of Christianity and its impact on church historiography is warranted. The notion of a polycentric map does not detract from the fact that we can only see the world from our own perspective, although the insights of others can surely broaden our vision. This implies that students of church history and scholars in the field must take their own particularity and context seriously. An ecumenical approach or 'World Christianity' perspective is therefore not to be posited over against confessional commitments, denominational histories, or a focus on local practices and congregational life. Moreover, I think church historians, like biblical scholars as well as systematic and practical theologians, ought to be more honest and forthright about the influence of their social location and confessional (or a-confessional or anti-confessional) stance on their theological views and presuppositions. A confessional stance and an ecumenical commitment are not mutually exclusive.[30]

e. *The focus on shared history, which attends to the way in which divisive histories are interwoven, holds much promise for South African church historiography*

"(T)he self returns to itself after numerous hermeneutic detours through the language of others, to find itself enlarged and enriched by the journey".[31] With these words Richard Kearney summarises well the methodology of the philosopher Paul Ricoeur. It is indeed Ricoeur's conviction that otherness enlarges and enriches identity, a conviction that is coupled with his reminder that we are also an other for another, as for instance expressed in the title of his book *Oneself as Another*.[32] These ideas, which have found general expression in the work of a wide variety of scholars over the last few decades, also hold promise, in my view, for the methodology of doing church history in South Africa today. It suggests that we can understand our own complex histories better in conversation with others and through an openness to their histories. Moreover, this entails the realisation that our respective histories are often interwoven and thus we are 'othered' in the others' histories.

I take the history of the Dutch Reformed Church and the Uniting Reformed Church in Southern Africa as an example. In many respects the history of these churches is a history of division. Much has already been written on this. But it is also a shared history, a history of interwoven memories. In our attempts to enter into discussion with the past of these churches in a responsible manner, it might be that the challenge and task now are precisely to revisit our histories anew in discussion with one another. Not isolation, but interaction, then becomes the hermeneutical key to unlock the past.

---

30  See, for instance, the comment by H Berkhof and OJ de Jong in their *Geschiedenis der Kerk* (Nijkerk: Callenbach, 1975): "Dit werk heeft er nooit een geheim van gemaakt dat het op reformatorische wijze het Evangelie wil verstaan. Het maakt er ook geen geheim van dat het de roeping tot eenheid wil dienen. Kerkgeschiedskrijving is oecumenisch. Anders is zij geen geschiedschrijving van Christus' kerk" (8).
31  Kearney, R, *On Paul Ricoeur: The Owl of Minerva* (Aldershot: Ashgate, 2004), 2.
32  Cf. Ricoeur, P, *Oneself as Another* (Chicago: University of Chicago Press, 1992). This work was originally published in French as *Soi-même comme un autre*.

Settings such as ecumenical faculties, where there is a diversity of ecclesial traditions, might be fruitful places to explore further the possibilities of joint memory work and historiography. This does not mean that denominations and faith traditions should take their own histories less seriously. Rather, a healthy ecumenical focus actually requires that you take your own particular identity even more seriously. However, an understanding of the interwovenness of our memories and histories requires, in fact, that we resist the temptation to think in isolation about what we regard as *our* past and *our* history. Therefore hospitality is also a virtue that is valuable in our attempt to deal with the past in a responsible manner.

The plea for a methodology of shared historiography also needs to be sensitive to the fragile nature of such an undertaking. We need to be aware about how what we view as founding moments, turning points or events worthy of celebration may represent a low point, indeed a wound or a scar, in the memory of another. As Paul Ricoeur has remarked: "What we celebrate under the heading of founding events are, essentially, violent acts legitimated after the fact by a precarious state of right ... The same events are thus found to signify glory for some, humiliation for others".[33] This reality reminds us that church historical discourse in South Africa requires a responsible historical hermeneutic.

## 3. CONCLUSION

In the beginning of this essay I mentioned the fact that our engagement with the past cannot be abstracted from our present commitments and future expectations. We also need to remind ourselves that the Christian 'future' is not to be abstracted from a faithful and creative historical engagement with the past. This engagement holds the promise of providing sources of creative renewal and reform. As the much-respected Methodist and ecumenical scholar Geoffrey Wainwright writes in an essay entitled "Back to the future":

> ... (S)everal of the most important movements of the twentieth-century history of the church and of theology have, as a matter of fact, looked towards the past in order to gain their bearings in the present and get guidance for the ongoing journey. My modest proposed thesis is that we shall have to continue in that direction – looking back with and through those movements into the full depth of God's history with the church.[34]

This essay is intended to affirm Wainwright's observation. One also needs to note that the movement 'back to the future' (or even 'back for the future') does not imply that we excuse the terrible abuses of the past, or repress the vivid beauty of Christian ideas and practices. Rather, it points to the importance of a responsible historical hermeneutic that is sensitive to the way in which the Christian past is "boiling with

---

33 Ricoeur, *Memory, History, Forgetting,* 82. See also his remark: "It is very important to remember that what is considered a founding event in our collective memory may be a wound in the memory of others". See Kearney, R and Dooley, M (eds.), *Questioning Ethics: Contemporary Debates in Philosophy* (London: Routledge, 1999), 5-11.
34 See Volf, M, Krieg, C and Kucharz, T (eds), *The Future of Theology: Essays in Honor of Jürgen Moltmann* (Grand Rapids: Eerdmans, 1995), 89.

life" (to use Margaret Miles's phrase).[35] Therefore Church History needs to be aware of the fact that, given the richness of life, it can never fully capture even the smallest slice of life from the past.[36] At the same time, Church history, as a theological discipline, needs to be haunted by the strange claim that the Word became flesh in history.

---

35  Cf. Miles, *The Word Made Flesh*, xv.
36  Franz Kafka reminds us of this fact in his short story "The next village": "My grandfather used to say: 'Life is astoundingly short'. To me, looking back over it, life seems so foreshortened that I scarcely understand, for instance, how a young man can decide to ride over to the next village without being afraid that – not to mention accidents – even the span of a normal happy life may fall far short of the time needed for such a journey". See Kafka, F, *The Complete Stories* (New York: Schocken Books, 1971), 404. For a reflection on Walter Benjamin's reading of Kafka's tale, see Stéphane Mosès, *The Angel of History: Rosenzweig, Benjamin, Scholem* (Stanford: Stanford University Press, 2009), 82-83.

# 7. ON COMMEMORATING: REMEMBERING THE REFORMATION AFTER 500 YEARS[1]

## 1. INTRODUCTION

On 31 October 1517 the Augustinian monk Martin Luther allegedly posted his 95 theses on the door of the castle church in Wittenberg, an event seen as a symbolic historical marker indicating the beginning of the 16$^{th}$-century Protestant Reformation. In 2017 the 500$^{th}$ anniversary of the Reformation will be commemorated worldwide through various conferences, church and cultural events, and publications. The Luther Decade was launched in 2008 already, focusing on a specific theme each year in the light of the legacy of the Reformation and the role of Martin Luther in particular.[2] What is interesting about the commemoration process thus far, as well as about the planned events and projects, is the fact that it is consciously ecumenical and global. As we read on a Reformation Anniversary website:

> While celebrations in early centuries were kept national and confessional, the upcoming anniversary ... ought to be shaped by openness, freedom and ecumenism. In 2017 we aren't just celebration 500 years of Reformation, but we are reminded of the role the Reformation played in the development of the modern age ... What started in Wittenberg in the 16$^{th}$ century changed Germany, Europe and the whole world.[3]

With regard to this ecumenical and global focus, it is worth mentioning a joint project of the Lutheran World Federation (LWF) and the Pontifical Council for Promoting Christian Unity (PCPCU). In 2013 The Lutheran-Roman Catholic Commission on Unity published their report *From Conflict to Communion: Lutheran-Catholic Common Commemoration of the Reformation in 2017*.[4] Already in the Foreword of this report we sense the ecumenical commitment to the unity of the church as well as the sense of the pain and harm caused by historical divisions and polarisation, thus seeking a way from "conflict to communion".[5] To commemorate the Reformation

---

1 This essay was read as a paper at the annual conference of the Church Historical Society of Southern Africa, held in Potchefstroom from 13-15 August 2015. The theme of the conference was "Remembrance and Commemoration". It was written before the 2017 Reformation commemorations and the original formulations are retained on the whole. This essay was originally published as "Commemoration, Rememoration and Reformation: Some Historical-hermeneutical Remarks in Light of the 1917 Reformation Celebrations of the Dutch Reformed Church" in *Studia Historiae Ecclesiasticae* 41/3, 2015:79-91.
2 See www.luther2017.de/en/ [accessed on 20 May 2017].
3 www.luther2017.de/en/2017/reformationsjubilaeum/ [accessed on 20 May 2017].
4 The Lutheran World Federation & The Pontifical Council for Promoting Christian Unity, *From Conflict to Communion: Lutheran-Catholic Common Commemoration of the Reformation in 2017* (Leipzig: Evangelische Verlangsanstalt/Bonifatius, 2013).
5 We read, for instance: "In 2017 we must confess openly that we have been guilty before Christ of damaging the unity of the church. This commemorative year presents us with two challenges: the purification and healing of memories, and the restoration of Christian unity in accordance with the truth of the gospel of Jesus Christ (Eph 4:4-6)". See *From Conflict to Communion*, 7.

in an ecumenical and global age, however, is no easy task, and the report mentions three main challenges which provide opportunities and obligations for the commemorative process:

> (1) It is the first commemoration to take place during the ecumenical age. Therefore, the common commemoration is an occasion to deepen communion between Catholics and Lutherans. (2) It is the first commemoration in the age of globalisation. Therefore, the common commemoration must incorporate the experiences and perspectives of Christians from South and North, East and West. (3) It is the first commemoration that must deal with the necessity of a new evangelisation marked by both the proliferation of new religious movements and, at the same time, the growth a secularisation in many places.[6]

These are indeed serious challenges to be dealt with in an attempt to commemorate the 16th-century Protestant Reformation in an ecumenical and global age. What is also of interest in the report is its sensitivity to the way in which political and church-political agendas had frequently shaped previous centennial commemorations. In 1617, for instance, the 100th anniversary helped to stabilise and revitalise the common identity of Lutherans and Reformed Christians at their joint celebrations, held in a polemical relationship to the Roman Catholic church. Luther became the liberator from the Roman yoke, while several centuries later, amidst the calamity of the First World War in 1917, Luther was portrayed as a German national hero.[7]

In this essay I do not offer a detailed reading or critique of the report *From Conflict to Communion*.[8] Rather, in the background is the question of how to commemorate the 16th-century Protestant Reformation in 2017 in Reformed circles in Southern Africa. But I concur with the emphasis in *From Conflict to Communion* on the need for a common commemoration over against isolationist celebrations that fuel insulation and polarisation, also in the light of past conflicts and the internal divisions within Reformed churches in Southern Africa as well as between various denominations and churches. Against this backdrop, this essay argues that the 2017 commemoration of the Reformation by the Reformed churches in Southern Africa should be accompanied by a self-critical reflection on the possible abuses associated with commemorations as such, as well as by a historical consciousness of the way in which past commemorations of the Reformation functioned in processes of identity construction and 'othering'. With this in mind, the essay proceeds in two parts. In the first part the aspect of commemoration itself is problematised by the critique of the possible abuse of memory associated with commemorations, as highlighted in the work of Tzvetan Todorov, including his distinction between commemoration and rememoration. The second part of the essay then turns to some historical documents that give us a glimpse into the 400th anniversary of the Reformation

---

6   *From Conflict to Communion*, 11.
7   *From Conflict to Communion*, 12.
8   See in this regard Oberdorfer, B, "Feiern? Gedenken? Büssen? Ökumenische Perspektiven auf das Reformationsjubilaum: Zur lutherisch-katholischen Studie 'Vom Konflik zur Gemeinschaft'", *Materialdienst des Konfessionskundlichen Instituts Bensheim* 64 (2014): 1, 3-8.

in 1917 in Reformed circles in South Africa, and specifically within the Dutch Reformed Church. Here I will draw especially on the Dutch Reformed Church's official publication *De Kerkbode*, as well as a booklet commissioned by the Federal Council of the Dutch Reformed Churches, and written by GBA Gerdener, entitled *Het Vierde Eeuwfeest* [*The Fourth Centenary*].[9]

## 2. COMMEMORATION AND THE ABUSE OF MEMORY (TZVETAN TODOROV)

A scholar who has written extensively on the abuses of memory, and has specifically indicted the frenzy of contemporary commemorations, is the Bulgarian-French writer, Tzvetan Todorov. Todorov wrote an influential essay *Les Abus de la mémoire*,[10] although here I will draw mainly on some perspectives on commemoration from his book *Hope and Memory: Reflections on the Twentieth Century*,[11] In the Preface to *Hope and Memory* Todorov writes: "Memory – one of the main themes of this book – should not be used only to celebrate one's own heroes, to mourns one's own dead, and to stigmatise the wrongs committed by others".[12] And memory is indeed a theme Todorov explores in his brief political history of the 20th century – a century that can be described as the age of totalitarian regimes. According to Todorov, the totalitarian regimes of the 20th century sought to achieve total control of memory.[13] What is of interest in Todorov's discussion of memory, furthermore, is his warning against the unconditional support of memory, because as he puts it, "the stakes of memory are too high for us to allow them to be dictated by enthusiasm or anger".[14] For Todorov memory, undefined, is neither good nor bad in itself and its benefits can be neutralised in several ways, for instance, through the sacralisation or the trivialisation of the past. Todorov observes: "We can fall into the frying pan of making the past *sacred* and thus isolating it completely from the present; and we can fall into the fire by making it *trivial*, by seeing the present exclusively through the lens of the past".[15] Put differently: "A sanctified past brings nothing to mind but itself; a trivialised past reminds of anything and everything".[16]

---

9   Gerdener, GBA, *Het Vierde Eeuwfeest. Gedenkschrift bij gelegenheid van de Vierhonderdste Viering van de Kerkhervorming* (Cape Town: De Zuid-Afrikaanse Bijbel Vereniging, 1917).
10  Todorov, T, *Les Abus de la mémoire* (Paris: Éditions Arléa, 1995).
11  Todorov, T, *Hope and Memory: Reflections on the Twentieth Century* (London: Atlantic Books, 2014 [2003]); first published in French as Todorov, T, *Mémoire du mal, tentation du bien: Enquêtesur le siècle* (Paris: Éditions Robert Laffont).
12  Todorov, *Hope and Memory*, xxi. Or as Todorov writes in *Memory as a Remedy for Evil*: "The memory of the past will serve no purpose if it is used to build an impassable wall between evil and us, identifying exclusively with irreproachable victims and driving the agents of evil outside the confines of humankind". Todorov, T, *Memory as a Remedy for Evil* (London: Seagull Books, 2010), 79, 80. And he ends this small book with the words: "The memory of the past could help us in this enterprise of taming evil, on the condition that we keep in mind that good and evil flow from the same sources and that in the world's best narratives they are not neatly divided" (88).
13  Todorov, *Hope and Memory*, 113. For a discussion of the anti-totalitarian humanism of Todorov (and Levinas), see Terreblanche, SJ, "Todorov, Levinas and anti-totalitarian humanism: A perspective on contemporary utopian thought", *HTS* 63/1 (2007): 301-325
14  Todorov, *Hope and Memory*, 119.
15  Todorov, *Hope and Memory*, 161.
16  Todorov, *Hope and Memory*, 164.

Todorov is clearly concerned with the abuses of memory, and opens space for the question of whether memory is necessarily a good thing and forgetting always a curse. [17] Of special concern for our purposes here is the distinction that Todorov makes between testimony, history and commemoration. According to Todorov, the traces of the past that live on in the present fall into a variety of discourses, and he highlights especially the language of testimony, the language of history and the language of commemoration. Testimony is the type of discourse that arises when we summon and recount memories as we give meaning to our lives and construct our identity. Although this form of memory-work may use documents or other material traces, it is by definition solitary work, and nobody can tell us what image to have of our own past. The historian, on the other hand, is attached to the discipline that seeks to recover and analyse the past, with the concomitant commitment to seek the truth. Todorov writes:

Historians often have reservations about testimonial literature. Not only do they attract lots of readers, but until they have been examined with the tools of historical scholarship (which often proves to be impossible), they have little truth value. Witnesses for their part, mistrust historians – because they weren't there, they didn't suffer physically, they were still in short pants or not even born when the event took place. This undeclared war can be settled, all the same, if we could grant that testimony, even if it does not respect the criterion of truth in the way that history must, nonetheless enriches historical discourse.[18]

But, Todorov continues, the past does not only live in the present through testimonial literature or historical inquiry, but also through commemoration. He observes: "Like the witness the commemorator is pursuing his or her personal interest; but in common with professional historians, celebrants operate in the public sphere and aspire to irrefutable truthfulness, as far as possible from the unreliability of personal accounts".[19] Whereas Todorov sees some possible complementarity between historians and witnesses, he is less optimistic about the compatibility of historians and celebrants, given the fundamental difference of aims and methods. Although the discourse of commemoration suggests objectivity and truthfulness, it is – according to Todorov – not objective at all. Todorov comments: "While history makes the past more complicated, commemoration makes it simpler, since it most often supplies us with heroes to worship or with enemies to detest, it deals in desecration and consecration".[20] He then makes a helpful distinction between rememoration and commemoration: "*Re*memoration is to try and grasp the truth of the past. *Com*memoration is to adapt the past to the needs of the present" (2014:133).

---

17   Todorov writes in this regard: "Memory should not be thought of as a mechanical recording of what happened. It has many forms and functions, and we have to choose between them; it develops in stages, each of which can be distorted or disturbed; it can be possessed by different people who derive different moral attitudes from it. Is memory necessarily a good thing? Is forgetting always a curse? Does the past always help us to understand the present, or can it serve to confuse our view of the here and the now? Are all uses of the past permissible?". Todorov, *Hope and Memory*, 3.
18   Todorov, *Hope and Memory*, 130.
19   Todorov, *Hope and Memory*, 132.
20   Todorov, *Hope and Memory*, 133.

In this regard Todorov defends the notion of revisionism, understood in a certain way. He does not mean the form of revisionism that is associated with negationism (for instance, that the gas chambers in German concentration camps did not exist), but rather in a way that sees historical truth as always subject to revision. For him this kind of revisionism stands over against pious or sanctified history, which is what the discourse of commemoration is made of. Todorov admits that commemoration may be inevitable, but for him it is not the best way to make the past live on in the present. In a democracy we need something other than sanitised and sanctified images of the past. As he puts it: "In our world human values, not monuments should be holy".[21] Or put differently, the use of memory should be linked to continuing responsible action in its name in the present: "It can be very gratifying to commemorate the victims of past crimes, but getting involved with the victims of today is much trickier".[22]

These statements reflect something of Todorov's overall concern to link memory to 'the good'. In his discussion on the uses and abuses of memory in his book *Memory, History, Forgetting*, Paul Ricoeur refers to Todorov's statement in *Les Abus de la mémoire* that the work of the historian "is necessarily guided by the search, not for truth, but for justice".[23] While Ricoeur has reservations about viewing truth and goodness as stark alternatives, he affirms the importance of the reorientation of the discussion of the abuses of memory under the auspices of the search for justice.[24] One is also reminded in this regard of the concluding words of Todorov's essay "The Uses and Abuses of Memory": "Far from remaining prisoners of the past, we must put it to the service of the present, just as memory – and forgetting – should be used in the service of justice".[25]

I mention Todorov's emphasis on the link between memory and justice and some of his critical comments concerning commemoration here because they foster a self-critical attitude towards possible abuses associated with remembering the past. If one reflects on commemoration, and specifically on the question of how to commemorate the Reformation in Southern Africa in 2017, one would be well advised to take heed of Todorov's distinction between rememoration and commemoration, and guard against simplifying the past in a way that entails not taking the messiness and complexities of history seriously. In the process we should challenge commemorative strategies that glorify or reify 'our own' and demonise 'the strange' or 'the other', often leading to us becoming oblivious to the urgent challenges posed by current injustices that require responsible action. In Todorov's words:

Ritual commemoration, when it only confirms a negative image of the other in the past or a positive image of the self, is ineffective as a tool for public education, and, what is worse, it is an easy way of giving us all a good conscience while averting our eyes from present emergencies … It is hard to find the path that skirts the pitfalls of sanctification and of trivialization, that leads us neither to serve only our

---

21 Todorov, *Hope and Memory*, 134.
22 Todorov, *Hope and Memory*, 175.
23 Ricoeur, P, *Memory, History, Forgetting* (Chicago: University of Chicago Press, 2004), 86.
24 Ricoeur, *Memory, History, Forgetting*, 86.
25 Todorov, T, "The Uses and Abuses of Memory", in Marchitello, H (ed.), *What Happens to History: The Renewal of Ethics in Contemporary Thought* (New York: Routledge, 2001).

own interests nor to give lessons only to others. But that strait and narrow path does exist.[26]

## 3. REVISITING THE 1917 COMMEMORATION OF THE REFORMATION IN THE DUTCH REFORMED CHURCH

In the previous section I called attention to some of the critical remarks raised by Todorov that challenge an uncritical enthusiasm for commemoration. The attempt to grapple with the question of how to commemorate or celebrate the Reformation in Reformed circles in Southern Africa in 2017 should, or so this essay argues, take this critique of commemoration seriously. One can argue further that this question is not situated in a historical vacuum and that any reflection on responsible processes of commemoration of the Reformation in Reformed circles should take cognisance of the complex and ambivalent history of the Reformed churches in Southern Africa, including the history of commemorated practices associated with the Reformation. In this light, the essay pays close attention to some texts from Dutch Reformed Church circles that relate to the 400th commemoration of the Reformation in 1917.

At the meeting of the Federal Council of Dutch Reformed Churches (the combined council of the various Dutch Reformed Synods) held in March 1917 in Graaff-Reinet, the commission tasked with the 400th anniversary of the Reformation (consisting of WA Joubert, DJ Pienaar, MW Odendaal and PS van Heerden) reported that this festival should be celebrated in a special way and that this occasion should be used to make congregations attentive to the meaning of Protestantism and the principles that lie at the heart of the Reformation. This was viewed as important for the following reasons:

a) A lack of principled conviction ("beginselvastheid") on the side of the nation (or people, *volk*), which the Roman Catholic Church ("de Roomsche kerk") knows how to utilise in its favour;

b) The powerful action of Roman Catholicism with regard to the founding of schools and proselytising ("proselieten-makerij");

c) The great ignorance among church members regarding the origin and history of the Protestant church;

d) A false conception of what freedom of religion entails, and the idea that Rome [i.e. the Roman Catholic Church] is not the same as in previous centuries and not concerned with the faith of Protestant believers.[27]

---

26  Todorov, *Hope and Memory*, 175, 176. Although Todorov acknowledge the right to affirm one's own identity, he speaks of the greater dignity associated with concern for the misfortune of others, and writes in this regard: "A French Jewish writer, André Schwarz-Bart, wrote a remarkable novel about the genocide of the Jews, *The Last of the Just*, and then devoted himself to the world of black slaves. When he was asked to account for this change, he replied: 'A great rabbi once asked: Why is the stork, whose name in Jewish [sic] is *hassida*, meaning loving, because it loves its own, why is it classified as an unclean bird? The rabbi replied: 'Because it gives its love only to its own'". See Todorov, *Hope and Memory*, 174.

27  Acts of the Federal Council of DR Churches (1917): 78 (my translation and parenthesis).

In reading this report one is struck by the way in which the celebrations are motivated in the light of the perceived threat posed by the Roman Catholic Church. The report also makes some suggestions on how the Reformation Festival is to be celebrated and suggests, among other things, that the government should be asked to declare 31 October 1917 a national public holiday;[28] that worship services and conferences with a focus on the Reformation should be held on the Sunday closest to the 31st of October; that a short booklet should be written on the Reformation and distributed to congregations; and that special collections should be taken at the commemorative events for needy congregations ("hulpbehoevende gemeenten").[29]

The commissioned booklet referred to in the recommendation was written by GBA Gerdener, who later became professor at the theological seminary at Stellenbosch and a well-known figure in church, mission and ecumenical circles. Towards the end of Gerdener's 125-page historical overview of the Reformation, entitled *Het Vierde Eeuwfeest. Gedenkschrift bij gelegenheid de Vierhonderste viering van de Kerkhervorming 1517-1917*, he asks the following questions: "Is the church situation in 1917 still the same as in 1517? Is there still a danger from the side of the Roman Catholic Church? Are there still persecution and heresies against which Protestants should protest?"[30] Gerdener feels, and thanks God for it, that the situation is indeed not the same in 1917 as in 1517. But, he continues, we should still be on our guard against the sly activities ("listige bedrijvigheid") of the Roman Catholic Church. He points to the fact that there have been no doctrinal changes in the Roman Catholic Church regarding the doctrines that Luther and Calvin protested against, and he lists some examples in this regard. And he calls his readers to guard against the Roman Catholic Church and its schools, pointing to the fact that the influence of the Roman Catholic Church had grown in the recent past, a fact that he finds surprising:

One can hardly believe that a church that allows for so little freedom and that has a tradition of cruelty and persecutions behind it can have an influence on our freedom-loving *volk*, a *volk* that has a great part of the blood of the Huguenots and the Sea Beggars in their veins ("dat voor 'n groot deel het bloed van Hugenoten en Geuzen in de aderen heft").[31]

And, Gerdener continues, it is not intolerance that motivates us to warn against the Roman schools and the Roman Church. Rome should not be fought with the weapons of violence, but with the weapons of the pure truth of the gospel. Some of the same sentiments expressed in the report of the commission tabled at the Federal Council of DR Churches are thus also found in the commissioned booklet.

The decision of the Federal Council was also published in full on 2 August 1917 in *De Kerkbode*, the official weekly DRC newspaper.[32] In the same edition we find a letter from AJ Louw (a moderator of one of the Synods) that encouraged joint celebrations between various Reformed congregations, and even with the two "Hollandse

---

28  This was indeed requested and the various provinces all responded positively, albeit in different ways. The replies from the various directors general of the provinces were published in *De Kerkbode*.
29  Acts of the Federal Council of DR Churches (1917): 78-79.
30  Gerdener, *Het Vierde Eeuwfeest*, 118.
31  Gerdener, *Het Vierde Eeuwfeest*, 122.
32  *De Kerkbode* (2 August 1917): 741-742.

kerke" (i.e. the other main white Afrikaans-speaking Reformed churches).[33] A month earlier the *De Kerkbode* had already reminded its readers about the upcoming commemoration of the Reformation and stated that it would publish various short articles ("vliegende blaadjes") in the months leading up to the celebrations around 31 October.[34]

In most of these writings the same polemical tone against the Roman Catholic Church that marked the Federal Council's report is present.[35] An article by Rev. A McGregor in *De Kerkbode* of 5 July, however, is an interesting exception. He asks: "In what spirit are we going to celebrate?" And then comments:

Certainly not in a merely polemical, anti-Roman Catholic spirit ("Seker tog in geen bloot polemischen, anti-roomsche geest"). Although we emphasise points of difference between us and the Roman Catholic church ... we rejoice that in terms of the fundamental truths – on the glory of God, human sin, the divinity of Christ, the atonement through the cross, the indwelling of the Spirit, life after death – we are one. We should not forget that our biggest enemy is not Roman Catholicism, but materialism and unbelief ... If we celebrate this Festival only in a polemical manner it will be a failure".[36]

In the following months several letters to the editor were published in *De Kerkbode* that protested against this statement. In *De Kerkbode* of 9 August, WPJ Poen writes that he read the comments by McGregor with astonishment, and that he could not believe his eyes when he read these words from one of the most learned ministers in the church. "We *one* with Rome with regard to *the glory of God*! How can the glory of God find the right expression when the Protestant doctrine of election is not only negated, but scolded as a hellish, God-dishonouring monstrosity? ("maar als een helsch, God-onteerende monstrositeit uitgekreten wordt?").[37] And he goes on to speak in a similar vein of all the other doctrinal matters that McGregor mentioned.[38]

*De Kerkbode* was also used as a mouthpiece to call upon congregations to make the most of the celebrations, and it sought to contribute theologically to these commemorations. On 18 October a special edition ("praguitgawe") of 60 pages was distributed as an addendum to the regular edition of *De Kerkbode*. This richly illustrated edition contains articles on "The Reformations and its Leaders" (extensive articles on both Luther and Calvin); "The Reformation in Geneva under Calvin"; "The Reformation in the Netherlands"; two articles on "The Reformation and the Huguenots"; an article aimed at the youth ("'Oom Willem Smit' on the Reformation"), "Reformation Hymns", "The Reformation's doctrine of the Church", "The Reformation and the Family"; and "The Reformation and Mission". This

---

33   Louw, AJ, "Het Vierde Eeuwfeest der Kerkhervorming, 1 Oct. 1917: De viering in de Transvaal", *De Kerkbode* (2 August, 1917): 743-744.
34   *De Kerkbode* (5 July 1917): 651.
35   See, for instance, the articles in *De Kerkbode* of 2 August, 9 August and 20 September 1917 by Rev. HE du Plessis.
36   McGregor, A, "Het Vierde Eeuwfeest der Hervorming", *De Kerkbode* (5 July 1917): 655.
37   Poen, WPJ, "Het Vierde Eeuwfeest der Kerkhervorming", *De Kerkbode* (9 August 1917): 783 (my translation and parenthesis).
38   The same objections are also found in a letter by P J Marais, published in *De Kerkbode* of 13 September 1917.

commemorative edition also included a sermon by Rev. PS van Heerden on "The Reformation – a new day: The night has passed". In the sermon he speaks of the darkness of the Middle Ages (with its night of ignorance, night of injustice and night of superstition), followed by the coming of day that dawned with the new emphasis on the Bible and on justification by faith. As children of the light, moreover, we have responsibilities. The sermon also conveys a sense of being beleaguered. "Enemies surround us. Life is a struggle. Therefore we must take up the weapons of the light, and stand in the full armour of God".[39]

The opening contribution in the commemorative booklet by Rev. DJ Pienaar, however, is quite self-critical. It starts with the words: "It is now a time of festivity, a time of joy, a time of jubilation for Protestantism" ("Het is thans feesttijd, vreugdetijd, jubeltijd voor het Protestantisme").[40] Yet, Pienaar continues, there are also circumstances that can invite the question of whether our exuberant tone should not change to one of lament, and whether the time of feasting should not change into a time of fasting.[41] The land of Luther and Calvin, the countries of the Reformation, are in mourning amidst the horrific and bloody realities of war. Pienaar is also sensitive to the fact that the Reformation created a break in the one body of Christ and therefore the celebrations cannot be a matter of unqualified joy. Yet Pienaar nevertheless believes that the Reformation can be commemorated with gratitude and joy. The self-critical sentiments by Pienaar, however, are the exception rather than the rule in the writings found in *De Kerkbode* in the months preceding the Reformation celebrations, and the dominant impression is rather of a polemicising discourse that sought to strengthen an isolationist and beleaguered identity.

It seems indeed the case that the Reformation was commemorated in a festive way around the time of 31 October 1917. *De Kerkbode* later reported on large events being held in Cape Town at the Groote Kerk, and in Johannesburg at the Civic Hall (with 3,000 people attending). From the extensive feedback in *De Kerkbode* on these events it seems that the same anti-Roman Catholic rhetoric persisted at these events as well.[42]

## 4. CONCLUSION

This brief survey of the glimpses one gets through *De Kerkbode* and other commemorative publications on the 1917 celebrations of the Reformation in the Dutch Reformed Church reveals a polemical stance against the Roman Catholic Church, with the focus more on "conflict" than on "communion" (to use words of the report *From Conflict to Communion* mentioned in the Introduction). Although not uncontested, this antithetical approach seems to be the dominant paradigm in the commemorative discourse. Maybe this is indicative of the Dutch Reformed church's struggle with the modernism and the liberalism that characterised theological

---

39   Van Heerden, PS, "De Hervorming – Een Nieuwe Dag. De Nacht Voorbijgegaan" in *Het Vierde Eeuwfeest der Kerkhervorming*, supplement to *De Kerkbode* (18 October 1917): 59.
40   Pienaar, DJ, "De Hervorming – Gods werk", in *Het Vierde Eeuwfeest der Kerkhervorming*, supplement to *De Kerkbode* (18 October, 1917), 1.
41   Pienaar, DJ, "De Hervorming – Gods werk", 1.
42   *De Kerkbode* (8 November, 1917): 1094-1095.

debates in the first decades of the 20th century, culminating in the Du Plessis case and a certain form of neo-Calvinism that became entrenched in its wake.[43]

What will the dominant mode characterising the 2017 celebrations within Reformed circles be in Southern Africa? Time will tell, but in the light of the above comments, I suggest that the following aspects should be kept in mind:

- The need for a self-critical engagement with the possible abuses associated with commemorations. This means, among other things, that commemoration should not be abstracted from rememoration. Amidst their differences, the link between personal testimony (memory), history and commemoration should be maintained. The pragmatic concerns associated with commemoration should not override an honest and hermeneutically responsible engagement with the past through historical inquiry, including sensitivity to the complex and ambivalent historical contexts in which past commemorations took place.
- One should guard against strategies of identity construction and 'othering' that blind one to urgent current challenges and opportunities. Hence the importance of asking the question: With what future in mind we are commemorating the Reformation? In terms of Todorov's work, this means that we ask about the ethics of commemoration. Are our commemorations linked to concerns for justice?
- The emphasis on common commemoration in an ecumenical and global age holds much promise for a deeper understanding of our Christian tradition and may lead to a new appreciation of the contributions that insights from the Protestant tradition can bring to the table in contemporary discourses on what lies at the heart of the nature and mission of the church in our world today.
- Celebrations that are not touched by a spirit of confession about the disunity of the church will be unauthentic and in the end produce simplistic categorisations.

With regard to this last point, a sermon by Dietrich Bonhoeffer comes to mind. In 1932, in the midst of trying times, he preached on Reformation Sunday in Berlin, using as his text Revelation 2:4-5, 7: "But I have this against you, that you have abandoned the love you had at first. Remember then from what you have fallen; repent, and do the works that you did first. If not, I will come to you and remove your lampstand from its place, unless you repent … Let anyone who has an ear listen to what the Spirit is saying to the churches. To everyone who conquers, I will give permission to eat from the tree of life that is in the paradise of God". Let me end with a quote from this remarkable sermon.

> The Protestant church is observing a special day. Protest is among its traditional obligations. It must protest against quite a variety of things, but protest it must. This time it is a strong protest against secularization in the form of godlessness, but of course also – perhaps especially this time – against Catholicism and its dangers (meaning, of course, only the political dangers) … Oh, how easily we protest, with passion and self-confidence, since we have a documented right to it. But God says:

---

43  See Vosloo, R R, "Konfessionele neo-Calvinisme na die Du Plessis-saak". *NGTT* 51(Supplementum), 2010: 275-288.

'I have this against you …,' meaning, 'I protest.' God protests – against whom? Against us and our protest! Can't we hear it? Protestantism is not about us and our protest against the world, but rather about God's protest against us.[44]

---

44  Bonhoeffer, D, *Berlin: 1932-1933 (Dietrich Bonhoeffer Works, Volume 12)* (Minneapolis: Fortress Press, 2009), 441.

# PART 2 –
# REVISITING SOME EPISODES IN THE HISTORY OF THE DUTCH REFORMED CHURCH (1916-1960)

# 8. ON POVERTY: THE DUTCH REFORMED CHURCH AND 'THE POOR WHITE PROBLEM'[1]

## 1. INTRODUCTION

In 1989 Francis Wilson and Mamphela Ramphele published *Uprooting Poverty: The South African Challenge*,[2] a book that won public acclaim and evoked much discussion. This book, which had its genesis in a time of great social upheaval, presented the report of the second Carnegie inquiry into poverty and development in Southern Africa. *Uprooting Poverty* drew on a process that had already started in January 1980 and included the work of a feasibility commission, several years of active research, a large conference at the University of Cape Town in 1984 (attended by some 450 people, with over 300 papers presented), and many other post-conference projects, papers and publications. The authors used this material to provide an overview and analysis of poverty in South Africa. The Preface to this book notes that its origins go back more than fifty years to the time of the Great Depression, when "the rulers of South Africa were troubled by the fact that a large numbers of whites, uprooted from the land during the previous generation of war, drought, pestilence, populations growth, and the capitalisation of agriculture, were pouring into the cities to live, ill-equipped for modern industrial society, in dire poverty".[3] In the context of these challenges posed by white poverty, a group of people from the church and the academy set up, with support from the Carnegie Corporation in New York, the Carnegie Commission on the Poor White Problem in South Africa, resulting in 1932 in the publication of an extensive five-volume report.

In this essay I do not want to discuss the second Carnegie report and its reception (albeit that this report and its reception – also in church circles – deserve continuing academic attention) or provide a comparison between the work of the first and the second Carnegie inquiry. Rather, I want to focus on some of the events leading to the first Carnegie Report and the way the Dutch Reformed Church (DRC) responded in its wake to the so-called 'poor white problem'. Special attention will be given to a National or People's Congress (*Volkskongres*) held in Kimberley in October 1934 and immediately followed by a church conference. The essay also refers to some earlier conferences that became precursors to the Carnegie report and the subsequent Kimberley conferences. Given the fact that the 1930s were also a period in which a form of neo-Calvinism found a stronger foothold within the Dutch Reformed Church, the last section of the essay offers some brief comments on aspects of the theological discourse around the role of the church in caring for the poor.

---

1  This essay was read as a paper at the annual meeting of the Church Historical Society of Southern Africa (CHSSA) in Durban, 29 June – 1 July 2011, and first published under the title "The Dutch Reformed Church and the poor white problem in the wake of the first Carnegie Report (1932): some church-historical and theological observations" in *Studia Historiae Ecclesiasticae* 37/2, September 2011:67-85.
2  Wilson, F and Ramphele, M, *Uprooting Poverty: The South African challenge* (Cape Town: David Philip, 1989).
3  Wilson and Ramphele, *Uprooting Poverty*, ix.

In *Uprooting Poverty* Wilson and Ramphele rightly observe that although the first Carnegie Commission noted that the problems of black poverty were no less acute than those of white poverty, the focus remained primarily on the whites. As the economy grew with the industrial developments of the Second World War and post-war years, poverty among whites receded dramatically. Although blacks were also drawn into the economy in increasing numbers, black poverty "remained acute, although largely unexamined".[4] It is indeed the case that the first Carnegie report and the conferences and projects preceding and following it had an exclusive focus on white poverty; however, even a cursory glance at the material from this period also reveals that the poor white problem ('armblanke-vraagstuk') was not viewed in isolation from what was perceived as the 'native problem ('die naturelle-vraagstuk') and that these two 'problems' should be understood as inextricably interwoven.

## 2. THE 'POOR WHITE PROBLEM' AND THE RESPONSE OF THE DRC BEFORE THE CARNEGIE REPORT

The significance of the 'poor white problem' is often highlighted in Afrikaner political historiography. As Herman Giliomee observes in his book *The Afrikaners: Biography of a People*: "The so-called poor white problem became the most pressing social issue in Afrikaner politics early in the 20$^{th}$ century and retained that status until the early 1940s, when the search for a new approach to the racial problem replaced it".[5]

In the literature on the poor white problem, and the church's response, attention is further drawn to the way in which the discovery of diamonds and gold created a new complex and competitive economic situation that also disrupted Afrikaner society.[6] How did the Dutch Reformed Church respond to this new reality? In Dutch Reformed Church historiography it is often noted that from the 1880s onwards the Dutch Reformed Church increasingly extended its synodical work regarding the care of the poor (armesorg) through the founding of several church institutions, such as agricultural settlements for poor families, houses for orphaned and poor children, as well as other institutions for people with special needs.[7] Given the new industrial

---

4   Wilson and Ramphele, *Uprooting Poverty*, x.
5   Giliomee, H, *The Afrikaners: Biography of a People* (Cape Town: Tafelberg, 2003), 315.
6   Niewoudt puts it as follows: "the once uncomplicated Afrikaner society [*"boeresamelewing"*] suddenly had to accommodate cosmopolitan communities with a variety of norms and cultures … A complicated economic world unfolded with stringent competition for the wealth of the land. But the Afrikaner found himself in a traumatic, unenviable situation: his origins in an uncomplicated, isolated rural farmer's community [*boeregemeenskap*] with its limited educational opportunities placed him in a highly unequal struggle". See De Klerk, JJ (ed.), *Die diens van barmhartigheid en die Nederduitse Gereformeerde Kerk: 'n Diakonologiese studie* (Kaapstad: N G Kerk-Uitgewers, 1990), 85. It is debatable just how uncomplicated the isolated existence of the Afrikaner was in the rural areas; nevertheless, the new situation could indeed be described as traumatic and had a huge impact on Afrikaner identity, as is seen in the traces of the consciousness of the poor white problem in Afrikaner historiography, political discourse and literature.
7   Cf. Hanekom, TN (ed.) *Ons Nederduitse Gereformeerde Kerk: Gedenkboek by ons Derde Eeufees 1952* (Kaapstad: N G Kerk-Uitgewers, 1952), 274; Lindeque, RC, *Gaan maak jy ook so: Die Maatskaplike werk van die Ned. Geref. Kerk* (Pretoria: NG Kerkboekhandel Transvaal, 1985), 56; Botha, LLN, *Die Maatskaplike Sorg van die N.G. Kerk in Suid-Afrika (1928-1953)* (Paarl: Paarlse Drukpers, 1957), 141, 142.

situation in South Africa after the discovery of diamonds and gold, and the growing migration of people from the rural areas to the cities, increasing concern for the poor became noticeable. A series of eight articles, for instance, were published by Rev. BPJ Marchand in 1893 in *De Volksbode* on "Onze armen, wat kan er voor hen gedaan worden?" ["Our poor, what can be done for them?"].[8] Following a conversation with the Cape Minister of Agriculture John X Merriman, Rev. Andrew Murray (then the moderator of the synod) took the lead in convening a church conference at Stellenbosch in 1893 on *"De Arme Blanken" ("The Poor Whites")*.[9] The focus of this conference was mainly on the need for better education and the establishment of working communities to provide employment. The poor white problem increasingly became part of the national agenda as well, and after the Anglo-Boer War (1899-1902) the deteriorating situation became, as could be expected, even more of a reason for concern and action.

After the first decade of the 20th century the church's response to white poverty became more deliberate and organised in the wake of growing urbanisation. In 1915 the Cape Synod called into being a synodical commission for *"inwendige Zending"* ("Internal Mission", which in 1919 became *"Die Algemene Armesorg-kommissie"*) and in 1916 Rev. AD Luckhoff was appointed as the organising secretary. The church's more organised response to white poverty is also reflected in several important conferences that were held on the 'poor white problem' prior to the 1934 Congress. These conferences provide a good window onto the discourse on the poor white problem and the Dutch Reformed Church's response to it.

The first important conference took place in Cradock on 22 and 23 December 1916 and was organised by the Cape church; its theme was "Die landelike nood en trek na die stede" ("The needs of the rural areas and the trek to the cities"). The 225 delegates also included important government officials, professors from the Theological Seminary at Stellenbosch, the editor of *Die Burger* (Dr DF Malan), representatives of the Dutch Reformed Church in Transvaal, the Free State and Natal, as well as from the other Afrikaner Reformed churches. At the conference the term 'poor whites' was defined as those whites who are poor in material possessions and personal development. Reference was also made to the fact that the 'poor whites' come from strong European descent, implying that the condition of white poverty is unnatural. Dr DF Malan put it this way in his presentation: "The poor whiteism of the Afrikaner ... does not derive from the land, because others live on it and become rich ... It is even less in our blood, because we are children of the resilient and, on the economic terrain, the most enterprising and prosperous peoples of Europe".[10] The conference also devoted attention to the scope and the reasons for the poor white problem, as well as to possible remedies for the situation. The conference closed with a paper by Rev. HP van der Merwe on the church as a moral factor in uplifting the poor (die kerk as sedelike faktor in die opheffing van die arme). In his dissertation on the social work of the Dutch Reformed Church, published in 1957, LLN Botha noted how one is immediately struck by the thoroughness, scientific character and clear

---

8    Cf. De Klerk, *Die diens van barmhartigheid*, 87.
9    Cf. Van der Watt, PB, *Die Nederduitse Gereformeerde Kerk 1824-1905* (Pretoria: N.G. Kerkboekhandel Transvaal, 1980), 91, 92.
10   Botha, *Die Maatskaplike Sorg van die N.G. Kerk in Suid-Afrika*, 158.

insights shining through the papers presented at the conference.[11] This remark is quite significant, since it indeed seems to be the case that what was viewed as a more scientific approach would became more and more prevalent in addressing the poor white problem. The Carnegie report represents a high point in this development. It is important to note that this more scientific approach did not entail the type of critical hermeneutics that could challenge an unhealthy coupling of the church alliance with the *volk* and the growing Afrikaner nationalism.

The Cradock conference became a precursor to similar conferences. From 15-18 June 1922 a conference was held in Stellenbosch that became known as the Education conference (Opvoedingskongres). The conference was attended by 100 delegates, led by Rev. D Wilcocks, who was also the chair of the Synodical Education Commission of the Dutch Reformed Church. The main theme is already announced on the title page of the conference proceedings: "How to save a poor child and make him [sic!] a useful citizen" ("Hoofgedachte: Hoe het arm kind te redden en van hem een nuttig burger te maken").

Whereas the Stellenbosch conference focused mainly on poverty and education, the conference held the following year in Bloemfontein (4-5 July 1923) had a broader focus. This conference, also known as the "joint conference" ("die gesamentlike kongres"), was attended by delegates from the three Afrikaner Reformed Churches, women's organisations and representatives of the state. In his opening speech the chairperson and moderator of the Dutch Reformed Church in the Free State, Rev. P van Heerden, affirmed the need for action, saying that in order to make the conference a success, one needs to see, feel and act. He emphasised that the poor white person is a brake on the wagon of the people's prosperity (volksvoorspoed). They need to be saved for the sake of their families and for the people (*volk*).[12] Also present at the conference was General JBM Hertzog, who spoke to the question of what the state could do to address the poor white problem. In the process he made a plea for dropping the term "poor whites", since the problem was not poor whites but unemployment. Hertzog also mentioned the important issues of the competition between white and coloured (kleurling) workers, but did not go into more detail. What should be noted as well is that Hertzog concluded his speech by saying that the problem is not merely an issue for whites, but for the whole of South Africa. In providing employment, justice would be done to the Europeans (whites) and the black population (die naturel). Hertzog acknowledged, however, that it would be difficult to solve the problem in such a way that justice is done to both races.[13] Another prominent figure who spoke at the conference was Dr DF Malan. In his speech he focused on the migration of the rural (white) population to the cities and towns, emphasising that this is not a passing phase and that something positive might come out of this Second Trek. After the conference Dr Malan wrote a series of editorials in *Die Burger* (between 10 and 24 July 1923) that were subsequently published in an influential brochure entitled *Die Groot Vlug: 'n Nabetragting van die Arm-blanke-Kongres, 1923, en van die Offisiële Sensusopgawe* (*The Great Flight: A Reflection on the Poor*

---

11  Botha, *Die Maatskaplike Sorg van die N.G. Kerk in Suid-Afrika*, 155.
12  *Gesamentlike Kongres oor die Arm Blanke Vraagstuk in die Raadsaal the Bloemfontein op 4 en 5 Julie 1923* (Bloemfontein: Nasioanle Pers Beperk, 1923), 3.
13  *Gesamentlike Kongres*, 5

*White Congress, 1923, and on the Official Census*).[14] The impact of the ideas expressed in these editorials and the brochure can hardly be over-estimated, since their influence was felt in many of the discussions on the so-called poor white problem in the years to come. It is not surprising that the first Carnegie report contains several citations from this pamphlet.

Although it is clear that the dominant view in 1923 was still that urbanisation should be controlled, the view that the church should adapt to the new situation became more and more prevalent. The title of a brochure by JR Albertyn captures this new reality: "Die boerekerk word stadskerk" ("The church of the rural Afrikaner becomes a city church").[15] Another aspect that came to the fore during the 1923 conference (for instance, in the speech by HP van der Merwe and in DF Malan's speech and later reflections) is the way in which the poor white problem was viewed as intertwined with the so-called native problem,[16] an aspect that would also come to the fore in the Carnegie Report of 1932.

## 3. THE CARNEGIE REPORT (1932)

At the conferences at Cradock, Stellenbosch and Bloemfontein the voices pleading for a more scientific approach to the poor white problem became increasingly more emphatic. In 1927 the president and the secretary of the Carnegie Corporation of New York visited South Africa. It was suggested by various groups that the Corporation should fund an investigation into the poor white problem in South Africa. The Dutch Reformed Churches also requested such an investigation, to which the Corporation responded positively. In addition to carrying the major share of the costs, the Carnegie Corporation also arranged for two prominent American sociologists, Dr KL Butterfield and Dr CW Coulter, to assist with the inquiry.[17] A Management Council (Raad van Beheer) was established in 1928, which included representatives of the Dutch Reformed Church, the Council for Research Grants and some additional members.[18] The Dutch Reformed Church also paid the salary of Dr JR Albertyn during the time of his active participation in the process as representative of the Dutch Reformed Church and report writer, while the Universities of Stellenbosch and Cape Town, as well as several other government and non-governmental organisations, provided the necessary funding that enabled some of their members to participate in the inquiry as well.

In 1932 the Commission published its findings in an extensive five-volume report. The first volume, by JFW Grosskopf, presented an economic report that focused on

---

14  Malan, DF, *Die Groot Vlug: 'n Nabetragting van die Arm-Blanke Kongres, 1923, en van die Offisiële Sensusopgawe* (1923).
15  Albertyn, JR, *Die Boerekerk word Stadskerk* (Cape Town: S.A. Bybelvereniging, 1942).
16  At the Cradock and the Bloemfontein conferences the aspect of the competition between white and black workers was discussed, and the notion of industrial segregation was proposed. See Greyling, PF, *Die Nederduitse Gereformeerde Kerk en Armesorg* (Kaapstad: Nasionale Pers Beperk, 1939), 294, 301.
17  Grosskopf, JFW, *Die armblanke-vraagstuk in Suid-Afrika: Verslag van die Carnegie-kommissie (Deel I). Ekonomiese verslag: Plattelandsverarming en Plaasverlating* (Stellenbosch: Pro Ecclesia-Drukkery, 1932), i.
18  Grosskopf, *Die armblanke-vraagstuk in Suid-Afrika*, i-ii.

poverty in the rural areas and the migration from farms. The second report was a psychological report on the poor white person, with RW Wilcocks as editor. Part 3 of the report was written by EG Malherbe and focused on education and the poor white person, while part 4 presented a medical report by WA Murray on the physical condition of poor whites. The fifth volume of the report was a two-part sociological report. The first part by JR Albertyn looked at the poor white person and society, while the second part by the well-known writer ME Rothmann concentrated on the role of the mothers and daughters in the poor white family. It is not the purpose of this paper to give a detailed analysis of the five volumes of the Carnegie report, although such an analysis from different perspectives (including studies informed by gender and postcolonial theories) would certainly still be worthwhile. I do, however, want to refer briefly to some of the joint findings and recommendations of the report, as well as to a section on the role of the church (in the report by JR Albertyn).

Each volume of the Carnegie report is introduced by the 124 joint findings and recommendation of the Commission, with the recommendations printed in italics. These findings and recommendations start with remarks on the nature and scope of the poor white problem, as well as possible reasons for the problem (which included, according to the report, insufficient adaptation to new economic realities and the inability of the education system to prepare people for these changes). The report further indicates some of the psychological traits of the poor white person, highlighting an isolationist mindset in the psyche of the poor white person. Given this diagnosis, the report recommended some steps towards improving education and reducing social isolation. Specific committees should be established and social workers trained to address the problem. The findings and recommendations also comment on the physical situation and diet of poor whites, as well as the role of the mother and daughter in family life. In addition to these aspects, the report comments on the social and moral life of poor whites, concluding with the recommendation that increased state subsidy and control of housing projects in the cities and especially the rural areas be urgently implemented. This is followed by a section on the relationship between the poor whites and black people; it states that unlimited competition between unschooled black workers and poor whites on the labour market, with the consequent low income that the poor white person then receives, has a demoralising effect on the latter. Regulations that limit this competition should aim to counter this,[19] although it is suggested that the reservation of jobs for the white person should only be a temporary measure during a learning period. The findings and recommendations section of the report also comments on the (white) migration from the rural areas to the cities and the adaptation that is needed in this regard, emphasising in the process the need for help through social work (maatskaplike werk). Regarding the intelligence of the poor white person, the report states that "the greatest part of the poor white population, as far as intelligence is concerned, falls within the borders of normalcy".[20] This was an important finding that was intended to emphasise the potential of better education. This aspect of the report received much publicity.[21]

---

19 Grosskopf, *Die armblanke-vraagstuk in Suid-Afrika*, xix.
20 Grosskopf, *Die armblanke-vraagstuk in Suid-Afrika*, xxiv.
21 See, for instance, the article in two instalments by the Afrikaner poet NP van Wyk Louw in *Die Huisgenoot*, 19 May and 15 September 1933, as referred to in Giliomee, *The*

The Carnegie report further makes the point that sustainable change cannot only be implemented on the level of the improvement of external economic conditions, since psychological change within the poor persons themselves is needed as well. Hence the emphasis on the need for deliberate social upliftment in which the state, voluntary organisations and the church should play a role. The more wealthy citizens need to be educated regarding their responsibilities towards the less fortunate, and the poor in turn should be educated in "thrift, self-sufficiency, temperance, health, a sense of togetherness, and racial pride".[22] The church's social preaching can play an important role in this regard and the report refers to the church's care of the poor in positive terms.[23] But the report also points to certain limitations. Despite all the activities of the church, it is still the case that the church, with its natural conservatism and slow processes (given the long time lapses between meetings, etc.), is not totally informed about the extensive and far-reaching recent social changes.[24]

Other important findings of the report included an emphasis on the need for continual systematic and detailed scientific inquiry into the poor white problem in all its facets and its phases of development. The report also recommends the founding of a department of social studies at one of the South African universities, where social workers can be trained, as well as the establishment of a state department for "social welfare" ("maatskaplike welvaart").[25]

## 4. THE DUTCH REFORMED CHURCH'S RESPONSE TO THE CARNEGIE REPORT

After the Carnegie report was published in 1932, the DRC appointed three study commissions to look carefully at the report and its findings, with a national congress (volkskongres) on the issue in mind.[26] As heads of these commissions were appointed RW Wilcocks, JR Albertyn and HF (some sources say HL) Verwoerd. At a large meeting convened in Cape Town in January 1934 (attended by about 70 men and women) about 40 smaller sub-commissions were appointed to study aspects of the report. The proposals from these sub-commissions were then sent back to the three main study commissions, which evaluated them and consolidated the suggestions

---

*Afrikaners*, 348.
22   Grosskopf, *Die armblanke-vraagstuk in Suid-Afrika*, xxix.
23   See Grosskopf, *Die armblanke-vraagstuk in Suid-Afrika*, xxix
24   In Volume 5 of the report (in the section that focuses on the role of the church) one finds, for instance, the following quotation from the brochure by DF Malan mentioned above, *Die Groot Vlug*: "Can it be that there are not enough people within the church with the necessary theoretical and practical knowledge of the principles of taking care of the poor to organise effectively? … Can it be that it never occurred to the church to train experts in this regard? Can it be that the church is not in touch, and cannot be in touch, with the serious and rapidly changing situation because its synods, which are supposed to give direction, meet so seldom that they have actually become non-entities in the life of the *volk*?". Albertyn, JR and Rothmann, ME, *Die armblanke-vraagstuk in Suid-Afrika: Verslag van die Carnegie-kommissie (Deel V). Sociologiese verslag* (Stellenbosch: Pro Ecclesia-Drukkery, 1932), 66; cf. Malan, *Die Groot Vlug* 10.
25   Grosskopf, *Die armblanke-vraagstuk in Suid-Afrika*, xxxii, xxxiii.
26   Cf. Botha, *Die Maatskaplike Sorg van die N.G. Kerk in Suid-Afrika*, 191.

into 99 recommendations.²⁷ Some proposals were also received from the public.²⁸ The stage was now set for the national congress, organised by the Armesorgraad (The Poor Relief Council) of the Federated Dutch Reformed Churches of South Africa, to be held in Kimberley from 2-5 October 1934. The executive organising committee consisted of Rev. JR Albertyn (chair), Rev. AD Luckhoff (Cape), Rev. PJ Pienaar (Free State), Rev. P du Toit (Transvaal), with co-organisers the three heads of the study commissions (Dr Wilcocks, Dr Albertyn and Dr Verwoerd). The build-up to the conference, and the conference itself, received much attention in the media, with editorials making the plea that the church and government should take hands in joint action to address the poor white problem. *Die Vaderland* even published a full-length sermon by Rev. P. du Toit.

After the conference a 314-page report on the proceedings was published that opens an important window onto the debates at the conference and the prevalent mood at the time. It is worth quoting Rev. Albertyn's remark in his introduction to the report:

> It is well to remember that no magic charm exists by which the evil can be exorcised. Poverty and its consequences – like sickness – we will always have with us. For neither is there an unfailing panacea. But even as the united medical profession is continually evolving new and more efficient methods of fighting disease and death, so also must Christian philanthropy constantly and patiently devise ever better means of alleviating social distress. What may well be expected of this conference is that all the great social institutions of the country: the state, education, the Churches, other philanthropic bodies, indeed that all citizens, each in his own sphere of labour, but acting in co-ordination with the rest, will in future present a united front to the common enemies of pauperism, misery and degradation.²⁹

If one reads through the report, which includes speeches delivered at the conference, the emphasis on the urgency of the matter and the need for decisive action is clearly evident. This is reflected in the Preface to the report written by the chair at the conference, Dr William Nicol, who states that inquiry (by which he refers to the Carnegie Commission report and the decisions taken at the Volkskongres) should be followed by action: "It is clear that inquiry is useless and our decisions taken in vain if they are not followed now by forceful action … Nobody can be indifferent regarding this call to the people".³⁰ The dedication page of the report reads: "Dedicated to you, kind reader, if you assist".

After Rev. PGJ Meiring opened the conference with a prayer, Rev. Nicol welcomed the delegates and called attention to the urgency of the situation. Whereas the statistic indicating that poor whites numbered around 80 000 people had shocked the audience at the 1916 Cradock congress, the recent figure of 250 000 might have suggested that no end was in sight. Nicol made a strong appeal to turn the situation

---

27   Du Toit, P (compiler), *Verslag van die volkskongres oor die armblankevraagstuk gehou te Kimberley, 2-5 Okt, 1934 / Report of the national conference on the poor white problem held at Kimberley, 2ⁿᵈ to 5ᵗʰ Oct., 1934.* (Cape Town: Nasionale Pers Beperk, 1934), 3.
28   Botha, *Die Maatskaplike Sorg van die N.G. Kerk in Suid-Afrika,* 192.
29   See Du Toit, *Verslag van die volkskongres,* 5.
30   Du Toit, *Verslag van die volkskongres,* Preface.

around – a situation, he stated, that affects everybody and that is everybody's business, adding that it is no wonder that people from all walks of life showed an interest in the congress. It is quite telling that Rev. Nicol remarks in his welcoming address that the church would like to look beyond its own people (*volk*), since the Christian faith is in its essence unselfish and seeks to extend a hand beyond its own family and *volk*. He continues: "With us in South Africa this is the case to an extraordinary degree. Our great calling is after all to the native races. But today we are actually forced to limit our attention to the needs of our own people. It will in any case be impossible to reach out a helping hand to others if we are sinking ourselves".[31] Nicol expressed the view that it would have been difficult at that stage to find a solution for the native problem before the poor white problem had been address sufficiently. He suggested four points as a framework for the deliberations at the conference. The first concerned the need for a great awakening among our people regarding the poor white problem. Everybody (parents, state, church) must work together. The soul of the people should be gripped by the idea: "We must save our people" ("Ons moet ons mense red").[32] The second point affirmed the need for intensive and continuous study of the problem, involving in the process the best brains in the country. A third point related to the need for the large-scale training of social workers, with universities and the church playing an important role. And, fourthly, since funds were sorely needed, a new spirit of sacrificial charity (offervaardigheid) should take hold of the *volk*.

The report of the conference testifies to the fact that these points indeed formed the framework for the discourse, as they are reflected in the various speeches and resolutions taken at the conference. It is beyond the scope of this essay to comment on all the speeches addressed to the congress (included speeches by the likes of HF Verwoerd and DF Malan as well as Dutch Reformed pastors such as Rev. DP van Huyssteen, Rev. AD Luckhoff and Rev. P du Toit), but one can note that the various speeches at the conference, as well as the resolutions taken, for the most part reflected the framework set out by Rev. Nicol in his words of welcome. The conference report also reflected the view that the poor white problem was closely intertwined with the so-called native problem. Rev. DP van Huyssteen put it as follows in his opening address: "The poor white problem and the native problem stand before us and beg for a solution and relief. Nobody can look at these two giant mountains without feeling a chill running down their spine".[33]

The *Volkskongres* approved 109 far-reaching resolutions. These resolutions were introduced, echoing Van Huyssteen's speech, by the "deep realization that the workmen labour in vain unless the Lord builds the house".[34] The report concluded

---

31 Du Toit, *Verslag van die volkskongres*, 12.
32 Du Toit, *Verslag van die volkskongres*, 13.
33 Du Toit, *Verslag van die volkskongres*, 26.
34 Du Toit, *Verslag van die volkskongres*, 292. Thee rubrics under which the report lists the resolutions already give one a sense of the issues addressed at the conference: the reorganisation of welfare work, housing, health services in rural areas, recreation and amusement, the subsidising of social work, indoor relief (binnemuurse liefdadigheid), care for the aged, child welfare and juvenile delinquency, measures for increasing male employment in existing urban occupations, the creation of greater opportunities for work, employment and care of female employees, the provision of temporary employment, temporary care of the unemployed by means of unemployment and health insurance,

with a few general recommendations that included the instruction to the Continuation Committee (Voortsettingskomitee) to bring the resolutions more prominently before the people, the plea to citizens for financial contributions, as well as a reference to the supreme influence of religion as an elevating factor in life.[35]

The *Volkskongres* was followed immediately by a church conference, also in Kimberley (6-7 October 1934). It has been argued that this conference represents the first attempt to prioritise and re-organise the church's principles regarding its care of the poor (armesorg).[36] This church congress had as its theme "Christelike armesorg en die hulpmiddels daartoe" ("Christian care of the poor and the means to do so"). According to the Preface to the report on the conference written by Rev. PJ Pienaar and published by the General Commission for Poor Relief of the Federated Dutch Reformed Churches (Algemene Armesorg-Kommissies van die Gefedereerde Ned. Geref. Kerke), several thousand copies of the report were distributed to church councils. On the first morning of the conference Rev. PJ van Vuuren spoke on the biblical foundation of the church's care of the poor; this was followed by Rev. P du Toit's speech on principles of constructive care of the poor. The rest of the day focused on the role of the church and its societies and institutions, the role of women in Christian care of the poor, and the training of Christian social workers. On Sunday 7 October Rev. Nicol was the preacher at a worship service in the Dutch Reformed Church in Kimberley. The conference concluded on the Sunday evening with speeches on the education of the more and less fortunate church members.

The Volkskongres and the church conference that followed it are rightly viewed as important events in the attempt to turn the tide of the poor white problem. The Kimberley conference of 1934 can indeed be seen as a significant historical marker. In his autobiography, significantly entitled *Met Toga en Troffel*, William Nicol remarks that the 1934 conference "will go down in history as the turning point in the treatment of the poor in our country".[37] And MM Niewoudt commented: "Today it can be said with confidence that the entire welfare system in South Africa can trace its roots to the Poor White Congress of 1934".[38]

What was the significance of the Kimberley conference of 1934 as a response to the Carnegie report of 1932 and the cumulative experience of the poor white problem in the previous decades? I want to make five remarks in this regard.

First, in the decades leading up to the Carnegie report pleas for a more scientific approach to the poor white problem became stronger, a move that found specific concretisation in the Carnegie report of 1932. In the DRC's response to the poor white problem it is clear that they affirmed the value of a more scientific approach.

---

increase of employment in rural areas through the general improvement of agriculture, special provision of employment in rural areas for the European poor, compulsory measures for adults, church settlement and labour colonies, general measures of a psycho-educational nature, organisation of the school system, enhanced standard of general education, the curriculum, centralisation of schools, backward and retarded children, and inculcation of desirable habits and attitudes (292-316).

35  Cf. Du Toit, *Verslag van die volkskongres*, 316-317.
36  Botha, *Die Maatskaplike Sorg van die N.G. Kerk in Suid-Afrika (1928-1953)*, 216.
37  Nicol, W, *Met Toga en Troffel: Die Lewe van 'n Stadspredikant* (Kaapstad: N.G. Kerk-uitgewers, 1958), 316.
38  See De Klerk, *Die diens van barmhartigheid*, 96.

In addition, a more professional approach was propagated that incorporated the expertise of well-trained social workers.[39] A closer link between church and university was established in the process. It is therefore not surprising that several of the influential pastors in the Dutch Reformed Church's work in care of the poor received honorary doctorates from universities (Dr AD Luckhoff, Dr DP van Huyssteen, Dr JR Albertyn and Dr P du Toit).[40] One should also note that the increasing industrialisation that contributed to the poverty in South Africa, among whites as much as among blacks, is linked to complex processes in modernity, with the responses to the problems also reflecting the influence of the presuppositions of modernity.

Second, the Kimberley conference points to the close co-operation between church and state. A report by H Veen on the Kimberley conference published in *Die Kerkbode* of 24 October 1934, for instance, mentions how the co-operation between church and state led to a great movement forward.[41]

Third, the Kimberley conferences affirmed the need for urgent action. In the Preface to the published report on the church conference, Rev. PJ Pienaar mentioned that the words "now or never" were often heard at the conference. He adds that "it will be fatal if this conference turns out to be a failure. Every attempt must be made to convince *volk*, church and state to add actions to words in order to address the poor white problem with energy".[42]

Fourth, the Kimberley conference affirmed many of the recommendations of the Carnegie report regarding institutional arrangements to address the poor white problem. The church also made a successful plea for an independent department of national welfare (Volkswelsyn), which was finally established in 1937. In 1939 a national congress was held in Bloemfontein,[43] resulting in the founding of the Rescue Action Society (Reddingsdaadbond), just months before the outbreak of World War II. Nicol comments: "These two things worked together so that a few years after that conference the term 'poor white' virtually disappeared from our vocabulary".[44] Urbanisation, however, remained a problem, as is seen in another national congress held in 1947 on "The urbanisation of the Afrikaner nation" ["Die verstedeliking van die Afrikanervolk"]. This conference, which was attended by 700 people, followed an inquiry into the problem of urbanisation that had already started in 1944. This resulted in the report *Kerk en Stad (Church and City)*.[45] From this conference also developed the well-known *Kerk en Volk* [*Church and volk*] series consisting of 12 publications.[46]

---

39   Cf. Nicol, W, *Met Toga en Troffel*, 316.
40   Cf. De Klerk, *Die diens van barmhartigheid*, 92.
41   Veen, H, "Die Praktiese Oplossing van die Armblanke-Probleem", *Die Kerkbode* (7 November 1934), 882884.
42   Alg. Armesorg-kommisies van die Gefedereerde Ned. Geref. Kerke 1932, *Verslag van die Kerklike Armesorg-konferensie Kimberley, 6 en 7 Oktober 1934* (Bloemfontein: Nasionale Pers Beperk, 1934), Preface.
43   Nicol, *Met Toga en Troffel*, 63.
44   Nicol, *Met Toga en Troffel*, 317.
45   Cf. Albertyn, *Die Boerekerk word Stadskerk*.
46   The books in this series (published by N.G. Kerkuitgewers van Suid Afrika) is: *Die trouring* (W Nicol); *Die jeug se lekkergoed* (JJ Müller); *Verdwaalde vroomheid* (CR Kotzé),

Fifth, the church's response to the Carnegie Report showed that many of the church leaders in the Dutch Reformed Church shared the view that the poor white problem is intertwined with what was seen as the native problem – a point that I have already emphasised in this essay. It can indeed be argued that the Carnegie report (and its reception) "sanctioned a particular social construction of poverty – as a white, Afrikaner problem which warranted state intervention and positive discrimination for whites against competing blacks. The invisibility and, at times, denial of black poverty went hand in hand with the mobilization of ethnic Afrikaner nationalism around the discourse of racial privilege which was to take fuller expression in the ideology and policies of apartheid".[47]

## 5. THE POOR WHITE PROBLEM AND NEO-CALVINISM?

The poor white problem in South Africa evoked strong responses – also from within the Dutch Reformed Church. In this essay I have highlighted some important episodes in this regard, emphasising in the process the DRC's role in the genesis and aftermath of the Carnegie report. One could, and in my view should, also ask about the theological resources that the DRC drew on to deal as church with the challenges posed by the poor white problem and the concomitant societal problems. We should further note that from the 1930s onwards a form of neo-Calvinism became a stronger influence in some Reformed Churches in South Africa. I have discussed this in more detail elsewhere,[48] but suffice it to say here that a form of neo-Calvinism became stronger in certain circles in South Africa – a neo-Calvinism that blended rather uncritically with a growing Afrikaner nationalism and cemented the identification between the DRC and the Afrikaner *volk*.

Something of this brand of Calvinism is reflected in journals such as *Die Gereformeerde Vaandel* (*The Reformed Banner*) and the extensive three-volume publication *Koers in die krisis* (*Direction in the Crisis*). In the first volume (published in 1935) one finds – not surprisingly – an article on "Die Calvinisme and die Armesorg" ["Calvinism and care of the poor"]. In this article Daniel Lategan (a professor from the Theological Seminary at Stellenbosch, who taught historical theology) rejects as insufficient the solutions proposed by philanthropy, the "social gospel", mere education, the state's programme of poor relief, or a socialist or communist ideal. A Calvinist approach, Lategan argues, will also not be able to provide a complete and lasting solution to the problem (since the poor will always be with us). But Lategan nevertheless states: "We have no doubt that Calvinism offers the most harmonious solution to the problem by tackling the problem at its roots, namely by addressing the

---

*My aardse paradys* (PJ Viljoen); *Reguit koers gehou* (GBA Gerdener); *Die twee volkspilare* (JR Albertyn), *Aanskou die rots* (P du Toit); *Die kerklike byekorf* (HS Theron); *'n Stad bo-op 'n berg* (AJV Burger); *Kerk en volk* (TN Hanekom); *Olie op die wonde* (HDA du Toit) and *Die kerk se skatte* (HJ Piek). Cf. Van der Watt, P B, *Die Nederduitse Gereformeerde Kerk 1905-1975* (Pretoria: N.G. Kerkboekhandel Transvaal, 1987), 291.

47 Christie, P and Gordon, A, "Politics, Poverty and Education in Rural South Africa", *British Journal of Sociology of Education* 13/4 (1992): 404.

48 See Vosloo, RR, "Konfessionele Neo-Calvinisme na die Du Plessis-saak", *NGTT* 51, Supplementum (2009): 275-288.

moral-religious worldview of the poor".⁴⁹ What does the Calvinist position entail? Such a Calvinist view is, according to Lategan (and he uses some creative adjectives in this regard): theistic (*teïsties*), since it acknowledge the sovereignty of God; charistic (*charisties*), since it has love as its main motive; individualistic (*individualisties*) and not collectivistic, hence the personal relationship with the poor person is important; realistic (*realisties*), therefore the church and state must acknowledge the real situation of the poor person; synergistic (*synergisties*), thus the church, school, media, employers, labour unions, etc. must work together; prophylactic (*prophylacties*), hence the aim should be on prevention as well; optimistic (*optimisties*), given the belief in the mighty saving love of God; salvific (*salutaristies*), therefore the main goal is the spiritual aspect, i.e. the salvation of the individual whose soul is valuable in God's eyes; protectionist (*proteksionisties*) in the sense that the workers are protected from exploitation by the employer and the state protects the workers by creating jobs, as well as protecting them from unhealthy competition with blacks by securing their rights; and not selfish (*egoisties*), meaning that the employers should pay the employee a fair wage. Lategan also adds to this list that the poor themselves are called upon to contribute to the solution of the problem. In addition Lategan echoes the Kuyperian view that the church and the state both have their own sphere of operation and their own calling. Lategan concludes by expressing his belief that the revival of Calvinism would take the nation closer to a solution for the poor white problem.

In the third volume of *Koers in die krisis* one finds an article again meaningfully entitled "'n Beknopte Aanduiding van die Armblanke-vraagstuk" ("A Concise Account of the Poor White Problem") by Prof. LJ Du Plessis, which is interestingly followed by an article on "Die Jode as Probleem" ("The Jews as Problem") and "Die Rassevraagstuk in Suid-Afrika" ("The Race Question in South Africa"). It is a question whether this brand of neo-Calvinism, with its emphasis on the dangers of whatever is alien to the *volk* (die volksvreemde) was really inspired by a thorough engagement with Calvin's thought.

The influence of a form of neo-Calvinism is also seen in the Carnegie report of 1932, especially in Volume 5, which includes a section on the role of the church and its social preaching. At one point in this section the report mentions the church's role to foster the virtues of courage and patience in times of trial; it then engages with the critique that the Calvinist worldview contributes towards a fatalistic attitude and lack of ambition among poor whites. The report challenges this perception, stating:

> Nearly all the received testimony contradicts such a conclusion. It is shown that Calvinist nations actually promoted the greatest activity on the societal terrain, and Calvinism emphasises just as strongly one's own activity as God's liberating work. Far from encouraging inactivity and sloth, Calvinism rather contributes to initiative and ambition. It adds steel to the blood. But what can be viewed as the fruit of Calvinist preaching is the almost inexplicable resignation, patience and courage that members of the church display amidst the greatest disasters.⁵⁰

---

49  Stoker, H G & Potgieter, F J M, *Koers in die krisis I* (Stellenbosch: Pro Ecclesia-Drukkery, 1935), 250.
50  Albertyn and Rothmann, *Die armblanke-vraagstuk in Suid-Afrika*, 69.

This remark is quite revealing and it provides a description of a more widespread view within the Dutch Reformed Church regarding a Calvinist worldview. Today one can ask what theological resources inform the DRC's current response to poverty in South Africa. Does Calvinism (in some or other form) still play a role? Perhaps a re-engagement with Calvin's economic and social thinking in Reformed circles today can play a valuable role in enriching the discourse.[51]

## 6. CONCLUSION

An article in the Afrikaans newspaper *Die Burger* (21 June 2011) had as its headline "White poverty rises by more than 150% since 1994". The article refers to a DVD on white poverty made by Cloete Breytenbach (the brother of the South African poet Breyten Breytenbach) and includes comments that recall the discourse on the poor white problem in the earlier decades of the 20th century. This is but one example of the fact that the so-called poor white problem is very much alive as a 'site of memory' in Afrikaner collective memory.[52] This emphasises, among other things, the need for a responsible historiography (including church and theological historiography) of the poor white problem. In the process one should take note of some critical voices. Sampie Terreblanche, for instance, has noted in his book *A History of Inequality in South Africa 1652-2002* that, while the poor white problem is often attributed to colonial exploitation and factors beyond the control of the Afrikaner, the intense class struggle between wealthier farmers and smaller landowners is often not acknowledged in Afrikaner historiography.[53] And any consideration of the poor white problem today should also engage critically with the way in which the poor white problem in the first part of the 20th century became intertwined with the co-called native problem in a way that led to a reductive response to poverty in South Africa. The challenges remain for churches, including the Dutch Reformed Church, to address poverty in South Africa today in an inclusive and comprehensive way. In this regard much can still be learned from the strong and weak points that come to the fore as one revisits the (church's) response to the so-called poor white problem in the early decades of the 20th century.

---

51  See especially the renewed influence of the work of André Biéler in this regard. The English translation of his book entitled *Calvin's Economic and Social Thought* (Geneva: WCC Publications, 2005) is an important source that could stimulate the conversation on Calvin's social and economic witness, not the least through the book's extensive quotations from Calvin's work. See also Dommen, E and Bratt, JD (eds.), *John Calvin Rediscovered. The Impact of His Social and Economic Thought* (Louisville: Westminster John Knox Press, 2007).

52  On the notion of 'site of memory', see, for instance, Nora, P, "Between Memory and History: Les lieux de mémoire", *Representations* 26 (1989): 7-24.

53  Terreblanche, S, *A History of Inequality in South Africa 1652-2002* (Pietermaritzburg: University of KwaZulu-Natal Press, 2002), 266. Terreblanche also writes: "Part of the rising Afrikaner consciousness about the 'poor white' Afrikaner upliftment was stimulated by a desire to protect them against impoverished coloureds. Unfortunately, no steps were taken to similarly uplift 'poor brown' people who were already exhibiting the syndrome of chronic community poverty" (267).

# 9. ON URBANISATION: THE DUTCH REFORMED CHURCH AND THE CITY[1]

## 1. INTRODUCTION

During the Second World War Rev. JR Albertyn, the general secretary of the Poor Relief Committee (Armesorgkommissie) of the Dutch Reformed Church in the Transvaal wrote a booklet entitled *Die Boerekerk word Stadskerk* (*The church of the rural Afrikaner becomes a city church*).[2] This revealing brochure, published in 1942,[3] ends with the following words:

> God's Word starts with a garden – Paradise – but ends with a city – the new Jerusalem. In the Old Testament one finds mainly the depiction of the agricultural era of the world, but in the New Testament it is the era of the city. This will also be the direction for our church. In the beginning the rural perspective was dominant in religion, but the centre of gravity has now shifted to the urban aspect. May the church have the necessary vision and faith to settle successfully in this new environment.[4]

What is striking about this quotation – and the booklet as a whole – is the sense of the historical (and even theological) progression from rural to city life. Although the booklet is clear on the pitfalls associated with urban reality, the author is nevertheless candid about the fact that the church should adapt to this new reality.

This booklet should be seen against the backdrop of the rapid urbanisation of the Afrikaner in the first half of the 20th century. In the early 1940s the Dutch Reformed Church responded to this challenge by hosting two church conferences, one in Johannesburg and one in Cape Town.[5] Albertyn also wrote a series of booklets at the request of the General Poor Relief Committee of the Dutch Reformed Church in Transvaal (or the "N.H. of G. Kerk"). This series was called the "'My Eie' Reeks" (the "My Own" series), and titles in this series of 12 booklets include *My Eie Lewensmaat* (*My Own Spouse*), *My Eie Nasie* (*My Own Nation*) and *My Eie Kerk* (*My Own Church*). The title of the first booklet in this series is relevant for the theme of this essay: *My Eie Boeresitplekkie of Sal Ek Stad Toe Trek?* (*My Own Boer Space, or Should I Move to the City?*). This series was intended, as stated in the Preface dated

---

1 This essay was read as a paper at the annual meeting of the Church Historical Society of Southern Africa (CHSSA) in Bloemfontein, 15-17 August 2013. The theme of the conference was "The African churches and the environment in historical perspective". One of the sub-themes was "The Church and the City". The essay was then published under the title "From a farm road to a public highway: The Dutch Reformed Church and the changing views regarding the city and urbanisation in the first half of the 20th century (1916-1947) in *Studia Historiae Ecclesiasticae* 39/2, December 2013:19-32.
2 Albertyn, JR, *Die Boerekerk word Stadskerk* (Cape Town: S.A. Bybelvereniging, 1942).
3 The booklet is not dated, but it was published as one of a series in *Die Kerkbode* in 1942. For an announcement of the publication of the booklet, see *Die Kerkbode*, 4 November 1942, 15.
4 Albertyn, *Die Boerekerk word Stadskerk*, 36.
5 See Albertyn, JR, Du Toit, P, and Theron, HS (eds), *Kerk en Stad: Verslag van Kommissie van Ondersoek oor Stadstoestande* (Stellenbosch: Pro Ecclesia, 1947), iii.

September 1941, not as books on the poor but as books addressed to the poor (the so-called "minderbevoorregtes" ("the less privileged")).[6] This project can be seen as a continuation of the attempt to deal with the 'poor white problem', as reflected in the report of the Carnegie Commission of 1932, and the *volk* and church congresses of 1934 in Kimberley.[7] In 1947 another influential national conference (volkskongres) was held in Johannesburg, this time dealing with the phenomenon of rapid Afrikaner urbanisation. This conference was preceded by the publication of an influential report on the situation of Afrikaners in the city, *Kerk en Stad* (*Church and City*).

In this essay I would like to attend more closely to some booklets by Rev. JR Albertyn from the 1940s, the *Kerk en Stad* report, and the published papers and decisions of the *Volkskongres* of 1947, since these texts gives us a glimpse onto the (changing) views on the city and urbanisation within the Dutch Reformed Church, as well as within broader Afrikaner society. In addition to the descriptions of the city and urbanisation, this essay is also interested in highlighting the possible theological convictions that come to the fore in the attempt to help people to deal with the challenges of a new environment. In his book *The Afrikaners: A Biography of a People* the historian Herman Giliomee rightly notes: "Urbanisation was a rapid, chaotic, and almost always traumatic experience".[8] In the previous chapter I argued that the so-called poor white problem, along with the church's response, was closely intertwined with views regarding the so-called "native problem".[9] In a similar vein one can ask what role racial views and attitudes played in the process of dealing with the challenges associated with Afrikaner urbanisation.

The way in which the Dutch Reformed Church responded to the challenges posed by Afrikaner migration to the city in the 1940s represents an important shift from the attitude during the first decades of the 20th century. This changing attitude was of course linked to the changing economic situation in South Africa, which attracted people to the cities. Before the Anglo-Boer War (1899-1902) the number of Afrikaners in the cities was fewer than 10 000, by 1920 it was around 100 000, and in 1945, according to the church census, around 400 000.[10] This new reality challenged the Dutch Reformed Church, which was in essence viewed as a "Boerekerk"[11] (an Afrikaner rural church), to reconfigure its identity and mission. This posed quite a challenge, since – in the eyes of many – South African society was marked by a

---

6   Albertyn, JR, *My Eie Boeresitplekkie of Sal ek Stad toe Trek* (Pretoria: Armesorgkommissie van die N.H. of G. Kerk, Transvaal, 1941), Preface.
7   See especially Volume 5 of the Carnegie Report, which deals with "Die Armblanke en die Maatskappy" ("The Poor Whites and Society"), as well as the report of the national conference (volkskongres) on the poor white problem held at Kimberley in October 1934; Albertyn, JR and Rothmann, E, *Die armblanke-vraagstuk in Suid-Afrika: Verslag van die Carnegie-kommissie (Deel V). Sociologiese verslag* (Stellenbosch: Pro Ecclesia-Drukkery, 1932).
8   Giliomee, H, *The Afrikaners: Biography of a People* (Cape Town: Tafelberg, 2003), 323.
9   See the previous chapter.
10  Cf. Botha, L L N, *Die Maatskaplike Sorg van die N.G. Kerk in Suid-Afrika (1928-1953)* (Paarl: Paarlse Drukpers, 1957): 202; Albertyn, Du Toit, and Theron, *Kerk en Stad*, iii; Giliomee, *The Afrikaners*, 323.
11  The term 'Boerekerk' refers to the church of the Boers (which refers to the white Afrikaners in general), but in this article the dominant meaning is a rural church or the church of Afrikaner farmers.

separation between rural and city life, with the perception that English-speaking white people lived mainly in the city and the Afrikaans-speaking white people lived mainly in the rural areas. The city was viewed as a hostile space for the Afrikaner.[12]

## 2. A SECOND TREK?

In the decades following the Anglo-Boer War the Dutch Reformed Church was clearly concerned about the fact that thousands of Afrikaans-speaking white people were leaving the farms and rural areas as a result of dire economic circumstance in search of work and new opportunities in the cities. In an attempt to deal with the 'poor white problem' the Dutch Reformed Church organised a major conference in 1916 in Cradock. This was the first of a series of conferences addressing this issue, with similar conferences later held at Stellenbosch (1922), Bloemfontein (1923) and – following the publication of the Carnegie report in 1932 – in Kimberley (1934). At the Cradock conference of 1916 the dominant call was still to work at finding solutions to try and keep the Afrikaner in the rural areas, and even help those who were in the cities to return.[13] The call was "Back to the Land" and city life was viewed as a graveyard for the Afrikaner soul.[14] Dr DF Malan, who was also one of the speakers at the Cradock conference, afterwards wrote a series of articles for the Afrikaans newspaper *Die Burger* (of which he was the editor), which were later published in a booklet, titled *De Achteruitgang van Ons Volk: De Oorzaken Daarvan en de Redmiddelen* (*The Decline of Our People: The Causes and the Remedies*). In a chapter with the heading "Terug naar het Land" ("Back to the Land"), Malan refers to the trek to the cities as a new or second Great Trek, and comments: "But, sadly, this trek is not from confinement to open space. It is the move from a condition of freedom and abundance to a condition of poverty and want. It is the trek from Canaan back to Egypt. It is the journey of the happy and prosperous landowner to the land of misery".[15]

Malan was also a speaker at the conference dealing with poor whites held in Bloemfontein in 1923, and here his contribution already reflects something of a shift in the approach to the reality of urbanisation. In this speech Malan states: "People already living in the cities is not, or need not be, something completely negative. It may be the foundation of a stronger Afrikaner nation (*volk*). No *volk* can be strong if it consists only of farmers".[16] Again he referred to the journey of the Israelites to Egypt, which he described as something "apparently evil, but it ensured their survival as a nation. We also see the trek to the cities as a vice [euwel], but something good might be born out of it".[17] After the Bloemfontein conference Malan again published some of the articles he wrote in the wake of the conference for *Die Burger* in booklet form, under the telling title *Die Groot Vlug* (*The Great Flight*). Malan opens this brochure by acknowledging that the poor white conference in Bloemfontein

---

12 Botha, *Die Maatskaplike Sorg van die N.G. Kerk in Suid-Afrika* (1928-1953), 202.
13 Botha, *Die Maatskaplike Sorg van die N.G. Kerk in Suid-Afrika* (1928-1953), 205.
14 Albertyn, Du Toit, and Theron, *Kerk en Stad*, 58.
15 Malan, DF, *De Achteruitgang van ons Volk: De Oorzaken Daarvan en de Redmiddelen* (1917), 21.
16 Malan, DF, *Die Groot Vlug: 'n Nabetragting van die Arm-Blanke Kongres, 1923, en van die Offisiële Sensusopgawe* (1923), 17.
17 Malan, *Die Groot Vlug*, 8.

took decisions that would, if implemented, go a long way to improve the conditions in the rural areas and curb the exodus to the cities. But he is also clear about the fact that this will not deal effectively with the problem, since a more comprehensive approach would be necessary, including a commission appointed by Parliament to deal exclusively with this issue. For Malan these people moving to the city were not merely motivated by a sense of adventure or attracted by the comforts and pleasures of city life. No, they were motivated by economic pressures.[18] And this booklet also indicates, as did his earlier writings, that Malan viewed racial segregation as an important way of ensuring the (financial) survival of white Afrikaners in the cities. As Richard Elphick notes in his book *The Equality of Believers*: "Malan's views on poor whites had narrowed into a white-centred theory that overshadowed his mission-derived concerns".[19]

Malan's views that the Afrikaner *volk* should face the challenges of urbanisation head-on became influential and over time the view became stronger – also in church circles – that they should adapt to this new reality. However, the sense of nostalgia for rural life, and the sense of the dangers associated with city life remained, but slowly the awareness grew that city life (and the church in the city) could also be a blessing, albeit a mixed blessing. As Giliomee summarises this new social reality: "(T)he Boer on the farm was a dying breed and the real challenge for Afrikaners lay in the cities".[20]

The centre of gravity was clearly shifting. Rev. JR Albertyn's call in his booklet *Die Boerekerk word Stadskerk* (1942) that the church should deal with this reality captures the new situation well:

> Our nation ("volk") was born and bred on the wide open plains. All that is dear in our cultural heritage, all that is typical of the Afrikaner nation, is inseparably bound to the land, the soil, rural life. Here the Afrikaans flame burns brightest and warmest … It is therefore with deepest sadness that we observe how farm life [die boerelewe] is moving into the background as it is replaced with a new life style. Yet our church, with its deeply rooted Calvinistic worldview, has always proven its close links with the soul of the nation [met die volksiel] and knows how to serve its needs. And this gives us hope: the rural church [boerekerk] must and will become a city church [stadskerk].[21]

This quotation reflects something of the nostalgia for rural life, but this nostalgia is interwoven with a kind of practical realism that acknowledges the need to deal with the inevitable, and even to make a virtue out of a vice.

---

18   Malan, *Die Groot Vlug*, 8.
19   Elphick, R, *The Equality of Believers: Protestant Missionaries and the Racial Politics of South Africa* (Scottsville: University of KwaZulu-Natal Press, 2012), 137.
20   Giliomee, *The Afrikaners*, 99.
21   Albertyn, *Die Boerekerk word Stadskerk*, 8-9.

## 3. CHURCH AND CITY (1947)

Towards the end of *Die Boerekerk word Stadskerk* (which was initially written as a series of articles for *Die Kerkbode*), Albertyn endorses the plea for a special commission of inquiry to deal with the Afrikaner migration to the cities and the implications of that for the church. Albertyn suspected that the ensuing report would be one of the most momentous ever submitted to the church.[22] In 1944 a decision was indeed taken to appoint a commission of inquiry by the Federated Dutch Reformed Churches to study the situation of the church and religious in the nine major cities of the Union of South Africa, namely Cape Town, Port Elizabeth, East London, Durban, Pietermaritzburg, Bloemfontein, Pretoria, Kimberley and Johannesburg ("die Witwatersrand"). The goal of this inquiry was to gather information on the economic, social and religious situation of the members of the Dutch Reformed Churches in the cities of the Union of South Africa, and to interpret these data to indicate the church's course of action for the future.[23] The inquiry was furthermore limited to urban whites, although the report states the need for reflection on the situation of black people in the cities and the significance of this for the church. However, the report referred to black urbanisation only as it impacted on white urbanisation, for instance, when dealing with the mixing of races and segregated neighbourhoods.[24] This inquiry into white urbanisation produced a report that was published in 1947 under the title *Kerk en Stad* (*Church and City*).

It is beyond the scope of this essay to offer a detailed description and evaluation of this influential report.[25] I do want to highlight, though, the way that the report describes life in the city as a mixed blessing, as well as the way it contrasts rural and city life. In the description of the characteristics of urban life, the report mentions some positive aspects such as the possibility of acquiring greater wealth, given the access to more jobs, and that children in the city also have access to better educational opportunities. In addition, city life provides the opportunity for character formation, since it requires virtues such as punctuality, orderliness and trustworthiness, and because the surrounding social problems call on one's social consciousness. There are also opportunities in the cities for enriching oneself through cultural activities, arts and science, as well as through greater access to the media and wider social communities. The report even mentions that in all past ages the great reform movements in the field of religion emerged in the cities of the world.[26] This more positive description of city life is countered by the reference to negative influences, such as materialism, secularisation, the disruption of family life and class differences.[27]

---

22  Albertyn, *Die Boerekerk word Stadskerk*, 36.
23  Albertyn, Du Toit, and Theron, *Kerk en Stad*, iii.
24  Albertyn, Du Toit, and Theron, *Kerk en Stad*, v.
25  The report was viewed as of monumental significance for church and national life and has been described as a milestone in the history of the development of the Dutch Reformed Church's societal care; see Botha, *Die Maatskaplike Sorg van die N.G. Kerk in Suid-Afrika*, 204. In the first month after its publication 5 000 copies of the report were sold; see *Volkskongres te Johannesburg 1-4 Julie 1947: Referate en Besluite* (1947), 1.
26  Albertyn, Du Toit, and Theron, *Kerk en Stad*, 37.
27  Albertyn, Du Toit, and Theron, *Kerk en Stad*, 38. In 1949, as a result of the recommendation of the Volkskongres of 1947, a national conference dealing with problems of public morality (maatskaplike euwels) was held. See *Om hulle ontwil: Referate van die kerklike*

The way in which the report differentiates between rural and city life is also quite telling:[28]

- In the life on the farm and in rural areas one finds a greater dependence on the Creator, given that the forces of nature cannot be controlled, while in the city a person is more dependent on people (like the employer, the trader, the government). In the process there is a danger that the Afrikaner can lose his connection to God.
- A second difference relates to a person's public position. In the rural area he [sic] is known personally by others, and this can keep him on course, but in the city he can disappear into the masses, and the anonymity of city life can lead to promiscuity and other excesses.
- The uniformity (gelyksoortigheid) of rural life is further contrasted with the heterogeneity (vreemdsoortigheid) of city life. In the city one finds a plurality of languages and races.
- A fourth difference is the stability of the rural areas compared to the constant change in the city. This can destabilise family life and undermine traditions.
- The report also contrasts frugal country life with the excesses and temptations of city life. The temptation to spend money at the 'bioscope', bar and dog races are specifically mentioned.
- In the city the personal independence of life on the farm gives way to subservience (knegskap). This can lead to feelings of humiliation and inferiority, resulting in a lack of confidence.
- The tranquillity of rural life is opposed to the restlessness of city life.
- The report also contrasts the racial apartheid in the rural areas with the mixing of races in the city. The report argues that the well-established Boer tradition of blood purity and the concomitant disapproval of any social contact with 'non-whites' has served the church well in the past, but urban poverty is a powerful force to obliterate the dividing lines between whites and blacks.
- Lastly, the report mentions that the honest, pious attitudes that prevail in the rural areas are exchanged in the city for a recklessness in religious and moral matters.[29]

The report clearly romanticises rural life and demonises city life, yet the goal does not seem to be to motivate a movement back to the countryside, but rather to make members aware of the fact that they should join city congregations, and that they need cultural support structures to maintain their balance in the cities. In addition, the report also mentions some characteristics of the Dutch Reformed Church that the church member in the city should remember and from which he or she can draw strength. These include the church's Calvinist view of life, its conservative nature, its high values and strict discipline, the thorough training of its pastors, its effective organisation, its slow pace in accepting change (which has advantages and

---

    *kongres van die Gefedereerde N.G. Kerke insake maatskaplike euwels, gehou te Johannesburg 6-8 Julie 1949* (Pretoria: Die Federale Raad vir Bestryding van Maatskaplike Euwels, 1949).
28  Albertyn, Du Toit, and Theron, *Kerk en Stad*, 42-47.
29  For a similar description of the contrast between rural and city life, see also Albertyn, *My Eie Boeresitplekkie*, 8-20.

disadvantages), and its suspicion of what is viewed as foreign.[30] In the light of the fact that this article seeks to highlight some underlying theological notions related to urbanisation, it is interesting to note how the report uses the church's Calvinist worldview as a way to deal with the changing situation. The report grounds the essence of Calvinism in the belief in the sovereignty and rule of God. Therefore, according to the report, the Afrikaner believes in the presence of God's hand in the current changes, even if he or she does not understand them: "Thus he recognizes the divine providence in the current trek towards the cities, and believes that he also has a calling in the city, for *volk* and church".[31]

The practical realism of the report also makes some suggestions regarding the way in which the church can make the most out of the opportunities provided by the city for church life. It can also be mentioned that the report suggests that the church can be of service by proclaiming social justice, and although it should be intimately involved in all labour issues, it should advocate for healthy labour laws, and work for better housing, health and working conditions.[32] It is suggested that the church should be more closely involved with the working classes.[33] The church should not only work for the poor, but also with the poor. *Church and City* further discusses the spiritual calling, the organisation, the ministry and the societal work of the church, as well as the role of the family, the youth and women workers within the city church.

The last chapters of the report address the social problems of the city church, the relationship between church and state, and the policy of the church for the future. These chapters affirm the view that the proposed solutions to deal with the problem of Afrikaner urbanisation included the rejection of the mixing of races and a critique of mixed neighbourhoods. We read, for instance: "Naturally the most important solution to the mixing of races is: *separate neighbourhoods*. This is the big issue that the church should campaign for".[34] Church councils too must strive for separate neighbourhoods.[35] The report clearly views the mixing of races as a threat to the Afrikaner *volk* and argues that the church should support racial *apartheid* in order to give each race the opportunity to develop in the best possible way within its own racial group (volksverband).[36] It is also suggested that the church should agitate for the demolition of the so-called slum areas.[37] The above remarks illustrate that the

---

30  Albertyn, Du Toit, and Theron, *Kerk en Stad*, 70-73.
31  Albertyn, Du Toit, and Theron, *Kerk en Stad*, 70.
32  Albertyn, Du Toit, and Theron, *Kerk en Stad*, 84.
33  The report refers to a study done by the Evangelical Lutheran Church in Berlin in 1931 on the reasons why 1 000 former members left the church. The main conclusion was that the church did not have a heart for justice and for helping the oppressed, but stood on the side of the status quo and the ruling classes. Instead of challenging unjust rulers, the church recommended that the poor and oppressed accept their situation patiently, in the hope of a better situation in the afterlife. See Albertyn, Du Toit, and Theron, *Kerk en Stad*, 308-309.
34  Albertyn, Du Toit, and Theron, *Kerk en Stad*, 333. The report also put forward as one of its recommendations: "The mixing of races is becoming a growing vice, and can be prevented through separate neighbourhoods, and – where possible – separate businesses for blacks and whites" (341).
35  Albertyn, Du Toit, and Theron, *Kerk en Stad*, 361.
36  Albertyn, Du Toit, and Theron, *Kerk en Stad*, 391.
37  Albertyn, Du Toit, and Theron, *Kerk en Stad*, 364.

church's attempts to deal with urbanisation were closely interwoven with arguments for racial *apartheid*.

## 4. THE NATIONAL CONGRESS (VOLKSKONGRES) IN JOHANNESBURG (1947)

The publication of *Church and City* was followed by a *Volkskongres* on "Die stadwaartse trek van die Afrikanernasie" ("The Afrikaner Nation's Trek to the City"), held from 1-4 July 1947 on the campus of the University of the Witwatersrand. At this conference Rev. Albertyn gave the opening address. He affirmed the continuity between this conference and previous conferences, such as those in Cradock, Stellenbosch, Bloemfontein and Kimberley. According to Albertyn, this influx to the cities represented a turning point in the history of the Afrikaner nation:

> The path of the nation ("volk") has reached a mountain top, from where new horizons unfold, but also where gaping gorges pose dangers ... The whole nature of the landscape has changed; where the road was relatively straight and flat in the past, it now leads through twists and turns. Or – to adapt the image a bit – the route in the past resembled a quiet, private road, used by the same kind of people, with ample time and opportunity for meeting and conversation with kindred spirits. But now suddenly the way has become a wide, public highway, where people race back and forth at a feverish pace, and where the traveller has to find his way with toil and trouble through the masses. With longing and yearning he might think back to the quiet old farm road, but what I want to emphasise is that he will never travel that road again. That has passed. And the sooner he adapts to the new circumstances, the better, otherwise he will be pushed aside.[38]

Albertyn's pragmatic approach boils down to the idea that the times are changing and the Afrikaner must change with the times. In terms of the metaphor used in the above quotation: the Afrikaner must adapt to the movement from the quiet and private farm road to the city's bustling public highways.

Several other speeches were made at the conference; the report of the conference contains 16 contributions, including speeches by Dr TC de Villiers on "Die Afrikaner se Landelike Herkoms en Sy Verstedeliking" ("The Afrikaner's Rural Origins and Urbanisation"), Dr S Pauw on "Die Afrikaner se Taak in die Stad" (" The Task of the Afrikaner in the City"),[39] Dr AJ van der Merwe on "Gevare van Sedelike en Godsdienstige Ontwrigting" (The Dangers of Moral and Religious Disruption"), Dr N Diederichs on "Beroepsarbeid" ("Occupational Labour"), Rev. HS Theron on "Die Gemeente in die Stad" ("The Congregation in the City") and Dr W Nicol on "Die Kerk in die Stad" ("The Church in the City"). The report concludes with 95 decisions taken at the conference. The first decision acknowledges the guidance of God's providence in the affairs of nations. It expresses the firm belief of the conference that

---

38  *Volkskongres*, 5.
39  Cf. Pauw, S, *Die Beroepsarbeid van die Afrikaner in die Stad* (Stellenbosch: Pro Ecclesia-Drukkery, 1946).

urbanisation is part of God's supreme rule ("albestuur"), and that *volk* and church have a calling and mission in the cities.

A series of decisions regarding the adaptation of Afrikaners to the city is in line with the racial ideas expressed in the *Church and City* report. The report of the *Volkskongres*, for instance, suggests that the Afrikaner in the city must join Afrikaner groupings (volkseie kringe).[40] In a series of decision related to racial policy, the congress states as its firm position that a conscious and extensive policy of racial separation (rasse-apartheid ) should be applied to every sphere of society.[41] The principle of guardianship (voogdyskap) is also affirmed, as well as the decision that the church should take the lead in defining a racial policy for the *volk*. These decisions on race policy make it clear that the problem of Afrikaner urbanisation was inextricably intertwined with the 'native problem ('die naturelle-vraagstuk'). It is also quite telling that one of the papers that was not included in the report is that of Dr G. Cronjé on "Racial Policy" ("Rassebeleid")[42], since it was to be expanded and be published on its own. Later that year the book *Regverdige rasse-apartheid (Just Racial Separation)* was indeed published (with the collaboration of Dr W Nicol and Prof. EP Groenewald), a book that became one of the important text in justifying apartheid, also on theological grounds.[43]

There can be no doubt that the *Church and City* report and the *Volkskongres* of 1947 represent pivotal episodes in South African (church) history. They received extensive media coverage, including in Christian media such as *Die Kerkbode*. Pastors in congregations reported and preached on the report and the conference. A recent publication by the Beyers Naudé Centre for Public Theology, entitled *Vreesloos Gehoorsaam (Fearlessly Obedient)*, presents a selection of the sermons of Beyers Naudé, including a sermon he preached in Pretoria in the wake of the 1947 conference.[44] It should be noted that within the Dutch Reformed family of churches people like Beyers Naudé would continue to reflect on the implications of white and black urbanisation for a just future for all in South Africa. Jaap Durand's book *Swartman, Stad, en Toekoms (The Black Man, the City and the Future)*[45] can also be mentioned as a pioneering book in this regard from within Reformed circles.

## 5. CONCLUSION

In the introduction to this essay I referred to Albertyn's statement that the Bible starts in a garden and ends in a city. I must admit that as a city person I like this idea, although I am suspicious of the idea of giving a theological warranty to a view that romanticises the city. Nevertheless, many of the challenges for the church currently lie in the city, hence continual theological reflection on the changing city landscape

---

40   *Volkskongres*, 119.
41   *Volkskongres*, 124.
42   See also the editor's article on "Ons Kerk in die Stad" ("Our Church in the City"), *Die Kerkbode* (23 July 1947): 4-5.
43   See Cronjé, G, *Regverdige Rasse-apartheid* (Stellenbosch: Die C.S.V. Boekhandel, 1946).
44   Coetzee, M, Hansen, LD and Vosloo, RR (eds.), *Vreesloos Gehoorsaam: 'n Keur uit Beyers Naudé se preke 1939-1997* (Stellenbosch: Sun Press 2013): 97-99.
45   Durand, JJF, *Swartman, Stad en Toekoms* (Cape Town: Tafelberg, 1970).

is necessary.[46] In the current discourse on urbanisation one should also take note of the fact that cities are often spaces of resistance to destructive forms of capitalism.[47] As the churches in South Africa today grapple with the challenges posed by the shifting urban landscape, one would do well to engage in a theologically and historically informed way with the past responses of churches to urbanisation, such as the response of the Dutch Reformed Church discussed in this essay. As in the 1930s and 1940s, people who flock to the cities for work are experiencing the city environment as a hostile and contested space. Given these struggles for economic and symbolic survival, our societies are vulnerable to ideological forces that claim to eradicate the messiness of our lives together amidst the forces of fundamentalism and globalisation. For the church this implies the need for continual discernment. In the process we would do well to take to heart the ending of Italo Calvino's novel *Invisible Cities*:

> The inferno of the living is not something that will be; if there is one, it is what is already here, the inferno where we live every day, that we form by being together. There are two ways to escape suffering it. The first is easy for many: accept the inferno and become such a part of it that you can no longer see it. The second is risky and demands constant vigilance and apprehension: see and learn to recognize who and what, in the midst of inferno, are not inferno, then make them endure, give them space.[48]

---

46  For a wonderful theological engagement with the shifts in urban culture, see Graham Ward's book *Cities of God* (London: Routledge, 2000).
47  See, for instance, the argument put forward in David Harvey's *Rebel Cities: From the Right to the City to the Urban Revolution* (London: Verso, 2012).
48  Calvino, I, *Invisible Cities* (Orlando: Harcourt Brace & Company, 1974), 165.

# 10. ON DIVISION: THE DUTCH REFORMED CHURCH AND SOME RESPONSES TO THE SECOND WORLD WAR[1]

## 1. INTRODUCTION

In 1936 a report was tabled at the Cape Synod of the Dutch Reformed Church (DRC) on "Oorlog en Vrede" ("War and Peace").[2] This document was augmented and approved by the Council of Dutch Reformed Churches (Raad van kerke) in 1937.[3] It saw the prevailing world crisis – with the tense relationships between nations – as resulting from a growing apostasy from God and God's Word,[4] and stated that Synod deeply mourned the current mistrust and suspicion between world nations. The Synod was further convinced that military violence would not provide a solution, and that governments should commit themselves to investigating the causes of the strife and tension, and seek to eradicate them through international negotiations, arbitration and the League of Nations. The document also asks the church to use its preaching ministry to convey a clear message on the need to break down the walls of misunderstanding, hate and enmity, and adopt a stance for peace. In addition to these recommendations, the report makes some further comments on what it viewed as the biblical view regarding war, arguing in the process that not all forms of war are unconditionally condemned by Scripture, and that in certain circumstances war could be morally permissible (i.e. according to the principles of a just war). Although pacifism was not viewed as a sustainable solution for world peace, the document does state that the church – which is called to proclaim a gospel of peace – must struggle against war; it should support every movement towards peace and should condemn both the glorification of war (oorlogsverheerliking) as well as the stoking of the flames of war (die aanvuur van die oorlogsgees).[5]

---

1  This essay was read as a paper at the annual conference of the Church Historical Society of South Africa, held in Pretoria from 16-18 August 2014. The theme of the conference was "War and Peace". It was later published under the title "Dealing with division: Some responses to World War II within the Dutch Reformed Church on synodical and congregational level (1936-1944)" in *Studia Historae Ecclesiasticae* 40/2, December 2014:57-70.
2  *Acta Synodi*, Dutch Reformed Church in South Africa (1936): 280
3  Acts of the Council of Churches (1937): 84-36. The Council of Dutch Reformed Churches was the body that represented the various Synods of the Dutch Reformed Churches before they formed one General Synod in 1962.
4  Philippe Denis refers to fact that many contributors to the influential Dutch Reformed newspaper *Die Kerkbode* saw sin in general as a cause of the war; Denis, P, "Divided Loyalties: Two Church Newspapers on the Second World War", *Journal of Theology for Southern Africa* 118 (March 2014): 114-127. The editor, MJ van der Westhuizen, for instance, wrote in September 1941 that war was God's punishment so that the nations could turn back to him. See Denis, "Divided Loyalties", 116; cf. Van der Westhuizen, M J, *Die Kerkbode* (September 1941): 394-395.
5  Acts of the Council of Churches (1937): 85; cf. Durand, J and Smit, D, *Geweld – Wat sê die kerk? Die verhaal van die NG kerk in die 20ste eeu – as illustrasie* (Bellville: UWC Printing Department, 1995), 111.

Although the ideas in this document were articulated, and were recommended, at a time when the possibility of war in Europe was on the rise, there was not yet a strong expectation that South Africa would be involved in such a possible war. This changed, however, after the outbreak of the war in September 1939 and the issue of South Africa's participation in this war as a member of the Commonwealth became a matter of intense debate that evoked deep emotional responses, especially in some Afrikaner circles. When the Prime Minister of the Union of South Africa, General JC Smuts, declared war in support of Britain, the issue came to a head, also within congregational settings in the Dutch Reformed Church. Most Dutch Reformed Church members were against participating in the war on behalf of the British empire and aligned themselves politically with Malan and Hertzog. In January 1940 Malan's National Party and Hertzog's supporters merged to form the *Herstigte Nasionale Party* (The Reconstituted National Party) under Hertzog's leadership and later Malan's.[6] For many the idea of siding with Britain – given the memory of the Anglo-Boer War – was unthinkable and a betrayal of the cause of Afrikaner nationalism. There were some sentiments expressing sympathy for National Socialism in Germany (as seen in movements such as the *Nuwe Orde vir Suid-Afrika*[7]), and around this time a right-wing paramilitary group known as the *Ossewabrandwag* (the Ox-Wagon Guard) also grew in prominence, especially in the Free State, where the opposition to Smuts was especially strong and outspoken.

The *Ossewabrandwag* was founded in the study of a pastor of the Dutch Reformed Church, Rev. CR Kotzé, in Bloemfontein,[8] and some members of the Dutch Reformed church associated with this movement or identified with its sentiments (although many would later become disillusioned). The Dutch Reformed Church, whose members were mostly against the war, thus increasingly had to deal with political divisions *within* its congregations. It should also be noted that the 1930s saw the rise of Afrikaner nationalism,[9] a movement that found strong expression in the symbolic

---

6   Giliomee, H, *The Afrikaners: Biography of a People* (Cape Town: Tafelberg, 2003), 441.
7   The *Nuwe Orde* (New Order) was formed in 1942 under the leadership of Oswald Pirow, and it advocated an Afrikaner variant of National Socialism. See Giliomee, *The Afrikaners*, 442.
8   Cf. Olivier, AR, "Die problematiek van die Tweede Wêreldoorlog met betrekking tot die Nederduitse Gereformeerde Kerk" (Stellenbosch: Unpublished Masters thesis, Stellenbosch University, 1981), 21.
9   It should be noted, though, that the phrase "the rise of Afrikaner nationalism" is not an uncontested notion and needs some qualification. One should consider in this regard Benedict Anderson's definition of "the nation," namely that "it is an imagined political community – and imagined as both inherently limited and sovereign". See Anderson, B, *Imagined Communities: Reflections on the Origin and Spread of Nationalism* (London: Verso, 1983), 6. For Anderson the nation is an *imagined* community "because the members of even the smallest nation will never know most of their fellow-members, meet them, or even hear of them, yet in the minds of each lives the image of their communion" (6). The nation is imagined – according to Anderson – as *limited* "because even the largest … has finite, if elastic, boundaries" and the nation is also imagined as *sovereign* "because the concept was born in an age in which Enlightenment and Reformation were destroying the legitimacy of the divinely-ordained, hierarchical dynastic realm" (7). According to Anderson's definition, the nation is also imagined as a *community*, "because, regardless of the actual inequality and exploitation that may prevail in each, the nation is always conceived as a deep, horizontal comradeship" (7). When speaking of the rise of Afrikaner

Ox-Wagon Trek of 1938. The *Ossewabrandwag*, in fact, saw itself as exemplifying the spirit of the 1938 celebrations.

This new political situation and the concomitant divisions within the Dutch Reformed Church confronted the church, as Jaap Durand and Dirkie Smit have rightly pointed out in an interesting article on "The Afrikaner Churches on War and Violence", with the same two problems that it had to deal with during the rebellion of 1914 and 1915,[10] namely the issue of "the unity of the Afrikaner people and their church and the issue of the legitimacy of the government, with the concomitant idea of the right to resistance".[11]

With their comment in mind, this essay is interested in looking more closely at the way in which the Dutch Reformed Church dealt with this challenge of the divisions amongst its members, and how the responses on synodical and congregational level were articulated in theological language, specifically at the time of the Second World War. Some work has already been done in this regard, for instance by Durand and Smit (not only in the article referred to above, but also in their more comprehensive book entitled *Kerk en Geweld*[12]). The Master's thesis by André Olivier on "Die problematiek van die Tweede Wêreldoorlog met betrekking to the Nederduitse Gereformeerde Kerk" could also be mentioned,[13] as well as Philippe Denis's article in the *Journal of Theology of Southern Africa*, which investigates the response to the war as reflected in the Roman Catholic periodical *The Southern Cross* and the Dutch Reformed Church's official newspaper *Die Kerkbode*.[14] In order to add further texture to the inquiry regarding the Dutch Reformed Church's response to certain challenges arising within the context of the Second World War, this essay will look especially at some important official synodical documents following the outbreak of the war and South Africa's decision to join the war, as well as at some sermons preached in Dutch Reformed congregations during these years – sermons in which pastors specifically referred to the war and the conflict and divisions within Afrikaner circles. With regard to the synodical documents, the focus will mainly fall on reports from the 1940 and 1944 synods of the Dutch Reformed Church in South Africa (Cape Church), as well as reports from the 1940 and 1944 synods of

---

nationalism, the way in which nationalism is "invented" and the nation functions as "an imagined community" should be kept in mind.

10   When Prime Minister Louis Botha was requested by the British government to occupy some strategic places in German South-West Africa after the outbreak of World War 1, several former Boer generals rebelled. Martial law was declared and the rebellion was crushed, leading to great disunity in Afrikaner society at large, but also within church circles. See Durand and Smit, *Geweld – Wat sê die kerk*, 33-36.

11   Durand, J and Smit, D, "The Afrikaner Churches on war and violence", in Villa-Vicencio, C (ed.), *Theology and Violence: The South African Debate* (Braamfontein: Skotaville Publishers), 38.

12   Durand, J and Smit, D, *Kerk en Geweld* (Belville: UWK, 1995). Although *Kerk en Geweld* was published only in 1995, the initial research and first draft had been completed in the mid-1980s and should therefore be read against the background of the state of emergency in South Africa and the various discourses on violence during this period. The article in the volume edited by Charles Villa-Vicencio (1987) offers a summary of the main argument of this book.

13   Olivier, *Die problematiek van die Tweede Wêreldoorlog met betrekking tot die Nederduitse Gereformeerde Kerk*.

14   Denis, P, "Divided Loyalties: Two Church Newspapers on the Second World War".

the Dutch Reformed Church of the Orange Free State. With regard to the sermons, I will draw on a sermon preached by Rev. Beyers Naudé, as published in *Vreesloos gehoorsaam: 'n Keur uit Beyers Naudé se preke 1939-1997* (*Fearlessly Obedient: A Selection from Beyers Naudé's Sermons 1939-1997*),[15] as well as on sermons preached by Rev. CR Kotzé, as published in *Die Bybel en ons Volkstryd: Preke tussen 1930 en 1946* (*The Bible and the Struggle of our Volk: Sermons between 1930 and 1946*).[16] These sermons indicate different responses to the crisis that the war created within Afrikaner (church) circles, and as such indicate the way in which the broader viewpoints and emotional debates in society and on synodical level also found resonance in congregational life, and more specifically in the preaching ministry of the church. These two pastors are also chosen because their congregations belonged to the Cape Synod and the Free State Synod respectively, and this juxtaposition opens up a space to address the question of how their sermons reflected or contradicted the official statements of their respective synods. Without claiming that the sermons of these two pastors are representative of the sermons preached during the war, they do open a window onto the range of theological language used during this period as a way of responding to the crisis of divisions within the ranks of the Dutch Reformed Church.

## 10. SOME DUTCH REFORMED CHURCH SYNODICAL DOCUMENTS ON WAR

Already on 28 September 1939 the moderatures of the four federated synods issued a joint declaration after the outbreak of the war. The message on the state of the *volk* ("in sake die 'Volkstoestand'") is tellingly addressed to members of the Dutch Reformed Church "and to the whole Afrikaner volk" ("en voorts aan die hele Afrikanervolk"). The nationalistic views in some Afrikaner circles of the time found strong resonance in this declaration (the declaration makes reference to the Voortrekker Festival of 1938 and the Huguenot festival in the preceding weeks). It stated that the Afrikaner nation has been willed by God and that it has a divine calling, and that God rules. The declaration calls for prayer, also for the government and the leaders of nations.[17]

How did the various Synods of the Dutch Reformed Church respond to the outbreak of the Second World War, and how did they view South Africa's participation in the war?

The question of South Africa's participation in the war was not discussed at the Natal Synod meeting in 1940, while the Transvaal Synod in the same year refrained from any direct comments.[18] The Cape Synod, however, was more vocal and affirmed the views expressed at the Synod in 1936 and at the meeting of the Council of Churches in 1937, including the rejection of "any glorification of war" ("alle oorlogsverheerliking") and stoking the flames of war ("die aanvuur van die oorlogsgees"). However, at this critical time the Synod refrained from making any comments on the possible causes of the war or the policies of the warring nations.

---

15    Coetzee, M, Hansen, LD, and Vosloo, RR (eds.), *Vreesloos Gehoorsaam: 'n Keur uit Beyers Naudé se preke 1939-1997* (Stellenbosch: Sun Press, 2013).
16    Kotzé, CR, *Die Bybel en ons Volkstryd: Preke tussen 1930 en 1946 geskryf en gelewer deur Wyle Ds. C. R. Kotzé* (Bloemfontein: SACUM Bpk, n.d.).
17    Cf. *Acta Synodi*, Dutch Reformed Church, Free State (1940): 158-160.
18    Van der Watt, PB, *Die Nederduitse Gereformeerde Kerk 1905-1975* (Pretoria: N.G. Boekhandel, 1987), 364.

This report rejects the view that the war against Germany is a "holy war" to protect Christendom. The report also testifies to the divisions within Afrikaner circles: "With great concern Synod takes note of the division and intolerance and even embitterment that is coming to the fore in our beloved Fatherland as a result of a war far beyond our borders and as a result of the policy adopted in this regard".[19]

The Synod further issued a call to the members of the DRC to act, without forfeiting their convictions, in a calm and dignified way, displaying their faith in God. A serious plea was made for people to guard against the temptation, in this volatile situation, to hurt the feelings of those with different opinions.[20]

Yet the report is clear that it wants to speak out against any direct or indirect pressure on the conscience of people. The report also speaks out against the financial costs of the war, stating that these funds could have been used for development work among the needy of the Afrikaner *volk*. In addition, it issues a warning against the misuse of religion in stoking the flames of war. The Synod also requested the government "with deep concern", in the light of the divisions and intolerance and even bitterness that have emerged "in our beloved country, to use its God-given authority to address the deep-seated differences of opinion that prevail".[21]

From the Acts of the Synod it is clear that the debate must have been emotional – although the report was accepted, many delegates voting against the decision to adopt the report and some abstained from voting on this issue; some even wanted their opposition to be noted: "We abstain from voting since we are convinced that if the Synod spoke out on this matter it would not be beneficial for our congregations, given the differences of opinion in them".[22]

At the meeting of the Dutch Reformed Synod of the Orange Free State of 1940 there was also a sense that the time was one of crisis. This is already evident in the opening speech by the moderator, Rev. JP van der Spuy, who spoke in rather apocalyptic terms of the turbulent times.[23] This synod accepted a document on "'n Skriftuurlike uiteensetting oor oorlog" ("A biblical exposition on war") after a discussion on some points put forward by those with conscientious objections to the participation of the *volk* in this war. This report opens, in Calvinistic fashion, with a strong emphasis on the sovereignty of God, quoting also from the Heidelberg Catechism (questions 26 and 27). From there the document proceeds to speak about the scriptural basis for government, emphasising that government has its origin in God (with reference to Romans 13, and also quoting article 36 of the *Confessio Belgica*). The view is thus that it is God that gives authority to the government, that the government has a calling in this regard, and that the citizen also has a calling to obey and pray for the government. But the report also says that there are limits to obedience to the government, referring in the process to the words of the apostles "We must obey God more than people" (cf. Acts 4:19 and 5:29). The report also affirms the typical 'just war' arguments, emphasising that Scripture does not prohibit all wars.[24]

---

19  *Acta Synodi*, Dutch Reformed Church in South Africa (1940): 284.
20  *Acta Synodi*, Dutch Reformed Church in South Africa (1940): 284.
21  *Acta Synodi*, Dutch Reformed Church in South Africa (1940): 284, 285.
22  *Acta Synodi*, Dutch Reformed Church in South Africa (1940): 285.
23  Cf. *Acta Synodi*, Dutch Reformed Church, Free State (1940): 347-351.
24  *Acta Synodi*, Dutch Reformed Church in South Africa (1940): 497-501.

Drawing on this report, the Synodical Commission of the Free State formulated "A Message to the Government concerning the Present War", which was adopted at the Synod meeting of 1944.[25] This message was addressed to General Smuts, but also sent to Malan, Hertzog and the media. These forthright comments took note of the declaration of war and then proceeded to challenge some of the claims and allegations that were made to defend it, such as that the war was being waged as part of a fight for the protection of Christendom and Christian values, and that Hitler had plans for world domination. With regard to the first claim, the message states that synod is not convinced by the claim that the German *volk* is a pagan nation set on destroying Christendom and Christian values. With regard to Hitler's ambitions, it states that the church does not know the motives of Hitler's heart. God is the sole judge of that. The document continues by stating in no uncertain terms that the *volk* has a negative view of participating in this war and that it sees its conscience as being compromised. The message to General Smuts affirms that the *volk* (it does not speak of the church here) honours the government because it is ordained by God (with reference to Romans 13). But – the message continues – for this very reason the *volk* has to resist when the government tramples on the rights to freedom of the *volk*. Once again it is stated: "The *volk* must always and in everything obey their God more than government (Acts 5:29)".[26] Jaap Durand and Dirkie Smit's comment in this regard are to the point: "The Synod's opposition to the government's war effort was clearly not motivated on theological or ethical grounds, but was political in nature, despite all efforts to give it a religious flavour. At the same time the old Reformed idea of the right to resist was altered beyond all recognition as the church came to be replaced by the *volk*, and the will of God by the will of the *volk*".[27]

What is interesting about the reports by the Cape and the Free State Synod is their sensitivity to the possible divisive potential of the political situation (this is especially evident in the report of the Cape Synod), while one also registers that both synods – although they affirmed the God-given authority of government – raised the point that obedience to government can be resisted in the name of obedience to God.

### 3. PREACHING IN THE TIME OF WAR AND STRIFE: CF BEYERS NAUDÉ AND CR KOTZÉ

A recent volume of selected sermons by Beyers Naudé, one of the important voices in the church's struggle against apartheid, includes a sermon on 2 Chronicles 11:1-4 that Naudé preached as a young pastor in 1943 in the Dutch Reformed congregation of Loxton.[28] The title of this sermon is "War against brother" and the background is clearly a quarrel within the congregation as a result of the upcoming election in which some supported the National Party while others supported the *Ossewabrandwag*, the

---

25 *Acta Synodi*, Dutch Reformed Church, Free State (1944): 49-52.
26 *Acta Synodi*, Dutch Reformed Church, Free State (1944): 52.
27 Durand, J and Smit, D, "The Afrikaner Churches on war and violence", 41. It should be noted that this report was never accepted by the Council of Churches. If one looks at the report on war and peace that was accepted by the Council of Churches in 1947, it is clear that the tone of the 1947 report is markedly different. See Acts of the Council of Churches (1947): 44-50.
28 Coetzee, Hansen and Vosloo, *Vreesloos Gehoorsaam*, 63-66.

paramilitary organisation that had sympathies with National Socialism in Germany. The fact that some members of the congregation belonged to this organisation created some division and strife. Naudé's sermon should be understood against the backdrop of the fact that the Synod of the Dutch Reformed Church called for a day of prayer in view of the coming elections. Naudé, who ministered to this Karroo congregation between 1942 and 1945, was well aware of the fact that this call for a day of prayer could lead to intensifying the conflict, and he therefore addressed these matters in his sermon. He opened his sermon by admitting that when he first heard about the day of prayer he had his doubts about whether it would be wise for the church to get involved in this fierce and emotional conflict in Afrikaner circles. Yet Naudé clearly states that it is his conviction that the church has a message for a time like this, and that the church should not be silent, since by remaining silent the church would either say that it has no message in this situation, or that it does not have the courage to proclaim this message wholeheartedly. For Naudé the message of the church should not be that it prays for the victory of one of the two sides, or that it could be the judge in the current political conflict. No, Naudé notes, the election is in God's hands. But the church has a message regarding the spirit in which elections should take place. Hence a new attitude is needed, namely that of Christian brotherhood. Naudé asked himself whether a spirit of brotherhood was present in this context, and his answer to this question is clear:

> I am afraid that if I have to answer this question myself then I would painfully have to answer: No! ... It is painful to be a spectator of or participant in one of the biggest bloodbaths the world has ever seen. And it is painful to read in the newspapers, attend meetings, overhear conversations in which a spirit of fierce hate and evil intolerance reigns like an all-consuming fire that burns out the little bit of love and goodwill left.[29]

Naudé's sermon, as well as the situation in Loxton, opens a small window onto the larger situation within the Dutch Reformed Church during the time of the Second World War. Although Naudé was against South Africa's participation in the War, he was aware of the divisive potential of the conflict. In Colleen Ryan's biography *Pilgrimage of Faith* we read that Naudé said in this regard: "The emergence of the *Ossewabrandwag* was seen as a very serious internal conflict in the Afrikaner community and we were asked in the Broederbond to try to reconcile these two conflicting viewpoints".[30] And in his autobiography, *My land van hoop (My Land of Hope)*, Naudé, moreover, writes:

> It was the war years, the time of the ransoming of petrol, also the time of the *Ossewabrandwag* [OB], and the tension between the National Party and the OB. There were fervent OB supporters in the congregation as well as in our division of the AB [Afrikaner Broederbond]. And I put it to myself: if this tension erupts further I will have to act between Afrikaner and Afrikaner. Emotions were running very high at this time. My view towards everybody was: Look, don't let your political

---

29  Coetzee, Hansen and Vosloo, *Vreesloos Gehoorsaam*, 64.
30  Ryan, C, *Beyers Naudé: Pilgrimage of Faith* (second edition) (Cape Town: David Philip, 2005), 33.

sentiments impair your sense of being an Afrikaner or the higher ideals of the Afrikaner *volk*.[31]

It is interesting to compare the sermon by Naudé on Christian brotherhood with the war-time sermons of a pastor from Bloemfontein, Rev. CR Kotzé (1881-1950). Christiaan Rudolph Kotzé was born in 1881 and after the outbreak of the Anglo-Boer War he immediately joined the Boer commandos. During the war he was wounded and banished as a prisoner of war to St Helena. He returned to South Africa six months after the peace treaty was signed, because he initially refused to pledge loyalty to the British throne. He served in several Dutch Reformed congregations and in 1934 he accepted a calling to serve in the Dutch Reformed Church in Bloemfontein (also known as the *Tweetoringkerk*), where he was a minister until his retirement in 1947.[32] He attended the Free State Synod meetings of 1940 and 1944, and was in favour of the release of those who were interned for their anti-war sentiments. As mentioned, he was a founding member of the *Ossewabrandwag*, although he later resigned from the organisation, but this did not lessen his commitment to the *volk* (for him church and *volk* were not in critical opposition). In 1955 selections from his sermons were published posthumously under the title *Die Bybel en ons Volkstryd (Preke 1930-1946)* (*The Bible and the Struggle of Our Volk (Sermons 1930-1946)*). In the Foreword to this book Prof. EA Venter wrote about him: "Although there was opposition and much strife, friend and foe knew that the DR Church Bloemfontein had a pastor who fears God, but no human".[33]

It is clear from these sermons that Kotzé was strongly opposed to the "reconciliation politics" ("konsiliasiepolitiek") of the 1930s, and he was a passionate advocate of Afrikaner nationalism against what he viewed as British imperialism. This is clear, for instance, in one of his sermons with the telling title: "God makes the nations and the Devil makes the Empire". He ends the sermon with the words:

> Balshazzar is dead; Daniel lives. Nero is dead; Paul lives. Milner is dead; Paul Kruger lives. The imperialists are dead *before* they are dead. Christian nationalist Afrikanerdom lives and lives ... God says: Flee from the empire's flattery and ballot boxes. Flee from the empire's

---

31  Naudé, B, *My land van hoop: Die lewe van Beyers Naudé* (Cape Town: Human & Rousseau, 1995), 36. One can also refer to the crisis around the so-called "rooi lussies" during this time. South African troops that voluntarily fought outside the borders of the country wore red bands on each shoulder of their uniform. For many Afrikaners these bands were like a red flag to a bull. Certain pastors even asked these soldiers to leave the church. Cf. Olivier, *Die problematiek van die Tweede Wêreldoorlog*, 69. Naudé also had to deal with this challenge in his congregation in Pretoria. See Naudé, *My land van hoop*, 37. Very interesting! We have always had a photograph of my father as a young soldier who volunteered to fight in Egypt in 1939 – this is the first time I have ever even *noticed* the two red bands on his shoulders. He met an Italian lady there, brought her back to SA as his wife... and I arrived on the scene soon after!

32  Cf. Kock, FA, "Wyle Ds. C.R. Kotzé: Sy heengaan was 'n verlies vir Kerk en Volk", *Die Kerkbode* (24 Januarie 1951): 162.

33  Kotzé, CR, *Die Bybel en ons Volkstryd: Preke tussen 1930 en 1946 geskryf en gelewer deur Wyle Ds. C. R. Kotzé* (Bloemfontein: SACUM Bpk Kotzé, n.d.).

influences. Flee from the traitors. Stay with the *volk* whom God has chosen for you.[34]

The book also includes 10 sermons preached between 1939 and 1945; according to the publisher, these sermons caused quite a stir, drawing large crowds to the *Tweetoringkerk* in Bloemfontein. In a sermon entitled "War" Kotzé uses as his text Ecclesiastes 3:3, 8: "A time to kill and a time to heal ... A time for war and a time for peace". Towards the end of the sermon he asks how the Second World War got started. He refers to the Peace of Versailles and sees it as an oppressive treaty that stole from Germany. Yet England declared war, thus the Second World War was started to keep looted goods. Therefore God's blessing could not be on this war. The view of the Christian therefore should be: "If a war is there for the sake of injustice, looting or oppression, I will have no part in it. A person must be obedient to the government, but we must be more obedient to God than to people".[35]

Also included among his war-time sermons is a sermon he preached around the time of the 1943 elections. In this sermon he called upon the congregation to make their choice by answering the question: "Where does your salvation lie? In nationalism or in the empire?" He continues:

From the earliest times the empire and nationalism have been involved in a struggle for life and death. On which side do pious men and women stand? ... Think of Moses against Pharaoh, Isaiah against the empire of Nineveh, Daniel against Nebuchadnezzar, Paul against the Roman empire. These are the people who wrote our Bible. Name *one single* imperialist God could use to write the Bible.[36]

The sermons of Ds Kotzé, as reflected in *Die Bybel en ons Volkstryd*, open a window onto some sentiments within the Dutch Reformed Church. There is a strong anti-imperial sentiment as well as an affirmation of the idea of resistance against government in obedience to God. The concepts of church and *volk*, furthermore, are clearly merged and fused.

## 4. CONCLUSION

In their study of the position of the Dutch Reformed Church towards war and violence in the 20th century Durand and Smit note: "The Afrikaner churches, like most other churches, do not have a well-defined, authoritative and essentially timeless position on issues of war and violence. They have responded to these issues, like most other churches, in a variety of particular circumstances and therefore with differing voices".[37]

During the first part of the 20th century there were strong sentiments within the Dutch Reformed Church favouring resistance to imperialism. Once can think, for instance, of some of the responses to the suppression of the rebellion of 1914-1915, the message to the government by the Free State Synod, and the sermons of Rev. CR Kotzé. What is interesting in his sermons is how they conflate church and *volk*, as is

---

34 Kotzé, *Die Bybel en ons Volkstryd*, 10-11.
35 Kotzé, *Die Bybel en ons Volkstryd*, 36.
36 Kotzé, *Die Bybel en ons Volkstryd*, 67.
37 Durand and Smit, "The Afrikaner Churches on war and violence", 31.

also seen in the 1944 report of the Free State Synod, albeit that Kotzé's strong rhetoric may not have been welcomed by all. In Kotzé's sermons the strong emphasis on the *volk* is coupled with strong anti-empire sentiments. The call to stay with the *volk* is linked to the call to flee from the empire. Kotzé's anti-war sentiments and language of resistance should thus be understood within this pro-*volk* and anti-empire framework.

It is beyond the scope of this essay to deal with the responses to war and violence in the second half of the 20th century, but it can be said that generally the church did not support those who opposed war and state violence, or who claimed the right to resist the government on moral or religious grounds. Biblical texts such as Romans 13 and Acts 5:29 were given a different emphasis in the latter part of the 20th century as apartheid theology became more deeply entrenched in the church.

I referred earlier to the sermons of Beyers Naudé when he was a pastor at Loxton. Naudé was clearly against South African participation in the war and at that stage shared the sentiments associated with the growing Afrikaner nationalism, and in this sense he reflected the position taken by the Cape Church at the Synod of 1940. In the sermon referred to earlier in this article, Naudé emphasised the need for Christian brotherhood. For Naudé Christian brotherhood is not to be equated with the brotherhood of one political party, or of people who have the same economic concerns, or share the same ideology, or long for the same form of government. No, Christian brotherhood means something deeper, namely that "we are all children of the one Father and therefore brothers [sic] in the one Jesus Christ".[38] But in this sermon – as in other sermons during this time – Naudé also strongly emphasises the notion of justice. There can be no unity if justice is not the basis of all our relationships and interactions. Hence his comment: "This is for me the big open wound, the sore place, the main cause of the painful events of our times: the lack of a truthful justice!".[39] One can argue that at this stage Naudé's emphasis on brotherhood and justice should be understood – in accordance with the spirit of the times and within the context in which he ministered – as operating within the confines of the Afrikaner *volk*. Yet he already had to grapple with the wider South African experience. Looking back at this time, Naudé later said:

Once a quarter or when there was communion or baptism, I conducted services in the little mission church in Loxton. Looking at the terrible poverty, the lack of any real or proper education, I began to ask myself: 'How can we justify this?' Whites were always justifying why the people got the wages they did, and that there was very little they could do about it. I started to question this ... This was also linked to my very strong sense of mission ... I said to myself, 'Part of your mission, certainly, is to uplift the people'.[40]

As is well-known, Naudé would later on radically question the legitimacy of the apartheid government and the theology of the church that was, in his view, blind to its own structural violence. And he would join the majority of South Africans in their resistance to apartheid, and in the process he in some sense also tapped into his own denomination's history of resistance. It is also interesting to note how his

---

38  Coetzee, Hansen and Vosloo, *Vreesloos Gehoorsaam*, 65.
39  Coetzee, Hansen and Vosloo, *Vreesloos Gehoorsaam*, 65.
40  Ryan, C, *Pilgrimage of Faith*, 33.

initial emphasis on the unity of the *volk* and brotherhood (during the time when he was still a member of the Afrikaner *Broederbond*), developed into an emphasis on (racial) reconciliation in South Africa, as well as how the seeds of the emphasis on justice in his thinking and preaching would grow into a broader and more inclusive understanding of justice.

The Dutch Reformed Church is facing new challenges in South Africa today, not the least of them being how to deal with the challenges posed by secularisation. At the same time the Dutch Reformed church is also grappling with internal divisions within the church as a result of different views on church reunification within the Dutch Reformed family of churches and on how to make the Belhar confession (with its emphasis on unity, reconciliation and justice) part of its confessional base. Given these challenges, one can ask: Is the concern for internal unity within the denomination – which might be similar to the concern for the unity of the *volk* during the Second World War – still the main pursuit that drives the theology behind fundamental church and synodical decisions? Or can the Dutch Reformed Church find the necessary (theological) resources to challenge narrow and reductive understandings of unity, reconciliation and justice?

# 11. ON READING SCRIPTURE: THE DUTCH REFORMEDCHURCH AND THE BIBLICAL JUSTIFICATION OF APARTHEID[1]

## 1. INTRODUCTION

Reformed theology in South Africa has an ambivalent history and legacy, also with regard to the way in which the Bible was read and interpreted. It is a well-known fact that the Bible was used in some Reformed circles to justify the policy and practice of apartheid. However, a few prominent pastors and academics also expressed strong criticism of the attempts to use the Bible in this way. The focus of this essay is on the way the Bible was used in the 1940s in some Reformed theological circles in South Africa to justify apartheid, with specific reference to some influential texts by prominent theologians such as JD du Toit (Totius) and EP Groenewald. In addition, the essay attends to some of the writings of theologians such as BJ Marais and BB Keet, who strongly opposed any attempt to justify apartheid in this manner. Also examined are the constructions of identity and otherness that seemed to operate in this discourse.

## 2. THE BIBLE, SEPARATION, SEGREGATION AND APARTHEID

'Give me a Bible text,' says the opponent of our colour policy, 'a text that proves that segregation is in agreement with the utterances of Holy Scripture.' 'I have no text,' is my answer. 'Then I have won the case, says the advocate for equality' … I answer: … 'I don't have a text, but I have the Bible, the whole Bible. My argumentation would proceed from Genesis to Revelation.[2]

With these words the well-known Afrikaans poet and Bible translator Prof. JD du Toit (better known as Totius) begins his famous address on "Die Godsdienstige Grondslag van ons Rassebeleid" ["The Religious Foundation of our Race Policy"] at the National People's Congress (Volkskongres) on Race Policy, held in Bloemfontein in 1944. Totius, a prominent theologian in the Gereformeerde Kerk (today known as the Reformed Churches in South Africa), goes on to present his argument to defend racial segregation on biblical grounds, starting – as promised – with Genesis.

In Genesis 1, Totius argues, we read that God creates a beautiful unity. But how does God do this? God acts as the *Hammabdil*, i.e. the Separator or Divider ("Skeidingmaker"). As the "great Divider", God separates light and darkness, the dry land from the waters, the living creatures according to their kind. God created things not as a mixed mass, but as separated and segregated. Drawing on Acts 17:26,

---

1 This essay is based on a paper that was read at Biblica's "Conversation on the Bible", held at the Stellenbosch Institute for Advanced Studies (STIAS), 24-25 March 2015, and was first published under the title "The Bible and the justification of apartheid in Reformed circles in the 1940s in South Africa: Some historical, hermeneutical and theological remarks" in *Stellenbosch Theological Journal* 1/2, 2015:195-215.

2 Du Toit, JD and Du Toit, S, *Die Afrikaanse Rassebeleid en die Skrif: Artikels van prof. dr. J.D. du Toit en prof. dr. S. du Toit* (tweede druk) (Potchefstroom: Pro Rege Bpk, 1955), 5.

Totius admits that God created the nations out of one blood, but notes that this verse further states that God determined the boundaries of their territory. However, in Genesis 11 we read how the tower builders, drawing on their own wisdom and in resistance to God's command ("in hulle eiewysheid en verset"), did not want to trek any further, and wanted to remain one nation with one language. But, according to Totius, God again acts as the "Divider" ("Skeidingmaker") by creating a confusion of languages and dispersing the nations over the whole earth (Genesis 11:9). Therefore the nations should stand their ground ("hulleself handhaaf") against this Babylonian spirit of unification ("die Babiloniese gees van eenmaking"). For Totius, God willed the coming into being of the nations, but not the formation of empires (cf. Daniel 7; Revelation 17:13). Given this emphasis on the idea that God (as Divider) created the nations, Totius then goes on to challenge the idea of "gelykstelling" (equalisation) between the races as defended by what he calls "die humaniteitsmense" ("the humanists), with their references to texts such as Colossians 3:11 and Galatians 3:28. The point for Totius here is that the unity depicted in these texts refers to a spiritual unity in Christ in which distinctions and separations remain intact.[3]

Readers of Totius's text today will probably be struck by his reference to Africa as a "dark swamp" ("donker moeras") that is set over against "civilisation", as well as his depiction of the Afrikaner nation ("Boerenasie") as a "new type" that came into being out of a remarkable and miraculous convergence of bloodlines.[4]

The heart of Totius's argument for racial separation lies in his emphasis on the idea that what God has separated we should not put together. God wills pluriformity, and unity is to be viewed as a spiritual unity in Christ. Hence he wants no equality of races ("geen gelykstelling"), because this reflects the Babylonian agenda of imposing equalisation where there is in fact no equality.[5]

The idea of "geen gelykstelling" stands out as a dominant motif in the discourse on racial issues in South Africa. It found expression, for instance, in the Mission Policy of the Dutch Reformed Church in 1935, where we read:

> The Afrikaner's traditional fear of equalisation ("gelykstelling") between black and white was born from his aversion to the idea of racial mixing. The Church declares itself straightforwardly opposed to this mixing and to everything that promotes it ... While the church does declare itself opposed to social equality ("gelykstelling") in the sense of a disregard for the racial and colour differences between blacks and whites in daily life, it wishes to encourage and promote social differentiation and cultural segregation to the benefit of both sections.[6]

Totius supports this idea of "geen gelykstelling," as well as the emphasis on another dominant motif in the discourse on race relationships, namely the aversion of

---

3  Du Toit and Du Toit, *Die Afrikaanse Rassebeleid en die Skrif*, 9-10.
4  Du Toit and Du Toit, *Die Afrikaanse Rassebeleid en die Skrif*, 13.
5  Du Toit and Du Toit, *Die Afrikaanse Rassebeleid en die Skrif*, 14.
6  See "Sendingbeleid van die Gefedereerde Ned. Geref. Kerke, 1935" in Lombard, RTJ, *Die Nederduitse Gereformeerde Kerke en Rassepolitiek, met spesiale verwysing na die jare 1948-1961* (Pretoria: NGK Boekhandel, 1981), 272-273. Cf. Elphick, R, *The Equality of Believers: Protestant Missionaries and the Racial Politics of South Africa* (Pietermaritzburg: University of Kwazulu-Natal Press, 2012), 232.

proponents of segregation to racial "blood mixing" ("bloedvermenging"). Totius is thus not only opposed to "gelykstelling," but also to "verbastering" (bastardisation) through miscegenation. In this regard Totius recommends a pamphlet by Rev. JG Strydom (who was also a speaker at the Volkskongres of 1944) on "Die rassevraagstuk en die toekoms van die blanke in Suid-Afrika" (The Race Question and the Future of Whites in South Africa), commenting that every household in South Africa should have a copy of this booklet. This booklet by Strydom, the mission secretary of the Dutch Reformed Church in the Orange Free State, was published in 1942 and copies were indeed sent to every church council in the Free State to distribute for free. This text makes for interesting reading. The target of Strydom's booklet is also the idea of bastardisation. Strydom reaches the conclusion "that the white man's survival can only be guaranteed if he ... maintains the strict policy of the old folks of *strict apartheid* in social life, and not sink to the level of the barbarian, and if mixed marriages are prohibited and interracial intercourse is severely punished".[7]

It is also noteworthy that Strydom argues for objectivity and justice in dealing with the race question: "On the political level one should deal with the race question in a purely objective manner, in order to let justice prevail".[8] However, for him it is the policy of apartheid that provides the only honest, just and practical policy ("die enigste eerlike, regverdige en praktiese beleid") for whites and blacks to live together in one country. Strydom challenges those who – in his view – falsely, and on biblical grounds, argue against social apartheid, and proffered his belief that one can argue on the basis of God's Word that God willed separate nations, albeit that all those who are saved are one in Christ. Moreover, Strydom argues that the policy of apartheid is the only policy that protects racial purity, an emphasis that Totius shares.[9]

In his address at the Volkskongres in 1944 Totius further refers to the idea of Christian guardianship ("Christelike voogdyskap"), another central motif in the discourse on race in South Africa in the 1940s.[10] He comments in this regard:

> Fellow South Africans, here is the calling from God on high, namely to nurture the native in his coming of age ... The wonderful God who

---

7   Strydom, JG, *Die Rassevraagstuk en die toekoms van die blankes in Suid-Afrika* (NG Kerk in die O.V.S, n.d.), 28.
8   Strydom, *Die Rassevraagstuk en die toekoms van die blankes in Suid-Afrika*, 28.
9   Strydom, *Die Rassevraagstuk en die toekoms van die blankes in Suid-Afrika*, 42.
10  It would be a mistake to think that the notion of guardianship (voogdyskap) was used by all commentators in the same way. Prof. Gerdener, an influential missiologist from Stellenbosch, also made the case for 'voogdyskap' in several of his editorials in the quarterly *Op die Horison* (*On the Horizon*) in the late 1930s and early 1940s, emphasising that guardianship requires fairness and sacrifice: "We should practise our guardianship as whites in a truly altruistic way, so that both sections of the population are convinced of our good will". See *Op die Horison* 1/2 (April 1939): 98. Several articles in the early 1940s in *Op die Horison* dealt with this concept of guardianship. Dr AH Murray, for instance, wrote on the "Voorwaardes van Voogdyskap" ("The Prerequisites for Guardianship" "*Conditions of Guardianship*"?), arguing that the notion of 'voogdyskap' should replace the word segregation in everyday parlance. And in June 1944 Rev. CB Brink wrote on "Die betekenis van Christelike voogdyskap" ("The Meaning of Christian Guardianship"), discussing in his article the basis and obligations of guardianship. See Brink, CB, "Die Betekenis van Christelike Voogdyskap", *Op die Horison* 6/2 (June 1944): 50-58.

guided our fathers as torch-bearers for black Africa will also lead and inspire us under possibly even more difficult conditions to be bringers of light where the darkness still prevails.[11]

The Volkskongres in Bloemfontein in 1944 was not the first time that a scriptural justification was given for apartheid.[12] What was important about the 1944 congress, though, was that it brought discussions that were found in a small circle of academics and pastors to a wider public. The decisions taken at the Volkskongres draw together several of the motifs already highlighted from Totius's address. The congress decided

> That it is to the benefit of whites as well as blacks that a policy of apartheid be followed ... And that it is the duty of the whites to act as guardians over the black races ... And that in the best interest of all races there shall be no further mixing of blood.[13]

The decisions of the Volkskongres are presented as defensible on scriptural, scientific and historical grounds. The argument is thus made that the policy is based on the Bible, that it is scientifically grounded ("wetenskaplik gefundeerd"), and that it is in line with the experience of centuries of close contact with the 'non-white' races (thus an argument derived from experience and history). We also see some clear evidence of 'construction of an enemy' in the congress decisions, with its critique of liberalism, communism, Roman Catholicism and 'foreign' mission societies, because the influence of these forces would lead to the eradication of natural boundaries and that this, in turn, will create social chaos.[14]

## 3. JUST RACIAL APARTHEID?

The 1944 congress was a key event in which the scriptural justification of apartheid was given a powerful explication and it was followed by the dissemination of these ideas to a wider audience. In 1947 another influential Volkskongres was held in Johannesburg, this time dealing with the rapid pace of Afrikaner urbanisation, including the challenges faced in a competitive labour market. This conference was preceded by the publication of an extensive and influential report called *Kerk en Stad* (*Church and City*) in 1947. The final chapters of this report affirmed the view that the proposed solutions to deal with the challenges of Afrikaner urbanisation included the rejection of the mixing of races and a critique of mixed neighbourhoods.[15] At the 1947 Volkskongres, which was held from 1-4 July 1947 at the campus of the University of the Witwatersrand, a series of decisions that relate to racial policy was

---

11  Du Toit and Du Toit, *Die Afrikaanse Rassebeleid en die Skrif*, 19-20.
12  See, for instance, Van der Merwe, WJ, "Segregasie en Aparte Woongebiede" ("Segregation and Separate Residential Areas"), *Op die Horison* (March 1942): 15-22.
13  For the official decisions of the congress, see "Die Rassebeleid van die Afrikaner: Besluite van die Volkskongres, Bloemfontein, September 1944" ("The Race Policy of the Afrikaner: Decisions of the Volkskongres, September 1944"), *Op die Horison* (March 1945): 16-23.
14  "Die rassebeleid van die Afrikaner", 22.
15  Albertyn, JR, Du Toit, P, and Theron, HS (eds), *Kerk en Stad: Verslag van Kommissie van Ondersoek oor Stadstoestande* [Church and City: Report of the Commission of Inquiry into Urban Conditions] (Stellenbosch: Pro Ecclesia, 1947).

taken. For instance, the congress stated as its firm position that a conscious and extensive policy of racial separation ("rasse-apartheid") should be applied to every sphere of society.[16]

One of the speakers at the 1947 conference was Dr Geoff Cronjé, a professor of sociology from the University of Pretoria. His paper on "Racial Policy" ("Rassebeleid") was later expanded and published in the book *Regverdige rasse-apartheid (Just Racial Apartheid)*, which included chapters by Dr W Nicol and Prof. EP Groenewald. Prof. Groenewald, a respected New Testament scholar from the University of Pretoria, used as the basis for his chapter on "Apartheid en Voogdyskap in die lig van die Heilige Skrif" ("Apartheid and Guardianship in light of Holy Scripture') his earlier study on this theme, a document that was accepted by the Transvaal Dutch Reformed Synod and the Council of Dutch Reformed Churches in 1947.

For the purposes of this essay I want to attend more closely to Groenewald's text included in *Regverdige Rasse-apartheid*.[17] Groenewald starts by linking the argument for apartheid to the argument from history. The idea of apartheid, Groenewald states, is built on experiences stretching back through generations. References are further made to the Mission Policy of 1935, which declares the church's opposition towards social "gelykstelling" (equality) and affirms the importance of the idea of guardianship. Groenewald also shows that the Volkskongresse in Bloemfontein in 1944 and in Johannesburg in 1947 affirmed the policy and practice of racial apartheid. Groenewald is aware that these ideas in defence of apartheid are also contested, hence he acknowledges that one also finds statements against the policy of apartheid and guardianship by some advocates of "justice" and "peace". Given these conflicting views, wisdom in this regard is to be sought not in the wisdom of the human being, but in God's Word as our tried and tested and infallible guideline ("as beproefte, onfeilbare rigsnoer").[18]

Fortunately, or so Groenewald argues, Scripture is rich in statements that could provide fixed principles to guide us in this matter. The first point that Groenewald makes is the affirmation that Scripture teaches the unity of humanity. However, Scripture also teaches that diversity derives from God. In Genesis 10 we read that the nations were divided after the flood. And in Genesis 11 we read that God created a confusion of languages through a deliberate act ("'n bewuste daad"). Drawing on Acts 17:26, Groenewald sees not merely the separated nations but also the geographical area for each nation as part of the providence of God. Groenewald

---

16  *Volkskongres te Johannesburg 1-4 Julie 1947. Referate en Besluite* [National Conference in Johannesburg 1-4 July 1947. Papers and Decisions], 124.
17  For engagements with Groenewald's text cf., among others, Botha, AJ, *Die evolusie van 'n volksteologie* (Bellville: UWK Drukkery, 1984), 198-201; Kinghorn, J (ed.), *Die NG Kerk en apartheid* (Johannesburg: Macmillan, 1986), 103-104; and Loubser, JA, *The Apartheid Bible: A Critical Review of Racial Theology in South Africa* (Cape Town: Maskew Miller Longman, 1987), 61-69.
18  Cronje, G (with Nicol, W and Groenewald, EP), *Regverdige Rasse-apartheid* (Stellenbosch: Die Christen-Studentevereningingsmaatskappy van Suid-Afrika, 1947), 43.

continues that only the nation that is able to maintain its (separate) identity can survive and be true to its divine destiny:

> History … confirms the truth that the peoples who protected their identity were able, in the name of the Lord, to bring blessings to themselves and their neighbours. Those who removed the divisions perished.[19]

Groenewald also argues that apartheid is not limited to one area of life, but must be extended to cover every aspect of life, including its national, social and religious aspects. Therefore Groenewald defends a national apartheid that respects the national borders between nations. The image of the vineyard in Isaiah 5, with its strong fence to secure safe growth, is used to justify the argument. Without a fence the vineyard will be destroyed by wild boars. Along with national apartheid, Groenewald also affirms social apartheid, since social assimilation leads to miscegenation and that in turn leads to religious apostasy. This idea is also applied to marriage. Hence Groenewald's conclusion: "An unlimited social mixing with people who do not belong to your own community leads to moral and spiritual harm … There can only be communion for the sake of the gospel".[20] This prohibition against social mixing is then further extended to the arenas of labour and jurisprudence. And with regard to religious apartheid, Groenewald feels that Scripture is so obvious in this regard that there is not even a need to argue for it.

Groenewald admits that there are certain exceptions to the rule of national, social and religious apartheid to be found in Scripture. He refers to the assimilation of Rahab into Israel, the marriage of Ruth with Boaz, and the mixed descent of Timothy. But these exceptions do not disqualify the rule.

What is important to note is that the defence of apartheid is also placed within a broader 'moral' argument. The decision to maintain apartheid in order to survive does not mean that a nation does not have any responsibility for others, specifically underdeveloped peoples ("met name teenoor 'n minderontwikkelde"). The affirmation of apartheid is coupled with the responsibility to act as guardian towards the less "mature" and "civilised" nations. But can this idea of guardianship be justified from the Bible? Here Groenewald refers to Galatians 4:2, where the word "guardian" or "ward" ("voog") occurs. The child, even if he is an heir, is placed in the care of guardians and managers for a time determined by the father. The guardian is there only for a while, until the child reaches maturity. This idea is then extrapolated by Groenewald from the individual to nations. Groenewald, moreover, qualifies this relationship as follows: "One should add that no nation that accepts, in the name of the Lord and justice, guardianship over another should do so out of self-exaltation and as demonstration of superiority".[21] But, continues Groenewald, there must be a certain response from the other, minor party in this relationship; they must show gratitude and respect to those who want to help them and lead them to maturity.[22] Groenewald concludes his defence of racial apartheid and guardianship

---

19 Cronje, *Regverdige Rasse-apartheid*, 48.
20 Cronje, *Regverdige Rasse-apartheid*, 54.
21 Cronje, *Regverdige Rasse-apartheid*, 64.
22 Cronje, *Regverdige Rasse-apartheid*, 64.

by stating "that the policy of apartheid and guardianship, as propounded by the Christian Afrikaner for non-whites, can be traced back to God's Word".[23]

The attempt to provide a scriptural justification for apartheid was also contested (as will be indicated in the next section of this article), but these ideas nevertheless made their way into official reports of the Dutch Reformed Church (such as the 1947 report of the Transvaal Synod of the DRC). It is therefore not surprising that in a series of editorials in *Die Kerkbode* (the official DRC newspaper) in September 1948 (a few months after the National Party won the general election with its slogan of 'apartheid') could speak of apartheid as "church policy" ("kerklike beleid") and also challenge attempts to characterise apartheid as unscriptural.[24] The Synod of 1949 accepted a report of the Committee on Race Relations that gave scriptural grounds for "our conception of the differences between and characteristics of the races". The gist of the report's findings lie in the statement that "the existence of the various races and nations was not only allowed by God, but was specifically willed and ordained by Him".[25]

## 4. CRITICAL VOICES AGAINST THE BIBLICAL JUSTIFICATION OF APARTHEID: BEN MARAIS AND BENNIE KEET

The attempt to give a biblical justification for apartheid found its fullest expression towards the end of the 1940s, albeit that earlier defences of apartheid as Scriptural could already be found in the late 1930s and early 1940s. But after 1944 more and more was written in this regard and the public debate on these issues, for instance in *Die Kerkbode*, became more pronounced.[26]

One of the earliest critiques of the attempt to justify the racial policy of segregation came from Rev. Ben Marais (who later became professor in Church History at the University of Pretoria). Already on 10 April 1940 he had written a letter to *Die*

---

23   Cronje, *Regverdige Rasse-apartheid*, 65.
24   See the editorials in *Die Kerkbode* (22 September 1948): 664-665 and *Die Kerkbode* (29 September 1948): 724-725.
25   See *Acta Synodi*, Dutch Reformed Church in South Africa (1949): 459.
26   See the letters on Scripture and racial apartheid by PV Pretorius, *Die Kerkbode* (2 June 1948): 1279; and BJ Marais, *Die Kerkbode* (14 July 1948): 1597; with both letters being critical of the attempt to defend apartheid on Scriptural grounds. This led to a strong polemic on "Die Skrif en Rasse-apartheid" ("Scripture and Racial Apartheid"), with letters by JF Britz, *Die Kerkbode* (4 August 1948): 265; FA Kock, *Die Kerkbode* (4 August 1948): 267; "Uit Die Vrystaat: Die Bybel en Rasse-Apartheid" (From the Free State: The Bible and Racial Apartheid"), *Die Kerkbode* (11 August 1948): 301-302; JF Cilié, *Die Kerkbode* (11 August 1948), 316; PJ Loots, *Die Kerkbode* (11 August 1948): 316; EA Venter, *Die Kerkbode* (11 August 1948): 317; SH Rossouw, *Die Kerkbode* (25 August 1948): 441-443; RH Venter, *Die Kerkbode* (8 September 1948), 572. This was followed by another letter from BJ Marais, *Die Kerkbode* (15 September 1948): 632-633, in which he responded to the criticisms of his position. See also further letters by LP Spies, *Die Kerkbode* (29 September 1948): 747-748; EA Venter, *Die Kerkbode* (6 October 1948): 807-808; and FA Kock, *Die Kerkbode* (13 October 1948): 875-876. The correspondence was concluded with a letter by PV Pistorius, *Die Kerkbode* (20 October 1948), 937-939. For more background on this correspondence, see also Van der Watt, PB, *Die Nederduitse Gereformeerde Kerk 1905-1975* (Pretoria: NG Kerkboekhandel, 1987), 90-91.

*Kerkbode* saying that there is no Scriptural justification for apartheid. And at the Transvaal Synod in 1944 he questioned the view that apartheid is grounded on the principles of God's Word purporting to teach racial apartheid and affirming the white man's role of guardian over the native.[27] Marais wrote several articles and letters pertaining to this topic, but for our purposes here I want to focus mainly on two texts, namely an article in *Op die Horison* in June 1947 (which was an address at a conference for pastors held in March 1947 in Pretoria), and an article published in 1950 in *Die Gereformeerde Vaandel* (*The Reformed Banner*).[28]

In an article "'n Kritiese beoordeling van die Standpunt van ons Kerk insake Rasseverhoudings met die Oog op Gebeure Oorsee" ("A critical evaluation of the view of our church regarding racial relations in the light of events abroad"), published in 1947 in *Op die Horison*, Marais gives a clear statement of his views. He starts out by admitting that there are differences of opinion on this matter. He recalls his ecumenical experience in Madras in 1938, where it became clear to him that world Christianity would never accept or understand the Dutch Reformed Church's policy on race. In reading Marais's text one has the feeling that he displays a more fully developed hermeneutical sensibility that some of his interlocutors. He writes, for instance: "I want to point out that our usual reference to the Old Testament in defence of apartheid is based on highly dubious grounds. We cannot simply transfer the prescriptions to Israel regarding 'separateness' to us or the English or the natives".[29]

Marais also held a different view on racial mixing from those of the defenders of apartheid on biblical grounds. Although he affirms that where there are great differences in type, culture, civilisation or religion, racial mixing is dangerous for several reasons, for Marais it is nevertheless untenable to claim – on biblical grounds – that God willed and divided the nations as a permanent and static condition. He continues: "There is today no race on earth without a mixed heritage. God built up, *especially through racial mixing*, a rich diversity of nations through the ages".[30] Marais draws his arguments against the biblical justification of apartheid from what he refers to as the general principles of the Christian doctrine view of brotherhood ("Christelike broederskapsleer"), which was also the theme of his doctoral dissertation.[31] God is the father of all people and they are all equal before God. The principle of the Kingdom is that of universalism. Therefore the church should be very careful in the way in which it justifies its racial policy with reference

---

27   Cf. Van der Watt, *Die Nederduitse Gereformeerde Kerk 1905-1975*, 81.
28   Cf. Coetzee, MH, *Die 'kritiese stem' teen apartheidsteologie in die Ned Geref Kerk (1905-1974): 'n Analise van die bydraes van Ben Marais en Beyers Naudé* (*The 'critical voice' opposed to apartheid theology in the Dutch Reformed Church (1905-1974): An analysis of the contributions of Ben Marais and Beyers Naudé*) (Wellington: Bybel-Media, 2010), 368-371.
29   Marais, BJ, "'n Kritiese beoordeling van die Standpunt van ons Kerk insake Rasseverhoudings met die Oog op Gebeure Oorsee", *Op die Horison* (1947): 67.
30   Marais, "'n Kritiese beoordeling", 48.
31   Marais, BJ, "Die Christelike Broederskapsleer: Sy Agtergrond en Toepassing in die Vroeë Kerk" ("The Doctrine of Christian Brotherhood: Its Background and Application in the Early Church") (Unpublished PhD dissertation, Stellenbosch University, two volumes, 1946). Prof. BB Keet was his promoter.

to Scripture and church history. Again Marais displays some hermeneutical caution and discernment:

> The way in which the matter is stated in South Africa, as if it is a matter of doctrine that Scripture teaches apartheid between whites and blacks, is certainly far-fetched and ungrounded. We overburden Scriptural passages by applying them directly and in an unqualified manner to our situation. There are justified conclusions that we can reach. But we need to be careful.[32]

Marais further states: "The Christian must thus be careful not to reify and revere the transient orders of family and volk, race and state, and view them as absolute".[33] Yet one should note that Marais did leave space for justifying racial apartheid "on the ground of very weighty practical considerations".[34] But he added the following qualification: "But the requirement of Christian brotherhood should not be discarded and it should not be driven by racial self-interest or a sense of racial superiority".[35] Marais also challenges the idea of permanent guardianship ("ewigdurende voogdyskap"). Marais's critique is at this stage certainly not a well-developed theological critique of the whole apartheid edifice. Yet his arguments were met with strong opposition, as is testified in the correspondence in *Die Kerkbode* following an extended letter that Marais wrote along similar lines to *Die Kerkbode* in 1948.

Marais maintained and developed his argument in an article on "Die Skrif en Rassebeleid" ("Scripture and Race Policy") in a volume of *Die Gereformeerde Vaandel* in 1950 which dealt with the apartheid issue ("die Apartheidsvraagstuk").[36] In this article Marais provides some hermeneutical pointers in dealing with this question. Marais points out the danger of wishful thinking that could lead us into accepting any argument as long as it fits our position.[37] He also indicates the need to let Scripture speak as a whole. In addition, he called attention to the way in which the Dutch Reformed Church was totally isolated in holding its position, also from the broader ecumenical church and world Christianity. Of special interest is the way in which Marais counters the argument made from history to justify apartheid (the argument that apartheid or segregation was the way of our fathers or previous generations) by going back in church history (and especially to the early church) to indicate an alternative to the logic of separation.

Marais summarises his conclusion by arguing that Scripture does not emphasise racial apartheid, but the apartheid of sin,[38] a point also made in his influential 1953 book entitled *Colour: Unsolved Problem of the West*: "What Scripture emphasises is not

---

32  Marais, "'n Kritiese beoordeling", 70.
33  Marais, "'n Kritiese beoordeling", 74.
34  Marais, "'n Kritiese beoordeling", 75.
35  Marais, "'n Kritiese beoordeling", 76.
36  Marais, BJ, "Die Skrif en Rasse-apartheid", *Die Gereformeerde Vaandel* 18/1 (February 1950): 14-25. This edition of *Die Gereformeerde Vaandel* also includes articles by EA Venter on "Die Heilige Skrif en die Apartheidsvraagstuk" ("Holy Scripture and the Question of Apartheid"), PV Pistorius "Ons Apartheidsbeleid en die Skrif" ("Our Apartheid Policy and Scritpure") and A van Schalkwyk on "Apartheid en die Kerklike-Godsdienstige Lewe van die Bantoe" (Apartheid and the Church-Religious Life of the Bantu").
37  Marais, "Die Skrif en Rasse-apartheid", 15.
38  Marais, "Die Skrif en Rasse-apartheid", 16.

racial apartheid, but apartheid as a result of sin".³⁹ Marais also does not deny the idea of guardianship, but does challenge certain views that are often associated with this notion. He argues, for instance: "Let our first consideration be: Not how can I secure and maintain the rights and privileges of the whites, but how can I fulfil my duty as guardian in the light of Scripture".⁴⁰

Another voice critical of the biblical justification of apartheid was that of Professor Bennie Keet, a theology professor at the Stellenbosch theological seminary. He attended the Synod of 1949 in Cape Town that accepted the report of the Committee on Race Relations, but could not participate in the discussion (since professors of theology were not official delegates). He did, however, write a four-part series for *Die Kerkbode* in which he explicated his views. Keet is clearly sceptical of the statement of the report that the declared policy of apartheid would lead to the spiritual flourishing of blacks.⁴¹ He is also highly critical of the way the report uses Scripture to justify political apartheid. Like Marais, Keet also found the isolation of the Dutch Reformed Church on this issue regrettable, since the church was in danger of becoming sectarian. Keet also engages Groenewald's arguments in *Regverdige Rasse-apartheid*, and is clearly in agreement with the arguments and hermeneutical assumptions already put forward by Marais. Keet further challenges the narrow focus on the "*volk*" as main identity marker when it comes to spiritual and national calling. With regard to the calling of Christians, he comments: "We live out our calling not in the first place because we are Afrikaners, but because we are *Christian-Afrikaners* ... (W)ithout the qualification Christian we will have no calling".⁴² It should also be noted that Keet defended to some extent the notion of "kerklike apartheid" (church apartheid) on practical grounds, but wanted to keep the idea alive that the walls of separation can be broken down. Therefore he mentions in closing some initiatives towards achieving unity, such as that the Dutch Reformed Mission Church ("Sendingkerk") be represented on the Federal Council ("Federale Raad"), as well as the need for the practice of joint celebration of the Lord's Supper by these churches divided along racial lines.

## 5. THE BIBLE, APARTHEID AND IDENTITY CONSTRUCTION

What can we learn from the way the Bible was read in the 1940s in South Africa to justify apartheid on biblical grounds as well as from the attempts to critique this reading? Here one should tread carefully, since the Bible was not read in the same way by the different proponents of a biblical justification of apartheid, and also not in the same way by those who critiqued apartheid. Yet it does seem as if certain identity constructions were at play in this regard. The various texts referred to above display an implicit or explicit understanding of the relationship between self and other, between sameness and difference, between identity and otherness. In conclusion, I want to make a few hermeneutical remarks that are in my view pertinent in this regard.

---

39  Marais, BJ, *Colour: Unsolved Problem of the West* (Cape Town: Howard B. Timmins, 1953), 293.
40  Marais, "Die Skrif en Rasse-apartheid", 25.
41  Keet, BB, "Die Heilige Skrif en Apartheid", *Die Kerkbode* (30 November 1949): 1005.
42  Keet, BB, "Die Heilige Skrif en Apartheid", *Die Kerkbode* (14 December 1949), 1087.

## a. Beleaguered identity

A close reading of the primary texts from the 1940s related to the theological justification and critique of apartheid reveals the challenges posed by the sense of what can be called "beleaguered identity". This is seen in the prevalence of the language of survival in these texts. Often the authors highlight the need for adopting a certain strategy vis-à-vis the other in order to survive or not to lose one's own identity. In addition, the language used for Africa as a zone of danger contributes to this sense of beleaguered identity (this is evident in Totius's and Strydom's depictions of 'dark Africa'). In the 1940s the process of rapid Afrikaner urbanisation also led to competition with black labour, and the church's role was (in part at least) to create a type of enclave in which (rural) Afrikaner identity was protected and extended into the future. What are the implications of this for the way Scripture was read? The answer to this question is not all that clear, but I think that one could deduce that this context created an affinity for 'survival texts' in which identity was protected through separation and segregation in order to survive. The anti-British empire language in many of the sermons preached during this time (see the sermons of CR Kotzé) also exemplifies this sense of a beleaguered identity.[43] The argument is even made, as seen in the statement by Groenewald already referred to above, that history confirms the idea that peoples who protected their identity (through upholding divisions) were able to bring blessings to themselves and their neighbours.

## b. Fixed identity

Another aspect that comes to the fore from reading these texts is the way in which identity was mostly understood in fixed categories. This understanding of identity as fixed and stable found expression in the aversion to 'blood mixing' and bastardisation. This notion of a fixed identity is linked to the perception of beleaguered identity in the sense that in order to survive in a hostile situation the self and the group must remain 'pure' and not be contaminated by the other. Any sense of identity as fluid or hybrid is completely absent in the writings of the proponents of the scriptural justification of apartheid. This fixed understanding of identity is often coupled with the romanticising of the Afrikaner bloodline, the so-called blood of the Huguenots and the Geuzen ("die Hugenote en die Geuse"). It is not surprising then that those texts which could possibly be used to affirm pure identity over against mixed identity would be pounced on in order to affirm a specific life and worldview. It is interesting that Ben Marais (as indicated in the discussion above) challenges this kind of identity construction when he deconstructs the critique against "blood mixing" ("bloedvermenging"), arguing that cultures and races are not static entities but that they have developed precisely through blood mixing.

---

43  See Kotzé, CR *Die Bybel en ons Volkstryd: Preke 1930-1946*. Bloemfontein: SACUM Beperk, n.d. In these sermons one finds the recurring emphasis on the need for strong walls to keep the nations apart. See, for instance, his sermon on "Die Volksmure" ("the walls of the *Volk*)", with Isaiah 60:18 as text (37-41).

### c. Isolationist identity

Another feature of the texts arguing for the biblical justification of apartheid is the way in which they seem to flow from an understanding of identity as isolationist and hermetic. This is seen in the way in which those who critique their reading are often depicted (including more critical ecumenical voices). One of the marks of Marais's and Keet's critique is that they seem to be aware of this isolation of the Dutch Reformed Church with regard to the policy of apartheid, and see this as a serious call to introspection and internal critique. The greater ecumenical sensitivity of Marais and Keet seems to make them more aware of the ideological temptations operative when we read Scripture.

### d. Polarised identity

Let me make a final remark with regard to identity construction in the discourse on the scriptural defence of apartheid. A strong sense of "us" versus "them" characterises the discourse. This is in a sense ironic, since the Afrikaner struggled for internal unity during the time of the Second World War (in the aftermath of the divisions that emerged from the decision that South Africa should join the war on the side of Britain). So Totius could affirm the need to keep together what God has put together (the unity of the volk) and to separate what God has separated (the white and black races in South Africa). And it is interesting to note how other worldviews such as liberalism, Roman Catholicism and communism were viewed as dangerous for challenging the belief that there should be no equality ("geen gelykstelling") between races and no racial mixing.

## 6. CONCLUSION

Rereading the texts from the 1940s raises the question of how our reading of the Bible is determined by beleaguered, fixed, isolationist and polarised identity constructions. And what difference does it make when we employ a hermeneutic marked by hospitality, hybridity, ecumenicity and reconciliation?

I have mixed feelings when reading these texts from the 1940s. It seems to me too easy to challenge or dismiss the proponents of the biblical justification of apartheid as simply immoral or evil, or as bad exegetes, or as people who were merely pawns in the hand of politicians. The more haunting questions for me became: Why were these ideas received so favourably in the church? And why were the dissenting voices not heard more widely and, when they were, often scapegoated? Are we aware of our own ideological distortions as we appropriate the Bible for our seemingly good causes today? It remains important to grapple with these questions as we reflect on the uses and abuses of the Bible in public discourse today.

# 12. ON ECUMENISM: THE DUTCH REFORMED CHURCH, BEYERS NAUDÉ AND THE GHOST OF COTTESLOE[1]

## 1. THE GHOST OF COTTESLOE?

After the shocking events at Sharpeville on 21 March 1960 when 69 people were killed and 180 wounded by the police during a protest march against the notorious pass laws, the World Council of Churches (WCC) initiated a process that eventually led to the Cottesloe Consultation. This consultation – held from 7-14 December 1960 at the Cottesloe hostel of the University of the Witwatersrand – was attended by representatives of the eight member churches of the WCC in South Africa. At the end of the conference the so-called Cottesloe Declaration was released. For many people today this document may not appear to be all that radical. However, it did contain statements such as:

> … We recognise that all racial groups who permanently inhabit our country are a part of our total population, and we regard them as indigenous …
>
> No-one who believes in Jesus Christ may be excluded from any church on the grounds of his colour or race …
>
> There are no Scriptural grounds for the prohibition of mixed marriages …
>
> We call attention to the disintegrating effects of migrant labour on African life …
>
> It is our conviction that the right to own land wherever he is domiciled, and to participate in the government of his country, is part of the dignity of the adult man …
>
> It is our conviction that there can be no objection in principle to the direct representation of Coloured people in Parliament …[2]

The Cottesloe consultation, and the resulting declaration, generated a flood of responses in the media. The consultation and the declaration were rightly perceived as a challenge to the government's policy of apartheid. The Prime Minister, Dr Hendrik Verwoerd, stepped into the church dispute, saying in his New Year Message:

> I do not intend to discuss recent announcements on colour policy by individual churchmen. It is, however, necessary to correct the wholly wrong impression – which has been created by antagonists to the policy of separate development – that certain Afrikaans churches have

---

1 This essay was read as a paper at the annual meeting of the Church Historical Society of Southern Africa (CHSSA) in Potchefstroom, 16-18 August 2010. It was first published under the title "The Dutch Reformed Church, Beyers Naudé and the ghost of Cottesloe" in *Studia Historiae Ecclesiasticae* 37/1, 2011:1-17.
2 World Council of Churches, *Mission in South Africa April-December 1960* (1960): 30-21; Hewson, LA (ed.), *Cottesloe Consultation: The Report of the Consultation Among South African Member Churches of the World Council of Churches* (Johannesburg, 1961): 74, 75.

thereby declared their standpoint ... The churches have, in fact, not yet spoken through their synods, at which the members as well as the whole of the clergy will be represented. The voice of the church has still to be heard ... May I express the hope that the names of our churches will not be dragged in unfairly into a debate which can as yet only be conducted by individuals.[3]

The Transvaal and Cape Synods of the Dutch Reformed Church (who as member churches of the WCC sent delegates to Cottesloe) would in fact reject the Cottesloe declaration at their respective synods in 1961, in the process casting a shadow on the reputation and integrity of many of the Cottesloe delegates. These synods furthermore took the decision to resign as members of the WCC. Thus the churches in a sense 'dealt' with Cottesloe, though we should also consider the remark made by the Afrikaans writer WA de Klerk in his book *The Puritans of Africa: A Story of Afrikanerdom:* "And yet, the ghost of Cottesloe would return to haunt the Afrikaner's wayward theologising. There was evidence that, in spite of the silencing, recantation, bowing of heads and deep cogitation, something remained. The Church could never quite be the same again".[4] De Klerk's words are often quoted in discussions on the impact of the Cottesloe church consultation.[5] And indeed Cottesloe remains an important historical marker that points to some unfinished business for the Dutch Reformed Church on an ecclesial, ecumenical and theological level.

Ten years after Cottesloe an editorial in the official Dutch Reformed Church newspaper *Die Kerkbode* (9 September 1970) referred to an upcoming conference of South African member churches of the World Alliance of Reformed Churches under the heading "'n Tweede Cottesloe?" ("A Second Cottesloe?"). More than 15 years after Cottesloe, shortly after the Soweto Riots in 1976, Charles Villa-Vicencio wrote in *South African Outlook* on "The Ghost of Cottesloe ... A Soweto Theological Postscript," stating that "Verwoerd could not silence the Cottesloe Ghost".[6] Nearly thirty years after Cottesloe (on 12 September 1990) a conference was held at the University of Pretoria on the theme "Cottesloe after 30 years" (speakers included JW Hofmeyr, CF Beyers Naudé and EPJ Kleynhans). A report on this conference in *Die Kerkbode* (21 September 1990) had as its heading: "Stofstorm rondom Cottesloe lê nog nie heeltemal nie" ("Dust storm around Cottesloe not quite settled yet"). These

---

3   Cf. The Sunday Times Political Reporter, "Verwoerd Enters Church Crisis", *The Sunday Times* (1 January 1960).
4   De Klerk, WA, *The Puritans of Africa: A Story of Afrikanerdom* (Harmondsworth: Penguin Books, 1975), 255.
5   Cf., for instance, De Gruchy, JW (with De Gruchy, S), *The Church Struggle in South Africa: 25th Anniversary Edition* (London: SCM Press, 2004), 66.
6   Villa-Vicencio, C, "The Ghost of Cottesloe ... A Soweto Theological Postscript", *South African Outlook* 106 (1976): 108-109. In this article Villa-Vicencio strongly challenges the theologised nationalism that he observes in the thought of people such as Dr AP Treurnicht. For Villa-Vicencio one alternative to such a national theology is "to give the Cottesloe Ghost new sinews and flesh and to begin to live again in obedience to the one true God" (109). Villa-Vicencio ends his article with the words: "The Cottesloe Ghost is still with us ... What we need is a new Cottesloe conference and the church to stand up in opposition to the false gospel and the worship of Baal. But this will not happen. The only alternative is the need for confessing communities to be established across our land to worship the God who is one and before whom there is no other" (109).

three examples (and others can be added) underline the perception that Cottesloe represents a symbolic historical marker of great importance for the (Dutch) Reformed and ecumenical church and theological life in South Africa. Cottesloe has undeniably become a site or place of memory (a *lieu de mémoire*) in the collective memory, to adopt notions from the influential work of theorists such as Maurice Halbwachs and Pierre Nora.[7]

The fact that Cottesloe functions as a significant 'site of memory' suggests that it was often recalled at crucial periods to reconfigure ecclesial and theological identity. In the early 1990s, for instance, parallels were drawn between the Cottesloe consultation and the Rustenburg conference.[8] In 2010 the conferences themes of both the Church Historical Society of Southern Africa and the Theological Society of South Africa (which met in Potchefstroom and Bloemfontein respectively) brought Cottesloe into conversation with the discussion on ecumenism (given also the centenary celebration of the 1910 Edinburgh World Mission Conference). These meetings created the opportunity to revisit Cottesloe after 50 years, not merely to gain more clarity about the events around the 1960 consultation and the declaration, but also to reflect on some of the challenges facing church, ecumenical and theological life in South Africa in our time. In this essay I do not want to focus on the events leading to the Cottesloe consultation or on the consultation itself. These topics have been discussed in great detail and from various perspectives elsewhere.[9] From a church historical perspective we are also fortunate to have the autobiographical accounts of influential figures such as Beyers Naudé, Alan Paton, FE O'Brien Geldenhuys and Willie Jonker on their experiences of Cottesloe and the circumstances around the

---

[7] See Halbwachs, M, *On Collective Memory* (Chicago: University of Chicago Press, 1992) and Nora, P, *Les lieux de mémoire* (7 volumes) (Paris: Gallimard, 1984-1992). For a translated text that gives a good description of Nora's project, see Nora, P, "Between Memory and History: Les lieux de mémoire", *Representations* 26 (1989): 7-24. For the use of the notion of sites of memory for church historical reflection, see Harinck, G, Paul, H, and Wallet, B, *Het gereformeerde geheuen: Protestantse herinneringsculturen in Nederland, 1850-2000* (Amsterdam: Uitgeverij Bert Bakker, 2009), as well as Markschies, C and Wolf, H (eds), *Erinnerungsorte des Christentums* (München: C H Beck, 2010).

[8] Frits Gaum's report on the same conference in *Die Kerkbode* (16 November 1990) had as its heading "Die lang reis van Cottesloe na Rustenburg" ("The long journey from Cottesloe to Rustenburg"). The fact that Cottesloe was viewed as an important historical marker is further seen in the title of De Gruchy's article "From Cottesloe to The Road to Damascus". See Loots, G (ed.) 1990, *Listening to South African Voices: Critical Reflection on Contemporary Theological Documents* (Proceedings of the Annual meeting of the Theological Society of Southern Africa held at the University of Port Elizabeth, 29-31 August 1990) (Cape Town: Woordkor, 1990), 13-14. Also telling is the title of the report published after the WCC Cape Town consultation: *From Cottesloe to Cape Town* (1991).

[9] Cf. Lückhoff, AH, *Cottesloe* (Cape Town: Tafelberg, 1978); Lombard, RTJ, *Die Nederduitse Gereformeerde Kerke en Rassepolitiek met spesiale verwysing na die jare 1948-1961* (*The Dutch Reformed Churches and Racial Politics, with special reference to the years 1948-1961*) (Pretoria: Unisa, 1974); De Gruchy, *The Church Struggle in South Africa*; Van der Watt, PB, *Die Nederduitse Gereformeerde Kerk 1905-1975* (Pretoria: N.G. Boekhandel, 1987); Hofmeyr, JW, "'n Beraad te midde van berade: Die historiese konteks van die Cottesloe-kerkeberaad herbeoordeel" ("A conference amid conferences: The historical context of the Cottesloe church conference re-assessed"), *Skrif en Kerk* 12/2 (1991): 142-258; Strauss, P, "Beginsel of Metode: Die Ned Geref Kerk en apartheid na Cottesloe" ("Principle or Method: The DRC and apartheid after Cottesloe"), *NGTT* 32/3 (1991): 437-446.

conference. In this essay I rather want to revisit some of the events that occurred in the Dutch Reformed Church in the aftermath of Cottesloe, with a special focus on the role of Beyers Naudé. In the process I will make reference to some of Naudé's newspaper articles, speeches and sermons, as well as some unpublished material. In the final section I will return to the question of whether the ghost of Cottesloe is still haunting the Dutch Reformed Church in our time.

## 2. THE AFTERMATH OF COTTESLOE

### a. Reactions to Cottesloe in the media and society

In a personal letter written to AH Lückhof in 1974 WA Visser t'Hooft (the General Secretary of the WCC who played an important role at Cottesloe) wrote that although the situation at the Cottesloe consultation was initially very tense, during the course of the conference – through the Bible study, the humour and the eating together – a sense of real brotherhood developed. There was a feeling that something important had happened.[10]

The view that something significant (and controversial) had happened at Cottesloe was definitely shared by the media. The consultation made headlines in newspapers such as *Die Transvaler*, *Die Vaderland*, *Die Burger* and *The Rand Daily Mail*. It is interesting to note that an editorial in *Die Burger* of 19 December 1960 was quite sympathetic to the decisions taken at Cottesloe, saying (among other things) that the church has the right and responsibility to test from time to time the prevailing political policy according to moral laws, and to challenge fearlessly the rulers of this world in the light of the fact that the church represents a higher authority.[11] But on the whole Lückhoff is right to conclude that the English newspapers responded mostly positively, while the Afrikaans newspapers (with the exception of the editorials in *Die Burger*) were sharply critical of the consultation and its declaration. In the correspondence columns of the Afrikaans newspapers the tone of the letters was predominantly harsh and critical, challenging (among other things) the delegates' mandate to vote for the Cottesloe resolutions. A cabinet minister's wife even wrote that pastors should keep out of politics and do more house visitations.[12]

One of the delegates of the Transvaal Synod to Cottesloe was Beyers Naudé. As a member of the organising committee, he was closely involved with the planning of the consultation. For him the aftermath of Cottesloe became an especially trying

---

10   Cf. Lückhoff, *Cottesloe*, 95. Not everybody, however, shared this feeling that something significant has happened at Cottesloe. Visser t'Hooft also refers to the delegates of the Nederduitsch Hervormde Kerk (NHK), who ate on their own. It was therefore not that surprising that after the consultation the NHK released a report in which they distanced themselves from several aspects of the Cottesloe declaration. For a discussion of the NHK's reaction after Cottesloe, see Lückhoff, *Cottesloe*, 97-103. In his autobiography *Journey Continued* Alan Paton notes: "John de Gruchy in his book *The Church Struggle in South Africa* writes that the members of the N.H.K. delegation 'tended to keep apart'. This is a very kind way of putting it. They did not tend to keep apart, they *did* keep apart". See Paton, A, *Journey Continued: An Autobiography* (Cape Town: David Philip, 1988), 213.
11   Cf. Lückhoff, *Cottesloe*, 103.
12   Cf. Lückhof, *Cottesloe*, 105.

time. In his autobiography *My land van hoop* (*My land of hope*) he gives an account of what he calls "die bitter nasleep van Cottesloe" ("the bitter after-effects of Cottesloe"). Naudé responded within days after the Cottesloe conference to some of the allegations made against the Cottesloe delegates in an article published in the Sunday newspaper *Dagbreek en Sondagnuus* (18 December 1960). In this article entitled "Afrikaans Churches in Danger of Confusion"[13] Naudé acknowledges that the discussions of the eight member churches of the WCC caused quite a stir and that they would have consequences. He comments: "It is abundantly clear that the findings of the deliberations are going to have far-reaching results for Church and State, for relationships between Afrikaans and English speaking, as well as the relationship between White and non-White. [They are] going to affect the future of every ecclesiastical, national and racial group most closely".[14]

In the rest of the article Naudé aims to set straight some of the interpretations regarding Cottesloe. He admits that the discussions do not necessarily reflect the official viewpoints of the churches concerned. Nevertheless, the findings are based on intensive study reports. Naudé further denies the allegations that the leaders of the World Council of Churches wished to prescribe terms to the conference or to influence it through lectures, addresses and proposals. The report was also not meant as an attack on the government: "If the report of the study contains, or implies, criticism of the policy of the Government, it stemmed from the formulation of Scriptural principle, and is in no way meant as an attack or as uncharitable criticism".[15] Naudé did realise, however, that the discussions and findings at Cottesloe placed the Afrikaner churches at a crossroads and that "the coming months are going to demand study and meditation of every minister of the Gospel as has perhaps never been asked before in our lifetime".[16]

On 28 December 1960 *Die Kerkbode*, with Andries Treurnicht as editor, joined the discussion on Cottesloe by asking the questions about when and on what issues the church must make its voice heard. The article ends – after questioning the decision about Coloured representation in Parliament – with the warning that some church leaders ought to speak in a lower prophetic tone. The responsibility to preach

---

13  Naudé, B, "Afrikaans Churches in Danger of Confusion", *Dagbreek en Sondagnuus* (18 December 1960). For the purposes of this article, I use the translated newspaper article as found in the Cottesloe documents of the Dutch Reformed Church Archives, Stellenbosch.
14  Naudé, "Afrikaans Churches in Danger of Confusion", 1.
15  Naudé, "Afrikaans Churches in Danger of Confusion", 2.
16  Naudé, "Afrikaans Churches in Danger of Confusion", 2. Naudé also wrote that ministers and spiritual leaders have to inform their members about the principles of the Bible regarding race relationships, for example, through congregational discussion and Bible groups. In addition, Naudé points to the fact that the consultation has great importance for inter-church relationships, and even for the witness of the churches throughout the whole of Africa. Naudé is also aware of possible dangers, such as serious divisions within the Afrikaner churches, or that Christians can cast doubts on one another's sincerity. Christians must guard against over-hasty conclusions and he adds that what is needed is honest, courageous and open-hearted discussion that is not merely confined to our own denomination. Naudé concludes his article on a trusting note: "Personally I believe that God is allowing great and good things to be born out of all the tension and confusion of the present to the benefit of His church. We as believers must continue in that belief. He that obeys God and His word need have no fear" (5). This theme of obedience to God would continue to be a central theological notion for Naudé in the stormy years to come.

justice to the social and political sphere admittedly belongs to the church, but when the church starts using political formulas, an impermissible *coup d'etat* has been carried out.[17]

I have already mentioned Hendrik Verwoerd's New Year address in which he said that the churches had not yet spoken on Cottesloe through their synods. Naudé comments in *My land van hoop* that after this statement few members of the church, especially in the Transvaal, dared to defend the Cottesloe decisions. Those who did write in favour of Cottesloe in the media for the most part used pseudonyms. The Afrikaner Broederbond also took a firm stand against the Cottesloe decisions via its circular letter.[18] Naudé, who was chairperson of the Broederbond cell in his area, was very upset by this interference. His comment on this matter is revealing: "It created a very serious crisis of conscience on the whole question of ultimate loyalty and ultimate disobedience. The authority of Scripture and the demands of the gospel were in conflict with my own nation and their political aspirations ... although not the final straw, unconsciously I was at the point where I said, 'If this is what the Broederbond can do, then it has become a very dangerous influence in my life'".[19]

During the heated discussions in the media after the Cottesloe consultation a number of protest meetings were held as well, to the dismay of many of the Cottesloe delegates. One of the targets during the storm that erupted after Cottesloe was the book *Vertraagde Aksie (Delayed Action)*, which was published before Cottesloe in Afrikaans and English and contained essays by Professors AS Geyer, BJ Marais, BB Keet and others. This controversial book dealt with church and race relationships in South Africa and was intended as an ecumenical witness. In his important essay "Die klok het al gelui" ("The bell has already tolled") Bennie Keet focuses on the question of the calling of the church in the light of the policy of apartheid, stating clearly his conviction that the time has come that the Afrikaner churches give notice to the government that they can no longer accept the policy of apartheid. Keet also asked in his essay that discussions be organised between whites and blacks on the highest level with the aim of finding the best solution in the striving for a multiracial South Africa. If this option was not taken up, the church had to do what the state was unwilling to do, namely to initiate mutual discussions. This raised the objection that the church was acting outside of its sphere, but desperate times called for desperate measures. The church has a prophetic calling towards the whole of life, including the political realm. According to Keet, the Afrikaner churches have rightly been

---

17 See *Die Kerkbode* (28 December 1960). In the editorial of 8 February 1961 Treurnicht again wrote on Cottesloe and said that members who are confused in light of the decisions of Cottesloe should know that the church still stands precisely where it stood in the past ("die kerk staan presies waar hy was"). He also reminded church council members that they must claim [assert?] their maturity and act accordingly. This is of course a valid point, although one can ask if the timing of this remark was not aimed at gaining the support of church council members against Cottesloe for the upcoming synod meetings. Cf. also Treurnicht's essays on Cottesloe in his book *Op die Keper* (Cape Town: Tafelberg-Uitgewers, 1965), 27-54.
18 Cf. Wilkens, I and Strydom, H, *The Super-Afrikaners: Inside the Afrikaner Broederbond* (Johannesburg: Jonathan Ball Publishers, 1980), 296.
19 Ryan, C, *Beyers Naudé: Pilgrimage of Faith* (Cape Town: David Philip, 1990), 64.

accused of neglecting their prophetic task regarding the policy of apartheid and its bitter fruits.[20]

Given this sort of criticism from Keet, it is understandable that *Delayed Action* became a target in the aftermath of Cottesloe. At a meeting of 2 000 people in the Brits Town Hall in early January 1961 a motion was accepted condemning the book. Speakers at the event included Dr FG van de Walt of the Gereformeerde Kerk, Prof. AD Pont (Nederduitsch Hervormde Kerk), and Prof. AB du Preez and Dr JD (Koot) Vorster of the Dutch Reformed Church. According to newspaper reports, Dr Vorster said that because ideas could spread like measles, he was glad about these kinds of meetings, "which showed what the true policy of the church was".[21] Dr Vorster became one of the most outspoken critics of Cottesloe, later describing the Cottesloe consultation as "the sharpest attack by the liberalistic element to destroy Afrikaner politics".[22]

The *Afrikanerkring* (an Afrikaner cultural organisation) also organised a protest meeting that was held on 24 January 1961 in a packed Silverton Town Hall. At this meeting, which was attended by about 1 500 people, a motion was accepted stating the meeting's unwavering trust in the church of the Afrikaner, as well as their confidence that when the respective synods of the Afrikaans churches discuss the Cottesloe decisions, they will unequivocally maintain the traditional policy of apartheid – a policy that was not viewed as contrary to the Word of God.[23] Mass meetings were organised on university campuses as well.[24]

### b. Cottesloe and the official Dutch Reformed Church meetings

In addition to these protest meetings, several church councils took a stand against Cottesloe, often including a call that the Dutch Reformed Church withdraw from the WCC. Beyers Naudé's own Aasvoëlkop congregation recommended withdrawal from the WCC, although they did state that, despite their disagreement with their minister, they express their thanks for his Christian example, integrity and sincerity.[25]

Influential church leaders such as JD Vorster and JS Gericke were especially vocal in the general critique of the Cottesloe decisions. From 22-24 March 1961 the biannual meeting of the Federal Council of the Dutch Reformed Churches met and this Council also rejected the statements that lay at the heart of the Cottesloe declaration. A lengthy three-part proposal, tabled by JD Vorster, can be seen as a recommitment to the policy of separate development and the view that this policy is based on Scripture. The proposal stated that separate development provides the only realistic solution for racial problems in South Africa. The motion further stated

---

20   See Geyser, AS et al. *Vertraagde Aksie* (Pretoria: published by authors, 1960), 10.
21   Cf. *The Rand Daily Mail* (7 January 1961).
22   Cf. Langner, D J, "Teen die hele wêreld vry: J.D. Vorster as 'n neo-Calvinis in die Nederduitse Gereformeerde Kerk 1935-1980" ("Free against the whole world: JD Vorster as a Neo-Calvinist in the Dutch Reformed Church 1935-1980") (Unpublished doctoral dissertation, University of the Free State, 2004), 114.
23   Cf. *Die Transvaler* 26 January 1961; see also *The Star* 25 January 1961).
24   About a thousand students met at the University of Pretoria, for instance, to discuss the political implications of the Cottesloe decisions. Here too a motion was accepted rejecting the Cottesloe findings. Cf. *Die Transvaler* (10 March 1961).
25   Cf. Ryan, *Beyers Naudé*, 65.

that integration on church level is not a demonstration of a belief in the community of saints and expressed its disappointment that the delegates made the decisions public before churches could discuss them.[26] Beyers Naudé and Frans Geldenhuys voted against parts of the proposal, although it is probably correct to say that at this stage Naudé did not support a full-scale rejection of apartheid.[27] At the same meeting of the Federal Council a motion (proposed by JS Gericke and IJ Viljoen) was accepted that the DRC resign as member church of the WCC.

Before the Transvaal Synod meeting an *ad hoc* committee was appointed to study the findings of Cottesloe and to reflect on the decision to withdraw from the WCC. Men with strong anti-Cottesloe sentiments played a dominant role in the committee. With this kind of build up to the Transvaal Synod, it certainly seemed unlikely that the synod would not reject the Cottesloe statement and that a decision would be taken to resign from the WCC. The election to the moderature already indicated the direction that the synod would take. Although the Cottesloe delegate Ds AM Meiring retained his position by a narrow margin, both Beyers Naudé and Frans Geldenhuys were ousted. Willie Jonker, who had just returned from theological studies in the Netherlands, replaced Frans Geldenhuys as actuarius. When Jonker seconded a motion for continued membership of the WCC there was, according to one observer, whispering from a certain corner: "We have chosen the wrong actuarius!"[28]

For two and a half days the synod discussed the Cottesloe decisions, with most of the speakers condemning the findings. On 10 April the delegates were called upon to respond. In his reflection on these events Willie Jonker mentioned how painful it was for him to see Naudé and Geldenhuys, but also those critical of Cottesloe such as Ds Brink and Professors EP Groenewald and AB du Preez, sitting in the front of the hall like people accused of committing a crime.

In his response at the synod meeting Beyers Naudé said that if any synod member could convince him that the decisions taken at Cottesloe were against the Word of God or the demands of the gospel, then he would admit that they were misguided. Without such evidence, he stood by his conviction to support the Cottesloe recommendations. Naudé later wrote that he realised that his statement would probably place his career as a minister in the Dutch Reformed Church under serious suspicion, but that he was filled with a deep sense of calm and peace at the same time. In the end the synod accepted a motion that rejected the decisions taken at Cottesloe and reaffirmed support for what was called a policy of "differentiation". Shortly afterwards the recommendation of the *ad hoc* commission that the Transvaal synod of the Dutch Reformed Church withdraw from the WCC was accepted.

By the time the Cape Synod convened on 19 October 1961 emotions were already less intense than in the months immediately following Cottesloe. However, the Cape Synod also adopted the Federal Council's rejection of Cottesloe as its own decision.

---

26 Cf. *Handelinge van die Raad van Kerke* (1961): 50-51.
27 One should also recall that after Cottesloe the delegates of the Transvaal Synod released a declaration (after consultation with the Cape Synod) that to some extent defended the idea of differentiation. See *Inligtingsburo van die Ned. Geref. Kerk* 17/12/60 (Dutch Reformed Church Archives, Stellenbosch).
28 Cf. Naudé, B, *My land van hoop: Die lewe van Beyers Naudé* (Cape Town: Human & Rousseau, 1995), 57.

With a resounding majority the Cape Synod too accepted the motion to resign from the WCC. Even a proposal that they maintain correspondence with the WCC was rejected. Thus both the Transvaal and the Cape synods rejected the findings of Cottesloe and recommended withdrawal from the WCC.[29]

### 3. COTTESLOE AND BEYERS NAUDÉ'S DECISION

In the year after Cottesloe several synods, synodical commissions and church councils categorically rejected the findings of Cottesloe. It was indeed, as Lückhoff has noted, a devastating defeat for the ecumenically-minded.[30] For Beyers Naudé Cottesloe and its aftermath represented – in his own admission – a turning point that eventually led to his decision to resign as minister of the Dutch Reformed congregation Aasvoëlkop in 1963 and to head the ecumenical Christian Institute. In Alan Paton's reflections on Cottesloe in his autobiography, he recalls an incident at the consultation when Beyers Naudé invited him for a private talk, saying that he must not give up because a great change is coming in the Dutch Reformed Church (NGK), especially among younger people. Paton adds: "Well, a great change did come about, but not in the NGK. It came about in the life of Beyers Naudé".[31]

Much has been written on the life of Beyers Naudé, including his decision to resign as minister and his farewell sermon on "Obedience to God," a sermon in which he used as his text Acts 5: 29 ("We must obey God rather than men"). For the purposes of this paper I want to consider briefly an unpublished sermon by Naudé that also used Acts 5: 29 as text. Among the sermons and speeches donated by Beyers's wife, Ilse Naudé, to the Beyers Naudé Centre for Public Theology at Stellenbosch, there is a typed sermon titled "Obedience: To Whom?" ("Gehoorsaam: Aan Wie?"). The scripture reading for this sermon is given as Acts 5: 17-42 and the inscription on the front page says: Linden 27 Nov 1960 / Piet Retief 16 December 1960. Thus Naudé most probably preached this sermon just before and just after Cottesloe.

In this sermon Naudé interprets the struggle between Peter (along with the apostles) and the religious authorities as a situation in which these Christians' highest loyalty was tested to the utmost. Obedience means submission to the highest authority.

---

29 For more extensive discussions of the Cape and Transvaal Synods see Lombard, *Die Nederduitse Gereformeerde Kerke en Rassepolitiek*, 336-343; Lückhoff, *Cottesloe*, 133-151; and Groenewald, "Die Transvaalse Kerk en die Cottesloe-beraad", 131-142.
30 Lückhoff, *Cottesloe*, 128.
31 Paton, *Journey Continued*, 215. Twenty-four years later Paton interviewed Naudé for *Leadership S.A.* He reminded Naudé of this statement and asked whether he still stands by his view regarding change in the DRC. Naude's response is revealing: "I think we have to accept the fact that the present official, appointed leadership of the N.G. Kerk will not change. The majority of these men are diehard, conservative and political figures ... Where our hope lies is among a small and influential number of theologians within the NGK who are working very hard behind the scenes to bring new theological insight and perspective to the theological students – the Dawid Bosches, Willie Jonkers and others – but they are doing it quietly behind the scenes for reasons which I can understand ... There is going to be a split in the NGK, a tremendous battle ...my feelings is that 24 years after Cottesloe there are at last deep stirrings within the hearts and the consciences of a number of theologians, theological students and lay people, who are saying that they cannot remain silent any longer". See Paton, *Journey Continued*, 216-217.

Furthermore, such obedience to God touches all aspects of life and requires holy respect for his Word. Naudé then turns to the topic of God's Word and race relations, with reference to some books critical of the current policy on race relations (although *Delayed Action* is not mentioned by name, its views are clearly implied). Naudé makes a plea that people should not dismiss these books out of hand, but should judge them in the light of God's Word. The time has come for the whole Christian church in South Africa to ask: "What is God's Word saying, and what does obedience to that Word demand? If the church comes to the conclusion that any of its views are not in accordance with Scripture, then the church does not only have the right but also the *duty* [this word double underlined in the original text] to state it honestly and courageously".[32] In the final part of the sermon Naudé refers explicitly to the Cottesloe conference. He comments: "If the delegates ... seek no other truth than that of the Word, then we can expect that God will do great things for his church and our country. But then we must also trust God when his guidance goes against our human viewpoints".[33] Naudé ends the sermon on a personal note with reference to the fact that his father taught them as children that your highest obedience is always owed to God, an obedience that must be shown towards his Word. Therefore his prayer: "May we as church and *volk* take this word to heart during this time: those who are obedient to God's Word do not have anything to fear".[34]

What this sermon makes clear, apart from opening a window onto Naudé's own piety, is that already before Cottesloe Naudé was having serious doubts about whether South African racial policies were in accordance with Scripture. When Naudé returns to this text in his farewell sermon in 1963, he returns to ideas that were not merely central to the ecumenical climate of the day, but that he had already internalised earlier, before and during the time of Cottesloe.

An unpublished speech entitled "The prophetic calling of the church in our day" ("Die profetiese roeping van die kerk in hierdie tyd"), delivered on 11 May 1961 (just weeks after the Transvaal synod) to pastors in Pretoria, also makes for interesting reading. "What strikes me," states Naudé's text, "is that the general approach of the man on the street ("die gewone man") is derived not from the perspective of Christianity, but from [the perspective] of the future of whites ("blankedom"); not so much to determine the prophetic calling of the church but to determine the political calling of the *volk*".[35] Naudé sees this as a grave danger. He is deeply aware of the importance of this moment for the church, hence his observation: "Never before in history was there a more urgent need for serious reflection on the nature, calling and future of the church as today".[36]

In this regard two aspects concerning race relations are emphasised by Naudé. The first aspect was related to the question of how the unity of the church finds

---

32 Naudé, B, "Gehoorsaamheid – Aan Wie?" (unpublished sermon, 1960), Beyers Naudé Archives, Stellenbosch. This sermon was later published in Coetzee, M, Hansen, L and Vosloo, R (eds), *Vreesloos gehoorsaam: 'n Keur uit Beyers Naudé se preke 1939-1997* (Stellenbosch: Sun Press, 2013), 153-157.
33 Naudé, "Gehoorsaamheid – Aan Wie?"
34 Naudé, "Gehoorsaamheid – Aan Wie?"
35 Naudé, B, "Die profetiese roeping van die kerk in hierdie tyd" (unpublished speech, 11 May 1961), Beyers Naudé Archives, Stellenbosch.
36 Naudé, "Die profetiese roeping van die kerk in hierdie tyd".

expression in society. The churches needed to take seriously the questions addressed to the (Dutch Reformed) church regarding membership, joint worship and mixed marriages. Shying away from these challenges would be fatal for the prophetic calling of the church. The second aspect that called for reflection was related to the 'apartheid' of which Scripture speaks and does not speak. In the New Testament eschatology the lines of separation are not between East or West, or white or black, but between faith and unbelief, church and world, God and Satan, Christ and the Antichrist. God does not guarantee the survival of a *volk* because it is white or black, but in as far as its serves the purposes of the Kingdom of God. In a spirit of serious reflection, continues Naudé, the church should preach in a clear voice on Christian justice, responsibility and love with regard to race relations. This task calls for study and prayer. Naudé is furthermore in favour of study circles, also with brothers from other Christian churches, to seek greater clarity in the light of God's Word. Naudé words run directly counter to the mentality that supported the termination of the Dutch Reformed Church's membership of the WCC. The prophetic calling of the church, however, is not only limited to reflection and preaching, but also requires embodiment ("belewing"). The church must let its voice be heard against all forms of social injustice and oppression. In words that have the same tenor as the later Belhar confession, Naudé states: "As Christian church the church must be an advocate for the poor, the oppressed, the hungry, the voiceless, the unjustly treated – notwithstanding whether they are white or black".[37] Moreover, to do this the church must be able to have empathy with the needs of people – not just talk about them, but with them. Naudé ends his speech with the prayer that South Africans will have a clear vision of their prophetic calling and live it out without fear.

Naudé's speech provides an important glimpse into his growing commitments after Cottesloe. In his autobiography *My land van hoop* Naudé writes in similar fashion that he realised two things in the aftermath of Cottesloe. First, the Dutch Reformed Church had placed itself on a path towards complete isolation as a church and ecumenically – in South Africa and abroad. Second, the decisions of the Dutch Reformed Church would result in this church not being able to perform its prophetic calling towards government, because of the influence of hidden powers.[38] It is my view that it is indeed on these two issues that the ghost of Cottesloe would continue to haunt the Dutch Reformed Church, even to this day.

## 4. THE RETURN OF THE GHOST?

Naudé rightly observed that response to Cottesloe had the effect of placing the Dutch Reformed Church on a road of isolation as a church and ecumenically, and that this hampered it in living out its prophetic calling vis-à-vis the state. In this respect the ghost of Cottesloe often returned to haunt the Dutch Reformed Church in the ensuing decades. Some have argued that Cottesloe did not bring an end to the Dutch Reformed Church's ecumenical relations, since the church remained a part of Reformed ecumenical bodies such as the Reformed Ecumenical Synod and the World Alliance of Reformed Churches.[39] However, the decision after Cottesloe

---

37  Naudé, "Die profetiese roeping van die kerk in hierdie tyd".
38  Naudé, *My land van hoop*, 59.
39  Strauss, "Beginsel of Metode", 440

to withdraw from the WCC did insulate the church from important voices in the ecumenical community.

In an article on "Cottesloe, Wêreldraad van Kerke en Ekumeniese Sending" ("Cottesloe, the World Council of Churches and the Ecumenical Mission"),[40] the South African theologian Jaap Durand notes that a true ecumenical vision should not be associated simply with the question of membership of the WCC. However, the important question was whether the Dutch Reformed Church was willing to live out its missional calling in ecumenical relations and, concomitantly, whether the Dutch Reformed Church was willing to approach the question of race relations from an ecumenical perspective.[41] Durand furthermore acknowledges the argument that withdrawal from the WCC was motivated by the concern about the organisational unity of the various Dutch Reformed synods. The question for Durand, however, was whether ulterior motives did not come into play as well – motives that unmistakably show a movement towards isolation. Durand ends his article by expressing the hope that if organisational unity on a synodical level were to materialise (which did happen in 1962), the church would receive with it an ecumenical vision, in the sense that the problems which the church was facing – also in terms of race relations – would not just be viewed as an issue for this church alone, but for the whole universal church of which it is a part. These prophetic words by Durand were not heeded by the church. In the decades to come an isolation-orientated mentality grew stronger, robbing the church in the process of important resources to confront the challenges facing it. The limits of such an isolationist mentality point to the continual need for what can be called an ethics of hospitality.[42] Hospitality, one could argue partly in conversation with Jacques Derrida, is not only about receiving angels but also about facing ghosts.

Together with its tendency towards ecumenical isolation, the Dutch Reformed Church's response to Cottesloe put a question mark behind the church's ability to fulfil its prophetic role towards the state. Beyers Naudé saw this matter as a question of one's ultimate loyalty and obedience. It is not surprising that some of the discussions around this issue in the early 1960s revolved around the question of loyalty. One is reminded here of AB du Preez's two-part article in *Die Kerkbode* (12 and 19 September 1962) on "Lojaliteit – 'n Verdwynende Deug" ("Loyalty – a disappearing virtue").[43] This article evoked several sharp responses, including a long letter from Ben Marais in which he faults Du Preez for the fact that he explains loyalty in the light of natural relationships. And in the following decades the Dutch Reformed Church indeed had to come to terms with the accusation that loyalty to the *volk* had clouded its prophetic judgment. One is reminded here of Alan Paton's

---

40  Durand, JJF, "Cottesloe, die Wêreldraad van Kerk en Ekumeniese Sending", *NGTT* (1961): 147-152.
41  Durand, "Cottesloe, die Wêreldraad van Kerk en Ekumeniese Sending", 152.
42  In his study on Cottesloe Lückhoff refers to Robert Bilheimer's visit to South Africa in September 1961 (Bilheimer played a vital role in making the consultation possible in the first place and visited South Africa several times). From correspondence between Bilheimer and Rev. AJ van Wijk, Lückhoff concludes that Bilheimer had been invited to speak to students at the Stellenbosch theological seminary, but that this invitation was withdrawn. Van Wijk apologised to Bilheimer for this "lack of hospitality and Christian charity". See Lückhoff, *Cottesloe*, 151.
43  Du Preez, AB, "Lojaliteit – 'n verdwynende deug", *Die Kerkbode* (12 and 19 September 1962).

remark: "If ever a church failed in its duty towards its country, it was the NGK That was because it saw its prime duty, after devotion to God, not as devotion to the country, but to the *volk*".[44] And one should consider De Gruchy's words too: "How different it might have been if Cottesloe had resulted in a united Christian witness. Years lost in the wilderness of repression and resistance, injustice, anger and frustration, might have been used to transform South Africa …".[45]

Beyers Naudé observed that it would take many years for the church to work through the shock of Cottesloe, not 10 or 15 years as he had silently hoped, but more than 30 bitter years.[46] But has the ghost of Cottesloe been put to rest? In some ways there have been some telling encounters with the ghost, for instance, through the *Church and Society* documents (1986, 1990) and through Willie Jonker's confession of guilt at the Rustenburg conference (1990), but given the fact that reunification has still not come to the Dutch Reformed family of churches, and that the church is probably still struggling to speak in a clear prophetic voice, one cannot but say that the spectre of Cottesloe is still a haunting presence today.

---

44   Paton, *Journey Continued*, 217.
45   De Gruchy, "From Cottesloe to Rustenburg and Beyond", 24.
46   Cf. Naudé, *My land van hoop*, 60.

# PART 3 – ENGAGING REFORMED THEOLOGIANS

# 13. ON CALVIN'S THEOLOGICAL HERITAGE IN SOUTH AFRICA: ENGAGING AN AMBIVALENT, CONTESTED AND PROMISING LEGACY[1]

## 1. INTRODUCTION

In an article, first read at the International Calvin conference in Geneva in May 2009, the South African Reformed theologian John de Gruchy comments:

> Held together by some common threads and family resemblances, Calvinism in South Africa is not a seamless garment but a patchwork quilt roughly woven together, in some places, badly soiled and in need of repair. There are perhaps as many reasons to decry Calvinism's significance in South African history as there are to regard it as in some ways formative. But one way or another it cannot be ignored when it comes to the making and unmaking of apartheid both as an ideology and a social reality.[2]

This remark attests to the fact that the legacy of John Calvin in South Africa is in many ways a complex, ambivalent and contested one. On the one hand, Calvinism became associated with the religious worldview that provided the theological underpinnings for the support of Afrikaner nationalism, and more specifically for the ideology of apartheid,[3] while on the other hand, one also finds traces of Calvin in anti-apartheid memory.[4]

---

1  This essay was presented as a paper in July 2009 in Aix-a-Provence at a confererence of the International Reformed Theology Institute (IRTI) that commemorated the 500th anniversary of the birth of John Calvin. The essay was originally published as "Calvin's Theological Heritage in South Africa: Engaging an Ambivalent, Contested and Promising Legacy" in Van den Belt, H (ed.), *Restoration through Redemption: John Calvin Revisited* (Leiden: Brill, 2013), 247-270.
2  De Gruchy, JW, "Calvin(ism) and Apartheid in South Africa in the Twentieth Century: The Making and Unmaking of a Racial Ideology" (Paper read at the International Calvin conference in Geneva in May 2009), 1. This paper was subsequently published in Backus, I and Benedict, P (eds), *Calvin and His Influence, 1509-2009* (Oxford University Press, New York, 2011), 306-18.
3  Trevor Huddleston, for instance, writes as follows in his well-known and moving account of his ministry as an Anglican priest in the 1940s and 1950s in the township of Sophiatown, Johannesburg, published under the title *Naught for Your Comfort* (London: Fontana Books, 1957): "The truth is that the Calvinistic doctrines upon which the faith of the Afrikaner is nourished, contained within themselves … exaggerations so distorting and so powerful that is very hard indeed to recognise the Christian faith they are supposed to enshrine. Here in the fantastic notion of the immutability of race, is present in a different form the predestination idea: the concept of an elect people of God, characteristic above all else of John Calvin … Calvinism, with its great insistence on 'election,' is the ideally suitable doctrine for White South Africa. It provides at the same moment a moral justification for White supremacy and an actual day-to-day reason for asserting it" (50).
4  For a more extensive discussion of this theme, see Vosloo, RR, "Calvin and Anti-Apartheid Memory in the Dutch Reformed Family of Churches in South Africa" in De Niet, J, Paul, H and Wallet, B (eds), *Sober, Strict, and Scriptural: Collective Memories of*

The story of Calvin's reception and influence in South Africa is thus a multifaceted story with several interwoven and conflicting strands.⁵ It is – like the story of Reformed life and theology in South Africa in general – a story of many stories.⁶ Actually, as Dirkie Smit has observed, it is difficult to speak of Calvinism in South Africa in the singular, given the divided and ambiguous history of the Reformed tradition in South Africa.⁷

In order to engage with the ambivalent and contested nature of Calvin's theological heritage in South Africa today, it is of vital importance not to speak a-historically about Calvin's legacy. In this regard, I will make a few brief historical theological comments on the viewpoints that linked Calvin and Calvinism to what is sometimes called Afrikaner civil religion. This is followed by a discussion of the ways in which Calvin was used by some theologians from the Dutch Reformed family of churches⁸

---

*John Calvin, 1800-2000* (Leiden: Brill, 2009), 217-244. Sections of this essay draw on that essay. Cf. also Vosloo, RR, "Remembering John Calvin in South Africa today?", *NGTT* 51, Supplementum (2010): 423-435.

5   For a discussion of how Calvin's legacy took shape in different ways in the South African context from 1652 onwards through various colonial settler communities (who brought different streams of the Reformed tradition to South Africa), as well as how these communities were shaped by the encounter with indigenous peoples, see De Gruchy, JW, "Calvin(ism) and Apartheid in South Africa in the Twentieth Century". See also Thom, G, "Calvinism in South Africa" in Reid, WS (ed.), *John Calvin: His Influence in the Western World* (Grand Rapids: Eerdmans, 1982), 345-363. For another discussion of Calvin's influence in South Africa, see Britz, D and D'Assonville, V, "Calvijn in Afrika" in Selderhuis, HJ (ed.), *Calvijn Handboek* (Kampen: Kok, 2008), 557-563.

6   Cf. Smit, DJ, "Reformed Theology in South Africa: A Story of Many Stories", *Acta Theologica* 12/1 (1992): 88-110, as well as Smit, DJ, "On Adventures and Misfortunes: More Stories about Reformed Theology in South Africa" in Harinck, G and Van Keulen, D (eds), *Vicissitudes of Reformed Theology in the Twentieth Century* (Studies in Reformed Theology, Vol. 9) (Zoetermeer: Meinema, 2004), 208-235. Compare also Smit, DJ, "What does it mean to live in South Africa and to be Reformed?", *Reformed World* 58/4 (2008): 263-283. These three articles can also be found Smit, DJ, *Essays on Being Reformed: Collected Essays 3*, Vosloo, RR (ed.) (Stellenbosch: SUN MeDIA, 2009), 201-258.

7   Smit, D J, "Morality and Politics – Secular or Sacred? Calvinist Traditions and Resources in Conflict in Recent South African Experiences" (Paper read at conference on "Das Politische Problem religiöser Liberalität in Christentum und Islam Konsultation", Berlin, 3-5 July 2009), 1. This paper has since been published in Smit, DJ, *Essays on Being Reformed: Collected Essays 3*, 513-549. WA de Klerk makes a similar point in his book *The Puritans in Africa: A History of Afrikanerdom* (Harmondsworth: Penguin Books, 1975) when he comments: "To say that the key to the Afrikaners is Calvinism is not enough. As is the case with all apostles, there are as many Calvins as there have been restatements or 'revisions' of the original philosophy" (125).

8   The term "Dutch Reformed family of churches" (which is not uncontested) refers to the Dutch Reformed Church, the Dutch Reformed Mission Church, the Dutch Reformed Church in Africa and the Reformed Church in Africa. These churches historically had mainly white, coloured, black and Indian members respectively. In 1994 the Dutch Reformed Mission Church and the largest part of the Dutch Reformed Church in Africa united to form the Uniting Reformed Church in Southern Africa. There are, of course, important theological strands in other Reformed churches in South Africa that reflected on the realities of apartheid South Africa in the light of Calvin's legacy, for instance the serious scholarly work by theologians of the Gereformeerde Kerk associated with the University of Potchefstroom, as well as the work by theologians within the mainly English-speaking Reformed Churches. One could also reflect on the reception of Calvin

to critique the theological presuppositions associated with Afrikaner neo-Calvinism. Against this historical theological backdrop, the final section of the essay offers a few searching remarks regarding the promise of reclaiming the legacy of Calvin amidst the challenges posed by South African context.

## 2. THE CALVINIST PARADIGM AND AFRIKANER CIVIL RELIGION

In an influential article "The roots and fruits of Afrikaner civil religion," written in 1983, the well-known South African missiologist David Bosch observes that it is still the dominant view that the religio-political views of the Afrikaner, which reached their maturity in the mid-20th century, have their roots in Calvinism. According to this view, which is often referred to as the "Calvinist paradigm", the outlook since the 17th century, and increasingly so during the subsequent centuries, has been inspired by a strictly Calvinist view of life. Bosch continues:

> This led them to regard themselves as a chosen people, to identify themselves with Israel of old, and to believe that they have been called by God to Christianize and civilize the original inhabitants of the subcontinent. This awareness of being a chosen people blended with the Calvinist doctrine of election and predestination and led to the belief that they – the Afrikaners – were the elect of God in contradistinction to the other races; because this was so, any form of 'gelykstelling' (=equal treatment) of Blacks and Whites would be contrary to the ordinances of God.[9]

The interesting point that Bosch makes with regard to the "Calvinist paradigm" is that it had been advocated not only by scholars critical of Afrikaner nationalism,[10] but also by some Afrikaner scholars, particularly since the 1870s, and even more from the 1930s onwards. As Bosch puts it in a later article: "Thus both friend and foe agreed that Calvinism shaped Afrikanerdom; the one, however, wished to prove how *bad* Calvinism was, the other how *good* it was".[11]

Bosch is also mindful of the fact that some scholars have challenged this so-called Calvinist paradigm. He attends especially to the meticulous scholarly critique of André du Toit, from which he quotes: "A critical investigation will show that there is simply no contemporary evidence for the presence among early Afrikaners of a set of popular beliefs that might be recognised as 'primitive Calvinism' nor of any

---

    in the Nederduitsch Hervormde Kerk, another Afrikaans-speaking Reformed church in South Africa.

9    Bosch, DJ, "The Roots and Fruits of Afrikaner Civil Religion" in Hofmeyr, JW and Vorster WS (eds) *New Faces of Africa: Essays in Honour of Ben (Barend Jacobus) Marais* (Pretoria: University of South Africa, 1984), 15.

10   Cf. Moodie, TD, *The Rise of Afrikanerdom: Power, Apartheid and the Afrikaner Civil Religion* (Berkeley: University of California Press, 1975) and Patterson, S, *The Last Trek: A Study of the Boer People and the Afrikaner Nation* (London: Routledge, 1957).

11   Bosch, DJ, "The Afrikaner and South Africa", *Theology Today* 43/2, 1986: 204. For a discussion of the features, failures and future of Calvinism in South Africa, see also Bosch, DJ, "A Calvinist perspective on the future of democracy in South Africa" in Nürnberger, K (ed.), *A Democratic Vision for South Africa* (Pietermaritzburg: Encounter Publications, 1991), 188-195.

ideology of a chosen people with a national mission: nothing of this kind appears in the accounts of travellers or other well-placed observers before the 1950s, nor are such views articulated at all by Afrikaners themselves before the last decades of the 19th century".[12] Although Bosch argues that Du Toit probably overstates his case, he nevertheless agrees that it is hard to refute Du Toit's central thesis that the 'Calvinist paradigm' cannot be historically substantiated. Furthermore, Bosch remarks that the picture of the heroes of Afrikaner history as devout Calvinists is probably overdrawn: "It is therefore most probable that those scholars are correct who contend that Afrikaners of the 18th and early 19th centuries were, at most, Calvinist only in a cultural sense and that very few of them actually lived according to the central tenets of the Calvinist faith".[13]

It is not possible to give a detailed discussion of the influence of Calvin and Calvinism on Afrikaner identity in this essay, but even the cursory remarks above demonstrate that an over-simplified description and uncritical acceptance of the 'Calvinist paradigm' is problematic. In order to understand Afrikaner 'civil religion'[14] (as it is associated with Afrikaner nationalism), one has to acknowledge a more complex interplay of forces. Bosch identifies three forces in this regard: "The religious roots of Afrikaner nationalism, as it reached maturity in the 1940s and 1950s, are ... to be traced back to the influences of orthodox evangelicalism, Kuyperian Calvinism, and

---

12   Bosch, "The Roots and Fruits of Afrikaner Civil Religion", 16. See also Du Toit, A, "No Chosen People: The Myth of the Calvinist Origins of Afrikaner Nationalism and Racial Ideology", *American Historical Review* 88/4 (1983): 920-952. In a later article Du Toit again asserts the fact that very little of the historical construction of the Calvinist paradigm will withstand rigorous critical scrutiny. See Du Toit, A, "Puritans in Africa? Afrikaner 'Calvinism' and Kuyperian Neo-Calvinism in Late Nineteenth Century South Africa," *Society for Comparative Study of History* 27 (1985): 209-240. Du Toit concludes his argument: "(I)n comparative and historical perspective the reputation of authentic Calvinism is quite overblown: it is meagre in substance and its historical foundation is shallow. The theory of an authentic Calvinist tradition going back to a primitive Calvinism nurtured in the isolated *trekboer* society of the open frontier, and ultimately derived from the golden age of 'seventeenth-century Calvinism' is a historical myth" (234) check original?. For a more recent discussion of the link between Calvinism and the idea of the Afrikaner as a chosen people, see Giliomee, H, *The Afrikaners: Biography of a People* (Cape Town: Tafelberg, 2003), 175-179. For a description of 'Calvinism' in the Afrikaner school of historiography, see also Britz, RM, "Die begrip 'Calvinisme' in die Afrikaanse geskiedskrywing. 'n Oorsigtelike tipering" ("The Concept 'Calvinism' in Afrikaans Historiography: An Overview"), *Skrif en Kerk* 15/2 (1994): 196-218.
13   Bosch, "The Roots and Fruits of Afrikaner Civil Religion", 18. See also Bosch, "The Afrikaner and South Africa", 206.
14   For a thorough discussion on the use and usefulness of the notion of 'civil religion' in South African discourse, see Dirkie Smit's article "Civil Religion – in South Africa?" in Smit, DJ, *Essays in Public Theology: Collected Essays 1*, Conradie, EM (ed.) (Stellenbosch: Sun Press, 2007), 101-123. See also Deist, FE, "Notes on the Context and Hermeneutic of Afrikaner Civil Religion" in Kritzinger JNJ and Saayman WA (eds), *Mission in Creative Tension: A Dialogue with David Bosch* (Pretoria: Missiological Society, 1990), 124-139. Deist later published an extensive study on the exposition of Scripture in the Dutch Reformed Church, with an informative chapter on "Calvinism and Biblical Science". See Deist, FE, *Ervaring, Rede en Metode in Skrifuitleg: 'n Wetenskapshistoriese ondersoek na die Skrifuitleg in die Ned. Geref. Kerk 1840-1990* (Experience, Reason and Method in Exegesis: A Scientific-historical Study of the Biblical Exegesis of the Dutch Reformed Church 1840-1990) (Pretoria: RGN, 1994), especially 155-260.

neo-Fichtean romanticism. It is, indeed, a curious blend of all three of these, having gleaned from what best suited the peculiar situation of the Afrikaner".[15]

Much has been written on these three influences on the development of Afrikaner nationalism, as well as on the formation of the identity of the Dutch Reformed Church.[16] Given our focus on the reception of Calvin and his legacy in South Africa, suffice it to say that it is also important to keep in mind that Kuyperian Calvinism (one can also speak of Afrikaner neo-Calvinism in this regard) underwent serious adaptation and distortion in the light of the way its proponents interpreted local needs.

From the 1930s onwards the South African version of Kuyperian Calvinism grew in strength. For instance, at the Theological Seminary of the Dutch Reformed Church at Stellenbosch a form of confessional neo-Calvinism became more evident. Calvinism became equated with a certain type of confessional orthodoxy.[17] It is a question whether this form of Calvinism was really infused with an in-depth engagement with Calvin, yet Calvin and Calvinism were definitely used as an identity markers and rhetorical devices. In addition, this strand of Calvinism rather uncritically embraced the rising tide of Afrikaner nationalism and patriotism.

This strand of Calvinism (to which prominent theologians of the Afrikaans-speaking Reformed Churches contributed) is especially reflected in an influential series called *Koers in die krisis* (*Direction in the Crisis*), of which the first volume was published in 1935 under the editorship of HG Stoker and FJM Potgieter.[18] This series consisted of a wide range of essays, including international contributions, collected by the Federation of Calvinist Student Organisations in South Africa. The aim of *Koers in die krisis* is well mirrored in the last paragraph of the editorial preface of the first volume: "May this work be to the honour of God and the benefit of the *volk*, and may it conquer the heart of our *volk*. And may it unite all the Calvinists in South Africa, whatever their church, province or profession, to common Calvinist action in South Africa!"[19]

Kuyperian Calvinism, or the way it was interpreted in South Africa, thus seemed to be congruent with the rapidly growing nationalism of the 1930s and 1940s. An

---

15  Bosch, "The Roots and Fruits of Afrikaner Civil Religion", 32.
16  See, for instance, Bosch, "The Roots and Fruits of Afrikaner Civil Religion", 25-32; Bosch, "The Afrikaner and South Africa", 208-213; Bax, DS, *A Different Gospel: A Critique of the Theology Behind Apartheid* (Johannesburg: Presbyterian Church of Southern Africa, 1979), 28-37; Botha, AJ, *Die evolusie van 'n volksteologie* (*The Evolution of a Theology of the Volk*) (Bellville: UWC, 1984), 164-187; Kinghorn, J (ed.), *Die NG Kerk en Apartheid* (*The Dutch Reformed Church and Apartheid*) (Johannesburg: Macmillan, 1986), 58-69; Jonker, W, "Kragvelde binne die Kerk" ("Forces within the Church"), *Aambeeld* 26/1 (1998): 11-14.
17  For a discussion of this strand of confessional (neo)Calvinism in the aftermath of the Du Plessis case, see Vosloo, RR, "Konfessionele Calvinisme na die Du Plessis-saak" ("Confessional Calvinism after the Du Plessis Case"), *NGTT* 51, Supplement 1 (January 2010): 275-288
18  See Stoker, HG and Potgieter FJM (eds), *Koers in die krisis I* (*Direction in the Crisis*) (Stellenbosch: Pro Ecclesia, 1935). See also Stoker, HG and Vorster, JD, *Koers in die krisis II* (Stellenbosch: Pro Ecclesia, 1940) and Stoker, HG and Vorster, JD, *Koers in die Krisis III* (Stellenbosch: Pro Ecclesia, 1941).
19  Stoker and Potgieter, *Koers in die Krisis I*, xii (my translation).

increasing number of young theologians from the Dutch Reformed Church and the Reformed Church (*Gereformeerde Kerk*) studied at the Free University of Amsterdam and a South African version of Kuyperian theology consequently became deeply entrenched. The Kuyperian notion of the separate spheres of life and the principle of the sovereignty of each of these spheres, together with the principle of diversity as something rooted in creation, was adapted to form an apartheid theology based on the principle of the diversity of people (with biblical support from texts such as Genesis 11 and Acts 17:26).[20]

## 3. CALVIN AGAINST CALVIN: PERSPECTIVES FROM THE WORK AND WITNESS OF BEYERS NAUDÉ AND WILLIE JONKER

The growing dominance in white Afrikaner Reformed churches of a more confessional (or confessionalistic) Calvinism, and the way it was linked to Afrikaner nationalism, were responsible for the fact that an exclusivist 'volkskerk' ecclesiology gained a stronger foothold in the Afrikaner churches. There were, however, a number of dissident voices in the 1940s and 1950s, such as Bennie Keet and Ben Marais, challenging what Jaap Durand described as "the seemingly monolithic theological structure of the Dutch Reformed Church".[21] From the 1960s onwards one can see how a few theologians and church leaders drew on a different understanding of Calvin. They were motivated by the need to critique the hegemony of the 'Calvin' who became associated with Afrikaner nationalism and apartheid discourse. The issue of Calvin's true legacy thus itself became a site of struggle. The efforts to develop an alternative reading of Calvin ought therefore to be situated rhetorically within this context. Within this context the image of a more 'ecumenical Calvin' emerges. In order to substantiate this claim, one might briefly recall aspects of the work and witness of Beyers Naudé and Willie Jonker, two prominent figures in church and public life in South Africa who, in their different ways, drew on Calvin and the Reformed tradition.

### a. Beyers Naudé

In 1969 Beyers Naudé wrote an article published in the *Rand Daily Mail* under the heading "What Calvin *really* stood for" in which he asserts: "Calvin did not proclaim or support an exclusive ideology based on the domination of any group, culture or race over others ... If he were to come alive and be in South Africa today, he would be the first to protest against and combat many of the concepts proclaimed by and posturing as Afrikaner Calvinism".[22] This remark underlines the fact that

---

20 See, for instance, Adonis, JC, "The Role of Abraham Kuyper in South Africa: A Critical Historical Evaluation" in Van der Kooi, C and De Bruijn, J (eds.), *Kuyper Reconsidered: Aspects of his Life and Work* (Amsterdam: VU Uitgeverij, 1999), 259-272, as well as, from a Dutch perspective, Harinck, G, "Abraham Kuyper, South Africa, and Apartheid", *The Princeton Seminary Bulletin* XXIII/2 (2002): 184-187.

21 Durand, JFF, "Afrikaner Piety and Dissent" in Villa-Vicencio, C and De Gruchy, JW, (eds.), *Resistance and Hope: South African Essays in Honour of Beyers Naudé* (Cape Town: David Philip / Grand Rapids: Eerdmans, 1985), 39.

22 Naudé, B, "What Calvin *really* stood for", *Rand Daily Mail* (29 April 1969): 13. This article was reprinted in Afrikaans in the journal *Pro Veritate*. See Beyers Naudé, "Waaroor het

it was important for many Reformed Christians to reclaim Calvin as a moral role-model and locate themselves in line with the basic tenets of his theology. This served as a strategy to give authority and legitimisation to their own position, as well as to disarm rhetorically and theologically those who in their eyes had distorted the tradition.

Naudé, who came from a very prominent Afrikaner family, brought his understanding of the Reformed tradition into critical conversation with his perception of the reasons for the Afrikaner's nationalistic outlook. In his article "What Calvin *really* stood for" Naudé responded to the fact that Calvin had been a point of focus in a notorious speech in parliament by Dr Albert Hertzog, the son of the former prime minister JBM Hertzog, who soon after this speech became the leader of the *Herstigde Nasionale Party* (a political party to the right of the ruling National Party). Hertzog argued that Afrikaner-Calvinism is not reconcilable with liberalism, as expressed by most of the English-speaking community in South Africa. On the other hand, an eminent Calvin scholar, Dr André Hugo, stated during a speech at the University of Cape Town that true Calvinism shows correspondences with what was known in South Africa as "liberalism". In his article Naudé argues that a comparison of these statements reveals conflicting views on Calvinism and that it is no wonder that the average citizen (Calvinist and non-Calvinist) is confused about what Calvin really said. In order to answer the question as to which of these opposing readings of Calvin is correct, Naudé asserts that the answer is only to be found through a careful and objective study of Calvin's pronouncements, writings and actions. There is no doubt in Naudé's mind that Dr Hertzog's use of Calvin, which drew on the neo-Calvinism of people such as the previous editor of *Die Kerkbode*, Dr Andries Treurnicht (who at that stage was the editor of the conservative newspaper *Hoofstad* and later became the leader of the Conservative Party, which broke away from the National Party in 1983), cannot be derived from Calvin himself. The main pillar for these arguments against liberalism is the claim that God established the diversity of nations at creation and at Babel, and that this 'biblical' principle is propounded by Calvin. According to Naudé, this use of the principle of diversity to sustain racial and national identity, and justify the separation of nations and races, has no grounds in Calvin's writings or in the Reformed Confessions.

Another line of critique that Naudé utilises against the position that uses Calvinism to affirm the ideology of apartheid and to critique English 'liberalism' is the affirmation of Calvin's ecumenical concern, not only towards German and Swiss Lutherans, but also towards the *English* Anglicans (Naudé himself emphasised the distinction). In this regard Naudé quotes at length from Calvin's famous letter of 29 March 1552 to the Archbishop of Canterbury, in which he responded to the invitation to a synod to discuss the possibility of greater unity between the churches of the Reformation. For Naudé, Calvin's ecumenical vision is at the heart of Calvin's thought, thus making Calvinism in essence an ecumenical movement. Naudé even asserts: "If Calvin were to come to life and live in South Africa today, I am convinced that he would be a staunch and active supporter of the Christian Institute of Southern Africa".[23] Here we see the focus on 'the ecumenical Calvin' as reaction against the ultra-conservative

---

dit eintlik vir Calvyn gegaan?", *Pro Veritate* (15 May 1969): 6-8.
23  Naudé, "What Calvin *really* stood for", 13.

depiction of Calvin in Afrikaner neo-Calvinism. In this regard one should keep in mind that Naudé's change of view regarding apartheid was deeply influenced by his contact with ecumenical bodies such as the World Council of Churches. Naudé's emphasis on the importance of ecumenism was furthermore related to his belief that church unification within the Dutch Reformed family of churches would serve as a powerful prophetic critique against apartheid.

Naudé is, moreover, interested in the question as to why there was no protest against the use of Calvinism to justify an unjust racial standpoint, noting the close historical intertwinement of the Dutch Reformed Church with the Afrikaner *volk*:

> It is an association so intimately linked and interwoven with all other areas of the life of the Afrikaner that any direct criticism by an Afrikaner on this very sensitive point would immediately be regarded as a betrayal of everything the Afrikaner holds dear, with resulting ostracism and expulsion from the Afrikaner community.[24]

Over against these uses of Calvin in Afrikaner neo-Calvinism Naudé wants to posit 'another Calvin'. Therefore Naudé makes a serious plea – and in this process he describes himself as "a staunch Calvinist" – to the members of the churches to reject the false views of this neo-Calvinism, since it does serious damage to a true understanding of Christianity in general and Calvinism in particular. Naudé concludes: "If only South Africa were to heed the true message of Calvin, how vastly different our whole ecclesiastical and political life would be".[25]

### b. Willie Jonker

The Stellenbosch theologian Willie Jonker is another important theological figure to consider in our reflection on the reception of Calvin in South Africa. Jonker was arguably, together with Johan Heyns, the most important Dutch Reformed systematic theologian in the latter part of the 20th century in South Africa. He is especially known for his confession of guilt for apartheid on behalf of the Dutch Reformed Church at the Rustenburg church conference in 1990, to which Archbishop Desmond Tutu responded with a word of forgiveness. Jonker wrote his doctoral dissertation under GC Berkouwer at the Free University of Amsterdam and after his return to South Africa he worked as a pastor in congregations in Johannesburg and Potchefstroom. The question of the unity of the church was central to his thinking, and he also did important research on church polity during the early 1960s, culminating in the work *Die Sendingbepalinge van die Ned. Gereformeerde Kerk in Transvaal* (*The Mission Ordinances of the Dutch Reformed Church in Transvaal*).[26] In this critique of the 1935 mission policy of the Dutch Reformed Church, which played such an important role in the attempt to provide a moral justification for apartheid, Jonker suggested a church denomination across colour lines. Jonker's thinking challenged the deeply rooted association between the Dutch Reformed Church and Afrikaner nationalism. He was soon branded as a 'liberal' and experienced the pain of rejection in a very

---

24 Naudé, "What Calvin *really* stood for", 13.
25 Naudé, "What Calvin *really* stood for", 13.
26 Jonker, WD, *Die Sendingbepalinge van die Ned. Gereformeerde Kerk in Transvaal* (Bloemfontein: Sendingboekhandel, 1962).

acute manner. After teaching theology at the University of South Africa (UNISA) in Pretoria for a brief period and at Kampen in the Netherlands, Jonker was called to Stellenbosch. His colleague was Prof. FJM Potgieter, who wrote his doctoral dissertation on Calvin under Valentijn Hepp at the Free University in Amsterdam.[27] There clearly was tension between Jonker's and Potgieter's views on apartheid. In his autobiography *Selfs die kerk kan verander* (*Even the Church Can Change*) Jonker writes that he could not help but see a fundamental interrelation between Potgieter's Kuyperian Calvinism and his right-wing political sentiments.[28]

Jonker's reading of Calvin moved in different direction from the one offered by Potgieter. In his essay "Die aktualiteit van die sosiale etiek" ("The Relevance of Social Ethics")[29] Jonker argues that Calvin's thought makes room for an approach to social ethics that does not slide into individualism or view the current social structure as an unchangeable and eternal order created by God. Therefore the church is not interested in a mere conservative restoration, but has the responsibility to deal with social and political questions in the light of God's Word.[30] For these insights Jonker also draws on André Biéler's work *La pensée économique et sociale de Calvin*. In an important footnote he affirms Biéler's view that Calvinism must be a permanent force for political and societal reformation and transformation. Christians must therefore always be a disturbing presence in society because of their protest against all forms of injustice. This is also the reason why Calvin addressed issues such as poverty and wealth, interest and wages.[31] For Jonker the consequences of the Reformed legacy, following in the footsteps of Calvin, are clearly evident for contemporary society:

> As long as we confess that Christ is the Lord and that his rule must be proclaimed over every inch of our earthy reality … we cannot close our eyes to injustice, poverty, oppression and frustration … The way of a pietistic escapism which argues that the church and politics have nothing to do with the burning social and political questions of the day is not an option for us.[32]

In an address at a conference in Geneva in 2007 on the theme "How to celebrate the legacy of John Calvin?" Dirkie Smit, who was a doctoral student under Jonker's supervision, reflects on the excitement they experienced as students at Stellenbosch when they heard Jonker speak on Calvin and read *The Institutes* with him. Smit, who currently is professor in Systematic Theology at Stellenbosch, writes about Jonker:

> He was also known as deeply Reformed, as steeped in Calvin and the Reformed confessions, but also as deeply critical of apartheid, as a

---

27 See Potgieter, FJM, *Die verhouding tussen teologie en die filosofie by Calvyn* (*The Relationship between Theology and Philosophy in Calvin's Thought*) (Amsterdam: NV Noord-Hollandsche Uitgevers Maatschappij, 1939).
28 Jonker, WD, *Selfs die kerk kan verander* (*Even the Church Can Change*) (Cape Town: Tafelberg, 1998), 126.
29 Jonker, WD, "Die aktualiteit van die sosiale etiek" ("The Relevance of Social Ethics") in Verhoef, PA, De Villiers, DW, and De Villiers, JL (eds), *Sol Iustitiae* (Cape Town: NGKU, 1973), 78-107.
30 See Jonker, "Die aktualiteit van die sosiale etiek", 85.
31 See Jonker, "Die aktualiteit van die sosiale etiek", 102.
32 See Jonker, "Die aktualiteit van die sosiale etiek", 96, 97 (my translation).

dissenter, as disloyal to the *volk*, perhaps even dangerous, as a personal friend of Beyers Naudé, Jaap Durand and others who were known to reject the pervasive ideology, as a public voice arguing for the visible unity of the church, for reconciliation instead of separation, for justice instead of self-preservation and self-privileging.[33]

For Smit and many of his contemporaries the writings of Jonker that appealed to Calvin and his legacy in order to make a plea for the reformation of the Reformed Churches in South Africa were highly influential. Smit comments on Jonker:

> He was appealing to the tradition against tradition. He was appealing to the community against the community. He was appealing to our deepest identity in order to critique our actual identity. He did that so often, in his lectures and in his sermons. He would often claim in so many words that there was something different in our tradition, even in the Dutch Reformed Church itself, something more than meets the eye, that there have been other people, other voices, and although they may now be completely silenced, temporarily suppressed and forgotten, their presence and their convictions are still there to guide us and to inspire us – like Calvin.[34]

Throughout his career Jonker consistently reflected on the challenges of society from a Reformed perspective, often with reference to Calvin and an emphasis on the important role of Scripture.[35] A reading of Jonker's work reveals especially his debt to Calvin's insights into the ecumenical nature of the church. Jonker can be viewed as an ecumenical theologian with an emphasis on the unity and catholicity of the church as a challenge to an uncritical relationship between church and *volk*.[36]

---

33  See Smit, DJ, "Why Do We Celebrate the Legacy of John Calvin? Views on Calvin's Ethics from a South African Perspective", *Reformed World* 57/4 (2007): 306-307. Jonker also wrote a revealing two-part series in *Die Kerkbode* (14 and 21 August 1974) under the title "Selfliefde en Selfhandhawing" ("Self-love and Self-preservation"). These articles, drawing specifically on Calvin, must be understood within the context of the emphasis on 'our own' (die eie) within Afrikaner nationalism.

34  Smit, "Why Do We Celebrate the Legacy of John Calvin?", 328.

35  See, for instance, Jonker, WD, "Heilige Skrif en sosiale etiek by Calvyn" (Holy Scripture and Calvin's Social Ethics), *Bulletin van die Suid-Afrikaanse Vereniging vir die Bevordering van Christelike Wetenskap* 39 (1973): 31-37 and Jonker, WD, "Die moderne belydenisbeweging in Suid-Afrika – en Calvyn" ("The Modern Confessing Movement in South Africa – and Calvin"), *In die Skriflig* 27/4 (1993): 443-461.

36  If 'ecumenical' is understood as a vague qualifier abstracted from soteriological concerns, the description of Jonker as an ecumenical theologian is problematic. See, in this regard Theron, PF, "Willie Jonker as Gereformeerd-Katolieke teoloog" ("Willie Jonker as Reformed-Catholic Theologian"), *NGTT* 51 (2010): 179-190. PF (Flip)Theron too is well-known in South African circles for articulating an ecclesiological vision that challenged church divisions along racial lines. For a short summary essay that captures well his thinking in this regard, see Theron, PF, "Die kerk as eskatologiese teken van eenheid" ("The Church as Eschatological Sign of Unity") in Meiring, P and Lederle, HI (eds), *Die eenheid van die kerk* (*The Unity of the Church*) (Cape Town: Tafelberg, 1979), 6-13.

## 4. BLACK AND REFORMED: A PAINFUL PARADOX

This brief discussion of aspects of Naudé's and Jonker's work and witness with reference to Calvin affirms that there were church leaders and theologians who challenged the dominant 'volkskerk' ecclesiology, often with an appeal to Calvin's own teaching and to the Reformed confessional tradition. In so-called black Reformed circles the theological inspiration for the struggle also came from the tradition of Calvin, Kuyper, Barth and the church struggle in Germany. Smit comments: "This of course had the result that controversies raged about the conflicting claims to represent this tradition – a major part of the struggle was the struggle between Calvin and Calvin, Kuyper and Kuyper, Barth and Barth, not to mention Calvin against Kuyper and Barth against Kuyper".[37]

In the midst of the painful reality of apartheid a central question in black Reformed circles was whether one could embrace Calvin in the light of the fact that 'Calvinism' was so closely tied up with Afrikaner nationalism. In a doctoral dissertation, completed at the theological seminary at Kampen in the Netherlands and significantly entitled "A Cry for Life: An Interpretation of 'Calvinism' and Calvin", LR Lekula Ntoane grappled with exactly this question. Ntoane refers to the fact that black Reformed Christians, who experienced the demonic and dehumanising effects of apartheid, could not do otherwise than to pose some serious questions: "Is 'Calvinism' truly and genuinely representative of Calvinian tradition? Are the views espoused in it a reflection of the teachings and intentions of its initiator? Are the views expressed both in 'Calvinism' and the Calvinian tradition reconcilable with the message of Jesus Christ? Is it worthwhile for black Christians who have adopted and embraced this tradition to remain loyal to it?"[38]

Another South African theologian who studied at Kampen is Allan Boesak, who later became moderator of the Dutch Reformed Mission Church and played a prominent role in the church struggle against apartheid, alongside influential figures like Desmond Tutu, Frank Chikane and Beyers Naudé. What makes Boesak of special interest for the purposes of this essay is the fact that he consciously and continuously referred to Calvin in his rhetoric against the injustices in apartheid South Africa. For instance, in his keynote address at the national conference of the South African Council of Churches (SACC) in July 1979 at Hammanskraal, Boesak quotes at length from Calvin to emphasise that God hears the cry of the oppressed, the cry "How long, O Lord?"[39] At this same conference the SACC adopted a resolution that encouraged acts of civil disobedience against the apartheid laws. The South African Minister of Justice, Alwyn Schlebusch, responded to this resolution by stating that the government is becoming impatient with such statements that threaten the stability of the country. Boesak responded by writing an open letter to Schlebusch, again drawing on Calvin.[40]

---

37　Smit, "Morality and Politics – Secular or Sacred?", 4.
38　Ntoane, LRL, *A Cry for Life: An Interpretation of "Calvinism" and Calvin* (Kampen, 1983), 124.
39　Boesak, AA, *Black and Reformed: Apartheid, Liberation, and the Calvinist Tradition*, Sweetman, L (ed.) (New York: Orbis Books, 1984), 23-24.
40　See Boesak, *Black and Reformed*, 32-41. In this letter Boesak addresses the routine warning by the government that pastors and churches must stay 'out of politics' and confine themselves to their "proper task," namely the preaching of the Gospel. For Boesak

In addition, Allan Boesak also played a leading role in the founding of the Alliance of Black Reformed Christians in South Africa (ABRECSA). At the first conference of ABRECSA at Hammanskraal in October 1981 Boesak gave an importance address entitled "Black and Reformed: Contradiction or Challenge?"[41] In this address Boesak asks the burning question: "What does it mean to be black and Reformed in South Africa today?"[42] For Boesak the fact that Reformed Christians, and specifically the Dutch Reformed Church, played such an important role in justifying apartheid theologically had the result that the use of the self-designation 'black and Reformed' expresses a painful paradox.

At the heart of Boesak's address is the question of the relation between the Reformed tradition and social justice. In this regard Boesak emphasises, by drawing on Calvin, that the government shows its Christian character not by good religious intentions, but by "the care of the poor, the protection of the weak and the needy, the suppression of the evil, the punishment of oppression, the equitable distribution of wealth, power, privileges and responsibilities".[43] For Boesak, Calvin's concern for social justice is, however, not reflected in the policies of those who claim spiritual kinship with him. Hence Boesak wants to use Calvin against the 'Calvinists'. Boesak continues to argue that South African history might have been different if Reformed Christians had taken Calvin's vision on human solidarity more seriously. Apart from his views on inter-human solidarity, Calvin also plays an important role in the section of Boesak's address where he attends more closely to a Reformed view on government. Boesak accepts Calvin's view that governments are instituted by God for the just and legitimate administration of the world. Therefore the government is not naturally an enemy. This view does not imply for Boesak a blind acceptance of government, but offers an important criterion for judging government. Governments must serve in a just and legitimate way. Boesak then notes that in terms of both the modern concept of democracy, and in terms of Calvin's understanding of legitimacy, the South African government is neither just nor legitimate. According to the Reformed tradition (and Boesak quotes Calvin at length in this regard), government is to be obeyed only "*insofar* as its laws and instructions are not in conflict with the word of God".[44] In the light of these remarks, Boesak returns towards the end of his address

---

the Gospel to be preached is not something meant only for the inner life, for the soul, but for the whole of human existence. The Lordship of Christ applies to all spheres of life, including the social, political and economic spheres. Boesak also wants to make it clear that he makes the plea for civil obedience as a Christian, and more specifically as a Reformed Christian, and that he has done nothing else but place himself "squarely within the Reformed tradition as that tradition has always understood sacred scripture on these matters" (35). It is Boesak's basic conviction that Christian obedience to the state or any earthly authority is always linked to obedience to God, and therefore the Christian's concern is whether the government accepts responsibility for justice. When justice is lacking, the government comes into conflict with God and then resistance is demanded and warranted. Boesak underlines this idea with a reference to the letter that Calvin wrote to King Francis, published as the prologue to his *Institutes*, from which he quotes: "For where the glory of God is not made the end of government, it is not a legitimate sovereignty, but a usurpation" (38).

41 For an edited version of this address, see Boesak, *Black and Reformed*, 83-99.
42 Boesak, *Black and Reformed*, 84.
43 Boesak, *Black and Reformed*, 90.
44 Boesak, *Black and Reformed*, 92.

to the idea of the painful paradox of being black and Reformed in South Africa. He affirms that black Reformed Christians have no reason to be ashamed of their tradition, but warns against the way in which adherents of this tradition have often displayed self-righteousness, arrogance and self-sufficiency in a way that leads to a harmful isolationism. Therefore his conviction that "the Reformed tradition has a future in this country only if black Reformed Christians are willing to take it up, make it truly their own, and let this tradition once again become what it was: a champion of the cause of the poor and the oppressed, clinging to the confession of the lordship of Christ and the supremacy of the word of God".[45]

I draw on this important address because it contains many of the ideas that also resonate throughout Boesak's numerous sermons and speeches during the church's struggle against apartheid.[46] Many of these ideas are also reflected in the ABRECSA charter adopted in 1981, especially in the section on the theological basis of the charter.[47] Of special importance is also the fact that the charter indicates the need for black Reformed Christians to contribute to the ecumenical field and, in this regard, a special opportunity arose with the World Alliance of Reformed Churches' meeting held at Ottawa, Canada in 1982. This meeting indeed became an important marker in the church's struggle against apartheid. A document written by Boesak was sent from ABRECSA to all the delegates before the meeting. This document, with the title "God Made Us All, But ... Racism and the World Alliance of Reformed Churches," is a plea for the World Alliance to play a more active role in the struggle against racism in South Africa. In this document racism is described as structured sinfulness with the added point that racism has made it impossible to share in the natural expression of unity within the body of Christ, namely the Lord's Supper. Here Boesak quotes Calvin at length:

> Now since he has only one body, of which he makes us all partakers, it is necessary that all of us be made one body by such participation ... We shall benefit very much from the sacrament if this thought is impressed and engraved upon our minds: that none of the brethren can be injured, despised, rejected, abused, or in any kind offended by us, without at the same time disagreeing with Christ; that we cannot love Christ without loving him in the brethren; that we ought to take the same care of our own brethren's bodies as

---

45  Boesak, *Black and Reformed*, 96.
46  See, for instance, Boesak, AA, *Die Vinger van God: Preke oor Geloof en die Politiek* (*The Finger of God: Sermons on Faith and Politics*) (Johannesburg: Ravan Press, 1979); *Walking on Thorns: Sermons on Christian Obedience* (Geneva, 1984); *If this is treason, I am guilty* (Grand Rapids: Eerdmans, 1987), and *Comfort and Protest: The Apocalypse from a South African Perspective* (Philadelphia, 1987). See also Boesak, A A, *The Tenderness of Conscience: African Renaissance and the Spirituality of Politics* (Stellenbosch: Sun Press, 2005). The many references to Calvin in this work by Boesak affirm the enduring impact of Calvin on his thought and rhetoric. The title of this work is, of course, taken from Kuyper's remark in his Stone lectures that "Calvinism understood that the world was not saved by ethical philosophizing, but only by the restoration of the tenderness of conscience" (as quoted by Boesak, *Tenderness of Conscience*, 213). See also the many references to Calvin in Boesak's latest book *Running with Horses: Reflections of an Accidental Politician* (Cape Town: Joho Publishers, 2009).
47  For the ABRECSA charter, see De Gruchy, JW and Villa-Vicencio, C (eds), *Apartheid is a Heresy* (Grand Rapids: Eerdmans, 1983), 161-165.

we take care of our own; for they are members of our body; and that, as no part of our body is touched by any feeling of pain which is not spread among all the rest, so we ought not to allow a brother to be affected by any evil, without being touched with compassion for him.[48]

These words gain special significance from the fact that controversy erupted at the Ottawa meeting when the delegations of the black Dutch Reformed Churches refused to share Holy Communion with the members of the white Dutch Reformed Church.[49]

The work of ABRECSA and the meeting at Ottawa, and the role of Allan Boesak in particular (who was elected president), prepared further ground for the process in which the the Dutch Reformed Mission Church called a *status confessionis* with regard to apartheid, leading to the adoption of the Belhar Confession.[50] A reading of the speeches, sermons and documents around these events shows that, while one must not overestimate the influence of Calvin in this regard, one does find that Calvin was put to rhetorical and theological use in the attempt to respond to the realities of apartheid South Africa.

## 5. THE PROMISE OF CALVIN'S LEGACY FOR SOUTH AFRICA TODAY?

Even a brief overview of Calvin's theological reception in 20th-century South Africa reveals the presence of many 'Calvins', including the depiction of Calvin as anti-liberal defender of the values of the *volk*, Calvin as ecumenical figure, and Calvin as advocate for social justice and civil disobedience. These different portrayals of Calvin ought to be kept in mind when considering the promise of Calvin's theological heritage amidst the challenges and opportunities posed by the current South African context.

At the end of August 2009 a conference was held at the Theological Faculty of Stellenbosch on the theme of "Calvin's relevance for today?". The conference programme identified some major opportunities and challenges that the Reformed tradition faced during the transformation of South African society, including:

> i) the opportunity to embody its own unity more visibly through renewal of its own structures and order, through common worship and

---

48   Boesak, *Black and Reformed*, 107. Cf. Calvin, J, *Institutes of the Christian Religion*, Volume 2, McNeill, JT (ed.), Battles, FL (trans.) (Louisville: Westminster John Knox Press, 1960), 4: 17/38, 1414, 1415.

49   For a discussion of these events see Pauw, JC, *Anti-apartheid Theology in the Dutch Reformed Family of Churches: A depth-hermeneutical analysis* (Amsterdam: Vrije Universiteit, 2007), 187-194.

50   For the draft confession of the Belhar Confession and the accompanying letter, as well as for some informative essays on the confession, see Cloete, GD and Smit, DJ, *A Moment of Truth: The Confession of the Dutch Reformed Mission Church* (Grand Rapids: Eerdmans,1984).

confession and through shared life and service, thereby overcoming destructive divisions of the past;

ii) the opportunity to proclaim and practice real reconciliation, thereby dealing with alienation and pain of yesterday and distance and distrust of today;

iii) the opportunity to witness publicly, through words and deeds, to God's compassionate justice, both through its own discipleship and calling on state, society and public opinion.[51]

Given the divisions, alienation and injustice associated with South Africa's apartheid past, it is indeed a challenge to embody unity, to proclaim and practice real reconciliation, and to witness publicly to God's compassionate justice. In response to these challenges, a critical and constructive engagement with Calvin's legacy can provide important theological resources. I would like to briefly highlight three aspects of Calvin's thought that hold particular promise, namely Calvin's commitment to the unity of the church, Calvin's affirmation of hospitality towards strangers, and Calvin's economic and social witness.

### a. Calvin's commitment to the unity of the church

In anticipation of the 500th anniversary of Calvin's birth, a group of scholars met in Geneva in April 2007 to reflect on the question "What is the significance of Calvin's legacy?" The report which followed from the consultation identified eight areas that were considered to be of particular interest for today. The last area that the report discusses deals with Calvin's commitment to the unity of the church, arguing that Calvin lived out his passionate commitment to the unity of the body of Christ within the reality of an already fragmented church. The report concludes:

> Calvin's thinking about the nature of Christian community, his willingness to mediate controversial matters such as the Lord's Supper, and his tireless efforts to build bridges at every level of church life, stand as a contemporary challenge. Calvin challenges churches to understand the causes of continuing separation and, in accordance with scripture, to strive towards visible unity by engaging in concrete ecumenical efforts, all for the sake of the gospel's credibility in the world, and the fidelity of the church's life and mission.[52]

---

51  For a discussion of a similar set of challenges, see Dirkie Smit's contribution on "South Africa" in the special "Calvin09" issue of *bulletin sek - feps* 2 (2009): 24-25.

52  "What is the significance of Calvin's legacy? Report on an International Consultation", *Reformed World* 57/4 (2007): 234-235. On Calvin's understanding of the unity of the church, see also Vischer, L, *Pia conspiratio: Calvin on the Unity of Christ's Church* (Geneva: John Knox Series 12, 2000). Cf. also Eva-Maria Faber's essay "Mutual Connectedness as a Gift and Task: On John Calvin's Understanding of the Church" in Hirzel, ME and Sallmann, M (eds), *John Calvin's Impact on Church and Society: 1509-2009* (Grand Rapids: Eerdmans, 2009), 122-144. Calvin was also interested in questions related to church order and the actual unity of the church. In South Africa, as elsewhere, the challenge remains to address issues of church unity and church polity in a responsible theological way. See also the influential study by W Nijenhuis, *Calvinus Oecumenicus. Calvijn en de eenheid der kerk in het licht van zijn briefwisseling* ('s Gravenhage: Martinus Nijhoff, 1959), as well as

These words are especially relevant to the South African context in the light of the long-standing divisions mainly along racial lines within the Dutch Reformed family of churches. In the discussion above I mentioned that Calvin's legacy in South Africa was often associated with a form of Afrikaner neo-Calvinism, which was characterised by a narrow confessionalism and an uncritical allegiance to a *volkskerk* ecclesiology. The question can still be asked today whether such an ecclesiology, albeit in a more subtle form, is still not one of the most important stumbling blocks on the road to church reunification.

In South Africa one furthermore finds a theological strand that challenged the hegemony of the 'Calvin' of Afrikaner neo-Calvinism, often drawing on a more ecumenical understanding of Calvin's theology (as is seen in the work and witness of Beyers Naudé and Willie Jonker, but the names of many others can also be mentioned). This strand, which found powerful expression in the Belhar confession with its focus on unity, reconciliation and justice, deserves in my view to be amplified within South African Reformed church life. Churches are faced with the challenge of overcoming destructive divisions of the past in the light of the confession that Christ's body is one, thereby giving visible form to this costly unity.

In 2006 a spirit of optimism regarding church reunification reigned, envisioning 2009 as the year in which this goal could be realised. A worship service glorifying God for the gift of reunification would have been a wonderful way for the Dutch Reformed family of churches to celebrate the 500th anniversary of Calvin's birth. Sadly this goal did not materialise, since enthusiasm for church reunification was by then at a low point. Therefore the celebration of Calvin's birth was not only an occasion for joy in the light of his rich theological heritage in South Africa, but also a time for mourning our painful divisions and lamenting our formal divisions. Yet at the same time Calvin's commitment to the unity of the church encourages us to keep on working toward the goal of reunification and reconciliation within the Dutch Reformed family of churches, inspired and sustained by a biblical and theological vision.

b. *The 'displaced Calvin' as resource for a graceful theology of hospitality*

May 2008 saw a violent outbreak of xenophobic attacks in South Africa. During that time I was working on a paper for our annual meeting of the Theological Society of South Africa, entitled "The Displaced Calvin: 'Refugee reality' as a Lens to Re-examine Calvin's Life, Theology and Legacy".[53] The rampant xenophobic violence that was then very much in the news caused me to look at Calvin in a different way. Given the fact that we are living in a world of growing migration, displacement and xenophobia, we may well discover that Calvin's life and theology, with all

---

Douglass, JD, "Calvin, Calvinism and Ecumenism", *Reformed World* 55/4 (2005): 295-310. For an engagement with Nijenhuis, Vischer and Douglass, see Koffeman, LJ, "Calvinus Oecumenicus? De O-factor van Calvijn" in Brouwer, RR, De Leede, B, and Spronk, K (eds), *Het calvinistisch ongemak: Calvijn als erflater en provocator van het Nederlandse protestantisme* (Kampen: Kok, 2009), 185200.

53  The conference theme for this particular theological society meeting was "Grace, Space, and Race: Towards a Theology of Place in (South) Africa Today". For my contribution at this conference, see the next chapter.

its limitations, may provide surprising insights that can aid in the reclaiming of a graceful theology of hospitality.

Such an endeavour is strengthened by the recognition of Calvin's own refugee experiences. Calvin himself was a refugee who ministered to other refugees in places like Strasbourg and Geneva. The impact of the 'refugee reality' on Calvin's ministry and theology contributes, in my view, to a more responsible – and exciting – interpretation of Calvin the theologian. It opens to door to rediscover certain neglected themes in his theology, such as exile and hospitality,[54] as well as to re-evaluate some much-discussed doctrines such as election and providence.[55]

In this regard, it remains important, however, to affirm the need for a sensitive historical hermeneutic that is mindful of the continuity and discontinuity between Calvin and our time, between 16$^{th}$-century religious refugees and 21$^{st}$-century economically and politically displaced persons.[56] Nevertheless, Calvin's engagement with reality was steeped in his reading of Scripture, and the Bible's emphasis on the need to show hospitality to 'the widows, orphans, and strangers' found many echoes in his sermons, letters, commentaries, *The Institutes* and other theological tracts. In this sense Calvin's life and theology may have continuing significance to sustain a Reformed theology of hospitality towards contemporary 'widows, orphans, and strangers'.[57]

Part of the challenge facing South Africa, and our globalising world, today has to do with the need to affirm ethnic identity and cultural diversity. Dealing with identity and difference is, however, no easy matter. The way some South African theologians used the legacy of Calvin to proceed from the emphasis on difference and diversity to separateness and exclusion serves as constant reminder not to abstract diversity talk from a deep concern for human dignity, hospitality and justice. In this regard

---

54  See, for instance, the Dutch theologian HJ Selderhuis's discussion of the 'exile motif' in Calvin's 1557 Commentary on the Psalms in his inaugural lecture *Calvijn als asielzoeker* (Apeldoorn: Theologische Universiteit, 1997), as well as in his book *Calvin's Theology of the Psalms* (Grand Rapids: Baker Academic, 2007).

55  Heiko Oberman has argued that in Calvin's case the puzzling doctrine of predestination was born out of the experience of exile. As he writes in his book *The Two Reformations* (New Haven: Yale University Press, 2003): "The Calvinist doctrine of predestination is the mighty bulwark of the Christian faithful against the fear that they will be unable to hold out against the pressure of persecution. Election is the Gospel's encouragement to those who have faith, not a message of doom for those who lack it. In particular, it responds to the anguish that Calvin had already felt in the early wave of persecution … Rather than providing grounds for arrogance, predestination offers all true Christians the hope that even under extreme distress they will persevere until the end" (114-115). Cf. Douglass, JD, "Pastor and Teacher of the Refugees: Calvin in the Work of Heiko A. Oberman" in Brady, TA *et al.* (eds), *The Work of Heiko A. Oberman: Papers from the Symposium of His Seventieth Birthday* (Leiden: Brill, 2003), 51-65.

56  Jacques Derrida rightfully reminds us that we ought to distinguish prudently between the categories of the foreigner in general, the immigrant, the exile, the deportee, and the stateless or displaced person. See his address to the International Parliament of Writers in 1996 in Strasbourg, published in Derrida, J, *Cosmopolitanism and Forgiveness* (London: Routledge, 2001).

57  "What is the significance of Calvin's legacy?", 234.

Calvin remains an important conversation partner – also for Reformed churches in South Africa.

### c. Calvin and social and economic justice

The year 2002 saw the celebration of 350 years of Reformed church life in South Africa.[58] During this year the book *A History of Inequality in South Africa 1652-2002* by the Stellenbosch economic historian Sampie Terreblanche was published.[59] In this work Terreblanche, who is from a Reformed background, traces in a detailed way the exploitation of indigenous peoples by dominant settler communities from the advent of European colonialism to the end of apartheid in 1994. He furthermore extends his discussion to the 'new South Africa', arguing that although the transition to democracy is a very significant political development, a similar socio-economic development has not yet followed. In addition, Terreblanche criticises the ruling ANC government for abandoning its redistributive ideals, as well as the corporate sector for its ruthless pursuit of its own interests.

Even those who may not fully agree with Terreblanche's analysis and proposals will have to admit the stark reality of economic inequality and injustice in South Africa. In such a context Reformed Christians and communities can indeed welcome the renewed interested in the economic and social witness of Calvin,[60] as well as the fact that the World Alliance of Reformed Churches has placed the issue of economic and ecological justice on its agenda. At the general assembly in Debrecen, Hungary in 1997, the WARC called for a *processus confessionis* regarding economic justice and ecological destruction. This process was continued in Accra, Ghana in 2004 with the Accra Declaration's strong, albeit controversial, criticism of the global economic system. This declaration draws on expressions from the Reformed confessional tradition, including the Belhar confession. Not surprisingly, these Reformed and ecumenical concerns on justice with regard to the economy and all of creation have found expression in the South African theological context.[61]

---

58  For a collection of essays reflecting on this heritage, see Coertzen, P (ed.), *350 Jaar Gereformeerd / 350 Years Reformed 1652-2002* (Bloemfontein: CLF, 2002).

59  See Terreblanche, S, *A History of Inequality in South Africa 1652-2002* (Pietermaritzburg: University of Natal Press, 2002).

60  See especially the renewed influence of the work of André Biéler in this regard. His book *Calvin's Economic and Social Thought* (Geneva: WCC Publications, 2005) is an important source that provides stimulus for the conversation on Calvin's social and economic witness, not the least through the book's extensive quotations from Calvin's work. See also Dommen, E and Bratt, JD, *John Calvin Rediscovered* (Louisville: Westminster John Knox, 2007), as well as the thought-provoking declaration "The Economic and Social Witness of Calvin for Christian Life Today: Statement of an International Consultation, Geneva, 3-6 November 2004", *Reformed World* 55/1 (March 2005): 3-7.

61  Cf. e.g. an interesting collaborative project between the Beyers Naudé Centre for Public Theology at Stellenbosch University and the Evangelischer Entwicklungsdienst (EED), together with the Evangelisch-reformierte Kirche and the Uniting Reformed Church in Southern Africa, called the Joint Globalisation Project. A book resulting from the consultations of this group has just been published, which includes contributions from different academic disciplines. See Boesak, AA and Hansen, L (eds), *Globalisation: The Politics of Empire, Justice and the Life of Faith* (Beyers Naudé Centre Series on Public Theology, Volume 40) (Stellenbosch: Sun Press, 2009). Of special interest is Matthias

Hopefully the renewed interest in Calvin's social and economic thought will continue to have an impact on Reformed theology and praxis in South Africa, leading to a critical and constructive engagement between Calvin's theology and our context. In appropriating insights from Calvin relevant to our current social and economic life, it is important not to extract from Calvin's thought a social and economic theory abstracted from his theological concerns. Moreover, the value of engaging Calvin as conversation partner in search for social and economic justice in our globalised world extends beyond his contribution to an adequate theological framework to the way in which his economic and social ideas found embodiment in offices and institutions. Calvin's Christian vision for church and society was a deeply public vision that required practical concretisation.

Within the South African context, as elsewhere, such a public Christian vision of compassionate justice, and the concomitant need for the church, in the words of the Belhar Confession, to "stand where the Lord stands, namely against injustice and with the wronged" and "to witness against all the powerful and privileged who selfishly seek their own interests and control and harm others" is often hampered by a growing movement towards a more consumer-driven privatised spirituality. This form of spirituality is vulnerable to a type of pietistic escapism that robs Christians of the resources for engaging with a deep Reformed theological commitment with the burning social, economic and political questions of the day. Such an escapist spirituality is not to be equated with Calvinist piety. The challenge remains for Reformed churches in South Africa today to find a way between, on the one hand, a narrow confessionalism, and on the other hand, a sentimental, privatised and often anti-theological (if not anti-intellectual) spirituality. In taking on this challenge, Reformed Christian communities in South Africa may well discover that Calvin's life and theology offer unexpectedly rich and as yet untapped resources.

---

Freudenberg's essay on "Economic and Social Ethics in the Work of John Calvin" (153-172), as well as Dirkie Smit's essay "Theological Assessment and Ecclesiological Implications of the Accra Document 'Covenanting for Justice in the Economy and Earth' – Tentative Comments for Discussion (173-184).

# 14. ON THE DISPLACED CALVIN: 'REFUGEE REALITY' AS A LENS TO EXAMINE CALVIN'S LIFE, THEOLOGY AND LEGACY[1]

## 1. INTRODUCTION

In his award-winning book *The Reformation: A History* the Oxford historian Diarmaid MacCulloch comments: "If one would have been justified in anticipating a good night out in the company of Martin Luther, the same cannot be said for the buttoned-up French exile who wanted to stop the citizens of Geneva dancing".[2] The "buttoned-up French exile" refers, of course, to John Calvin, whose name is indeed often associated with moral austerity. However, one also needs to note that the personality and theology of Calvin are much more complex than many of the caricatures and one-sided characterisations of the 16th-century Reformer suggest.

This fact partly explains the reason for the conflicting depictions of Calvin. As Carter Lindberg observes:

> He has been portrayed as both a narrow dogmatist and an ecumenical churchperson; a ruthless inquisitor and a sensitive, caring pastor; an ascetic, cold authoritarian and a compassionate humanist; a rigorous individualist and a social thinker; a plodding systematizer and the theologians' theologian who finally completed the doctrine of the trinity; a man dominated by logic and a man of contradictory traits and inconsistencies; a theoretician of capitalism and socialism; the tyrant of Geneva and a defender of freedom; a dictator and a revolutionary.[3]

It is not surprising, then, that the historian William Bouwsma identifies two Calvins who co-exist uncomfortably within the same historical personage.[4] The one is Calvin the philosopher and rationalist, a man of fixed principles who viewed Christianity as tending toward static orthodoxy. This philosophical Calvin craved anxiously for intelligibility, order and certainty. The other one Bouwsma identifies is Calvin the rhetorician and humanist. This Calvin was not so much seeking order and intelligibility, but was more "inclined to celebrate the paradoxes and mystery at the heart of human existence".[5] However one judges Bouwsma's portrait of the two Calvins, it rightly affirms the need to respect more complex portrayals of Calvin and

---

1 This essay was presented as a paper at the annual conference of the The Theological Society of South Africa held in Grahamstown, 18-20 June 2008, and was originally published as "The Displaced Calvin: 'Refugee Reality' as a Lens to Re-examine Calvin's Life, Theology and Legacy" in *Religion & Theology* 16, 2009:35-52.
2 MacCulloch, D, *The Reformation: A History* (London: Penguin Books, 2003), 241.
3 Lindberg, C, *The European Reformations* (Oxford: Blackwell, 1996), 250.
4 See Bouwsma, W, *John Calvin: A Sixteenth Century Portrait* (Oxford: Oxford University Press, 1988), especially 230-234.
5 Bouwsma, *John Calvin*, 231. Throughout his biography Bouwsma uses the spatial metaphors of the 'abyss' and the 'labyrinth' as heuristic devices to understand Calvin. According to Bouwsma, the philosophical Calvin "was chiefly driven by a terror that took shape for him in the form of the abyss" (230), while the humanistic Calvin "dreaded what he often described as entrapment in a labyrinth" (231).

to resist easy depictions that either overly romanticise or demonise the Reformer of Geneva.

This essay does not want to evaluate the different and often conflicting portrayals of Calvin by theologians and historians, but it does want to call attention to an important aspect of the life of the 'buttoned-up French exile', namely that he was an exile, a refugee who experienced displacement and a longing for his native land. In addition, he ministered as refugee to other refugees in cities such as Strasbourg and Geneva. But even Geneva was not his home. In Hillerbrand's words, "he was a stranger there, and his heart lay in the mission to propagate the gospel in his native land".[6] Calvin's experiences as a refugee and with refugees are not ignored in the broader scholarly conversation on Calvin's life and work. However, his 'refugee reality', as this experience will be referred to in this essay, has not yet received, in comparison to other themes, the thorough treatment that it deserves. This essay draws on scholarship that highlights this aspect of Calvin's social location and its impact on his theology, thus arguing for a re-evaluation of 'the displaced Calvin' as source and motivation for Reformed witness today.

The reality of socio-political and economic migration, immigration and displacement, and the concomitant xenophobia, have become important markers of life at the beginning of the 21st century, also in South Africa. Since one's depiction of historical figures also says something about one's own self-understanding and social landscape, it is important to acknowledge that our own experiences play a significant role in colouring our perceptions of the past. Although one must acknowledge the continuity between us and the 16th-century Calvin, it is also important to respect the strangeness of the past, thus also affirming the discontinuity between Calvin and us, between Calvin's world and ours. In the light of this methodological comment, the first part of this paper will offer a few brief biographical details that will amplify the centrality of the 'refugee reality' in Calvin's life. The second part of the paper, which affirms the close link between his biography and theology, will trace the impact of this experiential reality on Calvin's theology. Given the broad scope of such an undertaking, the focus in this section will be mainly on how this refugee reality may serve as a lens to aid our understanding of Calvin's reading of Scripture, as well as his doctrine of predestination. The first part of the paper gives a description of Calvin as refugee and his ministry to refugee communities, and the second part highlights – in conversation with scholars such as Selderhuis and Oberman – some implications of this fact for his theological project. The brief conclusion then suggests that, given the increasing levels of migration, displacement and xenophobia, the celebration of the legacy of Calvin requires a graceful theology of hospitality.

---

6   Hillerbrand, H, *The Division of Christendom: Christianity in the Sixteenth Century* (Louisville: Westminster John Knox Press, 2007), 290.

## 2. CALVIN, THE EXILE: SOME BIOGRAPHICAL REMARKS

### a. The pastor as exile

In November 2004 a diverse group of scholars gathered for a consultation of the World Alliance of Reformed Churches, the John Knox International Reformed Centre and the Faculty of Theology of the University of Geneva, with the aim of rediscovering Calvin's legacy amidst the economic and social realities of our time. The statement that resulted from this consultation starts with a striking introduction:

The pastor, an exile and resident alien, reached out to offer the strong hand of fellowship to a flock of refugees. This group spoke a language he knew, others later would speak different ones, but all shared the condition of having been uprooted from home and everything familiar. The young man remembered that from his own experience. Thankful to have been received into this community, these new exiles asked for prayers for the friends they have left far away, and help for themselves, in the name of the one Lord Jesus Christ and His gospel. Sometimes refugees might be able to bring with the means to set up a new life, but not this group. Some of them were able and willing to work but needed jobs. Others brought little more than their faith and their shattered lives: a widow still stunned by the murder of her husband and anxious about providing for their three small children, a man who had been crippled by torture wondering if he could bear to be dependent even on these generous unknown neighbours.[7]

The pastor depicted in this scene is, of course, John Calvin. The members of the consultation in 2004 believed that the picture they drew of Calvin and his ministry in the introduction to their statement was not a misrepresentation, and that the rediscovery of this Calvin can contribute something valuable to the witness of Reformed people and churches today.

Although the picture of Calvin as exile who ministered to refugees is probably not the dominant image of Calvin today, this paper argues that this is indeed an aspect of Calvin's life and work that needs to be rediscovered, albeit with the necessary hermeneutical sensitivity. The refugee experience was a central part of Calvin's life. His ministry to a congregation of refugees in Strasbourg had a major impact on his understanding of the church and ministry. Moreover, one cannot evaluate Calvin's ministry in Geneva without taking into account the crucial role played by the influx of refugees into that city. The cities associated with the life of Calvin – Basel, Strasbourg and Geneva – were all important centres for Protestant refugees and this social landscape left an important imprint on Calvin's theology and, in fact, on Protestantism as a whole.

### b. The refugee seeking refuge

The somewhat prosaic introduction to the statement of the 2004 Geneva consultation quoted above also mentions that the young pastor could identify with the uprooted

---

[7] For the text of the statement, see "The Economic and Social Witness of Calvin for Christian Life Today: Statement of an International Consultation, Geneva, 3-6 November 2004", *Reformed World* 55/1 (March 2005): 3-7.

refugees because he remembered similar experiences. This brings to mind the fact that Calvin himself earlier had to flee from Paris after the so-called 'Cop affair'. On 1 November 1533 (All Saints' Day) Nicolas Cop, the new rector of the Sorbonne and friend of Calvin, gave the customary address at the beginning of the academic year. In this address, which focused on the text of the Beatitude "Blessed are the poor in spirit", the young medical doctor commented on Erasmus's *Paraclesis* and Luther's *Kirchenpostilles*.[8] Cop also identified the 'poor in spirit with the persecuted evangelicals. The address was not favourably received by the Faculty, which wanted to uphold Catholic orthodoxy and saw the speech as Lutheran propaganda. Although there is doubt about whether Calvin was actually involved in writing the speech, as used to be held, he was nevertheless implicated in some way in the controversy that erupted after Cop's speech. Cop fled to Basel and a price was put on his head. Since Calvin's room was also searched and his papers confiscated, he followed Cop's example and left Paris. As one biographer of Calvin notes: "For the following year he was on the move, in danger, whether actual or, no less disturbing, imaginary. He was a known 'Lutheran', able and vocal".[9]

At the beginning of 1534 Calvin found refuge in the home of his friend Louis du Tillet, the canon of Angoulême cathedral in the south of France.[10] Although Calvin could probably not have spent more than four of five months there, some scholars have argued that through Du Tillet's splendid library he acquired greater knowledge of the church fathers. The precise whereabouts of Calvin during 1534 are difficult to ascertain precisely, but Calvin's need to hide at different places in France was ended by the events that followed 'the affair of the *Placards*'. These placards were posted all over Paris and other major towns in France, and they proclaimed a vehement attack on the Mass. The government acted immediately and arrests were made. Some people were even executed, including a friend of Calvin, Étienne de la Forge. These events explain why Calvin, accompanied by Du Tillet, fled to Basel in Switzerland, the city won for the Reformation by Oecolampadius.[11] Basel was at that stage already known as a safe haven for people with evangelical sympathies.[12] Here Calvin, who adopted the pseudonym Martinus Lucianus, seemed to adapt well to circumstances during his enforced exile. It is during this period that Calvin wrote prefaces in Latin and French for Pierre Robert's French translation of the Bible, and he completed the first edition of his *Christianae Religionis Institutio*, published in March 1536, but probably completed in August 1535. Calvin would later rework this major text several times, finally resulting in the definitive enlarged 1559 edition. The famous accompanying letter to *The Institutes* that Calvin addressed as *apologia* to King Francis must be read against the socio-political and religious context that caused, among other things, Protestant exiles like Calvin to seek refuge outside of France.

---

8    For a thorough description of these events, see Ganoczy, A, *The Young Calvin* (Philadelphia: The Westminster Press, 1987), 80-83.
9    Parker, THL, *John Calvin: A Biography* (London: J M Dent & Sons, 1975), 30.
10   In later years Calvin would experience much pain because of Du Tillet's decision to return to the Roman church.
11   See Parker, *John Calvin*, 32. At that time Erasmus, Wolfgang Capito, Sebastian Münster, Heinrich Bullinger, Guillaume Farel and Pierre Robert also lived in Basel.
12   See McGrath, A, *A Life of John Calvin: A Study in the Shaping of Western Culture* (Oxford: Blackwell, 1990), 75.

After a year or so in Basel, Calvin and Du Tillet left for Italy, visiting the court of Renée of France, the duchess of Ferrara. "To her flocked Reformists and Reformers, the fugitives after the affair of the Placards", writes Parker.[13] Calvin also sought refuge, and probably employment as scholar, in Ferrara.[14] However, after a Frenchman ostentatiously refused to go to the Mass on Good Friday in 1536, some arrests were made. In the ensuing commotion Calvin left Italy and went back to Basel, and from there to France. Since after the Edict of Lyon 'heretics' could live in France on the condition that within six months they be reconciled with Rome, Calvin could stay for a while in France, but after a few months he set out for Strasbourg. Because of hazardous circumstances he took a detour through the city of Geneva, resulting in the famous meeting with Farel, who through dubious rhetorical means convinced Calvin to stay in Geneva.

## c. "That Frenchman"

It is interesting to note that Calvin's name is not even mentioned in the first official reference to him in Genevan records (5 September 1536). It reads: "Master Guillaume Farel points out the necessity of the lectures begun by *that Frenchman* at St Peter's and requests that he be retained and supported. He was told that such support would be taken under advisement" (my emphasis).[15] Much has been written about Calvin's first stay in Geneva, but for our purposes here suffice it to say that he had to leave the city in 1538 because of conflicts with inhabitants who did not share the way in which Calvin and Farel envisioned and enacted reform. The Reformation scholar, Heiko Oberman, to whose writings I will turn more extensively later in the essay, has commented that Calvin's first stay in Geneva was not merely cut short because of the haste with which he and Farel drove reform, but that it was also in part "due to the Genevans' reaction and opposition to him as stranger from the outside".[16] The reference to "that Frenchman" (*ille Gallus*) in the records in the minutes of the city council is thus quite revealing.[17]

## d. A refugee among refugees in Strasbourg

Between his first and second stays in Geneva Calvin spent three happy and significant years in Strasbourg. Strasbourg was not at that time part of France, but given its strategic location close to the eastern French border, this city was one of the chief cities of refuge for the persecuted in France. It is here that Calvin became the minister of a French refugee congregation, consisting of some four or five hundred members. Parker writes about Calvin's new social location: "A happy situation for him; a Frenchman among Frenchmen, a refugee among refugees, a poor man among

---

13  Parker, *John Calvin*, 51.
14  On Calvin's relationship with the Duchess of Ferrara, which continued through later correspondence, see Barton, FW, *Calvin and the Duchess* (Louisville: Westminster John Knox Press, 1989).
15  Quoted in Hillerbrand, *The Division of Christendom*, 300-301. Hillerbrand comments in this regard: "Hardly an exuberant expression of welcome – and support" (301).
16  Oberman, HA, *The Two Reformations* (New Haven: Yale University Press, 2003), 147
17  See also Lindberg, *The European Reformations*, 257.

generally poor men".[18] In many ways this congregation of French refugees served as model for the Reformed Churches in Geneva, France and elsewhere.[19] Apart from his pastoral duties, and marrying Idelette van Bure, while he was in Strasbourg Calvin wrote his commentary on Romans (1540) and a new edition of the *Institutio* (published in 1539 in Latin and in 1541 in French), as well as his small treatise on the Lord's Supper (1541). In Strasbourg he also wrote his famous response to Cardinal Sadoleto's call that the Genevans return to the Roman church. Calvin's stay in Strasbourg was also important for the development of his ecclesiology, particularly through his contact with Bucer. Here he discovered a vision of the church of Christ in the diaspora. Oberman comments: "Calvin discovered the ecumenical church at his conversion ... But in Strasbourg he discovered a new mark of the church (*nota ecclesiae*): the authentic church of Christ ... is persecuted and dispersed".[20]

### e. Calvin and Geneva: an ambivalent relationship

Partly as a result of his eloquent reply to Sadoleto, Calvin was invited back by the Genevans. Calvin returned to Geneva in September 1541 to stay there until his death in 1564. The name of Calvin has become inextricably linked to Geneva. McGrath rightly notes: "To speak of Calvin is to speak of Geneva. Calvin would shape, and be shaped by, Geneva".[21] But Calvin's relationship to Geneva is also ambivalent. Bernard Cottret observes: "In Geneva's insularity he found refuge and an asylum; from there he drew his energy, his inspiration, his reason for hope. He also directed against the native Genevans his coldest and most inextinguishable anger".[22] For many years Calvin would consider himself as a temporary guest in Geneva – only accepting citizenship as late as 1559. Jeannine Olson captures well the ambivalent relationship between the displaced Calvin and Geneva: "Powerful as his influence was there, he was always somewhat a sojourner in a foreign land. In this sense he was but one of the many refugees living in Geneva with their eyes on their homeland, hoping that someday all of France would be evangelized ... Awaiting that day, he and his friends provided for the continuing stream of Protestant refugees from Roman Catholic areas by offering them food and shelter in Geneva".[23]

---

18  Parker, *John Calvin*, 68. In his biography of Calvin Selderhuis gives his chapter on Calvin's stay in Strasbourg the telling heading "De vluchteling" ("The Refugee"). See Selderhuis, H J, *Calvijn een mens* (Kampen: Kok, 2008), 111 -141. Cf. also Van 't Spijker, W, *Calvin: Biographie und Theologie* (Göttingen: Vandenhoeck und Ruprecht, 2001), 142-155 and Matthieu Arnold's article "Straatsburg" in Selderhuis, HJ (ed.), *Calvijn Handboek* (Kampen: Kok, 2008), 59-65.

19  Parker recalls the following testimony of a French-speaking refugee from the Low Countries with regard to the church in Strasbourg: "Everyone sings, men and women, and it is a lovely sight. Each has a music book in his hand. For five or six days at the beginning as I looked on this little company of exiles, I wept, not for sadness but for joy to hear them all singing so heartily, and as they sang giving thanks to God that he had led them to a place where his name is glorified". Parker, *John Calvin*, 69.

20  Oberman, *The Two Reformations*, 148

21  McGrath, *A Life of John Calvin*, 79.

22  Cottret, B, *Calvin: A Biography* (Grand Rapids: Eerdmans, 2000), 157.

23  Olson, JE, *Calvin and Social Welfare: Deacons and the Bourse Française* (London: Associated University Presses, 1989), 11.

Numerous studies deal with the relationship between Calvin and Geneva, including some very thorough and meticulous studies that draw on the rich Genevan archival documents.[24] It is not our goal here to attend to the fascinating and complex relationship between Calvin and Geneva, but for the argument of this paper it is important to note that the refugee reality was very much part of the life in Geneva. As Cottret writes about this city: "It was in the true sense a city of refuge, to which flowed the unsatisfied, the insatiable, the lovers of Jesus Christ, desirous of building an ideal Christian society".[25] And Carter Lindberg concurs: "Geneva not only welcomed refugees, it created them. At the center of all the praise and blame that swirled through and around Geneva stood John Calvin, himself a displaced person from France".[26]

During Calvin's second stay in Geneva, dramatic changes in the city's demography occurred.[27] Lindberg notes that between 1550 and 1562 Geneva received approximately 7 000 immigrants. This is quite significant in the light of the fact that there were only 10 000 citizens in Geneva at the time of Calvin's arrival. Some of these refugees were highly educated and wealthy, including printers such as Robert Estienne, lawyers such as Germain Colladon, and businessmen such as Laurant de Normandie.[28] Calvin was aided by the continuous influx of religious refugees, since they generally supported him. The vast majority of these immigrants were from France, with some English and Italian immigrants as well, and for many of them Geneva was more than a safe haven: "To them Geneva was not just a shelter, it was as close to the city of God as earthly pilgrims could get".[29] Thus, the people to whom Calvin preached and lectured consisted increasingly of refugees. Calvin welcomed these religious refugees as brothers and sisters. Bouwsma calls attention to the fact that Calvin saw no duty as "more pleasing and acceptable to God" than the Scriptural obligation "to be kind and dutiful to fugitives and exiles, and especially to believers who are banished for their confession of the Word".[30] For Calvin such hospitality also implied the need for establishing institutions to deal with the plight of the refugees.[31]

---

24  See, for instance, Monter, EW, *Calvin's Geneva* (New York: John Wiley, 1967); Innes, WC, *Social Concerns in Calvin's Geneva* (Allison Park: Pickwick Publications, 1983); Naphy, WG, *Calvin and the Consolidation of the Genevan Reformation* (Louisville: Westminster John Knox Press, 1994); Naphy WG, "Calvin's Geneva" in McKim, DK, *The Cambridge Companion to John Calvin* (Cambridge: Cambridge: University Press, 2004), 25-37; and the work of Robert Kingdon and others on the consistory registers, cf. Kingdon, RM, Watt, IM, Lambert, T (eds), *Registers of the Consistory of Geneva at the Time of Calvin 1542-1544 Vol. 1* (Grand Rapids: Eerdmans, 2000).
25  Cottret, *Calvin*, 109.
26  Lindberg, *The European Reformations*, 249.
27  McGrath, drawing on Perrenaud's *La population de Genève*, notes that whereas Geneva had about 13 100 inhabitants in 1550, by 1560 the population has risen to 21 400, with the main reason for this increase being the arrival of a large number of Protestant refugees seeking safety. McGrath, *A Life of John Calvin*, 121.
28  For a discussion of the refugees' economic contribution, see also Biéler, A, *Calvin's Economic and Social Thought* (Geneva: WCC, 2005), 132-134.
29  Lindberg, *The European Reformations*, 265.
30  Quoted by Bouwsma, *John Calvin*, 25. See also Calvin's commentary on Isaiah 16.4.
31  The hospitality to refugees was, for instance, institutionalised into a welfare fund known as the *Bourse française* or 'the French fund for poor foreigners'. For an extensive

Without doubt, the increasing number of French refugees strengthened Calvin's pastorate in Geneva. In 1549, for instance, the *Compagnie des éstrangers* (the society of refugees) undertook to support a professional scribe whose whole work was to transcribe his sermons.[32] However, the startling increase in population was also "accompanied by a xenophobia that hardly spared Calvin, often the first target of anti-French campaigns".[33] Naphy also notes that "xenophobia and confessional solidarity grew as one".[34] Anti-French sentiments had already become evident earlier in the late 1540s, expressed in statements such as "Frenchmen ought to be thrown into the Rhone River".[35] Many Genevans increasingly feared that the immigrants would become permanent residents, thus upsetting the power structure of the city. These immigrants were also often blamed for the rise in the cost of living.[36] The tension that started in 1546 exploded in late 1554, with anti-French xenophobia leading to riots and attacks on refugees. Calvin became involved in this factional struggle.[37]

One should also note that that the refugees played no minor role in the decisive battle for power in Geneva in the 1550s, culminating in 1555 in Calvin's victory over his opponents, the so-called libertines, who included people such as Francois Favre, Philibert Berthelier and Ami Perrin. These frictions and conflicts centred on the Consistory's power of excommunication. Over against his opponents, Calvin insisted that the Consistory, the Genevan institution that exercised discipline, alone had the power to excommunicate unrepentant sinners – thus not the city council. This conflict was influenced by a decision of the council, made for economic reasons, to admit suitable (read wealthy) refugees to bourgeois status, thus entitling them to vote.[38] The Perrinists (as Calvin's opponents were also called) tried to block the voting rights, but to no avail. Thus the influx of (wealthy) refugees, who generally supported Calvin, played an important role in consolidating Calvin's power in Geneva. On the other hand, though, the immigrants who found refuge in Geneva should not be romanticised. Parker comments: "Mixed with the immigrants who

---

      discussion of the *Bourse française*, see Olson, *Calvin and Social Welfare*. The French fund became a fundamental institution next to the Consistory and the ministerial association of the Venerable Company of Pastors. It was administrated by deacons and pastors and financed independently of the city council.

32   See Parker, *John Calvin*, 91.
33   Cottret, *Calvin*, 160. Cottret adds: "However, the importance of these feelings of resentment must not be exaggerated; the graft of the Protestant refugees onto the ancient Genevan stock was a success" (160). Cottret also notes that the influx of the French and Italian refugees led to a spirit of enterprise that transformed Geneva economically, introducing clock making, weaving, and the silk industry. It also contributed to the adoption of French at the expense of the native Franco-Provençal (161).
34   Naphy in McKim, *The Cambridge Companion to John Calvin*, 32. Naphy also argues that the influx of refugees threatened the city's social fabric: "The refugees' skills and wealth upset Geneva's economy. Prices, rents, and property values increased. The arrival of noble refugees with their prejudices and societal expectations exacerbated the situation" (32).
35   This is a statement by Francois Mestrat in June 1547. For this and other remarks against the "accursed Frenchmen", which included Calvin, see Cottret, *Calvin*, 187-188.
36   See Bouwsma, *John Calvin*, 25, who refers to Monter, *Calvin's Geneva*, 82. The cost of living indeed increased in this period, which would be known as the great price rise.
37   See Naphy in McKim, *The Cambridge Companion to John Calvin*, 33-34.
38   McGrath, *A Life of John Calvin*, 122.

had genuinely fled from persecution, there were also some strange characters and, we may conjecture, not a few French secret agents".[39]

These few brief historical remarks testify to the important imprint that the refugee reality made on the social landscape of cities like Strasbourg and Geneva, as well as on the life and ministry of Calvin. The refugee reality also impacted heavily on the spread of Calvinism. As McGrath writes: "The phenomenon of the refugee and the place of refuge played no small part in the propagation of Calvinism ... During their period of exile, such refugees often absorbed Calvin's outlook, and upon their return to the native lands, proceeded to propagate Calvinism".[40] Not only was Geneva a place of asylum for refugees, but Calvin also maintained an interest in the confession and organisation of the refugee congregations that were started elsewhere. These congregations were often the sites of conflicts and rivalry, also externally with Lutheran congregations. Calvin had a strong interest in these churches and their controversies, as his letters testify.[41]

## 3. THE REFUGEE REALITY AND CALVIN'S THEOLOGY

It is the argument of this essay that Calvin's refugee experience does not merely help us to gain valuable historical or psychological insight into Calvin's life, and to build up sociological knowledge of life in 16th-century Strasbourg or Geneva, but also that it serves as an important lens in understanding Calvin's theology. This is not to say that this is the only lens for interpreting Calvin's theological ideas. This essay makes the more modest claim that the necessary sensitivity to the impact of the refugee reality on Calvin's theology can contribute towards a more responsible – and exciting – interpretation of Calvin the theologian. It may contribute to a rediscovery of certain neglected themes in his theology, such as exile and hospitality, as well as a re-evaluation of well-worn doctrines, such as election and providence. In addition, this paper wants to affirm that Calvin's refugee experience did not only impact on his theology, but that his reading of Scripture and his theological insights also influenced his response to his own exile, as well as his response to the refugees he ministered to. This dialectical relationship between theology and life, or Scripture and ethics, must be maintained.

In order to illustrate something of the impact of Calvin's refugee experience on his theology, this section of the essay will limit itself to two aspects of Calvin's work, namely his reading of Scripture, and specifically his Commentary on the Psalms, and secondly, his doctrine of predestination.

---

39   Parker, *John Calvin*, 142. One of these agents, Jacques Spifame, lived next door to Calvin from 1559. He was beheaded in 1566. Many of the immigrants also did not agree with Calvin on doctrinal issues. In this regard one can recall the famous conflict between Calvin and Bolsec on the doctrine of predestination, and of course the much-discussed case against Servetus.
40   McGrath, *A Life of Calvin*, 198.
41   For a discussion of Calvin's correspondence with the refugee congregations, see Nijenhuis, W, *Calvinus Oecumenicus: Calvijn en de eenheid der kerk in het light van zijn briefwisseling* ('S Gravenhage: Martinus Nijhoff, 1959), 77-91.

## a. The motif of exile in Calvin's Commentary on the Psalms

In his inaugural lecture as professor at the *Theologische Universiteit van de Christelijke Gereformeerde Kerken* in Apeldoorn in 1997, the Dutch theologian HJ Selderhuis offered a very interesting reading of Calvin's 1557 Commentary on the Psalms. This lecture, which has been published under the title *Calvijn als asielzoeker*[42] (*Calvin as Asylum Seeker*), views Calvin's Commentary on the Psalms as a distillation of his theology and as a source for his biography. After placing the Commentary on the Psalms in its historical context,[43] Selderhuis argues convincingly that Calvin recognised himself in the figure of David, without idealising him, and that he also identified the situation in which the church of Geneva found itself with the situation of Israel. Thus in an indirect way Calvin's Commentary on the Psalms gives us much biographical information about Calvin, who was not eager to speak about himself. What is especially important for the concerns of this essay is that Selderhuis identifies an important motive in the way Calvin draws the parallel between David and himself, and the Genevan congregation and Israel, namely the exile motif ("het ballingschap-motief").[44] In Calvin's description of David he mirrors his own experiences of exile, loss and displacement.

Selderhuis also refers to the fact that Calvin the asylum seeker became a minister to other asylum seekers.[45] It is therefore not a surprise that the notion of 'asylum' is often found in Calvin's Commentary on the Psalms. Selderhuis calls attention to the fact that 'asylum' is used nine times by Calvin in the commentary on the first 50 psalms and that this term clearly has a juridical meaning for him. Selderhuis also argues that Calvin not only saw a parallel between David and himself, but also between David and the other Reformed refugees who were unjustly displaced. In similar vein, Calvin saw himself as connected in his own exile with his exiled brothers and sisters.[46]

According to Selderhuis, the exile motif is seen in the way that the situation of Calvin and his congregation serves as an image of the situation of the church and the believer on earth. Selderhuis summarises this point from Calvin's commentary on the Psalms: "We are asylum seekers, that is to say, we are outside of our Fatherland. We live and work here, but this is not our home: we live here temporarily in anticipation of our

---

42   Selderhuis, HJ, *Calvijn als asielzoeker* (Apeldoorn: Theologische Universiteit, 1997). For Selderhuis's more extensive treatment of Calvin's engagement with the Psalms, see Selderhuis, HJ, *Calvin's Theology of the Psalms* (Grand Rapids: Baker Academic, 2007), as well as his essay "Calvin's view of the Bible as the word" in *Reformed World* 57/4 (Dec 2007): 270-285.

43   Calvin published his Commentary on the Psalms in 1557, in the last phase of his life. Selderhuis notes that Calvin started to lecture on the Psalms in 1552 and commenced writing his commentary in 1553. However, he had preached on the Psalms every Sunday afternoon since 1549 already. The influx of refugees during this period meant that the people to whom Calvin preached and lectured consisted increasingly of refugees. In addition, Calvin also kept in his thoughts the plight of the persecuted believers in his native France. See Selderhuis, *Calvijn als azielsoeker*, 10.

44   Selderhuis, *Calvijn als asielzoeker*, 19.

45   Selderhuis, *Calvijn als asielzoeker*, 20.

46   Selderhuis writes in *Calvijn als asielzoeker*, 21: "de azielzoeker op de kansel en op katheder is één met die asielzoekers in de kerk en in de collegebanken".

return home".⁴⁷ The exile motif furthermore reaches past biography to theology: "We are not only physically but also spiritually dispersed and disturbed; through our sins we are outside of paradise in the desert and out of this situation we can seek asylum from God, through God's grace".⁴⁸ For Calvin, those who have found asylum from God carry their cross in this world, leading to new forms of exile. Thus for Calvin, those who have found asylum at once become asylum seekers again, since they must carry their cross, resulting in new forms of exile. Moreover, they can continuously seek asylum through the compassion and care of God.⁴⁹

Selderhuis's discussion of the exile motif in Calvin's Commentary on the Psalms is important, because it affirms the impact of Calvin's refugee experience on his reading of Scripture, as well as the way that Calvin's reading of Scripture influenced his theological assessment of his context. Scott Hendrix also sees a link between Calvin's refugee experience and his reading of Scripture: "Calvin's agenda had personal roots in his own refugee experience that caused him to read the biblical story in a different way and 'to discover God as the first refugee, trekking with the people of Israel through the desert'".⁵⁰ Although one certainly has to be careful not to overburden this motive of exile, or the 'refugee reality', as an interpretative lens to gain an insight into Calvin's life and theology, it nonetheless challenges certain reductions of Calvin's theology and holds promise for a new exploration of Calvin's legacy.

### b. The 'Reformation of the refugees' and Calvin's doctrine of predestination

Calvin's refugee experience also holds promise for revisiting his controversial doctrine of predestination, a doctrine often viewed as an abstract speculative system. However, the highly respected Reformation scholar Heiko Oberman has argued persuasively that in Calvin's case the puzzling doctrine of predestination was born out of his experience of exile.

> The Calvinist doctrine of predestination is the mighty bulwark of the Christian faithful against the fear that they will be unable to hold out against the pressure of persecution. Election is the Gospel's encouragement to those who have faith, not a message of doom for those who lack it. In particular, it responds to the anguish that Calvin already had felt in the early wave of persecution … Rather than providing grounds for arrogance, predestination offers all true Christians the hope that even under extreme distress they will persevere until the end.⁵¹

---

47   Selderhuis, *Calvijn als asielzoeker*, 27-28, with reference to a footnote in Calvin's commentary on the introduction to Ps 37 ("… *peregrinantur in mundo* …").
48   Selderhuis, *Calvijn als asielzoeker*, 28, with reference to a footnote in Calvin's commentary on Psalm 32:1 ("…*ad gratiae asylum confugere*…").
49   See Selderhuis, *Calvijn as asielzoeker*, 28, with reference to a footnote in Calvin's commentary of Psalm 25:11 ("… *ad misericordiae Dei asylum confugere*…").
50   Hendrix, SH, *Recultivating the Vineyard: The Reformation Agendas of Christianization* (Louisville: Westminster John Knox Press, 2004), 88. Hendrix refers here to the work of Heiko Oberman. See Oberman, H, "*Initia Calvini*: The Matrix of Calvin's Reformation" in Neuser, WH (ed.), *Calvinus Sacrae Scripturae Professor* (Grand Rapids: Eerdmans, 1994), 151.
51   Oberman, *The Two Reformations*, 114-115.

It is only later, argues Oberman, when the refugees became settlers and citizens, that the scriptural insights fostered by this experience were developed into a systematic theology that "lost touch with its initial purpose and hardened its doctrinal crust".[52]

According to Oberman, Calvin's apparently abstract doctrine of predestination – or more accurately, election – must therefore be understood as "a matter of existential faith for the exiles who, far from home, in a language arising from their experience of banishment, 'traveled through the wilderness'".[53] Oberman also sees Calvin's fundamental experience of exile as the experience within which and from which he reads Scripture, quoting in this regard from Calvin's commentary on Jeremiah 22: 28: "And we know that it is a hard lot when one is driven far away from his own country".[54]

In order to do justice to Oberman's emphasis on the importance of the experience of exile and banishment as a lens into Calvin's theology, in particular his doctrine of predestination, it is necessary to attend more closely to his influential historical demarcation of the three different epochs of the Reformation.[55] The first epoch of the Reformation is the reformation of Luther, which had its base in the monastery but also reached out to the territory and the kingdom. The second Reformation was the Reformation of the cities, and cities like Strasbourg, Zurich, Nuremberg and others became the laboratories for applying the ideas of reform. The third Reformation, which Oberman describes as "the Reformation of the refugees", began after the defeat of the Protestant princes in 1548 and 1549, when the cities were recatholicised and many Protestant citizens either adapted to the circumstances or fled. The expulsion of numerous Protestants through the city gates created a metamorphosis of Protestant self-understanding. Many ideas arose during this period that would be misunderstood and misconstrued once Calvinism again gained a firm footing in places such as the Netherlands, the Palatinate, Scotland and the United States (and we may add, South Africa). These misinterpretations or reductions stem from the fact that Calvin's ideas became disembedded from the historical and experiential context that gave them their intelligibility.

Oberman sees Calvin as a transitional figure between the second and the third Reformation. Calvin was indeed the city Reformer in Geneva, but although he was very much involved in the local context of Geneva, he also envisioned the expansion

---

52 Oberman, *The Two Reformations*, 115.
53 Oberman, *The Two Reformations*, 118.
54 Oberman, *The Two Reformations*, 119. Oberman continues on the same page with the following prayer from Calvin's commentary on Jeremiah 20:47: "Since You promised us rest nowhere but in your heavenly kingdom, so grant, almighty God, that on our earthly pilgrimage we may consent not have an abiding city but to be driven here and there, and despite all that still call upon You with a quiet spirit. Permit us to carry on our wayfare, which you have designed to train and to test us, that we might be firm and steadfast in this warfare until at last we arrive at that rest which has been obtained for us by the blood of Your only-begotten Son. Amen". For the discussion on Oberman that follows I will mainly draw on the chapter "Calvin's Legacy: Its Greatness and Limitations" in his posthumously published *The Two Reformations*. This chapter is a translation of an earlier lecture, published as Oberman, HA, *De erfenis van Calvijn: Grootheid en grenzen* (Kampen: Kok, 1988).
55 See also in this regard his chapter "One Epoch – Three Reformations" in Oberman, HA, *The Reformation: Roots and Ramifications* (Edinburgh: T & T Clark, 1994), 201-220.

of the Reformation through the whole of Europe. For Oberman this explains the fact that Calvin liked to conclude his sermons with the brief prayer: "May this grace be bestowed on all the peoples of the earth".[56]

It is within this historical epoch of 'the Reformation of the refugees' (or third Reformation) that Oberman places the development of the dogma of election and predestination. Oberman emphasises that this new political and social context of the third Reformation produced new theological accents and insights, because the experience of diaspora led people to view the Gospel with new eyes. During the later, national phase of Calvinism, many of these insights disappeared or were adjusted. However, within the context of 'the Reformation of the Refugees' the doctrine of election had great pastoral power. As Oberman writes: "For those who had no permanent place of residence, not even a fixed stone on which to lay their heads, neither valid passport nor a residence permit, predestination became their identity card".[57] In this context the doctrine of election, which Calvin called the *providentia specialissima*, was experienced in a special way as a confirmation of God's guidance and protection amidst the challenges of life in dispersion. The doctrine provided comfort and assurance. Oberman argues: "The church in-flight discovered the comfort of providence and election. This is evident in Calvin's heartfelt cry, 'We have no other place of refuge than his providence'".[58] And furthermore: "The doctrine of election becomes not merely a limitation but an abomination when it is uprooted and displaced in its turn, torn from its biblical context in the pilgrimage of the church on its journey from the burning bush to the final feast around the throne of the Lamb".[59]

## 4. CELEBRATING THE LEGACY OF THE DISPLACED CALVIN

In anticipation of the 500th anniversary of Calvin's birth in 2009, a group of scholars met in Geneva in April 2007 to reflect on the question "Who was John Calvin and what is his legacy in the light of the critical issues facing the Reformed churches and the world today?" The report which followed the consultation challenges some of the stereotypes associated with Calvin, arguing also that one should not draw an

---

56    Oberman, *The Two Reformations*, 148.
57    Oberman, *The Two Reformations*, 157.
58    Oberman, *The Two Reformations*, 149. Naphy (in McKim, *The Cambridge Companion to John Calvin*, 33) offers a similar argument: "To Protestants being persecuted for their faith, these doctrines were of great comfort. Calvin, ever-conscious of the plight of his fellow French Protestants, knew the power of this doctrine. It insured that sufferings, persecutions, exile, deprivation, and even death were not meaningless but, ultimately, were part of God's plan for believers".
59    Oberman, *The Two Reformations*, 150. With a play on Luther's famous words shortly before his death "Wir sind Bettler, Hoc est verum", Oberman concludes his fascinating discussion on Calvin's legacy with the words: "We are beggars. Nous sommes de gueux. Hoc est verum. We are destitute. And that is the truth" (168). It is also interesting to note that in an *In Memoriam* column of the *American Historical Association* (February 2002) for Oberman, who had died on 22 April 2001, the authors (Susan Karant-Nunn and Richard Cosgrove) mention that Oberman's earliest childhood memories were of the Jewish refugees who passed through the Oberman house as part of a covert network to find a safe haven for them. This tempts us, once again, to speculate on the enigmatic (and dialectical) relationship between biography and theology.

idealised picture of Calvin.[60] In addition, the report identifies eight areas that are viewed as of particular interest today, and that may provide fresh access to Calvin's legacy.[61] One of the areas identified in the report relates to Calvin's insistence on God's gift of creation. This section refers to God's will for creation's flourishing and adds that this vision includes "a compassionate commitment to love, justice, responsible care and hospitality towards widows, orphans, and strangers".[62]

In the light of the opportunity to reflect anew on the legacy of (the displaced) Calvin, our historical and theological engagement with his witness will also be influenced by our social location. Amidst a world of growing migration, displacement and xenophobia, we may well discover that Calvin's life and theology, with all its limitations, may provide surprising insights that can aid in the reclaiming of a graceful theology of hospitality. Such an endeavour will be strengthened by the recognition of Calvin's own refugee experiences and the way it serves as lens to reveal his theological ideas. Calvin's engagement with reality was steeped in his reading of Scripture, and the Bible's emphasis on the need to show hospitality to 'the widows, orphans, and strangers' found many echoes in his sermons, letters, commentaries, *The Institutes* and other theological tracts. In this sense Calvin's life and theology may have continuing significance to sustain a theology of hospitality towards contemporary 'widows, orphans, and strangers', or in the interpretative language of the report of the 2007 Genevan consultation, "those who are defenseless, displaced, hungry, lonely, silenced, betrayed, powerless, sick, broken in body and spirit, and all those who suffer in our globalising and polarising world".[63]

---

60  For the report, see "What is the significance of Calvin's legacy?" in *Reformed World* 57/4 (Dec 2007): 231-236. The report states: "Calvin was not a saint ... his response to conflicts was often harsh and his role in the execution of Servetus was, indeed, more than dubious" (232).

61  The eight areas the report emphasised are: Calvin's commitment to proclaiming the glory of God; Calvin's determination to place Jesus Christ at the forefront of all our thinking and living; Calvin's emphasis on the Holy Spirit in creation and salvation; Calvin's engagement with Scripture; Calvin's determination that God's will be brought to bear on all areas of life; Calvin's insistence on God's gift of creation; Calvin's realisation that the church is called to discern, in ongoing ways, its relation to the principalities and powers of the world; and Calvin's commitment to the unity of the church.

62  "What is the significance of Calvin's legacy?", 234.

63  "What is the significance of Calvin's legacy?", 234.

# 15. ON CALVIN AND THE MIRROR OF THE STRANGER: 'REFUGEE REALITY' AND THE GIFT OF RECOGNITION[1]

## 1. INTRODUCTION

The reference in the title of this essay to 'the mirror of the stranger' is taken from a remark by the 16th-century Reformer and exiled refugee John Calvin: "We cannot but behold our own face as it were in a glass in the person that is poor and despised ... though he were the furthest stranger in the world. Let a Moor or a Barbarian come among us, and yet inasmuch as he is a man, he brings with him a looking glass wherein we may see that he is our brother and our neighbour".[2]

This comment by Calvin, taken from his sermon on Galatians 6:9-11, is often quoted in studies related to hospitality and recognition. In her book *Making Room: Recovering Hospitality in the Christian Tradition* Christine Pohl, for instance, refers to this quotation, arguing in the process that since for Calvin every person bears God's image, our common humanity provides a basis for recognition and respect. Furthermore, for Calvin the fundamental dignity of the other person is not undermined by wrongdoing or neediness.[3]

Given the reference to the "poor and despised" in Calvin's remark in his sermon on Galatians 6:9-11, it is also not surprising that this quotation features in several studies by scholars from the Reformed tradition as they grapple with issues related to social justice and economic inequality. In a chapter on "The Rich and the Poor" in his book *Until Justice and Peace Embrace* the Reformed philosopher Nicholas Wolterstorff, for instance, argues with reference to this quotation that fundamental to Calvin's reflections on poverty was his conviction that every human being is created in the

---

1   This essay was read as a paper at an international conference on migration and aggression in Europe, held in February 2016 in Emden, Germany. It was originally published as "The Mirror of the Stranger: On Calvin, 'the Refugee Reality' and the Gift of Recogntion" in Detmers, A and Dreßler, S (eds), *Fremde(s) Aushalten: Migration und Aggression in Europa* (Solingen: Foedus Verlag, 2016), 39-52.
2   Calvin, J, *Sermons on Galatians* (Albany, OR: AGES Software), 588. Calvin's sermons on Galatians were first translated into English by Arthur Golding in the year 1574. For a more recent translation, see *John Calvin's Sermons on Galatians*, Childress, K (trans.) (Edinburgh: Banner of Truth, 1997): "For whilst we are human beings, we must see our own face reflected, as by a mirror, in the faces of the poor and the despised, who can go no further and are trembling under their burdens, even if they are people who are most alien to us. If a Moor or a Barbarian comes to us, because he is a man, he is a mirror in which we see reflected the fact that he is our brother and our neighbour" (626).
3   Pohl, CD, *Making Room: Recovering Hospitality in the Christian Tradition* (Grand Rapids: Eerdmans, 1999), 65. For Calvin's remark, Pohl quotes from Leith, JH, *John Calvin's Doctrine of the Christian Life* (Louisville: Westminster/John Knox Press, 1989), 186. Within the broader discourse on hospitality, Calvin's remark in his sermon on Galatians 6:9-11 is also quoted, with reference to Pohl, in Smith, DI and Carvill, B, *The Gift of the Stranger: Faith, Hospitality, and Foreign Language Learning* (Grand Rapids: Eerdmans, 2000), 85.

image of God and that the commandment to love one another is grounded in this recognition of our common humanity.[4]

In the quotation taken from Calvin's sermon on Galatians 6:9-11 referred to at the beginning of this essay we find reference to the image or metaphor of a mirror. Calvin states that we see our own face as in a mirror (*comme en un miroir*) in the person who is poor and despised, even if this person is the furthest stranger in the world. If a stranger comes into your midst, the stranger brings something with him or her, namely a looking glass or mirror, in which we can see or contemplate the fact that this stranger is our brother or sister, and a neighbour. The image of the mirror is, of course, a well-known metaphor in Calvin's thought, often utilised in his writings and sermons, and much has been written in this regard. In this essay I want to comment in a bit more detail on Calvin's sermon on Galatians 6:9-11, also against the broader background of his use of the mirror metaphor. In the final part of the essay I bring some of Calvin's remarks drawn from his sermons on Galatians, as well as from some of his other writings, into conversation with some pertinent emphases on the notion of recognition drawn from, among others, the work of the French philosopher Paul Ricoeur and the South African psychologist Pumla Gobodo-Madikizela.

Calvin preached his 43 sermons on Galatians between 14 November 1557 and 8 May 1558.[5] These sermons were taken down in shorthand by Denis Reaguenier, a professional scribe who was hired by the French emigrants in Geneva. The transcribed sermons were published and sold, and the income earned from this was donated to the fund that provided relief for the poor French-speaking refugees.

Calvin was, of course, himself a refugee and a significant part of his ministry was devoted to exiled refugees. In the previous chapter I discussed briefly some biographical details that amplify the centrality of what I refer to as 'the refugee reality' in Calvin's life, also arguing, in conversation with the work of Herman Selderhuis and Heiko Oberman, that sensitivity to Calvin as displaced refugee can serve as a lens to aid our understanding of his way of engaging with Scripture, as well as doctrines such as election and providence.[6] I wrote this last mentioned essay during an outbreak of xenophobic violence in South Africa in May 2008 and this fact left its mark on the article. It is most probably true that the current challenges and crises created by migration and xenophobia will impact on our engagement with historical

---

4    Wolterstorff, N, *Until Justice and Peace Embrace* (Grand Rapids: Eerdmans, 1983), 78. Cf. also Wolterstorff's essay "The Wounds of God: Calvin's Theology of Social Injustice" in Wolterstorff, N, *Hearing the Call: Liturgy, Justice, Church, and World* (Grand Rapids: Eerdmans, 20011), 122-144. This article was first published under the same title in *The Reformed Journal* 37:6 (June 1987): 14-22. Wolterstorff draws in his discussion on Ronald Wallace's study *Calvin's Doctrine on the Christian life*, in which Wallace comments, in the light of Calvin's remark: "This recognition that we possess a common humanity, which has its basis in the recognition of the image of God in all men, itself forms the basis of the command in the Law, and in the teaching of Jesus, 'to love our neighbour as ourselves.' In this world, all men, whoever they may be, are neighbours". See Wallace, RS, *Calvin's Doctrine of the Christian Life* (Tyler: Geneva Divinity School Press, 1959/ 1982), 150.
5    Calvin's study of Paul's letter to the Galatians began in 1546, with his commentary on Galatians being published in 1548. In November 1557 he returned to Galatians as part of his preaching ministry. See Calvin, *Sermons on Galatians*, 8-9.
6    See the previous chapter.

texts, figures and contexts, such as Calvin's writings and life in 16th-century Europe. This fact might lead to hasty comparisons and half-baked conclusions. Hence the need remains for a responsible historical hermeneutic in dealing today with the Reformed legacy. Yet it is also true that the current global crisis associated with refugees and migrants can sharpen our sensibilities, enabling us to engage in new ways with the various sources within our respective traditions as we search for responsible speech and embodiment regarding hospitality, discernment and recognition.

## 2. AS IN A MIRROR ...

Before turning in more detail to Calvin's sermon on Galatians 6: 9-11 (and the reference to the mirror metaphor in this sermon), it is important to note that Calvin uses the mirror metaphor extensively as a linguistic, rhetorical and theological device throughout his writings. Gerrit Neven, for instance, observes that the metaphor of the mirror is found four times in the 1536 *Institutes* and 13 times in the 1541 edition.[7] And according to Eric Kayayan, it occurs 32 times in the French text of the final edition of the *Institutes*.[8] Even a quick glance at these references reveals that the mirror metaphor often functions as an epistemological notion, relating the image of the mirror to the act of knowing, as well as to the nature of our knowledge of God and the self. It is therefore not surprising that scholars have often commented on this feature. Cornelius van der Kooi has, for instance, indicated in his study *Als in een Spiegel: God kennen volgens Calvijn en Barth* that the metaphor of the mirror in Calvin's thought points to a plurality of concrete ways in which knowledge of God arises and is sustained. As such, it functions as a locus where God reveals His will towards humanity.[9]

The metaphor of the mirror is often linked with the Calvinian idea of accommodation.[10] Given the limitations of our human capacities, we cannot understand God. There are limits to our knowledge. We indeed see "through a glass darkly" (1 Corinthians 13: 9, 12). Yet for Calvin we can gain indirect knowledge through fleeting glimpses of the Divine in a way similar to the way in which we register the images we see when

---

7   Neven, GW, "De Kwintessens van Calvijn" in Brouwer, RR, De Leede, B, and Spronk, K (eds), *Het Calvinistisch ongemak: Calvijn als erflater en provocator van het Nederlandse Protestantisme* (Kampen: Kok, 2009), 73-97, here 80.
8   Kayayan, E, "The mirror metaphor in Calvin's Institutes: A central epistemological notion?", *In die Skriflig* 30:4 (1996): 419-441, here 419. Kayayan's argument is that "as a linguistic and rhetorical device, the metaphor of the mirror fulfils the function of key towards knowledge, and is used as a prominent epistemological vehicle" (421). On the perceptual character of faith in Calvin's thinking, see Pitkin, B, *What Pure Eyes Could See: Calvin's Doctrine of Faith in Its Exegetical Context* (Oxford: Oxford University Press, 1999).
9   Van der Kooi, C, *Als in een Spiegel – God kennen volgens Calvijn en Barth: Een tweeluik* (Kampen: Kok, 2002), 22-23. For Van der Kooi's more extended discussion on the use of the metaphor of the mirror in Calvin's thought, see especially pages 58-64.
10  Much has been written on the *accommodatio Dei* in Calvin's work; see, for instance, Battles, FL, "God was accommodating Himself to human capacity", *Interpretation* 31 (1977): 19-38; Balserak, J, *Divinity Compromised: A Study of Divine Accommodation in the Thought of John Calvin* (Dordrecht: Springer, 2006) and "Accommodatio Dei" in Selderhuis, H (ed.), *The Calvin Handbook* (Grand Rapids: Eerdmans, 2009), 372-378; and Huijgen, A, *Familiar Knowledge: Divine Accommodation in John Calvin's Theology* (Göttingen: Vandenhoeck & Ruprecht, 2009).

looking into a mirror. In these mirrors the gracious God accommodates himself to our limited capacities.[11]

What are these mirrors? For Calvin the whole of creation is seen as a mirror in which we can behold the glory of God. As he observes in the 1559 *Institutes*: "You cannot in one glance survey this most vast and beautiful system of the universe, in its wide expanse, without being completely overwhelmed by its brightness … this skilful ordering of the universe is for us a sort of mirror in which we can contemplate God, who is otherwise invisible".[12] Scripture too is seen as a mirror: "In short, let us remember that that invisible God, whose wisdom, power, and righteousness are incomprehensible, set before us Moses' history as a mirror in which his living likeness glows".[13] And with regard to the law, Calvin writes: "The law is like a mirror. In it we contemplate our weakness, then the iniquity arising from this, and finally the curse coming from both – just as a mirror shows us the spots on our face".[14]

The mirror metaphor is also used with regard to the person and work of Christ. In his discussion of election, for instance, Calvin remarks: "Christ, then, is the mirror wherein we must, and without self-deception may, contemplate our own election".[15] And with regard to the risen Christ, Calvin writes: "in this mirror the living image of the resurrection is visible to us, so it is a firm foundation to support our minds".[16] In addition, Calvin also says with regard to the sacraments that we "might call them mirrors in which we may contemplate the richness of God's grace, which he lavishes upon us".[17]

Even these selected and cursory references to Calvin's use of the mirror metaphor underscores that it functions as an important (epistemological) notion in his thinking. As Keesecker puts it in a devotional article: "John Calvin looked into the mirror of creation, the Word, and the Word made flesh and beheld the splendour of the invisible God".[18] But what about our fellow human beings, including strangers and even our enemies? Do they also serve as mirrors in which we can see the splendour of the invisible God? With this question in mind we turn in more detail to Calvin's sermon on Galatians 6:9-11.

### 3. CALVIN'S SERMON ON GALATIANS 6:9-11

In his 41st sermon on Galatians, and his fourth on Galatians 6, Calvin provides an exposition of Galatians 6:9-11. The text from Galatians reads: "Let us not be weary of well doing: for in convenient season we shall reap without weariness. Therefore while we have time let us do good to all men, but chiefly to them that are of the

---

11 Cf. Keesecker, WF, "John Calvin's Mirror", *Theology Today* 17/3 (October 1960): 288-289, here 288.
12 John Calvin, *Institutes of the Christian Religion, Volume One*, McNeill, JT (ed.), Battles, FL (trans.) (Louisville: Westminster John Knox Press, 1960), 1.5.1, 52-53.
13 Calvin, *Institutes* 1.14.1, 160.
14 Calvin, *Institutes* 2.7.7, 305.
15 Calvin, *Institutes*, 3.24.5, 970.
16 Calvin, *Institutes*, 3.25.3, 991.
17 Calvin, *Institutes*, 4.14.6, 1281.
18 Keesecker, "John Calvin's Mirror", 289.

household of faith. You see how large a letter I have written to you with mine own hand".

Calvin already engaged with this text in his Commentary on Galatians (1547-1550), but the sermon is more than four times the length of the commentary.[19] In the first part of the sermon Calvin underscores Paul's exhortation that we should do good and thus apply God's gifts in the service of all men. Calvin refers in this regard to our natural inclination to seek our own profit, but views this as the way for all to perish.[20] But, Calvin continues, if we discharge ourselves of earthly care and look up to the Kingdom of God, even if it may seem that we shall be made poor and diminished in the process, our treasure shall not perish because it is kept in God's hand. Therefore we should not become weary of doing good. Calvin seems thoroughly conscious of the temptations and reasoning that holds us back from doing good to all people, and recognises that there will always be excuses to evade well-doing.[21] Yet amidst these temptations and excuses we should not grow weary of doing good, "rather having an eye unto GOD, than to the unworthiness of the persons that are to be succored".[22]

Calvin continues his sermon by commenting on Galatians 6 verse 10: "Therefore while we have time and leisure let us do good to all men, but chiefly to them that are of the household of faith". What struck me in reading Calvin's sermon is the fact that Calvin spends most of his time in the sermon on reiterating and emphasising the point of doing good to all people, rather than on emphasising the phrase "especially the household of faith". The latter phrase is not used rhetorically to argue for any parochial concerns. Calvin seems mainly concerned here about the way we look at our fellow human beings, encouraging his hearers in the process to recognise the image of God in all human beings and our concomitant common humanity:

> For we must not look what every man is, nor what he deserveth: but we must mount up higher and consider that God hath set us in this world to the end we should be united and knit together: and that forasmuch he hath imprinted his image in us, and we have all one common nature: the same ought to move us to succor one another.[23]

---

19  Calvin, *Sermons on Galatians*, 9.
20  Calvin, *Sermons on Galatians*, 586. "We are of the opinion that all is lost, if every man seek not his own profit, and be given wholly to himself. But it is clean contrary ... Contrariwise there is a way for all to perish, namely if we be too gripple with the riches of this world, so as we have no care nor regard but of our own profit: we shall gather corruption, that is to say, all shall perish" (581).
21  Calvin observes in this regard: "Hereupon also we are tempted to seek excuses. For we will allege [on the one side] that we cannot tell whither the party that complaineth have such need as he speaketh of, or whither he be so greatly to be pitied: and on the other side that the world is so wicked and ungratious, that a man cannot tell to whom to do good, and that oftentimes the good turn is lost, and there is such unthankfulness, that it is better to let those complainants to endure hunger and thirst, than to give them occasion to offend God". Calvin, *Sermons on Galatians*, 582-583.
22  Calvin, *Sermons on Galatians*, 583.
23  Calvin, *Sermons on Galatians*, 588.

Calvin goes on to argue that if we shy away from doing good to all, not offering relief to any, we should reconsider our identity (or 'shape' or 'figure'), since we don't act as if belonging to humankind. Hence the statement already quoted in this essay:

> (F)or so long as we be of mankind, we cannot but behold our own face as it were in a glass in the person that is poor and despised, who is not able to hold out any longer, but lieth groaning under his burden, yea though he were the furthest stranger in the world. Let a Moor or a Barbarian come among us, and yet inasmuch as he is a man, he brings with him a looking glass wherein we may see that he is our brother and our neighbour.[24]

Calvin often uses the metaphor of the mirror in his sermons on Galatians. We find, for instance, references to God's word as a mirror,[25] Abraham is "taken as the mirror of all perfection,"[26] and the Gospel is described as "the true looking glass wherein we behold Jesus Christ as it were in the face".[27] Here the image of the mirror is applied as part of the exhortation to do good to all people. If we are not inhuman we will see our own face, that is to say that we will recognise our own humanity in the other, in the person who is poor and despised, in the stranger. Even (and especially) people whom we view as alien to ourselves (say, people with a different culture, religion or language – Calvin speaks here of the Moor and the Barbarian) carry with them a mirror, indeed act in some way as a mirror, in which is manifested the fact that they are a brother or a sister and a neighbour.

For Calvin we are therefore bound to all human beings without difference, since we are all one flesh. And Calvin refers in this regard to Isaiah 58:7: "Thou shalt not despise thine own

Flesh".[28] In his commentary on the book of Isaiah Calvin also links – again using the mirror metaphor – the recognition of our own likeness in all human beings to what it means to be human. He writes: "Here we ought to observe that the term flesh, by which he means all men universally, not a single one of whom we can behold, without seeing, as in a mirror, 'our own flesh,' It is therefore a proof of the greatest inhumanity, to despise those in whom we are constrained to recognise our own likeness".[29]

If people shy away from doing good to all people, they not only despise God and reject his word, "but also are ugly monsters, because they consider not that there ought be community among all men".[30] The endeavour to do good to all people also includes those whom we view as unworthy and even our enemies. Calvin acknowledges this is no easy matter and contrary to our natural inclination, but he challenges his hearers to extend their understanding of "neighbour," reiterating the fact that we are of one flesh: "Therefore the furthest strangers in the world are

---

24 Calvin, *Sermons on Galatians*, 588.
25 Calvin, *Sermons on Galatians*, 211
26 Calvin, *Sermons on Galatians*, 187.
27 Calvin, *Sermons on Galatians*, 410.
28 Calvin, *Sermons on Galatians*, 588.
29 *Calvin's Commentary on Isaiah*, 234.
30 Calvin, *Sermons on Galatians*, 588.

neighbors near enough unto us, though they be neither our parents, our kinsfolk, nor our acquaintance. And why? For we be all of one flesh, and we bear all one mark, which ought to persuade us to do what we possibly can for another".[31]

In his sermon on Galatians 6:9-11 Calvin thus takes the word "all" in the call "to do good to all men" very seriously and extends the understanding of neighbour to include strangers, and even enemies. Calvin does acknowledge what he calls a "certain nearer alliance" between the household folk of faith,[32] following the text from Galatians 6:10, yet he does not labour this point in a way that weakens his emphasis on the need to do good to all human beings, given the fact that we are of one flesh.[33]

## 4. THE RECOGNITION OF STRANGENESS AND SAMENESS, AND THE POETICS OF AGAPE

In his sermon on Galatians 6:9-11 Calvin thus extends the mirror metaphor to argue that the other person, even those who are the furthest strangers or most alien to us, carry a mirror in which we should recognise our common humanity and that we are of one flesh. Since God has stamped or imprinted his image on us, we have one common nature.

Calvin makes the same point in a well-known passage in his discussion of the love of our neighbour (notwithstanding whether we deem them worthy or not) in his chapter on the denial of ourselves as the sum of Christian life in Book 3 of the *Institutes*:

> Therefore, whatever man you meet who needs your aid, you have no reason to refuse to help him. Say, "He is a stranger"; but the Lord has given him a mark that ought to be familiar to you by virtue of the fact that he forbids you to despise your own flesh [Isa. 58:7]. Say, "he is contemptible and worthless"; but the Lord shows him to be one whom he has deigned to give the beauty of his image.[34]

---

31 Calvin, *Sermons on Galatians*, 589. Calvin makes the same point in his 35th sermon, on Galatians 5:14-18: "Therefore we be all formed after his image, and we bear his mark. Besides this, we be all of one nature, and that ought to hold us in true unity and brotherhood ... And although men on their side deserve not to be counted and taken for neighbors, we show it is good reason that God should overweigh our naughtiness. We see that such as are our enemies and labor to devour us, do notwithstanding not cease to be our neighbors, in respect of the order that hath set" (496).
32 Calvin, *Sermons on Galatians*, 591.
33 Calvin makes the point strongly that we should not say that we don't know our brothers and sisters, but should look differently at them, because God looks differently at us: "Ye see that God our sovereign Lord looketh down upon us that are but wretched worms of the earth and filthiness: yea, and he not only vouchsafeth to say: I know your: but also protesteth, I have adopted you for my children, ye be my workmanship, ye be mine heirs, ye be after a sort my members". Calvin even says that those "who are so strange in withdrawing themselves from their brethren, and will not in any wise communicate with them, deserved well to be wiped out of the book of life". Calvin, *Sermons on Galatians*, 591.
34 Calvin, *Institutes*, 696.

We should therefore see the beauty of God's image in the needy person and stranger, even – Calvin continues – in our enemies. As Calvin puts it in the same paragraph:

> Assuredly there is but one way in which to achieve what is not merely difficult but utterly against human nature: to love those who hate us, to repay their evil deeds with benefits, to return blessings for reproaches [Matt. 5:44]. It is that we remember not to consider men's evil intentions but to look upon the image of God in them, which cancels and effaces their transgressions, and with its beauty and dignity allures us to love and embrace them.[35]

Thus, for Calvin it is important that when we look at others we see that they are bearers of the image of God. This fact should motivate us towards love of neighbour and in the process we should enlarge our understanding of neighbour to include strangers and even enemies.[36] John Leith sums up Calvin's position regarding the Christian social life well: "Human beings are united not only by a common flesh, but also by the image of God, which is imprinted on all".[37]

In the beginning of this essay I referred to the fact that Calvin was a refugee and that his life and ministry were marked by what can be termed the 'refugee reality'. As Heiko Oberman puts is: "Calvin did not serve a parish, a territory, or a country. He did not understand his own position as that of ... the people's priest of the Genevan city state. He did not receive his calling from the city council ... Reading the scriptures as an exiled refugee in the light of his own experiences, he addressed his listeners and readers not as citizens of Geneva or any other European region, but rather as uprooted wayfarers who had signed up for the hazardous trek to the Eternal city".[38] One might even be tempted to say that Oberman's argument for what he termed the third Reformation, or the Reformation of the refugees (following the defeat of the Protestant Princes in 1548 and 1549 and the expulsion of many Protestant through

---

35 Calvin, *Institutes*, 697. Cf. Randall Zachman's remark: "Therefore, if we rightly direct our love, we must first turn our eyes not to man, the sight of whom would more often engender hate than love, but to God, who bids us extend to all the love we bear in him, that this might be an unchanging principle: whatever the character of the man, we must yet love him because we love God". Randall C. Zachman, "'Deny Yourself and Take up Your Cross': John Calvin on the Christian Life", *International Journal of Systematic Theology* 11/4 (October 2009): 468-482, here 473.

36 Cf. also in this regard the following questions and answers from the "Catechism of the Church in Geneva":
Minister: What do you understand by the term neighbour?
Child: Not only kindred and friends, or those connected with us by any necessary tie, but also those who are unknown to us, and even enemies.
M: But what connection have these with us?
C: They are certainly joined by that bond by which God gathers the whole at once, But it is a tie, sacred and inviolable, which cannot be loosed by depravity.

See Reid, JKS (ed.), *Calvin's Theological Treatises* (Philadelphia: The Westminster Press, 1954), 89.

37 John Leith, *John Calvin's doctrine of the Christian Life* (Louisville: Westminster John Knox Press, 1989), 187.

38 Oberman, HA, "*Europa afflicta*: The Reformation of the Refugees", *Archiv für Reformationsgeschichte* 83 (Dec 1992): 91- 111, here 102-103. Cf. also Oberman, HA, *John Calvin and the Reformation of the Refugees* (Geneva: Droz, 2009).

the city gates),[39] explains something of the difference in tone and pathos between Calvin's earlier commentary and the later sermon on Galatians 6:9-11. Moreover, it is highly probable, given the influx of refugees to Geneva in the 1550s, that Calvin often had to engage with xenophobic attitudes and narrow nationalistic concerns. One should certainly guard against overusing the idea of 'the refugee reality' as an interpretive lens onto Calvin's life and thought. However, it does challenge us to revisit Calvin with this emphasis in mind, also as we rethink the promise of Reformed theology to respond to the pressing challenges of our globalising and polarising world.

The current global crisis pertaining to migrants and refugees certainly raises pertinent and difficult questions, and there is an evident need for fair laws and policies, the protection of the rights of citizens and refugees, and just institutions regulating and dealing with this crisis. Moreover, it is certainly true that the discourse on migration and refugees is often accompanied by harmful strategies of 'othering' such as racism and xenophobia.

In their book *Imagined Liberation: Xenophobia, Citizenship and Identity in South Africa, Germany and Canada*, sociologists Heribert Adam and Kogila Moodley have rightly argued for the importance of political literacy as a strategy to combat xenophobia.[40] Elsewhere I have argued, drawing on the work of the French philosopher Paul Ricoeur, that such a strategy could also incorporate an emphasis on the notion of mutual recognition, since racism and xenophobia have at their heart the posture of non-recognition or misrecognition.[41] In one of his last books, entitled *The Course of Recognition*, Ricoeur places mutual recognition between what he calls the prose of justice and the poetics of love or agape. In conversation with the work of Axel Honneth, Ricoeur grapples with the question: When does a subject deem him- or herself truly recognised? In the process Ricoeur puts forward the following thesis: "The alternative to the idea of struggle in the process of mutual recognition is to be sought in peaceful experiences of mutual recognition, based on the symbolic mediations as exempt from the juridical as from the commercial order of exchange".[42] The contribution of Ricoeur, in my view, lies in the fact that in his attempt to find a way between justice and love, he interrogates the conflictual nature of the struggle for recognition with the telos of peace in mind. In the process notions associated with the 'poetics of agape' receive their rightful place.

I think this emphasis on the 'poetics of agape' amidst the reality of violence and aggression resonates well with Calvin's discussion on the love of the neighbour already referred to earlier in the paper. This is not to say that the 'prose of justice' is not important, but that if we separated it as a formal rule from the 'hymn' of agape something will be lost in the process. Amidst the challenges posed by the migration of refugees in our global world today, the theological emphasis on the

---

39   See Oberman, HA, *The Two Reformations: The Journey from the Last Days to the New World* (New Haven: Yale University Press, 2003), 147.
40   Adam, H and Moodley, K, *Imagined Liberation: Xenophobia, Citizenship and Identity in South Africa, Germany and Canada* (Stellenbosch: Sun Press, 2013).
41   Vosloo, RR, "Between the Prose of Justice and the Poetics of Love? Reading Ricoeur on Mutual Recognition in the Light of Harmful Strategies of 'Othering'", Études Ricoueriennes/ Ricoeur Studies 6/2 (2015): 105-117.
42   Paul Ricoeur, *The Course of Recognition* (Cambridge: Harvard University Press, 2005), 216.

need to love our neighbour (and to understand 'neighbour' in its widest sense), as well as love the stranger, still can have currency in our public discourse. We are reminded in this regard of Calvin's remark in his commentary on Leviticus 19:18: "Not only those with whom we have some connection are called our neighbours, but all without exception; for the whole human race forms one body, of which we are all members, and consequently should be bound together by mutual ties; for we must bear in mind that even those who are most alienated from us, should be cherished and aided even as our own flesh; since we have seen elsewhere that sojourners and strangers are placed in the same category (with our relations); and Christ sufficiently confirms this in the case of the Samaritan".[43]

The discussion around the politics of recognition raises some tough questions. Christian theology has rich resources to draw upon in its search to develop an adequate theology or ethic of recognition and hospitality, and the Reformed tradition too can contribute richly to this discourse. In the process we should hear the biblical call to embody hospitality to strangers and to recognise the otherness of the other and the strangeness of the stranger in the process. We should affirm difference and not reduce otherness to sameness. We should guard against the reification of the language of the 'own' over against that which is different or strange. In the South African context the logic of apartheid was built on the type of beleaguered identity that sought to protect the 'own' and insulate it from 'the strange'. Yet at the same time apartheid thinking, also in the way it was theologically justified, had difficulty in recognising racial equality (even 'the equality of believers', to use the title of a book by Richard Elphick[44]) or people's shared humanity. One cannot but wonder how different the history of South Africa would have been, given also the ambivalent history of Reformed churches in the country, if Reformed Christians took to heart Calvin's remark and recognised in the face of the other a common humanity, and affirmed the dignity of the other as being created in the image of God? Maybe some of Calvin's fundamental insights, as expressed in his sermon on Galatians 6:9-11, can also challenge some of our own harmful strategies of othering as we seek to respond to the distress of the displaced in our interwoven contexts today.

## 5. CONCLUSION

In her book *A Human Being Died That Night: A South African Woman Confronts the Legacy of Apartheid*, Pumla Gobodo-Madikizela, a psychologist involved with the Truth and Reconciliation Commission and who has subsequently done important research on themes such as trauma, memory and forgiveness, describes her interviews with Eugene de Kock (also nicknamed 'Prime Evil'), the notorious commanding officer of the apartheid regime's death squads. During one of the interviews Gobodo-Madikizela reached out, in a compassionate gesture, to touch De Kock's hand. She describes her own mixed emotions as she realised that she

---

43  John Calvin, *Commentary on Leviticus* [see http://biblehub.com/commentaries/calvin/leviticus/19.htm].
44  Richard Elphick, *The Equality of Believers* (Pietermaritzburg: University of KwaZulu-Natal Press, 2012).

was touching "the physical body that had made evil happen".[45] Gobodo-Madikizela also admits to the fact that in these interviews she experienced something of De Kock's "other side," a side she was more afraid of confronting, namely "a human being capable of feeling, crying, and knowing pain".[46] During a later meeting De Kock thanked her for their earlier meeting and then he said: "You know, Pumla, that was my trigger hand you touched".[47] In her perceptive reflection on this unsettling incident, Gobodo-Madikizela makes the following telling remark:

> My action may well have been the first time a black person touched him out of compassion. He had previously met black people only as enemies, across the barrel of a gun or, for those who were on his side of the firing line, as comrades in murder. Perhaps de Kock *recognized my touch as a kind of threshold crossing*, a new experience for him" (my emphasis).[48]

Gobodo-Madikizela seems to be well aware of the ambivalence of this encounter. Nevertheless she ends her chapter on "The Trigger Hand" with some remarkable sentences in which she recognises De Kock's humanity, as well as his own search to affirm it:

> His world was a cold world, where eyes of death stared accusingly at him, a world littered with corpses and graves – graves of the unknown dead, dismembered or blown-up bodies. But for the horrific singularity of his acts, de Kock was a desperate soul seeking to affirm to himself that he is still part of the human universe.[49]

The incident recounted briefly above bears testimony to the moral power of gestures of recognition in which the dignity and humanity of another person are acknowledged and affirmed. It is certainly difficult to recognise amidst strife and even violence the common humanity between ourselves and others. We shy away from looking in the mirror held up, to use Calvin's language, by the poor or the stranger, and even the enemy.

We should also remind ourselves that we are not only challenged to look into the mirror of the stranger, but that as strangers to others and as human beings bearing the image of God, we are mirrors ourselves. As recipients of God's grace we are called to mirror his glory in gratitude. Or as Brian Gerrish writes: "While the entire created order reflects God's glory as in a mirror and in this sense 'images' God, man is set apart from the mute creation by his ability to reflect God's glory in a conscious response of thankfulness".[50]

---

45  Pumla Gobodo-Madikizela, *A Human Being Died That Night: A South African Woman Confronts the Legacy of Apartheid* (Boston/ New York: Houghton Mifflin Company, 2003)
46  Gobodo-Madikizela, *A Human Being Died That Night*, 38.
47  Gobodo-Madikizela, *A Human Being Died That Night*, 39.
48  Gobodo-Madikizela, *A Human Being Died That Night*, 42.
49  Gobodo-Madikizela, *A Human Being Died That Night*, 47.
50  Gerrish, BA, "The Mirror of God's Goodness: Man in the Theology of Calvin", *Concordia Theological Quarterly* 45/3 (July 1981): 211-222, here 215.

# 16. ON BEYERS NAUDÉ: REVISITING A LEGACY OF HOSPITALITY AND TRUTH-TELLING[1]

## 1. INTRODUCTION

I first heard the name of Beyers Naudé when, as a high school student, I overheard a conversation in which he was branded as a dangerous communist. This perception of Beyers Naudé was reinforced for many white South Africans in later years by the infamous photograph showing Beyers Naudé at a funeral in Cradock against the backdrop of a communist flag. While Naudé later noted in his autobiography, *My land van hoop* (*My Land of Hope*), that he was unaware of the presence of this flag, the name Beyers Naudé was for many not equated with the unrelenting search for truth and justice, but was linked to labels like communist, traitor and dissident. This symbolises something of the enclosed mindset within the Afrikaner community that continued to demonise any voices that dared to critique the unjust and inhuman system of apartheid.

My prior perceptions of Beyers Naudé were markedly challenged in the late 1980s by a visit to the home of Beyers and Ilse Naudé in Greenside, Johannesburg. This visit, which was in later years followed by other meetings with Oom Bey, was part of a series of student ecumenical tours organised by the Dutch Reformed Student Church in Stellenbosch. Carel Anthonissen, one of the pastors at this congregation, played an important role in organising these encounters. He had also previously been pastor at the Dutch Reformed congregation Aasvoëlkop in Johannesburg (the congregation which Naudé left in 1963) and he knew the Naudés well. For many of us these tours were powerful, emotional and liberating events that shattered many of the deeply-embedded myths and preconceived ideas with which we grew up. They also opened new and exciting vistas by bringing us into contact with communities and people who embodied, through their struggle and witness, something that felt genuine, joyous and hopeful. Visiting Beyers and Ilse Naudé's Greenside home was an encounter that has left a deep and lasting impression on me. We were struck by Oom Bey's clear and straightforward conversation. We experienced that he took us seriously, that he was willing to engage with us, facing even the toughest issues. One recollection that comes to mind with regard to these visits is the generous hospitality of the Naudés. It was our experience that they opened their home as well as their hearts to us. For me, their hospitality was even more significant in the light of the fact that Beyers Naudé previously spent seven years under house arrest and thus was confined to his home. In this essay I will use the related notions of 'hospitality' and 'home' as lenses to reflect on the legacy of Beyers Naudé, as well as reflecting on the implications of this legacy for us today.

---

1     This essay was read as a contribution to a conference hosted by the Beyers Naudé Centre for Public Theology at Stellenbosch University in August 2005 under the title "Oom Bey for the future". My contribution was published as "Hospitality and Truth-telling: Revisiting the Witness of Beyers Naudé" in Hansen, L and Vosloo, R (eds), *Oom Bey for the Future: Engaging the Witness of Beyers Naudé* (Stellenbosch: Sun Press, 2006:129136.

## 2. ON HOSPITALITY AND THE HOME

Hospitality is the welcoming openness towards the other and otherness – towards the stranger, strangeness and even estrangement. One finds the concept and practice of hospitality, in one form or another, in most cultures and religions. This lead Jacques Derrida to say, "Hospitality – this is culture itself".[2] Nevertheless, history is also littered with many monuments to inhospitality and exclusion. Apartheid and neo-apartheid can be viewed as forms of anti-hospitality that emphasise enclosed constructions of identity, with the concomitant inability to engage with the other and otherness, also otherness within the self. In the process self and community easily become insulated from the gift of meaningful communion.

Hospitality is strongly associated with metaphors relating to the home. It recalls the idea of an open home in which there is space for others. One can argue, furthermore, that an ethos of hospitality also challenges false constructions of 'home'. Phil Cohen suggests in his book *Home Rules: Some Reflections on Racism and Nationalism in Everyday Life* that all xenophobia has the ideal of a secure home as its sense-giving metaphor.[3] The image of a secure home transforms that which is 'not-home' or 'outside of home' into a terrain fraught with danger whose inhabitants are viewed as a constant threat.[4] In the process the home becomes a defensible space; something to be protected against the onslaughts of the stranger. The home becomes a place in the midst of chaos where order and decency reign. While it is certainly true that the home is, and must be, a space that denotes safety and enjoyment, there is a real danger that a mindset focused on security can construct 'home' as the exclusive space *par excellence*. It is thus necessary to challenge certain constructions of the notion of 'home'. We need to be critical of formulations that construct 'home' as an enclosed space that excludes the other and otherness. The philosopher Emmanuel Levinas (in a remarkable paragraph entitled "The dwelling" in his book *Totality and Infinity*) makes the important point that even the home is not 'owned'. One is a guest in one's own home. One is never the master of the house. Levinas writes: "The home that founds possession is not a possession in the same sense as the moveable goods it can collect and keep. It is possessed because it already and henceforth is hospitable to its proprietor".[5] Hospitality (or, what Levinas calls, "the welcome") precedes ownership. Levinas also writes: "Recollection in a home open to the Other – hospitality – is the concrete and initial fact of human recollection and separation; it coincides with the desire for the Other absolutely transcendent".[6] This suggests that the banning of otherness and the Other from the home (both physically and mentally) is, in a certain sense, a sign of being closed to the advent of the transcendent. In the

---

2   Derrida, J, *Acts of Religion*, Anidjar, G (ed.) (New York: Routledge, 2002), 361. Derrida makes this remark in a chapter meaningfully entitled "Hostipitality" (he uses this term to show the ambiguity of hospitality – *hostis* means enemy). Derrida's remark about hospitality as culture is preceded by his statement, "Not only is there a culture of hospitality, but there is no culture that is not also a culture of hospitality". Derrida, *Acts of Religion*, 361.
3   Cohen, P, *Home Rules: Some Reflections on Racism and Nationalism in Everyday Life* (London: University of East London, The New Ethnicities Unit, 1993). See also Bauman, Z, *Life in Fragments: Essays on Postmodern Morality* (Oxford: Blackwell, 1995), 135.
4   Bauman, *Life in Fragments*, 135.
5   Levinas, E, *Totality and Infinity* (Pittsburgh, PA: Duquesne University Press, 1961), 157.
6   Levinas, *Totality and Infinity*, 172.

process the Other is not only excluded, the self is also imprisoned. It is the home that is open to the Other that is ethical, that is a home in the true sense of the word.[7]

I previously referred to the hospitality our group of students experienced at the home of the Naudés in Greenside, an experience shared by many others. However, these reflections on the home and hospitality also point to more than the opening of one's domicile to the other. It is also closely intertwined with the willingness to open one's *identity* to the other, and also to see oneself *as* another (to use the title of an influential book by Paul Ricoeur). Our reflection on the legacy of Beyers Naudé cannot be separated from the way in which his life serves as a courageous prophetic critique of the destructive mindset of enclosed identity. His life serves as a testimony to the hope that arises when one risks one's life for the sake of truth and justice. While he grew up in the context of a house typified by a strict sense of Afrikaner identity, he allowed himself in the course of his life to be opened to other people, and other ideas, and to act boldly (and some might add, often naively) in the light of these encounters. It is ironic that the banning order, which had the goal of limiting his influence, actually lead to many more such encounters in his own home, where visitors where to be encouraged by his welcoming openness and pastoral concern.

The story of Beyers Naudé's house arrest, what he would later call his "seven lean years", is well-known. After the Soweto protests of 1976 and the death of Steve Biko in the following year, the Christian Institute, together with several other organisations, was banned in 1977. The offices of the CI were raided and closed, and many documents were confiscated. A banning order was served on Naudé that prohibited free social contact with others and put tremendous strain on his family life and friendships: he could not leave the magisterial district of Johannesburg; he could meet with only one person socially at a time; he could not attend meetings; he could not speak in public or write anything for publication; and it was considered unlawful to quote him. But for Naudé this was also a time of enrichment through counselling and reflection. He wrote:

> Through all these years there was a constant contact between myself and others. One by one they came, black and white, old and young, early in the morning and late at night … in and through it I gained tremendous insight into the life, the needs, the hopes and fears of many different people.[8]

Naudé also mentions that during this time he reflected more deeply than ever before on the rise and crisis of the Afrikaner people, on the English liberal tradition, on the situation facing both black and white students to discover for themselves what future they would like to face, on the growth of black political power and the emergence of

---

7   Cf. Vosloo, R, *Engele as Gaste? Oor gasvryheid teenoor die ander* (Wellington: Lux Verbi.BM, 2006), 39-41.
8   Naudé, CFB, "My Seven Lean Years", JTSA 51 (1985): 5. See also Ryan, C, *Beyers Naudé: Pilgrimage of Faith* (Cape Town: David Philip/ Grand Rapids: Eerdmans/ Trenton: Africa World Press, 1990), 1-3, 193-203. Also Naudé, *My land van hoop*, 109-123.

trade unions, and on the position of churches and the role of Christian faith in our country. After the lifting of the banning order, Naudé wrote:

> My seven lean years were over – the longest and leanest years of my life. No, I am wrong: Upon reflection I realize that in all probability they were the most difficult, but certainly the most enriching experience of my life because the banning brought to fruition many latent insights, feeling, visions and hopes.[9]

One cannot help but note the irony. The power of an open heart prevailed against attempts to imprison it. As the proverb goes: "If there is room in the heart, there is room in the house".[10] The legacy of Beyers Naudé encourages us to continue to critique enclosed notions of identity. Today we are faced with new kinds of enclosed mentalities that find subtle expression in our constructions of notions such as 'the home', 'the family' and 'the market'. Driven by the powerful hegemony of the market, we are tempted, for instance, to live isolated and consumer-driven lives, closing our eyes and hearts to injustice in our globalising world. Or we are tempted to succumb to a lifestyle that seeks to find security in the midst of perceived chaos and change in a fundamentalist attitude. I realise that the label of fundamentalism is not always helpful and that it cannot be separated from globalisation, but nevertheless we need to be mindful of the temptation of fundamentalism (in all its different guises). The danger of fundamentalism – or however we name false and fearful reactions to change that seek solace in fixed rules and final answers without sensitivity to complexity and ambiguity – is that it uglifies the self, it turns community into sect, and God into a projection of our fears. In short: it stifles life.

The notion of hospitality encompasses a critique of these false construction of identity. It implies a welcoming openness towards the other and otherness, an openness that cannot be separated from sensitivity to justice. Towards the end of his autobiography (published in 1995) Naudé looks to the future and mentions four interdependent priorities that express his concerns, i.e. the ecumenical movement, economic justice, the problem of corruption, and the challenge of seeking truth and reconciliation. In the section on economic justice, he notes that he is struck in his reading of the Old and the New Testament by the commands given with regard to the care for the poor, widows, strangers, refugees and the marginalised. He also asks the question: "Is wealthy Sandton, just a few kilometres away from poverty-stricken Alexandra … not a striking, visible symptom of the problem not only South Africa, but a large part of the world is struggling with today".[11] In reflecting today on the theme of "Oom Bey for the future" this haunting question on economic justice continues to ask for response. We are challenged to face this seemingly overwhelming

---

9   Naudé, "My Seven Lean Years", 14.
10  Quoted in Hallie, P, *Tales of Good and Evil: Help and Harm* (New York: HarperCollins, 1997), 54. Cf. Pohl, C, *Making Room: Recovering Hospitality as a Christian Tradition* (Grand Rapids: Eerdmans), 150.
11  Naudé, *My land van hoop*, 145. This question becomes particularly poignant by the fact that Beyers Naudé's funeral was held at Aasvoëlkop Congregation in a wealthy suburb in Johannesburg, the same congregation that he left in 1963, but that his ashes were then taken to Alexandra. This is a challenging gesture for the Dutch Reformed Church family. It can also be read as a wider challenge to see the interconnectedness of the destinies of rich and poor, first and third worlds.

task in courageous and creative ways. But maybe we can also drink from the wells of wisdom left by Beyers Naudé. It is worth keeping in mind the words that he spoke at a lecture at Rhodes university on 1 April 1985:

> Listen first to the voice of the voiceless, hear the cry of the oppressed, consider the power of the powerless ... become involved in a new society in which the recognition of human dignity, human rights and human responsibility forms the basis on which the future of the country is built.[12]

## 3. BEING WELCOMED

Reflecting on "Oom Bey for the future" in the light of the notion of just hospitality does not only focus on the exclusion that the Naudés' experienced, or the welcoming openness that they embodied. One also has to acknowledge the immense hospitality given to them by the communities in which they also found acceptance. The stories of these welcoming communities need to be remembered and retold. It is unthinkable to try and apprehend the legacy of Beyers Naudé without reference to the role played by these communities in sustaining his witness. In this regard we can think of the acceptance found within the broader ecumenical movement, within resistance communities, and specifically within the congregation in Alexandra. This reminds us that hospitality is not only about welcoming, but also, and maybe even primarily, about *being welcomed*, about *receiving* hospitality. It is about hosts becoming guests and guests becoming hosts in a way that challenges and subverts oppressive and limiting hierarchies of power.

Beyers Naudé ends his autobiography with a short section in which he mentions the invitation by the Dutch Reformed Church congregation Aasvoëlkop to come and preach there on 13 August 1995 (32 years after his painful separation from the congregation). For Naudé this was an emotional event, a sign of hope, a symbol of the reconciliation needed within the Dutch Reformed Church family, the reconciliation also necessary for all churches and for our country. The section has the meaningful heading "Tuiskoms" ("Homecoming"). Upon reading these words, one cannot help but be saddened by the lack of progress in this regard within the Dutch Reformed family of churches. The legacy of Beyers Naudé continues to challenge churches (also the churches within the whole family of Dutch Reformed Churches) to embody hospitality through the willingness to risk with each other in vulnerability and obedience. This implies the willingness to welcome, to re-welcome and to be welcomed. One can also recall here the words of a friend of Beyers Naudé, the theologian Willie Jonker, at the end of his autobiography, *Selfs die kerk kan verander* (*Even the Church can Change*). Jonker writes:

> While the struggle of the past forty years was mainly to challenge the way in which the DRC was a *volkskerk*, the following decades will probably involve the development of unity within the Dutch Reformed

---

12   Naudé, *My land van hoop*, 126.

Church family, as well as the conservation of the Reformed character of these churches and their prophetic role in society.[13]

## 4. TRUTH-TELLING, THE CHILD AND THE FUTURE

Hospitality is not to be equated with a mere romanticised openness towards otherness. Moreover, hospitality cannot be separated from truth-telling. It is about being *pro veritate*, for the truth. It is about confessing the truth,[14] about living the truth. Therefore one must be careful not to make a false separation between a pastoral and a prophetic responsibility. Those who are willing 'to tell the truth' are often the best pastors. The way in which Beyers Naudé combined truth-telling (often in a rather reckless manner) with pastoral concern, serves as an important reminder not to erect false dichotomies that merely serve the status quo and result in the neglect of the prophetic task.

Hospitality and truth-telling: these are two words that resonate with me when I think of the witness and legacy of Beyers Naudé. The challenge is to embody these concepts in new in creative way in our complex and changing world. This probably requires different arguments and actions than those spoken and performed by Beyers Naudé. Maybe our time asks for greater hermeneutical sensitivity and for a thicker theological description of reality. Nonetheless the words and witness of Beyers Naudé, and the communities sustaining him, will continue to be a guiding light in this regard.

I think that the legacy of Beyers Naude is best honoured when his witness is not abstracted from his life. As Charles Villa-Vicencio reminds us:

> Contrary to the opinion of those who admire him from a distance and turn him into a mystical icon of their cult, he is a human being. He has made his mistakes. He can be a stubbornly independent person, quite reckless with passionate abandon, and over-enthusiastic about ideas that cannot work. He can be a terrible judge of human character, and then fiercely loyal to colleagues and friends even in the face of the most damning evidence against them. All this has at times had a way of driving his closest friends to near despair.[15]

And Jean Knighton-Fitt refers in a biography on Theo and Helen Kotzé, entitled *Beyond Fear*, to the remark of a colleague, by no means unlovingly expressed, that

---

13   Jonker, W, *Selfs die kerk kan verander* (Kaapstad: Tafelberg, 1998), 221 (my translation).
14   Beyers Naudé saw important parallels between the situation in South Africa and in Nazi Germany. In 1965 he wrote a number of articles in *Pro Veritate* arguing that it is time for a "Confessing Church". See "Die tyd vir "n 'belydende kerk' is daar" (July 15 1965); "Nogeens die 'belydende kerk'" (November 1965) and "Nou juis die 'belydende kerk'" (December 15 1965). Here he challenges what he saw as the dangerous silence of the churches: "Why did you remain silent when you had to talk? ... And will the church not be reproached by name where God demands with good reason that the prophetic voice be heard to bear witness against all violations of law and justice, love and truth?" (December 15 1965): 4.
15   Villa-Vicencio, C and De Gruchy, JW, *Resistance and Hope: South African Essays in Honor of Beyers Naudé* (Grand Rapids: Eerdmans, 1985), 13.

"Beyers was unable to say 'no', and that mixed up with his magnanimity was an excessive naiveté about people's contributions. He embraced a lot of fools as well as prophets!"[16]

Beyers Naudé had the 'will to embrace' (to use Miroslav Volf's term[17]) and it may be that he embraced prophets as well as fools. This suggests the need to combine embrace with discernment, or hospitality with wisdom. Also with regard to hospitality we need, as Richard Kearney notes, at crucial moments "to discern the other in the alien and the alien in the other".[18] Although such discernment is certainly necessary, there is also something valuable in a certain naiveté and childlikeness. Maybe the attraction of (and reaction against) the life of Beyers Naudé partly resided in the fact that this person, who was for many a kind of parent figure, remained in some ways childlike. This led to a certain recklessness, but maybe it was also this quality that made it possible for him to hope, to believe in the future, to see the Kingdom. As Bonhoeffer writes:

> To-let-oneself-be-defined by means of the future is the eschatological possibility of the child. The child (full of anxiety and bliss) sees itself in the power of what 'future things' will bring, and for that reason it can only live in the present ... It is only out of the future that the present can be lived.[19]

The legacy of Beyers Naudé calls us to embody hospitality and truth-telling in new and creative ways. But it also helps us to be open to the surprise of the future. This is the gift that enables what Kierkegaard called the passion for the possible, or maybe even more importantly, the passion for the seemingly impossible.

---

16   Knighton-Fitt, J, *Beyond Fear* (Cape Town: Pretext, 2003), 140.
17   Volf, M, *Exclusion and Embrace: A Theological Exploration of Identity, Otherness, and Reconciliation* (Nashville: Abingdon Press, 1996), 29.
18   Kearney, R, *Strangers, Gods, and Monsters: Interpreting Otherness* (London: Routledge, 2013), 67.
19   Bonhoeffer, D, *Act and Being* (Minneapolis: Fortress Press, 1996), 159.

# 17. ON DIRKIE SMIT: TAKE, READ ... INTERPRET, CONFESS[1]

To read and to listen – together with others – to the Word that is a lamp unto our feet and a light unto our path is not simply a game, it is not a conversation where everything is eventually tolerated and where everything is eventually affirmed – often with an appeal to Scripture itself. For the church there indeed come times of decision-making, times of profound solemnity, times of confession ... These are times when it will be necessary to ask for boundaries to what is possible in the name of the message of the Bible, the truth of the gospel, and the credibility of the church. These are times when it will be necessary to ask for the rules for a responsible interpretation of the Scriptures, for a true theological hermeneutic, for the reading of the Bible according to the rule of faith, like the early church, which includes the rule of love and the rule of hope in the Triune God. These are times when the church prays together for the illumination and guidance of the Holy Spirit of the Father and the Son.[2]

## 1. DIRKIE SMIT AS READER

As one of Dirkie Smit's doctoral students, I had the privilege of borrowing many books from him. I am part of a large group of students whose studies, and later thinking, were motivated and sustained by these borrowed books (most of which have hopefully been returned by now!). These were often books that had only recently been published and were therefore not yet available in bookstores or in libraries. For many of us, it was precisely these books that further awakened our passion for theology.

The books and articles that we borrowed from Dirkie Smit and read made one thing clear: Dirkie Smit is an excellent reader. Besides having the ability to read quickly and with comprehension, he is also an utterly observant reader. The way in which he underlines the text, highlights the importance of certain parts and makes short marginal notes all bear witness to this trait. Smit also has the ability to read *between* the lines and he continuously attempts to understand the intention and ethos of authors by interpreting their words, quotations and passing remarks. He also likes to read *beneath* the lines, in the footnotes, and the Afrikaans word "kry" ("get") would often appear next to the literature cited by an author – an indication that he desires to follow up the references, to read more, to understand better and to continue the conversation. To read is for Dirkie Smit thus an act that signifies that you are part of a conversation – a conversation that started before you where there, *and* that will continue after your own participation.

---

1  This essay was originally published in Afrikaans under the title "Neem, lees ... vertolk, bely! Kantaantekeninge by die teologie van Dirkie Smit" in *NGTT* 48/1&2, 2007:397-411.
2  Smit, D J, *Neem Lees! Hoe ons die Bybel hoor en verstaan* (Wellington: Lux Verbi, 2006), 230.

Probably one of the reasons why Smit's theological work has such a significant influence in theological circles in South Africa – and also internationally – has to do with the way in which his reading and writing habits clearly reveal a respect for the riches as well as the complexity of Christian conversations throughout the ages, and in different contexts. The reading and interpretation of texts becomes a way to participate in these conversations. Dirkie Smit's love of reading, however, should not be mistaken for the mere curiosity of a consumer, but should be seen as being part of his ongoing pursuit to understand and interpret texts, and to integrate them with everyday life.

A reflection on Dirkie Smit's reading habits naturally brings one to questions about his understanding of the nature and task of theology. In his important inaugural lecture as professor at Stellenbosch University, "In diens van die tale Kanaäns? Oor sistematiese teologie vandag" ("Serving the language of Canaan? On systematic theology today"),[3] Smit begins with the question: "What does the theologian actually do?" and then immediately follows up with the statement: "A simple answer is not that easy".[4] The opportunity to reflect on the theology of Dirkie Smit opens up the space to ask: What does Dirkie Smit actually do? And to this question one must also hastily respond: a simple answer is not that easy. There are indeed numerous angles one could take in contemplating Dirkie Smit's theological method. In this essay one aspect will be examined closely, namely the important place of the act of reading in his theology. When highlighting the word "read" as a key verb, however, it quickly becomes clear that it is in need of further qualification. For Smit, the reading of texts can after all not be separated from the interpretation of them. Reading and interpretation furthermore ask for embodiment. They cannot be separated from the confessing body. Reading, interpreting, confessing… In my opinion, something of Dirkie Smit's theological logic comes to the fore in the coherence and interplay of these actions. In this essay these three verbs will be used as heuristic lenses to add a few side notes to the theology of Dirkie Smit.

## 2. READ: TO LISTEN TO THE WORD OF GOD TOGETHER

### a. Theology and the reading of the Bible

In a contribution to a *Festschrift* for Willie Jonker, published under the title *Koninkryk, kerk, kosmos* (*Kingdom, church, cosmos*), Dirkie Smit writes that Jonker preferred to be known as a Scriptural theologian (Skrifteoloog) and that he consciously conveyed to students the view that they too should be Scriptural theologians.[5] As one of Willie Jonker's students, Dirkie Smit came to embody something of this, not in the first place by pleading for the infallible authority of the Bible, but through his attempt to

---

3 Smit's inaugural lecture at Stellenbosch University was published as Smit, D J, "In diens van die tale Kanaäns? Oor sistematiese teologie vandag", *NGTT* 43, 1/2 (2002): 94-127.
4 Smit, "In diens van die tale Kanaäns?", 94.
5 Smit, D J, "' …om saam met al die heiliges Christus te ken'. Persoonlike indrukke van 'n ekumeniese waarheidsoeke" ("'To know Christ with all of the Saints'… Personal impressions of an ecumenical pursuit of truth"), in Theron, PF, Jonker, WD and Kinghorn, J (eds), *Koninkryk, kerk en kosmos: huldigingsbundel ter ere van Prof WD Jonker* (Bloemfontein: Pro-Christo, 1989), 11-32, here 11.

use the Bible exegetically, hermeneutically and homiletically in a responsible way. This is confirmed by his numerous contributions in the influential *Woord teen die Lig* (*Word against the Light*) series (which he co-edited with Coenie Burger and Bethel Muller). For many ministers it was exactly these thorough studies that affirmed that preaching cannot be done without proper exegesis and responsible hermeneutical work. In this regard, Dirkie Smit's writings were exemplary of an attempt to do continued theological training in a way that closely links Scripture and theology with one another. Even a cursory reading of Smit's dozens of contributions (over 90 sermon studies and at least 9 introductory articles) reflects his sustained practice of engaging Scripture. In the process he offers a motivation for and invitation to minsters and congregants to read more deeply and widely. Smit also wrote numerous books on specific passages of the Bible, books that often developed out of his preaching in congregations.[6] From these books, and from his sermon meditations (as well as in theological publications, often with fellow authors), and also from his numerous talks in congregations, it is clear that, for Smit, the reading and interpretation of the Bible are integrally connected to his understanding of the task of the theologian.

It is well known that Calvin did not want to his influential *Institutes* to be read apart from the Bible. It was, in fact, written to assist one in reading the Bible and not as a book to be read instead of the Bible. Considering that Smit has been deeply influenced by Calvin in terms of the importance of the Bible, it comes as no surprise to read in the Foreword to *Neem, Lees! Hoe ons die Bybel hoor en verstaan* (*Take, Read! How we hear and understand the Bible*) that that the book is meant to serve as an invitation for people to read and listen to the Bible *themselves*: "This is a book *about* the Bible, which invites people *to* the Bible".[7]

In *Neem, Lees!* Smit offers a comprehensive discussion on how the Bible has been read throughout the ages (a historical aspect), how texts are read (a systematic aspect), how the Bible has something meaningful to say about our lives (an ethical aspect), and how we could think about the Bible in the light of a number of metaphors found in the biblical texts themselves (a practical aspect). It is, however, quite significant that this book about the Bible that wants to invite people *to* the Bible also contains, towards the end, a number of sermon meditations on certain passages from the Bible. This emphasis, along with his more systematic work in the book, serves as witness to the fact that there is a theological hermeneutic at work in Smit's thought that binds together theology and the interpretation of Scripture. One can therefore say that Smit, like his teacher Willie Jonker, is indeed a Scriptural theologian.

### b. To read the Bible together

When studying Dirkie Smit's work, it also becomes clear that, for him, the reading of the Bible and the reading of theology are not the activities of an isolated individual or researcher in seclusion. Therefore the title of a book of Gregory Jones and Stephen

---

6  See in this regard, for example, his books *Christus is die Heer!* (on the letter to the Colossians) (Kaapstad: Lux Verbi, 1986); *Die geloof dan is …* (on the book of Hebrews) (Kaapstad: Lux Verbi, 1987); *Hoop in lewe en lyding* (on 1 Peter) (Kaapstad: Lux Verbi, 1988); *Wat sien ons in die spieël?* (on Jacob) (Kaapstad: Lux Verbi, 1994); *Gesigte van die liefde* (on the fruits of the Spirit) (Kaapstad: Lux Verbi, 1998).
7  Smit, *Neem, Lees!*, 8.

Fowl appealed to him: *Reading in Communion*.[8] It is clearly very important for Smit that the Bible should be read *together*. According to him, this importance of reading in community and communion has a deep theological foundation. In the abovementioned article on the theology of Willie Jonker, Smit refers to the way in which Jonker's work is marked by what could be called an *ecumenical* pursuit of truth.[9] A strong case can therefore be made that such an ecumenical pursuit of truth also lies at the heart of Smit's understanding of the nature and task of theology. Smit is clearly an ecumenical theologian. His hermeneutic is an ecumenical hermeneutic and his ecclesiology is an ecumenical ecclesiology. One could even argue that his convictions concerning the importance of ecumenism have intensified over the years. In this regard one can refer to his numerous discussions of ecumenical documents,[10] as well as his appreciative writings on ecumenical theologians such as Geoffrey Wainwright and Edmund Schlink.[11] Both Smit's ecumenical hermeneutic and his ecumenical ecclesiology are, however, closely intertwined with a "catholic" pursuit of truth. The focus on the importance of reading the Bible together, and on the communal practice of theology, is driven by a deep understanding of the unity of the church, of the important interplay between truth and unity.

What he writes about Jonker, is also applicable to himself:

> The passion for unity is not just a general-philosophical principle, but operates in the service of the pathos of truth. It has nothing to do with a search for unity on the grounds of non-theological interests, such as the unity of the nation, or the social-political interests of the group, or the general spirit of reconciliation in society. It also does not originate from a general attitude of tolerance, relativism and pluralism. *It is through and through a search for unity in the truth of the gospel.*[12]

Smit's emphasis on the importance of 'reading in community in search of the truth' can surely not be detached from the context of apartheid South Africa. It was in fact a reality of the nature of apartheid that people read the Bible on their own. Through the dramatic way in which the Bible was used to justify *and* to oppose apartheid, it became apparent that the Bible itself is a 'site of struggle' – something Smit would

---

8   See Fowl, SE and Jones, LG, *Reading in Community* (Eugene OR: Wipf and Stock Publishers, 1998).
9   The title of Smit's contribution – which can be translated as "To know Christ with all of the Saints… Personal impressions of an ecumenical pursuit of truth" – is already significant.
10  See e.g. Smit, DJ, "A time for confession? On the WARC project 'Reformed faith and economic justice'", *NGTT* 3&4 (2003): 478-499; and Smit, DJ, "Ecumenical hermeneutics? Historical benchmarks and current challenges of a concept" in Fröchtling, A and Phaswana, N (eds), *Being (the church) beyond the South-North divide: Identities, othernesses and embodied hermeneutics in partnership discourses South Africa-Germany* (Münster: LIT, 2003), 23-48.
11  See e.g. Smit, D J, "On Edmund Schlink's ecumenical systematic theology", Unpublished lecture at the Center of Theological Inquiry, Princeton, New Jersey (15 March 2006); and Smit, DJ "Visie, motief, weë - Geoffrey Wainwright oor die eenheid van die kerk" ("Vision, motif, routes – Geoffrey Wainwright on the unity of the church), *Skrif en Kerk*, 2 (1999): 414-440.
12  Smit, "' …om saam met al die heiliges Christus te ken', 22.

often reflect on.¹³ For Smit, the core question is how the Bible can be read in a theologically responsible way, amidst diverse and often conflicting interpretations. An important part of the answer to this question is the conviction that we need one another to read the Bible responsibly, especially in the light of the confusion following Babel, which results in people not hearing one another.¹⁴

What applies to the reading of the Bible is also relevant for the practice of theology. Theology is a communal activity. Smit writes that it is precisely this truth that became increasingly important for him and his generation, during apartheid South Africa:

> (W)e learnt that theology is something we do in communion, together – with the mothers and fathers of the tradition, with the brothers and sisters of the ecumenical church, with the victims of our communities and societies, with 'the destitute, the poor, and the wronged'.¹⁵

Throughout the years Smit would also then often take the lead in bringing people together to discuss texts and to reflect on book proposals. This community-creating quality of Smit's work is probably one of his greatest contributions and is closely linked with his ecumenical pursuit for truth.

### c. To read the Bible for today

In Dirkie Smit's book *Neem, Lees!* there are a number of revealing quotations that precede the table of contents. One of these quotations is from Robert Louis Wilken's book *The Spirit of Early Christian Thought: Seeking the Face of God*:

> Any effort to mount an interpretation of the Bible that ignores its first readers is doomed to end up with a bouquet of fragments that are neither the book of the church nor the imaginative wellspring of literature, art, and music. Uprooted from the soil that feeds them, they are like cut flowers whose colors have faded.¹⁶

---

13  See e.g. Smit, DJ, *Neem Lees!*; Smit, DJ, "Rhetoric and Ethic? A Reformed Perspective on the Politics of Reading the Bible", in Alston, W and Welker, M (eds), *Reformed theology: Identity and Ecumenicity II*, (Grand Rapids: Wm B Eerdmans, 2007), 385-418; and Smit, DJ, "On the Christian life", The Josephine So Lectures on Culture and Ethics, China Graduate School of Theology, Hong Kong (3-7 January, 2005).

14  Smit often uses the Babel metaphor when writing on hermeneutics and ethics. See e.g. Smit, DJ, "'Pidgin or Pentecost?' On translation and transformation", *Scriptura* 58 (1996): 305-328; Smit, DJ, "Etiese spraakverwarring in Suid-Afrika vandag" ("Ethical speech confusion in South Africa today"), *NGTT* 1 (1995): 87-98; Smit, D J, "Oor die skepping van 'n grammatika van saamleef" ("On the creation of a grammar of living together"), *HTS* 51/1 (March 1995): 85-107; Smit, DJ, "Het Suid-Afrika 'n gemeenskaplike morele taal nodig?" ("Does South Africa need a common moral language?"), *HTS* 51/1 (March 1995): 65-84; Smit, DJ, "Etiek na Babel? Vrae rondom moraliteit en die openbare gesprek in Suid-Afrika vandag" ("Ethics after Babel? Questions around morality and the public debate in South Africa today"), *NGTT* 1 (1994): 82-92; Smit, DJ (with Cloete, GD), "Its name was called Babel …", *JTSA* 86 (March 1994): 81-87. At one stage there was a print of Brueghel's famous portrayal of the tower of Babel against the wall in his office.

15  Smit, DJ, "Belonging: Doing Theology Together", Unpublished article (2007): 8.

16  Smit, *Neem Lees!*; the quotation comes from Wilken, RL, *The Spirit of Early Christian Thought: Seeking the Face of God* (New Haven: Yale University Press, 2003), xvii.

Smit's use of this quotation accentuates his belief that any reading of the Bible should always take the context of the first readers (as well as the contexts of readers throughout the ages) into proper consideration. The first part of *Neem, Lees!* is also then a historical investigation into the ways in which the Bible was read at different times and in different contexts. Smit is, however, not only interested in the contexts in which the biblical text developed and took shape. There is also an emphasis in Smit's work on the fact that the Bible speaks today, in the present moment. This conviction is clearly reflected in another quotation that appears in the beginning of *Neem, Lees!*, this time from Karl Barth's *The Epistle to the Romans* on the hermeneutics of the Reformers. The full quotation reads:

> By genuine understanding and interpretation I mean the creative energy which Luther exercised with intuitive certainty in his exegesis: which underlines the systematic interpretation of Calvin. Place modern work side by side with that of Calvin: How energetically Calvin, having first established with stands in the text, sets himself the task of rethinking all of the material and wrestling with it, until the walls that separate the 16$^{th}$ century from the 1$^{st}$ become transparent! Paul speaks and the person in the 16$^{th}$ century hears. The conversation between the original record and reader moves around the subject matter, until a distinction between yesterday and to-day becomes impossible. If people persuade themselves that Calvin's method can be dismissed as old-fashioned, they betray themselves as people who have never worked on the interpretation of Scripture.[17]

This quotation makes the point clear that the reading and interpretation of the Bible are connected to the belief that the Bible also speaks *today*. In a discussion of Calvin's hermeneutics, Smit points to the fact that Calvin (in contrast with, for example, Erasmus and Bullinger), never specifically wrote about hermeneutics. Smit mentions that the reason for this probably has to do with the fact that Calvin "was deeply convinced that the living, triune God still speaks to us through the Bible today".[18] This conviction lies at the heart of Calvin's theological hermeneutic. In the light of this belief, theology is understood as a continuous *listening* to the Word. The message of the Gospel, the message of the Word, can never be encapsulated conclusively. No, the living promises of the Gospel should always be heard anew. For Calvin, grammar and rhetoric are undoubtedly of importance in the search for the meaning of the text. There is, however, also an emphasis on the *meaningfulness* of the text, on what the text has to say to the congregation *today*. This emphasis on the significance, usefulness or meaningfulness (the *usus*) of the text, makes it possible for the Bible to surprise us, for something new to happen. But this emphasis cannot be separated from the belief in the faithfulness of the living God: "The same God speaks in his faithfulness to us today … in reading and in listening".[19]

Calvin's distinction between the meaning and meaningfulness of the Bible is important in Smit's thought. While acknowledging the complexity of the reading

---

17   Smit, *Neem Lees!*; the quotation comes from Barth, K, *The Epistle to the Romans (6th Edition)* (Oxford: Oxford University, 1968), 7.
18   Smit, *Neem Lees!*, 68.
19   Smit, *Neem, Lees!*, 53.

and interpretation process, there is indeed an expectation that the horizons of the historical text and the present context can fuse into one another: "Through all human weakness and even 'treason', the world still *hears*, and the congregation *lives* from that which is *heard*".[20]

## 3. INTERPRET: TO INTERPRET THE WORD OF GOD RESPONSIBLY

### a. Theology as bibliography

Before offering a few remarks on Dirkie Smit's view of interpretation, it is perhaps first necessary to say something about him as interpreter. It was mentioned earlier that many students' and colleagues' love for theology was kindled and strengthened by books that were lent to them by Dirkie Smit. It was, however, not only the books themselves that were of value, but also the way in which Smit could situate each one of them within a larger framework. Smit has the ability to interpret, to build bridges of understanding between texts and people.[21] In the process difficult arguments and complex viewpoints are explained in a clear way. Smit's impressive analytical abilities make him a *systematic* theologian in the best sense of the word. A distinction needs to be drawn, however, between a systematic theologian and a system theologian. For, like Jaap Durand, Dirkie Smit does not believe that theology has to do with systems. Hence his remark:

> The Christian faith knows no absolute truths. Dogmatics does not study dogmas. Systematic theology does not have systems. In fact, there are probably few disciplines in the university that are less dogmatic than dogmatics, less systematic than systematic theology.[22]

Despite the comprehensive nature of Smit's work, it certainly does not form a closed system. It rather represents, to reference the title of an anthology of NP Van Wyk Louw memorial lectures, a "circle left open" ("oopgelate kring").[23] It is precisely this *open-ended* nature of Smit's thought that can sometimes be frustrating for readers. The reader follows the analysis and arguments with great excitement and approval, just to be left with the feeling that the piece of writing ends somewhat bluntly, as Smit does not give any final answers, or offer a definite resolution to what he has said. This probably has to do with Smit's understanding of the dialogical function of theology. He sees his own role as interpreter within the context of a larger and ongoing conversation. For this reason he loves to buy books, to read widely and to converse with discussion partners. In the process Smit attempts to understand, to

---

20 Smit, *Neem, Lees!*, 167.
21 This is probably one of the reasons why he is such a popular speaker among both ministers and congregants who are interested in theology. In this regard, one can think of the many talks he has given at courses and church seminars – often with a large pile of books next to him – books that he would discuss with enthusiasm, insight and humour. His wide exposure to different theological contexts can also be mentioned in this regard. Specifically his knowledge of the worlds of German and American theology has been of great value to many students and colleagues throughout the years.
22 Smit, "In diens van die tale Kanaäns?", 102.
23 See Van Rensburg, FIJ (ed.), *Oopgelate kring: N.P. van Wyk Louw gedenklesings 1-11* (Kaapstad: Tafelberg, 1982).

gain a general overview, to place particular viewpoints within larger frameworks. Most of his publications are therefore extensive descriptions of his reading. Theology is in part also bibliography. One can also refer to his extended use of footnotes in this regard. In Dirkie Smit's work the boundary between the main text and the footnotes is – for methodological reasons – highly porous.[24]

This style of theologising naturally exposes the theologian to the temptation to function as some sort of all-seer or *panopticon* (to use the well-known term by Michel Foucault, who follows Bentham in this regard[25]). I think, though, that it is precisely Smit's openness to continued conversation that safeguards his theological method against any form of panopticism. Perhaps, a more appropriate image is that of the *episkopos* (the overseer) who offers visionary and responsible leadership. This does not mean that there has been no evaluation, but that, in the evaluation process, other viewpoints are always treated with integrity and respect. Here too we find traces of an ecumenical pursuit of truth: the search for a biblical or evangelical logic. Through all of this Smit has an underlying trust in the fact that theology *matters*. In a time when it has become easy – also for the theologian – to turn away from theology, Smit embodies a sort of unapologetic *practising* of theology, which issues from his inherent belief in the importance of theology. This focus on the importance of theology is, however, not a heroic or arrogant exaltation of theology. Towards the end of his inaugural lecture Smit mentions the German scholar, Friedrich Schleiermacher, who referred to himself throughout his life as a *student* of theology. Smit writes:

> Even though this does not apply to other professors any longer, it still applies to *those in theology*, that we are professors in the literal sense of the word, people who openly profess, with confidence and assurance, and hopefully in teaching *and* in life, what they believe and stand for, but who are therefore also permanent students of theology, full of wonder and longing, and searching for truth. If we ever think or pretend that we *know*, theology should be freed of us.[26]

b.  The complexity of interpretation

An attempt to reflect on Dirkie Smit's role as interpreter also asks one to devote attention to his views on interpretation – specifically his views on the interpretation of the Bible. Perhaps the great value of Dirkie Smit's contribution with regard to the question of the interpretation of the Bible lies in the fact that he does not attempt to offer cheap and oversimplified answers. He would rather increase the number of questions. The following quotation is representative of this:

> The question is: to which community-of-interpretation, to which tradition, to which group, to which 'polis' does the Bible properly

---

24  For this reason he decided to talk about the importance of the footnote when he received the Andrew Murray Prize in 2003 for the best theological article. Smit received the prize for his inaugural lecture "In diens van die tale Kanaäns? Oor sistematiese teologie vandag". This article has 118 footnotes. Smit would surely not have minded if one could make footnotes to footnotes.
25  See e.g. Rabinow, P (ed.), *The Foucault Reader* (New York: Pantheon Books, 1984): 206-203.
26  Smit, "In diens van die tale Kanaäns?", 102.

belong? Where can we expect to learn how to read and interpret the Bible properly, responsibly? Who are the real readers of the Bible? To whom does the Bible belong – to the church, as many would claim? Or to the academy and biblical scholarship? Or to society as a whole, as a classic of human orientation, wisdom and life? And if the answer is indeed the church, then which church, which faith community, which denominational tradition – if they are also disagreeing, even struggling with each one another, over the message of the Bible?[27]

Smit is thus fully aware of the contentious nature of any appeal to the Bible. In apartheid South Africa the Bible was indeed used in conflicting ways. From this, it became clear how difficult it is to justify a viewpoint by appealing to the authority of the Bible. These complex issues were discussed extensively in New Testament circles, and Smit himself would also take part in the conversation. From his contributions in this regard Smit's conviction seems to be that questions regarding the ethics of interpretation are important.[28] In *Neem, Lees!* he again refers to the importance of an ethics of interpretation with the underlying assumption that any interpretation of the Bible should be regarded as:

> ... a social and political act, which has consequences for people's lives, and therefore ought to be done with an ethical responsibility, and that any form of speaking on behalf of the Bible or writing about the Bible – sermons, spiritual literature, diaries, theology – must be accompanied with ethical responsibility, treated with suspicion and self-criticism, and should only be done with great modesty, humility, caution and with an openness to advice from others.[29]

For Smit the issue of responsible interpretation is indeed important.[30] And he therefore also has an interest in the rhetoric of interpretation and the importance of

---

27  Smit, "On the Christian Life", 87. See also Smit, *Neem Lees!*, 87.
28  In this regard, see Smit, DJ, "Interpreter interpreted. A reader's reception off Lategan's legacy", in Breytenbach, C, Punt, J, and Thom, J (eds), *The New Testament interpreted: Essays in Honor of Bernard Lategan* (Leiden: Brill, 2006); Smit, D J, "Reading the Bible and the (un)nofficial interpretive culture", *Neotestamentica* 28 (2) (1994): 309-321; Smit, DJ, "The Bible and ethos in a new South Africa", *Scriptura* 37 (1991): 51-67; Smit, DJ, "Wat beteken 'die Bybel sê'? 'n Tipologie van leserskonstrukte" ("What does 'the Bible says' mean? A typology of readers' constructs"), *HTS* 47/1 (1991): 167-185; Smit, DJ, "Ethics and interpretation and South Africa", *Scriptura* 33 (99): 29-43; Smit, DJ, "Ethics and interpretation; new voices from the USA", *Scriptura* 33 (99): 16-28; and "Wat is Gereformeerde spiritualiteit?" ("What is a Reformed spirituality"), *NGTT* 2 (April 1988): 182-193.
29  Smit, *Neem Lees!*, 85.
30  In many articles throughout the years Smit would specifically focus on this subject of the ethics of interpretation. See e.g. his article on the responsibility of translation: Smit, "Pidgin or Pentecost?"; his article on the responsibility of writing theology: Smit, DJ (with Wessels, GF), "An ethics of writing? On writing as a social activity", *Scriptura* 57 (1996): 125-138; the articles he wrote with Bethel Müller on the responsibility of preaching: Smit, DJ (with Müller, BA), "Public worship: a tale of two stories", in Mouton, J & Lategan, BC (eds), *The Relevance of Theology for the 1990s* (Pretoria: HSRC, 1994), 385-408; "Om lesings te lees ... 'n Kategorieë-sisteem vir die analise van preke en godsdienstige uitsendings as lees- en kommunikasiegebeurtenisse" ("On reading readings ... A categorial system for

questions such as: Who reads? On behalf of whom? And Why? Although Smit often takes a critical stance towards a certain use of a hermeneutic of suspicion and the way in which some modernist (and post-modernist) reading strategies have come to exert an influence in our day and age, there are nonetheless also traces of a critical hermeneutic in his own thought. The Bible is indeed never read in a blind, naïve way. Hence, his remark:

> The question is how do we understand what we read? The Bible also speaks in many languages. The Bible is a complex witness, a library of books, written throughout the ages, under different circumstances, by numerous writers, in diverse genres, organized according to different logics, declared authoritative in complex ways and with inscrutable motives, canonized in different ways – and all of this applies only to the origin of the Bible, without saying anything about the even more complex history of its interpretation.[31]

This is why theology lives more from listening and hearing, than from knowing and speaking.

### c. A theological hermeneutic?

Together with this remark, it should also be mentioned that for Smit hermeneutics is a deeply *theological* activity. In a very interesting article, "Rhetoric and Ethic? A Reformed Perspective on the Politics of Reading the Bible", Smit asks what a Reformed perspective on the reading of the Bible entails, with a specific focus on Calvin's hermeneutics. On Calvin he writes: "Hermeneutics, for Calvin, is theology, not merely its preparation, and theology, for Calvin, is hermeneutics, not merely its material".[32] Without going into the details of Smit's engaging discussion, it can be mentioned how, towards the end of the article, he makes it clear that Calvin's theological hermeneutics cannot be equated with what today is called fundamentalism, liberalism, Biblicism, legalism or moralism. There is, though, the question concerning the so-called unity of the Bible. Smit writes:

> There can be no doubt that for Calvin, exegesis is not only free, but in fact called to concentrate on the meaning, the sense, of the pluriform and complex detail of the biblical texts with all possible human skills,

---

the analysis of sermons and religious broadcasts as reading and communication events"), *Scriptura* 11 (1993): 36-68; "South African radio and television as contexts for exegesis: A case study of interpretive practices in South African public worship", *Scriptura* S9 (1992): 73-86; "Godsdiens in die openbaar. Tendense in die Afrikaanse godsdiensprogramme van die SAUK" ("Religion in public: Trends in the Afrikaans religious programmes of the SABC"), *NGTT* 4 (1991): 652-665; his article on the responsible use of the Bible in forming ethical judgments: Smit, "The Bible and ethos in a new South Africa"; and his article on the responsible use of church documents: Smit, DJ (with De Villiers, DE), "Hoe Christens in Suid-Afrika by mekaar verby praat ... Oor vier morele spreekwyses in die Suid- Afrikaanse kerklike konteks" ("The way Christians in South Africa talk past one another ... On four ways of moral speaking in the South African church context"), *Skrif en kerk* (1994): 228-247.

31   Smit, "In diens van die tale Kanaäns?", 109.
32   Smit, "Rhetoric and Ethic?", 388.

methodologies and knowledge ... But then, according to Calvin, all this detail must somehow be assembled again, gathered ... The crucial question is, therefore, *how this gathering takes place, if at all*?[33]

It is probably easier to say how such a gathering of fragments does *not* take place. But Smit holds the view, like Calvin, that it *is* possible. How is it possible for Calvin? Smit answers:

> Clearly, because of his theological conviction that the same living Triune God is still speaking through these words, because of his trust that the same faithful God of the covenant of grace, because of his faith in the real presence of Christ, still fulfilling, through spoken and visible words, his three-fold office, promising, exhorting, and (trans)forming readers until today, through this message.[34]

We are thus dealing here with a transformative, theological hermeneutic. At this moment, there is indeed a growing number of voices calling for a theological interpretation of the Bible. Smit himself refers in the bibliography of *Neem, Lees!*, with the noteworthy title "Nóg stories oor ánder se stories" ("Yet more stories about the stories of others") to a number of commentary series that deliberately aim at being *theological*, for example NT Wright's *Everyone* series, the *Brazos Theological Commentary on the Bible* and Eerdmans' *Two Horizons* commentaries.[35] According to Smit, it is still too early to judge whether these products will make a lasting contribution. It is already clear, however, that the term 'theological hermeneutics' can be interpreted in many ways. It would therefore come as no surprise if Smit also raises questions about the underlying ethics of interpretations of a theological-hermeneutical reading of the Bible, as these approaches develop in the future.

## 4. CONFESS; TO EMBODY THE WORD OF GOD TODAY

### a. A confessional hermeneutics?

For Dirkie Smit both the reading and interpretation of the Bible are part of a complex hermeneutical process in which an attempt is made to hear the Gospel's message for today in a responsible manner. This process is not an exercise that can take place without some form of response and appropriation. 'Reading' and 'interpreting' are closely connected to 'confessing'. This notion of *confession* is indeed of central importance in Smit's understanding of the church and of theology. Theology is not the mere repetition of yesterday's truths. He writes:

> It is with this insight, that it is not enough to merely repeat what others, including the Holy Scriptures, have said before, and that it is also not possible to redirect and systematise the content of the Scriptures to form a corpus of timeless and perennial truth-propositions that can be consulted like a juridical codex or repository of truths and proofs, but

---

33  Smit, "Rhetoric and Ethic?", 415.
34  Smit, "Rhetoric and Ethic?", 416.
35  Smit, *Neem Lees!*, 320.

that they live with the necessity, the challenge – yes, on the ground of what the Scripture and its interpreters before them confessed – to read the signs of the times in each new situation, and to talk about the challenges and opportunities of each new day in the languages of Canaan, that the church struggles throughout the ages.[36]

For Dirkie Smit, this insight is articulated in the notion that faith asks for confession. To confess is to consent to, and to repeat in and through one's own words and life, that which has been heard in the Scriptures and in tradition.

A large portion of Dirkie Smit's work is devoted to this notion of confession, and he has indeed written extensively on the creeds and the confessions. On a number of occasions he has also presented Pentecost series on, for example, the different segments of the Nicene Creed. Through the years he would also reflect deeply on the nature and function of the Reformed confessions.[37] For him, the Reformed tradition is indeed a confessing tradition. Smit is, however, adamant about the fact that the creeds and confessions should not be seen as ahistorical documents consisting of timeless propositions. No, the Reformed engagement with confessions "takes historicity and contextuality very seriously".[38] There is thus a certain temporality and spatiality at work in Smit's thinking, which does not regard faith as something detached from time and context. Similar to the biblical texts, the confessions ask to be interpreted responsibly, by always taking historicity and contextuality into account. Smit states that "a hermeneutic of tradition is necessary in order to hear and obey the powerful and living witness of the confessions in the present time".[39] Confession is therefore also for the here and now, for our time, for and in Africa.

This focus on the historical context in which the confessions originated, as well as the context in which the confessions are appropriated, does not mean that the

---

36   Smit, "In diens van die tale Kanaäns?", 104.
37   See e.g. Smit, DJ, "'Bevrydende waarheid?' – Nagedink oor die aard van die Gereformeerde belydenis" "'Truth that liberates?' – Reflecting on the nature of the Reformed confession"), *Acta Theologica* 26, Vol. 1 (2006): 134-158; Smit, DJ, "Barmen and Belhar in conversation – A South African perspective", *NGTT* 47, 1&2 (2006): 291-302; "Die Gereformeerde siening van belydenis? Enkele algemene gedagtes" ("The Reformed view of confession? Some general thoughts"), unpublished article (2006); Smit, "On the Christian life"; Smit, "A time for confession?"; Smit, DJ, "'Christ transforming culture?' Nagedink oor die aard van die gereformeerde geloof" ("'Christ transforming culture?' Reflecting on the nature of Reformed faith"), in *Essentialia et Hodierna. Oblata P C Potgieter* (Acta Theologica Supplementum 3) (2002): 125-149; Smit, D J, "Bely en beliggaam" ("Confess and embody"), in Coertzen, P (ed.) *350 jaar Gereformeerd/350 Years Reformed* (Bloemfontein: CLF, 2002), 357-371; Smit, DJ, "Social transformation and confessing the faith? Karl Barth's views on confession revisited", *Scriptura* 72/1 (2000): 67-85; Smit, DJ, "A status confessionis in South Africa?", *JTSA*, Vol. 47 (1984): 2146; Smit, DJ, "… op 'n besondere wyse die God van die noodlydende, die arme en die veronregte.." ("… in a special way the God of the destitute, the poor and the wronged …", in Cloete, GD and Smit, DJ (eds), *'n Oomblik van waarheid* (*A Moment of Truth*) (Kaapstad: Tafelberg, 1984), 62-75; and Smit, DJ, "Wat beteken *status confessionis*?" ("What does *status confessionis* mean?", in Cloete, GD & Smit, DJ (eds), *'n Oomblik van waarheid* (Kaapstad: Tafelberg, 1984): 16-40.
38   Smit, "Die Gereformeerde siening van Belydenis?", 6.
39   Smit, "Die Gereformeerde siening van Belydenis?", 6.

authority of confessions is bound to social and historical contexts. Times of social transformation can be the motivation for confession (with Reformed confessions this is almost always the case), but the confessions can never be determined by this. In accordance with Barth, Smit writes:

> The historical context is present in the confession, sometimes implicitly, in the form of the No embedded in the Yes, but it never becomes the authority to which confession appeals. The intention and claim of Reformed confession is always to witness to truth that is above the historical context and to faith that properly belongs to the whole church, and will remain so. The reason is that Reformed confession rests on the authority of the living God who speaks through Word and Spirit ... What is ultimately at stake is the characteristic Reformed way of seeing the Word of God, the way Reformed believers think about reading, interpreting, hearing and preaching God's Word.[40]

In Smit's reflections on the Reformed tradition of confession, Karl Barth is thus also an important conversation partner. In an article "Social Transformation and Confessing the Faith: Karl Barth's views on confession revisited", Smit gives a comprehensive description of Barth's views on confession. He refers to a number of important speeches by Barth, such as one in September 1923 before the entire assembly of the *Reformierter Bund* in Emden on the subject, "Reformierte Lehre, ihr Wesen und ihre Aufgabe",[41] and his influential speech before the World Alliance of Reformed Churches' meeting in Cardiff in 1925 on the possibility and desirability of compiling a universal confession. In the light of his views on the nature of Reformed

---

40   Smit, "Social transformation and confessing the faith?", 81.
41   In this speech Barth asks what it means to take Reformed teaching and theology seriously. He goes on to reject three responses to this question, namely an antiquarian response, an ideological response and an emotional response. The antiquarian response sees the term "Reformed" as something that belongs to your identity, to your own tradition and practices. According to this view, the church should thus 'remain' Reformed, i.e. remain as it currently is. But the Reformed tradition, Barth holds, has a far greater openness towards the future. As a confessing tradition, there is, for example, always the possibility to write or adopt new confessions (if members of the church come to new insights). Another response, Barth writes, is an ideological one, which chooses certain themes, practices, slogans and institutions and calls them "Reformed". This group wants others to "become" more Reformed. Barth discusses a number of Reformed 'truths' and institutional forms that are seen in this way. Barth, however, also rejects this response. Smit summarises the reason for this as follows: "the church does not live from (a plurality) of truths, but from the *one* truth, which is not an idea, a principle, a doctrine ... but *the willingness to listen*, again and anew". Barth lastly also rejects what he calls an emotional response. Some, he writes, want to 'feel' more Reformed. They usually display great admiration for the 'fathers' and 'heroes' of the Reformed tradition. In this response, 'spirituality' (*Frömmigkeit*) is an important word. Barth, however, defends what has come to be known in history as "the principle of Scripture". In Reformed teachings and confessions certain things are said, because – in the light of the Word – one does not have any other choice. This 'principle' is not a formal principle, however, but a present reality. It cuts to the core of Reformed teaching, namely that God speaks. Barth accordingly makes the following observation about modern Protestantists: "they are caught in a prison, built on the four pillars of orthodoxy, pietism, enlightenment and religiosity". See Smit, "Social transformation and confessing the faith?", 71-72.

confessions, Barth was of opinion that this assembly could not and should not write a universal confession. Both of these speeches by Barth contains insights on the Reformed tradition that Smit would continually reflect on and integrate into his own views on Reformed identity throughout the years. In the Cardiff speech Barth gives his well-known definition of a Reformed confession:

> A Reformed confession of faith is the spontaneously and publically formulated presentation to the Christian church in general of a provisionally granted insight from the revelation of Jesus Christ attested to in Holy Scripture alone by a geographically circumscribed Christian fellowship which, until further notice, authoritatively defines it character to outsiders and which, until further action, gives direction to its own doctrine and life.[42]

In Dirkie Smit's numerous publications and speeches on Reformed theology, these words by Barth play a very important role. Smit accentuates the way in which this definition underlines the binding power of the confession. Smit also points to the significance of the phrase "until further notice" in Barth's definition. Like Barth, Smit is of opinion that the confessions possess a *relative authority* (with both words accentuated). A confession has authority because it represents the way in which previous generations heard the Word of God, but it also has a relative authority because it is subject to the authority of Scripture. Confessions should continuously be measured according to Scripture. Smit writes:

> The confession has authority because it has the authority of the Word of God behind it, yes, but it is all for the time being, currently, at this moment, with the present guidance and light, with the present spiritual insight and discernment. It is in principle always possible that the Spirit and the Word may bring the faith community to a different insight and conviction.[43]

In a fundamental way, all confessions are subject to the actual authority of the living Word.

According to Smit's view of confession, the emphasis is thus on the (historical) moment, but also on the fact that this moment is a moment of *truth*.[44] And this pursuit of truth is closely connected to the way one thinks about the reading, interpretation, hearing and preaching of the Word. Times of decision-making and truth are indeed times that ask for the responsible reading and interpretation of the Bible, for a true theological hermeneutic.

---

42   See Smit, "Social transformation and confessing the faith?", 72.
43   Smit, "Die Gereformeerde siening van Belydenis?", 5.
44   See also his work on the idea of the status confessionis: e.g. Smit, "A *status confessionis* in South Africa?", and Smit, Wat beteken *status confessionis*?". His own involvement in the process – also the writing process – surrounding the Confession of Belhar is well known. His work in this regard shows great continuity with his later writings on the nature of Reformed confessions. For the connection between Belhar and Barmen, Barth and other confessions, see Smit, "Social transformation and confessing the faith?", and Smit, "Bevrydende waarheid?".

### b. Confess and embody

In Barth's famous definition of Reformed confessions, he refers to the fact that confessions give direction to the teaching and life of the church. Smit also remarks that "(a)n extraordinary characteristic of Reformed confessions is the deep and reciprocal relationship between truth and life, between faith and ethics, between confession and act, between word and deed".[45] The act of confession is thus also a call to embodiment. The confession should be *lived out*. It has everything to do with the *praxis* of Christian and church life:

> The confession stretches out over ... the structure, the form, the institutionalising of the church that hears the gospel in such a way and confesses, and the confession stretches out over the ethics, the life, the conduct, the personal, social and political life of those who hear the gospel in such a way and confess.[46]

In the light of this one can point to the intrinsic relation between confession, on the one hand, and ecclesiology and ethics, on the other. It is thus quite possible, in contemplating a practical-theological ecclesiology and a contextual theological ethics, to build on, for example, the Barmen declaration or the confession of Belhar. It strengthens the connection between theological orientation and ecclesiastical or ethical embodiment. Smit's views on ecclesiology and ethics are indeed deeply connected to his understanding of the relation between confession and embodiment.

Smit would, for example, often refer to Calvin who, after he was convinced by Farel in 1536 to stay in Geneva, wrote three documents in the course of only a few months which would contribute to the reform of the congregation: a memorandum with the key points for a church order, a catechism, and a confession to which all members had to commit themselves as a foundation for life in the city.[47] For Calvin the order is arranged on the basis of the confession. In 1541 he again wrote three documents: a catechism, a liturgical guide and a few rules of order. Confession and embodiment thus go together. Renewal in confession leads to renewal in the church order.

Confession asks for embodiment. Smit states:

> It is therefore not surprising that within the Reformed tradition there have often been attempts to write new church orders through which these new insights from the gospel and the new confessions of their faith could be embodied. The confession called for embodiment, for more than that just ad hoc, instantaneous deeds of thankful obedience, for public, visible and lasting church structures, organisational forms, that would continuously enable and promote a life of thankfulness.[48]

The question of how the church should be ordered is thus also a question regarding confession, and is closely connected to the understanding of the church as a confessing community. This embodiment of the confession in church structures and ordinances forms part of an acknowledgement that confession and life are connected

---

45  Smit, "Die Gereformeerde siening van Belydenis?", 9.
46  Smit, "Die Gereformeerde siening van Belydenis?", 10.
47  Cf. e.g. Smit, "Bely en Beliggaam".
48  Smit, "Bely en Beliggaam", 358.

to one another. Towards the end of his important article "Bely en beliggaam", Smit writes: "After confession and after the first embodiment in the church order, for the Reformed faith the actual embodiment in life follows".[49]

### c. Confess and belong

In an article "On Belonging: Doing Theology Together", Smit points to the fact that at the heart of apartheid theology one could find an apartheid ecclesiology. The question is indeed to whom does the church belong: "Radically put, is the church the church of the *volk*, or the church of the Triune God?".[50] Since the time of Calvin, it has after all been a central claim of the Reformed faith that the church does not belong to itself. It is directly opposed to the idea of "our own". As the first question and answer of the Heidelberg Catechism clearly states: our deepest comfort lies therein that we do not belong to ourselves, but to Jesus Christ. For Smit, this fact – that the church does not belong to itself, but in Christ to the Triune God – is of decisive importance for our thinking about the church. Smit furthermore notes that almost all Christians would agree with this, but that the test will lie in concrete ecclesiologies, in everyday practices, and in specific historical circumstances. Smit continues by saying that the specific test in South Africa (which is sometimes referred to as 'the acid test'), takes form in the question of whether the church should visibly become one, and how this should be done. Today, in the midst of conversations on church reunification, it is important to take note of Smit's reminder that the the process around visible unity is closely related to the question of to whom we belong as church.

The Christian life is about the embodiment of the truth that we belong to the Triune God. Being Christian and being church has to do with 'belonging'. It also has significant implications for the way one thinks about theology. Theology is done in community:

> Theology is the ongoing work of the church of Jesus Christ, and this church does not belong to any nation or to the arbitrary wishes, needs and interests of particular groups who may decide to form a congregation or denomination, but to the Triune God of the whole church, history and the world. It is in belonging to this community that we can do theology together.[51]

This comment once again confirms Smit's fundamental belief in the necessity and integrity of an ecumenical pursuit of truth.

---

49  Smit, "Bely en Beliggaam", 371.
50  See Smit, "Belonging: Doing Theology Together", 5.
51  See Smit, "Belonging: Doing Theology Together", 8.

# 18. FOR JOHN DE GRUCHY: DEMOCRACY IS COMING TO THE RSA[1]

## 1. THE COMING OF DEMOCRACY

The title of this essay is a reference to the Canadian songwriter and poet Leonard Cohen's song "Democracy" (from his album *The Future*). Each stanza ends with the words "Democracy is coming to the USA". Although the album was only released in 1992, Cohen often alluded to the fact that the song developed around the time of the fall of the Berlin wall, a time when there were high hopes for a new world order of peace and justice. In an interview conducted in 1993 Cohen commented further:

> So while Eastern Europe was liberating itself, and the wall was coming down ... I said to myself: 'Is democracy really coming to the East?' And I had to answer truthfully 'No, I don't think it is!' And then I had to ask myself 'Where is democracy coming? What is democracy' ... And that's when I came upon the line 'Democracy is coming the USA', which of course has an irony. 'What do you meant to say, that it is not there already?' Well no. It isn't really there already, it is the ideal, it is the fate.[2]

The time that Cohen was working on this song was of course also the time during which a radical political transition was underway in South Africa. The country was on the bumpy road towards its first truly democratic elections in 1994, and during this time that the concept of democracy was widely discussed. Looking back, one can ask whether there was enough of a theological engagement with the notion of democracy during that time. One should recall, though, some projects and publications, such as the booklet *Die keuse vir 'n inklusiewe demokrasie: 'n teologies-eties studie oor toepaslike gemeenskapswaardes* (*The choice for an inclusive democracy: A theological-ethical study on relevant community values*) by Bernard Lategan, Johann Kinghorn, Lourens du Plessis and Etienne de Villiers (published by the Centre for Hermeneutics in Stellenbosch in 1987),[3] the collection *A Democratic Vision for South Africa* edited by Klaus Nürnberger

---

[1] This essay was presented as a paper at a conference of the Theological Society of South Africa (TSSA), on the theme "Citizens or Subjects? Theological and ethical reflections on participatory democracy in South Africa", held in Potchefstroom, 18-20 June 2014. The essay was orginally published under the title "'Democracy is coming to the RSA': On democracy, theology, and futural historicity" in *Verbum et Ecclesia* 37/1, 2016, 1-7.

[2] Interview with Leonard Cohen "Bob Harriss Show" (26/5/93). See http://www.leonardcohen-prologues.com/democracy.htm [Accessed on 14 June 2014]. Cohen adds: "But if it's coming to any place, its coming to America first, the cradle of the best and the worst".

[3] Lategan, B, Kinghorn J, Du Plessis, L, De Villiers, E, *Die keuse vir 'n inklusiewe demokrasie: 'n Teologies-etiese studie oor toepaslike gemeenskapswardes vir Suid-Afrika* (Stellenbosch: Sentrum vir Hermeneutiek, 1987). For a further development of the project, see Kinghorn, J, *'n Tuiste vir Almal: 'n sosiaal-teologiese studie oor 'n gesamentlike demokrasie in Suid-Afrika* (Stellenbosch; Sentrum vir Konstektuele Hermeneutiek, 1990).

(published in 1990),[4] and John de Gruchy's book *Christianity and Democracy*,[5] which was completed around the time that Nelson Mandela was inaugurated in May 1994 as South Africa's first democratically elected president.

The celebration of 20 years of democracy in South Africa in 2014 calls for sustained theological and ethical reflection. In this essay I would like to focus not so much on the coming of democracy to South Africa, or on the current state of our political dispensation, or on the future of democracy in South Africa. Rather, I want to offer some reflections that relate the concept of democracy – as an open-ended tradition – to notions dealing with historicity and the future, such as 'democracy to come', 'promise' and 'a democratic vision'. I will argue that although these notions are rightfully associated with the future, they also imply that democracy should not be disconnected from an emphasis on an inheritance from the past.

With this emphasis in mind, the first part of the essay attends to the French philosopher Jacques Derrida's intriguing phrase 'democracy to come,' drawing mainly but not exclusively on his text "The Reason of the Strongest (Are There Rogue States?)" in his book *Rogues: Two Essays on Reason* (first published in France under the title *Voyous*).[6] The second part of the essay takes a closer look at some aspects of the work of the South African theologian John de Gruchy on democracy. Special attention is given to De Gruchy's distinction between a democratic *system* and a democratic *vision*. Although Derrida's and De Gruchy's writings on democracy originate from different social locations, are conducted in different genres, and are situated in different theoretical discourses, they do share – amidst their differences – an emphasis on the open-endedness of democracy. One could speak in this regard of democracy's futural historicity. The third and final part of the essay brings some of the insights taken from the engagement with Derrida and De Gruchy into conversation with the continuing challenges facing theological discourse on democracy in South Africa today.

## 2. "DEMOCRACY TO COME" (JACQUES DERRIDA)

Although one can argue that politics is never absent from Derrida's work, and one should acknowledge the fact that Derrida often resisted the idea that his thinking had taken a political and ethical turn, it is true that there is a more explicit focus on politics (and ethics) in his later work. One key political idea that emerges in his later work is the thought-provoking concept "democracy to come" (*la démocratie à venir*). He developed this concept in a number of works and interviews from the early 1990s onwards, including *Spectres of Marx* (1993, a book dedicated to Chris Hani), *The Politics of Friendship* (1994), and most extensively in his essay "The Reason of the Strongest" (included in his book *Rogues: Two Essays on Reason*, the last book published during his lifetime). In this essay – first presented at a conference at Cerisy

---

4   Nürnberger, K (ed.), *A Democratic Vision for South Africa: Political Realism and Christian Responsibility* (NIR Reader No. 3) (Pietermaritzburg: Encounter Publications, 1991).
5   De Gruchy, JW, *Christianity and Democracy: A Theology for a Just World Order* (Cape Town: David Philip/ Cambridge: Cambridge University Press, 1995).
6   Derrida, J, *Rogues: Two Essays on Reason* (Stanford: Stanford University Press, 2005).

in 2002[7] in the aftermath of the attacks of 11 September 2001 – Derrida acknowledges that the strange syntagma "democracy to come" is an expression in which he often sought a sort of refuge.[8] But what does this enigmatic phrase mean?

On one level one can say that there is for Derrida an indeterminacy and open-endedness to democracy, as the verb "to come" indicates. The phrase 'democracy to come' implies, as Matthias Fritsch has argued, "a link between democracy and the promise of a future to come, an unownable and unknowable future".[9] The futural aspect of the 'to come' suggests not merely that democracy is coming in the future, but also that in some way the future is coming to democracy. Derrida often distinguishes between 'le futur' and 'l'avenir'. Whereas the first term refers to the future time that is in a sense predictable and foreseeable, 'l'avenir' ('à venir'; the futural 'to come') points to an unpredictable and unexpected event that can interrupt and transform, and hence also holds a certain promise.[10]

The phrase 'democracy to come' thus for Derrida points to the fact that democracy is not some stable and fixed concept or tradition, but that it is continually open to change and transformation. Within democracy there is an inherent instability, plasticity and drive to perfectibility (or pervertibility).[11] Democracy is always in the process of striving to become (more) democratic. In order to illuminate Derrida's use of the concept 'democracy to come', it is necessary to acknowledge the close interrelation between this term and another intriguing concept that plays a pivotal role in Derrida's later theology, namely the idea of 'autoimmunity'.[12] Autoimmunity – a term taken from biology – can be described as the process in which an entity attacks its own defences in order to defend itself. In a dialogue with Giovanna Borradori, Derrida gives the following succinct description: "(A)n autoimmunitary process is the strange behaviour where a living being, in quasi-*suicidal* fashion , 'itself' works to destroy its own protection, to immunise itself *against* its 'own' immunity".[13]

---

7   For more background information about this conference and Derrida's role, see Peeters, B, *Derrida: A Biography* (Cambridge: Polity Press, 2013), 515-517.
8   Derrida, *Rogues*, 8.
9   Fritsch, M, "Derrida's Democracy to Come", *Constellations* 9/4 (2002): 574-597, here 577.
10  In a documentary on Derrida's life (*Derrida*, 2002, directed by Amy Ziering and Kirby Dick), Derrida comments as follows "In general, I try and distinguish between what one calls the future and *l'avenir* [the 'to come]. The future is that which – tomorrow, later, next century – will be. There is a future which is predictable, programmed, scheduled, foreseeable. But there is a future, *l'avenir* (to come), which refers to someone who comes whose arrival is totally unexpected. For me, that is the real future. That which is totally unpredictable. The Other who comes without my being able to anticipate their arrival. So if there is a real future, beyond the other known future, it is *l'avenir* in that it is the coming of the Other when I am completely unable to foresee their arrival".
11  Although one can describe Derrida as a friend of democracy, he does draw attention to the aporetic character of democracy and the dangers contained within it. Cf. Patton, P, "Derrida, Politics and Democracy to Come", *Philosophy Compass* 2/6 (2007): 766-780, here 767.
12  Derrida began using the concept of autoimmunity in the mid-1990s. See in this regard his important essay "Faith and Knowledge: The Two Sources of 'Religion at the Limits of Reason Alone'" (first published in French in 1996 and in English in 1998) in Derrida, J, *Acts of Religion*, Anidjar, G (ed.) (New York, Routledge, 2002)
13  Borradori, G, *Philosophy in a Time of Terror: Dialogues with Jürgen Habermas and Jacques Derrida* (Chicago and London: University of Chicago Press, 2003), 94.

In "The Reason of the Strongest" Derrida illustrates the term 'autoimmunity' with reference to a couple of examples. The first example is taken from post-colonial Algeria where the democratic electoral process of 1992 was interrupted because of fears that it could result in the formation of a fundamentalist Islamist government, which might have introduced antidemocratic laws. If so, this would have been an example where democracy democratically served the move to an anti-democratic regime. This possibility is real for all democracies, Derrida argues, since "the *alternative to* democracy can always be *represented* as a democratic *alternative*".[14] The Algerian example to suspend provisionally the elections in sovereign fashion is for Derrida typical of all assaults on democracy that take place in the name of democracy, seemingly for democracy's own good.

Derrida's second example of autoimmunity at work in democratic processes invokes the attacks of 11 September 2001. Derrida comments on the fact that the largely democratic culture and legal system of the United States makes the country relatively open to others, including the suicidal pilots that were trained on American soil.[15] The threat to democracy experienced in the aftermath of 9/11, Derrida argues, resulted in the fact that democracy attacks part of itself, restricting in the process some democratic freedoms and rights, and transferring unchecked power to security police and the surveillance apparatus of the state.[16]

For Derrida, democracy is not merely autoimmune in the sense that it turns against itself and its own inherent values of freedom and openness in the light of real or perceived threats, but also that it turns against itself through constantly putting itself into question. Inherent in democracy is a form of self-critique that is linked to the fact that democracy seeks perfecting itself. Derrida writes:

> The expression 'democracy to come' takes into account the absolute and intrinsic historicity of the only system that welcomes in itself, in its very concept, that expression of autoimmunity called the right to self-critique and perfectibility. Democracy is the only system, the only constitutional paradigm, in which, in principle, one has or assumes the right to criticize everything publicly, including the idea of democracy, its concept, its history, and its name. Including the idea of the constitutional paradigm and the absolute authority of law. It is thus the only paradigm that is universalizable, hence its chance and its fragility.[17]

One can thus say that autoimmunity does not only involve, as Samir Haddad has rightly pointed out, the occurrence of what is often viewed as antidemocratic

---

14  Derrida, *Rogues*, 31.
15  Derrida, *Rogues*, 40.
16  In Derrida's words: "(W)e see an American administration, potentially followed by others in Europe and the rest of the world, claiming that in the war it is waging against the 'axis of evil', against the enemies of freedom and the assassins of democracy throughout the world, it must restrict within its own country certain so-called democratic freedoms and the exercise of certain rights by, for example, increasing the powers of police investigation and interrogations, without anyone, any democrat, being really able to oppose such measures". Derrida, *Rogues*, 40.
17  Derrida, *Rogues*, 86-87.

measures, but also accounts for what is regarded by many as prodemocratic.[18] These prodemocratic accounts of self-critique and openness underline an attitude of hospitality within democracy that makes democracy vulnerable. The infinite perfectibility of democracy thus brings with it danger and risk. Yet to speak of democracy to come is to inscribe within democracy the promise of an open future associated with radical hospitality.

It is beyond the scope of this essay to give a detailed description of Derrida's complex discussion of the notion 'democracy to come', but suffice it to say that for Derrida democracy to come indicates a promise of infinite perfectibility that implies a continuing critique of the way democracy is formalised and institutionalised. Ideas such as freedom and equality are inscribed as promise within democracy. This promise is inscribed within history (with democracy thus being a political dispensation open to its own historicity), opening up an endless process of transformation.

What are the implications of Derrida's concept of 'democracy to come'? A possible answer to this question relates to the fact that it challenges any lazy equation of democracy with a specific regime or practice, and continually calls for an interruptive and transformative engagement with democracy in the here and the now. As Derrida puts it:

> The expression 'democracy to come' does indeed translate or call for a militant and interminable political critique. A weapon aimed at the enemies of democracy, it protests against all naïveté and every political abuse, every rhetoric that would present as a present or existing democracy, as a de facto democracy, what remains inadequate to the democratic demand, whether nearby or far away, at home or somewhere else in the world, anywhere that a discourse on human rights and on democracy remains little more than an obscene alibi so long as it tolerates the terrible plight of so many millions of human beings suffering from malnutrition, disease, and humiliation, grossly deprived not only of bread and water but of equality and freedom, dispossessed of the rights of all, of everyone, of anyone.[19]

The ethical and political thrust of Derrida's understanding of 'democracy to come' is clear in the above quotation, and throughout his writings Derrida emphasises the way in which 'democracy to come' is inextricably linked to justice.[20]

Moreover, democracy is for Derrida radically historical yet is always coming. As he writes towards the end of his book *Politics of Friendship*:

> For democracy remains to come; this is the essence in so far as it remains indefinitely perfectible, hence always insufficient and future, but, belonging to the time of the promise, it will always remain, in each of

---

18   Haddad, S, *Derrida and the Inheritance of Democracy* (Bloomington: Indiana University Press, 2013), 60.
19   Derrida, *Rogues*, 86.
20   Cf. Derrida, *Rogues*, 88. Here Derrida points to the conjunction between democracy and justice in his works *Specters of Marx* and *Politics of Friendship*.

its future times, to come: even when there is democracy, it never exists, it is never present, it remains the theme of a non-presentable concept.[21]

The fact that 'democracy to come' hesitates endlessly does not mean for Derrida that it merely offers a neutral conceptual analysis or leads to paralysis; rather, it also attempts to win support and adherence; it seeks performativity. "The *to* of the 'to come' wavers between imperative injunction (the call to performance) and the patient *perhaps* of messianicity".[22] Democracy to come indicates that we do not know what democracy is, that we should be careful to identify it with any political regime, that it is (always) to come, and at the same time that the openness to this futural 'to come' has transformative potential; it promise an event, a change of heart, within history, within the here and the now.

## 3. A DEMOCRATIC VISION (JOHN DE GRUCHY)

In the second part of the essay, I want to draw attention to the work of the South African theologian John de Gruchy who has engaged extensively from a theological perspective with the notion of democracy since the early 1990s, the period of transition to democracy in South Africa. For De Gruchy – as for Derrida – democracy is an open-ended tradition that is in need of constant interruption and transformation in the concrete here and now in the light of a future vision or vision of the future.

In his book *Christianity and Democracy: A Theology for a Just World Order*, De Gruchy makes a helpful distinction between the democratic *system* and the democratic *vision*. He explains:

> By democratic *system* we mean those constitutional principles and procedures, symbols and convictions, which have developed over the centuries and which have become an essential part of any genuine democracy whatever its precise historical form. When we speak about a democratic *vision*, we refer to that hope for a society in which all people are truly equal and yet where difference is respected; a society in which all people are truly free, but where social responsibility rather than individual self-interest prevails; and a society which is truly just, and therefore one in which the vast gulf between rich and poor has been overcome.[23]

This distinction implies, among other things, that a democratic system is birthed and sustained by a democratic vision, and that a democratic system is in constant need of asking the question whether it adequately gives form to a democratic vision.[24]

---

21 Derrida, *Politics of Friendship*, 306.
22 Derrida, *Rogues*, 91. Or as Paul Patton writes about "democracy to come": "In effect, the phrase is not simply constative but also performative: it is both an open-ended description function and a demand for more democracy". Patton, *Derrida, Politics and Democracy to Come*, 773.
23 De Gruchy, JW, *Christianity and Democracy: A Theology for a Just World Order* (Cape Town: David Philip/ Cambridge: Cambridge University Press, 1995), 7.
24 It should be noted though that De Gruchy does not vilify the idea of a democratic system in order to affirm the promise of a democratic vision. He writes: "It may be argued that while the democratic system has derived from the liberal trajectory in the development

What exactly such a democratic vision entails, however, is in itself often highly contested, albeit that there is often also some form of consensus about the values that are associated with such a vision. De Gruchy links the democratic vision to the hope for a society in which there is true equality, true freedom and true justice. Moreover, it is an equality that respects difference, it is a freedom that is linked to social responsibility, and it is a justice which seeks to overcome economic inequality.[25] Or as he put it elsewhere: "If we regard democracy simply as a system of governance, we fail to appreciate its character as an open-ended process that is ever seeking to become more inclusive, more just, and more global in response to the needs and hopes of society".[26]

In the previous section I referred to the specific way in which Derrida emphasises the open-endedness or open future of democracy. De Gruchy too views democracy as an open-ended tradition: "Like all living traditions, democracy is a 'narrative of an argument' which is open to change and development, retrieval and renewal".[27] He quotes approvingly John Dewey's remark that the task of democracy "is one that can have no end, the task of democracy is forever that of the creation of a freer and more human experience in which all share and to which all contribute".[28] And, adds De Gruchy: "That is the democratic vision which democratic systems should seek to serve".[29]

De Gruchy wrote *Christianity and Democracy* around the time of the first truly democratic elections in South Africa in 1994, completing it in the week of Nelson Mandela's presidential inauguration. During that time South Africa was clearly in need of a truly participatory democratic system, and a theological engagement with the concept of democracy was timely. Although many pastors, church members and theologians were aloof with respect to the political discourse and praxis surrounding the democratic transition in South Africa, De Gruchy was among those theologians and church leaders who amplified Nelson Mandela's call that the churches should be midwives of democracy.[30]

Even though De Gruchy agrees – in some sense at least – with Stanley Hauerwas's oft-quoted remark that the church "does not exist to provide an ethos for democracy or any other form of social organisation"[31], he also argues that this statement

---

of democracy, the prophetic vision has been expressed in the socialist trajectory. But whatever their past relations there is today the clear need to embody the best of both and move beyond them in search of new models of a just and democratic world order". De Gruchy, *Christianity and Democracy*, 275.

25  See De Gruchy, *Christianity and Democracy*, 7.
26  De Gruchy, JW, "Democracy", in Scott, P and Cavanaugh, W T, *The Blackwell Companion to Political Theology* (Oxford: Blackwell, 2004), 441.
27  De Gruchy, *Christianity and Democracy*, 15,16.
28  Quoted in De Gruchy, *Christianity and Democracy*, 39.
29  De Gruchy, *Christianity and Democracy*, 39.
30  In a speech on 14 December 1992 at a meeting of the Free Ethiopian Church of Southern Africa, Mandela called on churches "to join other agents of change and transformation in the difficult task of acting as a midwife to the birth of our democracy". See De Gruchy, *Christianity and Democracy*, 218. Cf. also De Gruchy JW, "Midwives of Democracy", *Journal of Theology for Southern Africa* 86 (1994):14-25.
31  De Gruchy, *Christianity and Democracy*, 8. See Hauerwas, S, *A Community of Character: Towards a Constructive Social Ethic* (Notre Dame: University of Notre Dame Press,

should not imply that all systems of government are equally acceptable from a Christian perspective. De Gruchy is furthermore interested in highlighting some deep connections between Christianity and democracy. In his historical account of the relationship between Christianity and democracy he argues that democracy should not be only linked to what happened in Athens in the 5th century BCE, but that Christianity, and specifically the vision of the Hebrew prophets, provided the matrix for the development of a democratic vision. It was in the womb of Western Christendom that democracy gestated, and although the relationship between Christianity and democracy is ambiguous, Christianity did also contribute to the democratic vision through its prophetic witness, even if this witness was often severely compromised. Yet De Gruchy also states:

> ... however much Christianity provided the matrix for the gestation of democracy, or through its praxis has enabled its birth in different contexts, it has been its witness to the prophetic vision as interpreted through the reign of God in Jesus Christ that has been its lasting contribution ... Moreover, it is the eschatological message of the prophets, their concrete utopianism in which hope and justice have been inseparably related, which has provided Christianity with its resources in the public sphere and enabled it to remain in tension or critical solidarity with political systems.[32]

Although De Gruchy also highlights the promise of a social understanding of the doctrine of the Trinity for the Christian tradition's critical and constructive engagement with democracy,[33] for him it is especially in the prophetic vision as interpreted through the reign of God in Jesus Christ where the deep connection between Christianity and democracy is to be found. It is this prophetic vision that informs and constantly challenges a democratic vision of a just, free and equal society. De Gruchy admits that this "concrete utopia" is always beyond full realisation, and in this sense he shares an important concern underlying Derrida's use of the concept 'democracy to come'. However, De Gruchy also adds that "every victory for human equality, freedom, justice, peace, and the integrity of creation, is a step towards its fulfilment".[34] Although democracy might be the best political system available for the embodying of what he calls "penultimate expressions of the vision of shalom",[35] it is not to be equated with the kingdom of God.

For De Gruchy the democratic vision is furthermore in need of some important moral and spiritual commitments. Democracy requires a democratic ethos, and although it is not the main task of the church to provide the ethos for democracy or other political systems, it is also true that a democratic vision suffers if it is not sustained by some sort of moral and spiritual force.[36]

---

1981), 35.
32  De Gruchy, *Christianity and Democracy*, 275. In his book *A Theological Odyssey: My Life in Writing* (Stellenbosch: Sun Media, 2014), De Gruchy uses the first part of this quotation as motto for his chapter on "Democracy, Reconciliation & Restoring Justice".
33  See De Gruchy, *Christianity and Democracy*, 11-12, 238-248.
34  De Gruchy, *Christianity and Democracy*, 274.
35  De Gruchy, *Christianity and Democracy*, 276.
36  De Gruchy emphasises that democracy is dependent on the participation of all citizens, and even if this is an ideal, it is an ideal worth striving for. He adds: "Perhaps that is why

## 4. FUTURAL HISTORICITY, THEOLOGY AND DEMOCRACY IN SOUTH AFRICA

In his book entitled *A Rumour of Spring* the seasoned journalist Max du Preez gives an interesting analysis of the 20 years of democracy after 1994 in our "multiply wounded, multiply traumatised" country.[37] At the heart of Du Preez's analysis is a concern for the future of democracy in South African, hence his question: "(A) re we facing a spring of hope, growth and cohesion, or an Arab Spring Aftermath with popular uprisings, economic ruin and instability?"[38] Although Du Preez takes a hard look at the state of democracy in South Africa, he does not think that South Africa is facing anything like the harsh consequences of an Arab Spring. Part of his optimism lies in what he sees as the reawakening of civil society. Hence his forecast: "My weather report says the winter will persist for a while, but there is a promise of an eventual spring. It might be accompanied by a few thunderstorms, though".[39]

It is not my purpose here to comment on the state of democracy in our country, or indeed worldwide,[40] but in closing I want to make four brief remarks that I think are important to keep in mind in the attempt to provide a constructive and critical theological engagement with the discourse on democracy, also in South Africa, drawing in the process on some insights from the thoughts of Derrida and De Gruchy.

The first remark relates to the open future of democracy. By viewing democracy as an open-ended tradition, one challenges the view that sees democracy as something fixed, static and stable. Derrida's use of the notion of 'democracy to come' invites us to acknowledge the unstable and aporetic nature of democracy. We should not think too hastily that we know what democracy is, or describe too quickly a specific government as democratic or undemocratic. Processes of democratisation have the potential to demythologise harmful ideologies, but one should also remember, as Dirkie Smit has argued, that democracy itself can become ideological when used "as self-evident expressions and for the purposes of new ideological language, mystifying and obscuring, legitimating new collective interest".[41] The radical character of a 'democracy to come' with its emphasis on (impossible) unconditional hospitality (Derrida), or a democratic vision with its emphasis on true equality, freedom and justice (De Gruchy), should continue to haunt political systems, including so-called democratic regimes. The interruptive, disruptive and transformative potential of this future vision for a just political dispensation should not be underestimated. Christian

---

some writers insist that democracy is ultimately dependent upon the development of a spirituality in which human freedom, genuine community, and the willingness to share undergird political programs and actions". De Gruchy, "Democracy", 453.

37  Du Preez, M, *A Rumour of Spring: South Africa after 20 Years of Democracy* (Cape Town: Zebra Press, 2013). The phrase "multiply wounded, multiply traumatised" is taken from the heading of the first chapter of Du Preez's book, and Du Preez, in turn, draws for this notion on the work of Nicaraguan psychologist Martha Cabrera.
38  Du Preez, *Rumour of Spring*, 3.
39  Du Preez, *Rumour of Spring*, 279.
40  See in this regard the provocative set of essays by Giorgio Agamben, Alain Badiou, Daniel Bensaïd, Wendy Brown, Jean-Luc Nancy, Jacques Rancière, Kristin Ross and Slavoj Žižek in Agamben, G et al., *Democracy in what state?* (New York: Columbia University Press, 2012).
41  Smit, DJ, "The demythologisation of ideology", Nürnberger, K (ed.), *A Democratic Vision for South Africa* (Pietermaritzburg: Encounter Publications, 1991), 280-296, here 296.

theology can indeed, as De Gruchy has pointed out, draw on rich theological notions such as the prophetic vision of the peaceful reign of God in Christ to challenge and enliven a democratic vision in order to foster a culture that respects the life, dignity and wellbeing of humans and the rest of creation.

Secondly, the emphasis on the futural openness of democracy should not invite a vague utopianism, but should be viewed as closely connected with the present and the past. In speaking of the vision of the prophetic tradition in the Scriptures, De Gruchy uses the helpful phrase "concrete utopianism". This reminds us that this vision seeks form and embodiment in the here and the now. In addition, we should not merely think of democracy as something informed and sustained by a vision of the future, but also as an inheritance from the past. Samir Haddad has convincingly argued that there is a connection between Derrida's 'democracy to come' and a certain relation to the past, and that inheritance plays a pivotal role in Derrida's thought on democracy.[42] Haddad comments:

> In addition to evoking an openness to the future, Derrida's writings on democracy also contain the injunction to inherit, and so one is reminded that the passive dimension in democracy to come does not entail doing nothing at all. There is a lot to do, for there is a call to examine democracy's history, its historicity, to negotiate this history and all it produces.[43]

In other words, democracy to come has a futural openness, but this openness has the structure of a futural *historicity*, a historicity that emphasises an inheritance from the past and a repetition (which is always a re-appropriation of the tradition) in the present. If I can bring this into conversation with some challenges arising from the South African democratisation process: our actions should not only be informed by a future vision of what democracy can be, but by the memory of a specific history, a history of undemocratic exclusion and the struggle towards greater equality, freedom and justice. In our discussion on the current state and future of democracy in South Africa, and on possible theological responses, we should be acutely aware that our discourse and actions are situated within a very specific historical reality and that a sensitivity to this reality should mark our remarks and shape our thoughts and actions.

A third aspect that I think requires in-depth theological engagement (although I will merely mention it here) relates to the thorny relationship between democracy and sovereignty. Several readers of Derrida's work on 'democracy to come' have highlighted the way in which Derrida seeks to disassociate this concept from the principle of sovereignty. As Alex Thomson observes: "Derrida's ultimate target in *Rogues* may not be democracy after all, but sovereignty, and with it our sense of propriety, of sanctity and security, of the supposedly legitimate force wielded over any body, state, or identity".[44] It is the case that democracy seems to depend on sovereignty; it is difficult to imagine democracy without political control over one's territory. Yet it might be that the deepest pathos underlying Derrida's 'democracy

---

42  See Haddad, *Derrida and the Inheritance of Democracy*, especially 2, and also 65-72.
43  Haddad, *Derrida and the Inheritance of Democracy*, 72.
44  Thomson, A, "What's to Become of 'Democracy to Come'?" (2005). http://pmc.iath.virginia.edu/text-only/issue.505/15.3thomson.txt [Accessed on 12 June 2014].

to come' is his dream of a democracy without sovereignty. John D. Caputo, who has written much on Derrida and also in the spirit of Derrida, asks some poignant questions along these lines:

> (M)ust democracy be a sovereignty? Or is the very idea of sovereignty incompatible with a true or radical democracy? Might it be that wherever democracy tries to come, sovereignty would have to go? Do we not require a *new* democratic revolution, not a revolution *to* democracy, but a revolution *in* democracy, once that turns the screw of democracy once again and turns it *into* democracy.[45]

Caputo is of the opinion that a radical democratic revolution would not entail jettisoning theology, but rather requires "a parallel radicalisation of theology", one in which we imagine "the coming of God without sovereignty".[46] Some theologians, like Graham Ward, have also argued that the fragility of the history of democracy, as well as the fact that some scholars now describe our current situation as postdemocratic, underline the need "to revisit the theological foundations of sovereignty".[47] In my view an engagement with Trinitarian theology offers rich resources for a theological engagement with sovereignty. And a theological engagement with sovereignty should also take into account the Reformed theologian John de Gruchy's remark that:

> Sovereignty is not only a royal metaphor which separated God from the world, thereby legitimising hierarchy and paving the way for a theocratic-style tyranny; it is also a prophetic metaphor which, when applied to God, de-absolutizes and relativizes all other claimants to absolute power ... Thus, whatever the inadequacy of sovereignty as a divine attribute, we dare not surrender the theological claim that is being made.[48]

A fourth and final remark relates to the fact that a democratic system and vision are envisaged and sustained by people who embody a democratic ethos. In his forthcoming book *A Theological Odyssey: My Life in Writing*, John de Gruchy engages

---

[45] Caputo, JD, "Without Sovereignty, Without Being: Unconditionality, the Coming God and Derrida's Democracy to Come", *JCRT* 4/3 (2003): 9-26, here 11. Cf. also Michael Naas's article, "'One Nation Indivisible': Jacques Derrida on the Autoimmunity of Democracy and the Sovereignty of God", *Research in Phenomenology* 36 (2006): 15-44.

[46] Caputo, "Without Sovereignty, Without Being", 13. For a fuller development of Caputo's thought in this regard, see Caputo, JD, *The Weakness of God: A Theology of the Event* (Bloomington and Indianapolis: Indiana University Press, 2006), especially 1-41.

[47] Ward, G, *The Politics of Discipleship: Becoming Postmaterial Citizens* (Grand Rapids: Baker Academic, 2009), 39. Ward draws on the work of Colin Crouch, who has written extensively on the so-called postdemocratic condition, and has highlighted four characteristics. The first feature is that the will of the people is not so much obtained but created, with politics being dominated by media presentation. A second feature of postdemocracy is that the political sphere is dominated by economic questions. A third characteristic of the postdemocratic condition is that there is not simply a decline in political participation, but indeed active forms of depoliticisation. And fourth, there is a crisis of representation in the sense that the interests of a powerful minority attract far more attention than their numbers justify, and politicians represent not their constituencies but the concerns of influential lobbyists. See Ward, *The Politics of Discipleship*, 63-72.

[48] De Gruchy, *Christianity and Democracy*, 257-258.

with Dietrich Bonhoeffer's response to William Paton's book *The Church and the New Order* (drafted in 1941), in which Bonhoeffer emphasised that a return to a full-fledge democracy would be unwise for post-war Europe, because democracy "can only grow in a soil which has been prepared by along spiritual tradition".[49] For Bonhoeffer a genuinely democratic order required a deeper spiritual foundation and value commitment than that provided by liberalism. In conversation with Bonhoeffer, De Gruchy state his own position:

> Going with but also beyond Bonhoeffer, I believe that democracy at its best is an open-ended project of transformative praxis in which the rule of law, the development of shared moral values and the protection of human rights are affirmed, in which differences of culture and gender are respected, and in which the economic market is reconstructed in the interests of overcoming the explosion of poverty and the destruction of the environment.[50]

Maybe this emphasis on a moral and spiritual force needed to sustain democracy invites us to re-contextualise Leonard Cohen's song mentioned in the Introduction to this essay:

> It's coming to South Africa first,
> The cradle of the best and of the worst.
> It's here they got the range
> and the machinery for change
> and it's here they got the spiritual thirst.
> It's here the family's broken
> and it's here the lonely say
> that the heart has got to open
> in a fundamental way
> Democracy is coming to the RSA.

---

49 De Gruchy, *A Theological Odyssey*, 109. Cf. Bonhoeffer, D, *Conspiracy and Imprisonment: 1940-1945* (DBWE 16) (Minneapolis: Fortress Press, 2006), 536.

50 De Gruchy, *A Theological Odyssey*, 110. De Gruchy continues: "It is a vision of a truly equal, responsibly free and socially just world order. As such it challenges and prods us towards the ongoing transformation of present democratic systems in the struggle for fuller and more adequate expressions of the democratic vision in which human dignity and social justice are fundamental. I believe that this vision is embodied in the South African Constitution and that for this reason it must be respected, defended and implemented if we are to achieve the democratic transformation for which we hope and struggle" (110).

# PART 4 –
# REVISITING REFORMED PRACTICES AND CONFESSIONAL DOCUMENTS

# 19. ON THE LORD'S SUPPER: THE 'WELCOME TABLE', EXCLUSION AND THE REFORMED TRADITION[1]

## 1. INTRODUCTION

In a chapter entitled "De Kerk" ("The Church") in Bram van de Beek's book *Is God terug?* (*Is God back?*) he states his deep-seated conviction that the Lord's Supper is central to the life of a Christian and the church. He therefore advocates frequent celebration of the Lord's Supper – at least weekly or even more often.[2] In the same chapter he also writes about the need for church discipline ("tucht") as an ecclesial practice.[3] In honour of Bram van de Beek I want to address some questions regarding the relationship between the Lord's Supper, hospitality and church discipline. At the heart of my reflection is a concern with finding a way to relate a focus on the Lord's Supper as a feast of radical inclusion and hospitality to the need to protect the integrity of the meal through disciplined practices. I offer these reflections in the hope and confidence that Bram van de Beek's work on ecclesiology will provide important theological insights and pointers in this regard, given – among other things – his profound knowledge of the Reformed tradition.

One could argue that the Lord's table is not a table of separation and exclusion, but can be described as 'the welcome table' (to use the title of a well-known short story by Alice Walker).[4] The unconditional acceptance of all participants at the Lord's Supper affirms the visible unity of the body of Christ and the grace of the Host. The Lord's Supper is thus inextricably linked to the notion of hospitality, as well as to the need to challenge certain reductive practices of exclusion and restricted access. One can even ask whether the exclusion of people from the table as part of church discipline does not often result in a form of moral gatekeeping that threatens to negate the welcoming character of God's grace. In this essay I want to affirm the importance of viewing the Lord's Supper as a welcome and welcoming table.

---

1  This essay was read at a meeting of the "Reformed History and Theology" group at the American Academy of Religion in San Diego in November 2007, and later published as "The Welcoming Table? The Lord's Supper, Exclusion, and the Reformed Tradition" in Van der Borght, E and Van Geest, P (eds), *Strangers and Pilgrims on Earth: Essays in Honour of Abraham van de Beek* (Leiden: Brill, 2012), 483-501.
2  Van de Beek, A, *Is God terug?* (Zoetermeer: Meinema, 2010), 92. Van de Beek writes: "Het centrale moment van het leven van een christen zou de viering van het avondmaal moet zijn en dan niet eenmaal in de drie maanden, maar minstens wekelijks en liefst nog vaker. Het is onvoorstelbaar dat er kerklijke gemeenschappen zijn die eenmaal in de drie maanden een avondsmaalviering genoeg vinden. Kan dat ooit de viering van de liefde zijn? Meer nog: kan dat ooit de viering van het leven zijn?" (92). [The central moment of the life of a Christian ought to be the celebration of the Lord's Supper, and not only once every three months, but weekly, and even more frequently. It is unthinkable that some ecclesial communities find a quarterly celebration sufficient. Can that ever be enough to celebrate love. Indeed, can that be a celebration of life?]
3  Van de Beek comments: "Het wordt hoog tijd dat de kerk weer tucht gaat uitoefenen en dan niet pas als een dominee beweert dat God niet bestaat". Van de Beek, *Is God terug?*, 97. [It is high time that the church again exercises its discipline, and not wait until a pastor claims that God does not exist]
4  See Walker, A, *In Love and Trouble* (San Diego: Harvest, 1967).

This particular emphasis is highlighted by referring to the way in which a synodical decision by the Dutch Reformed Church in South Africa in 1857 legitimised separate worship and separate celebrations of the Lord's Supper along class and race lines. In the first part of the essay I revisit this decision and its historical context, drawing in part on the work of the late Chris Loff, as a way to point to the need not to separate the Lord's Supper from notions of inclusion and hospitality. With this historical example in mind, the rest of the essay elaborates on, and complicates, this emphasis on the Lord's Supper as a welcoming table by drawing on certain aspects of the thought of the German Reformed theologian Michael Welker and the 16th-century Reformer John Calvin. The last section of the essay offers a few concluding remarks on the Lord's Supper as a practice of hospitality among other disciplined practices that enable, and are enabled by, the visible unity of the body of Christ in time.

## 2. SEPARATE TABLES: THE DECISION OF 1857

In November 1857 the synod of the Dutch Reformed Church in South Africa took a decision that would later prove to have great historical significance. This decision reads as follows (in translation):

> Synod regards it as desirable and Scriptural that our members out of heathendom should be accepted and incorporated within our existing congregations, wherever this can happen; but where this measure could, *as a result of the weakness of some*, obstruct the advance of the cause of Christ amongst the heathen, then congregations consisting of heathen converts, or which may still so be formed, shall enjoy their Christian privileges in a separate building or institution.[5]

Although this decision affirms that ideally and in the light of Scripture, the coloured and black converts to Christianity should be incorporated into the existing Dutch Reformed congregations, it did open the door for exceptions by making allowance for the 'weakness of some' (i.e. the prejudices of some white members). Over time, however, this "state of exception"[6] paved the way for establishing a situation in which the exception became the rule. What was viewed as a temporary measure became the status quo.

What was the background of the infamous 1857 decision? In 1855 a group of 45 white members approached the church council of the congregation of Stockenström in the Eastern Cape (where the white members were in the minority) with a request that separate communion services be held for them.[7] This request was denied by the

---

5   *Acta Synodi*, Dutch Reformed Church (1857): 168.
6   For a discussion on the use of the notion of 'state of exception' in political theory, see Agamben, G, *State of Exception* (Chicago: University of Chicago Press, 2005). For a reading of Agamben on "the state of exception" with reference to an episode in South African religious history, see Vosloo, R, "The state of exception and religious freedom: Revisiting the Church-State confrontation correspondence and statements of 1988" in *Studia Historiae Ecclesiasticae* 34/1, 2008:193-210.
7   Stockenström's congregation grew from a community of Khoi people established on the banks of the Kat River (near Grahamstown in the Eastern Cape). At first the London Missionary Society ministered to this community, but in 1831 it joined the Dutch Reformed

church council. The group made a second appeal in which they asked that they at least be served by white church council members after the Lord's Supper had been celebrated by the rest of the congregation. With reference to texts such as Romans 14:1 ("Welcome those who are weak in faith"), they asked in their appeal that the church council must not be too harsh on their 'weaknesses'.

Although the church council allowed that white church council members be chosen, they did not agree to the separate celebration of the sacrament. The presbytery of Albany – under which the congregation of Stockenström resorted – took notice of the request of the white minority group and suggested that, because of the weakness and prejudices of these members, the church council should allow that one or more tables be set afterwards to serve them. How do these events relate to the synod of 1857? According to Chris Loff, there was an elder from Malmesbury who was aware of the event in Stockenström from a report in the official Dutch Reformed Church newspaper *De Gereformeerde Kerkbode*; this elder requested that the decision of the presbytery of Albany be read to the synod of 1857 during a debate about a request from the congregation of Ceres (in the Western Cape) for a separate building for coloured members.[8] The debate evinced two positions. On the one hand, there were those who felt that (racial) prejudices must be challenged. On the other hand, some pleaded for a policy of caution, most likely claiming that these practices of separate communion services were already prevalent in many congregations. When the synod reconvened the next day, Rev. Andrew Murray Senior, made the proposal (quoted above) aimed at resolving the thorny issue. He proposed that while the synod ideally wants to see that converts from heathendom be accepted and incorporated into the existing congregations, 'because of the weakness of some' separate worship services could be allowed to advance the cause of Christ among the heathen. The matter was brought to a vote and accepted with a large majority. From these complex series of events it is thus evident that the separate celebration of the Lord's Supper by different racial groups was related to the discussion on separate worship services in separate buildings. In principle the synod rejected separate services, but in practice this decision, which may originally have been well-intentioned, legitimised separation. Although one must not isolate this decision by the synod from its historical context or over-emphasise its significance, it did play some role in paving the way for the

---

Church as its first black congregation. In the following decades the white members of the Dutch Reformed Church who moved into the area joined the Stockenström congregation. For an account of the historical background of the synod decision of 1857, see Loff, C, "The history of a heresy" in De Gruchy, JW and Villa-Vicencio, C (eds), *Apartheid is a heresy* (Grand Rapids: Eerdmans, 1983), 10-23. See also Pauw, CJ, *Anti-apartheid theology in the Dutch Reformed Family of Churches: A depth-hermeneutical analysis* (Amsterdam: Vrije Universiteit, 2007), 71-76. For an engagement with the decision of the Synod of 1857 within the context of a discussion of the ethics of reading Scripture, see Fowl, SE and Jones, LG, *Reading in Communion: Scripture & Ethics in Christian Life* (Grand Rapids: Eerdmans, 1991), 96-99.

8   The presbytery of Albany decided "that to the Honourable Church Council of Stockenström it be recommended, in order to meet the prejudice and weakness halfway, that after Holy Communion had been administered to the older members of the congregation, one or more tables be administered for the new or white members". See the *Minutes of the DRC Presbytery of Albanie*, 194; cf. Loff, "The history of a heresy", 18.

establishment of separate Dutch Reformed Churches along racial lines.[9] Moreover, the mission policy of the Dutch Reformed Church continued to play a major role in providing the moral underpinnings for the theological legitimisation of the policy of apartheid.

It is also important to note that the decision of 1857 deviated from a previous decision by the synod of 1829 in which the synod maintained that Holy Communion was to be administrated simultaneously to all members without distinction of colour or origin, because this practice was an unshakeable principle built on the infallible Word of God. A pastor from the Somerset West congregation tabled this issue at the synod of 1829, because the church council was of the opinion that Holy Communion must be administered separately (as was already the practice in some other congregations). Like the decision of 1857, the historical background to this decision of 1829 entails a dramatic narrative,[10] but suffice it to say that the background events in this case also emphasised that the joint celebration of the Lord's Supper by people of different races and origins brought racial prejudices and tensions to the fore. While the decision of 1829, whatever the motivation, maintained that separate celebrations of Holy Communion are unacceptable, the 'weakness of some' decision of 1857 would play a role in normalising prejudices and opening the door to more blatant forms of class and race injustice.

---

9   The first separate Dutch Reformed Church was the Dutch Reformed Mission Church in 1881. This was followed by the Dutch Reformed Church in Africa (1910, 1932, 1951, 1952) and the Reformed Church in Africa (1965). These churches had mainly coloured, black and Indian members respectively. In 1994 the Dutch Reformed Mission Church and the largest part of the Dutch Reformed Church in Africa united to form the Uniting Reformed Church in Southern Africa (URCSA).

10  The background events to the inquiry from Rev. Spijker of the Somerset West congregation (or Somerset-Hottentots Holland congregation, as it was then called) at the synod of 1829 had to do with the demand of a certain Bentura Visser (referred to as a "bastaard", i.e. a person of mixed blood) to be served Holy Communion simultaneously with the other members. He had applied for membership shortly before and this was granted because one of the elders presented a good testimonial. The issue was also raised whether he could receive Holy Communion with the rest of the congregation. Rev. Spijker was clear that this must be the case, but some congregation members referred to the practice in other congregations, in which the white members were served first (men before women) and then the black members. Rev. Spijker felt this was wrong, but because the practices of some other congregations (such as Stellenbosch) carried some weight, he accepted the decision of the church council. When Bentura Visser took Holy Communion for the first time, he did so together with the white members. Some white members, however, were very unhappy because he dared to receive the sacrament together with 'born Christians'. A heated debate followed in which one church member even referred to a (mis)translation of Deuteronomy 23:3 ("A bastard shall not enter into the congregation of the Lord, even to the tenth generation"). The Somerset West case was dealt with at the presbytery meeting of Cape Town, which advised that, according to the Bible and the spirit of Christianity, exceptions cannot be made regarding the joint celebration of Holy Communion. This was also the decision of the synod of 1829. In his very interesting discussion of these events, church historian Chris Loff also points to the fact that the decision of 1829 might also have been influenced by the presence of a public state officer (known as the "Kommisaris Politiek"), who felt that this matter must not turn into an issue that led to conflict at the synod. See Loff, "The history of a heresy", 16-17.

In 2007 – precisely 150 years after the event – the decision of 1857 once again featured in the ecclesial and public discourse in South Africa. The Western Cape synod of the Dutch Reformed Church accepted a proposal (October 2007) with a large majority that the synod should revoke the 1857 decision based on 'the weakness of some'.[11] The documents that motivated this proposal state that in effect the decision has already been reversed by previous decisions that underlined the commitment to church reunification.[12] Nevertheless, the documents make the case that that particular decision had led directly and indirectly to much pain and humiliation in the lives of many children of God, people created in God's image. The 2007 decision also acknowledges that the 1857 decision made it very difficult for the Dutch Reformed Church to speak in a biblically and theologically sound way about the unity and mission of the church. The documents prepared for the 2007 proposal moreover argue that the primary theological error of the 1857 decision was that the synod legitimised an understanding of the church in which faith in the Christ of the Scriptures was not viewed as the only condition for church membership. The 1857 decision was seriously flawed in that it allowed for a depiction of the church, worship and celebration of the sacraments in which human prejudices and natural creation ordinances such as culture, race and language received greater prominence than the Word of God. The recommendation to the synod of 2007 expresses the hope that the revocation of the 1857 decision would serve the Dutch Reformed Church well by placing its current reunification process on a new track in which the church could think together as sisters and brothers about the future of the church, its calling and its unity.[13]

At the 2007 meeting of the Western Cape synod of the Dutch Reformed Church Allan Boesak (as Moderator of the Western Cape Synod of the Uniting Reformed Church) made the following significant comments in his acceptance speech in which he described the revocation of this decision of the synod of 1857 as a moment of great historical and theological value, something to be accepted with gratitude and joy. Boesak said:

> [This decision] repairs and reconfirms our communion ("verbondenheid") with Christ and with each other through Baptism and Holy Communion, so that we can pray with John Calvin that this sacrament will be so engraved within our hearts that we will know that Christ only has one body, of which He made us all partakers, and that none of the brothers (and sisters) can be injured, despised, rejected, abused, or in any kind offended by us, without at the same time injuring, despising, rejecting or abusing Christ ... we cannot love Christ without loving Him in our brothers and sisters ... because we are members of the same body.[14]

---

11   A similar decision was also taken by the Eastern Cape synod in 2007.
12   The Dutch Reformed family of churches is currently in a process of reunification. For many people this process is painfully slow, although some still cherish the hope that it will came to fruition in the near future.
13   It is, of course, a question whether one can really revoke a decision from the past in this way, but the decision was clearly aimed at making a symbolic gesture.
14   *Handelinge van die Vyf en veertigste vergadering van die Sinode van die Ned Geref Kerk in Suid-Afrika (Wes-en Suid-Kaapland)* 15-19 Oktober 2007, 115.

Boesak continued:

> This decision is a sacred renewal of the *memoria Christi*. From now on the Lord's Supper will not remind us any longer of the 'weakness of some', but of the unlimited grace of God in Jesus Christ and the power of that grace that is enough for us ... The decision of 1857 was taken in the sign of exclusivity and human weakness; the decision of 2007 is taken in the sign of the inclusivity of God's embrace.[15]

This very brief account of the 1857 decision of the synod of the Dutch Reformed Church, and of its symbolic revocation 150 years later along with the responses this evoked, highlights the point that the Lord's Supper should not should not be the cause of reminding us of exclusion fuelled by (racial) prejudice, but should be viewed as a sign of God's unconditional embrace. If one underlines this close link between the Lord's Supper and hospitality – given the view that the Lord's Supper is a feast of unconditional acceptance – one can still ask the question: How should one view the church's discipline practices that are often intertwined with exclusion from the Lord's Supper? There is clearly a difference between exclusion from the table on the basis of class and racial prejudice and the exclusion resulting from church discipline, but the important question of how to think in theological terms about the relationship between hospitality and church discipline (with regard to the Lord's Supper) remains.

## 3. THE FEAST OF UNCONDITIONAL ACCEPTANCE?

In his book *What Happens in Holy Communion?* Michael Welker makes the following statement as a possible answer to the question posed in the title of his book: "*Holy communion is an event of unconditional acceptance of all the participants*" (his emphasis).[16]

The question can be asked, however, how such a statement relates to Scriptural passages such as 1 Corinthians 14:27-29, where we read: "Whoever, therefore, eats the bread or drinks the cup of the Lord in an unworthy manner will be answerable for the body and blood of the Lord. Examine yourselves, and only then eat of the bread and drink of the cup. For all who eat and drink without discerning the body, eat and drink judgment against themselves ..."

According to Welker, the lack of clarity about the meaning of phrases such as "examine yourselves" and "in an unworthy manner" has had the fateful consequence that the Supper could no longer be understood as a feast of reconciliation, rejoicing and peace. He argues: "Instead it came across to many persons as an anxiety-producing means of moral gatekeeping. In a sad irony, the feast of unconditional acceptance of human beings by God and among each other was misused for intrahuman control".[17] In the process the Lord's Supper was often reduced to paralysing self-examination

---

15 *Handelinge* 2007, 115, 116.
16 Welker, M, *What Happens in Holy Communion?* (Grand Rapids: Eerdmans, 2000), 69.
17 Welker, *What Happens in Holy Communion?*, 70. For similar arguments see also Moltmann, J, *The Church in the Power of the Spirit: A Contribution to Messianic Ecclesiology* (London: SCM Press, 1977), 242-260.

and condescending clerical control.[18] In the light of this unhealthy understanding of the Lord's Supper, Welker makes two important remarks. First, "in the celebration of the Supper, God unconditionally accepts human beings who, in a threatened world, have fallen under the power of sin".[19] This includes even the enemies of communion with Christ. Welker stresses the point that Jesus did not celebrate the Last Supper with his disciples simply "because they were the small, faithful apostolic elite, the few irreproachable models of integrity, the glorious Twelve, to whom the administration of Jesus' legacy is entrusted on the basis their moral and religious blamelessness".[20] No, the first recipients of Jesus' supper were Judas "who betrayed Him", Peter, "who denied Him", and the disciples, "who abandoned Him and fled". They all participated fully in "the night of betrayal". Thus one can argue that Jesus' pre-Easter practice of table fellowship, which demonstrated acceptance of the community's enemies and sinners, "reaches an exemplary apex in Jesus' celebration of the last supper".[21]

In addition to this comment on the unconditional acceptance of all participants in Holy Communion, Welker also makes a second remark, namely that the church of Christ (i.e. the Christians who make up that church), "must take care that this meal is celebrated in accordance with the meal's identity".[22] Therefore the celebration of the meal should not contradict or pervert the meal's identity. This implies that human beings ought to judge for themselves whether they do in fact embody in their celebration of the sacrament the unconditional acceptance of all participants. Where pride or lack of love reigns, for instance, they should excuse themselves from the Supper. Welker emphasises that it is important that each person judge himself or herself, but he also states that "no one has the power and the authorisation to exclude a particular person or a particular group of persons from participation in the Supper!"[23] Welker calls attention to the fact that it is exactly because of the misuse of the Supper in order to exercise moral control and oppressive domination over others that Paul expresses his reproach in 1 Corinthians.[24]

---

18 For Van de Beek's more sympathetic engagement with the phenomenon of hesitation in taking the Lord's Supper ("avondsmaalhuiver"), see his essay "Ambt en avondmaal" in Van de Beek, A, *Tussen traditie en vervreemding: over kerk en christenzijn in een veranderende cultuur* (Nijkerk: Callenbach, 1985), 115-125.
19 Welker, *What Happens in Holy Communion?*, 71.
20 Welker, *What Happens in Holy Communion?*, 71.
21 Welker, *What Happens in Holy Communion?*, 72.
22 Welker, *What Happens in Holy Communion?*, 71.
23 Welker, *What Happens in Holy Communion?*, 71.
24 Welker devotes a few pages in *What Happens in Holy Communion?* to a discussion of the question of what the "unworthy eating and drinking" in Corinthians refers to. He considers two interpretative options that rest on subtle translation differences. The first option accepts that the church in Corinth first ate a normal meal and then celebrated the Supper. The more wealthy members arrived earlier and satisfied their hunger. By the time the poor arrived, there were only bits and pieces left. Paul's reproach then urges the more affluent members to have this meal at home prior to religious communion. Welker also discusses a second interpretative option that draws on the work of the New Testament scholar Otto Hofius. According to this interpretation, the unsociable behaviour of the wealthy is also demonstrated in the celebration of the Supper itself, which in Paul's time included a full meal. Welker refers to Hofius's discussion, which argues that the decisive Greek word in 1 Corinthians need not be understood temporally as "taking

It is clear that Welker wants to protect the celebration of the Lord's Supper from reductive moralisation. In light of his understanding of the relation between law and gospel, he emphasises the importance of safeguarding the strict interconnection between justice (all participants are placed on an equal footing), the acceptance of the weak and sinners, and thanksgiving to God for God's goodness, preservation and deliverance. All practices that obscure these intentions and interconnections make human beings "unworthy" to receive the sacrament. For Welker, Holy communion is thus an event of unconditional acceptance of all participants and not a test case to express the moral self-assertion of the community. When persons deny or mask – in whatever way – this unconditional acceptance, they are celebrating the meal "unworthily". Therefore Welker remarks: "The self-denominated 'righteous' who want to sit in judgment over others must instead judge whether *they themselves* are taking seriously the radicality and breadth of the reconciling work of God and Jesus Christ in the Supper!"[25]

Notwithstanding his emphasis on Holy Communion as an event of unconditional acceptance of all the participants, Welker does seem to be aware of the tensions that often arise between the 'acceptance of the weak' and the preservation of the cultic form. He comments that "little gestures can express deficient mutual acceptance, can demonstrate inequality and justice, or can wound the sensibilities of the weak, and thereby pervert the Supper. Therefore cultic clarity and integrity are important".[26] This argument points to the need for pastoral oversight in dealing with questions such as "May we celebrate holy communion with grape juice as well?" and "Must we use the common cup or individual glasses?" It is therefore important to address the issue of the 'weaknesses of some'. But an overburdened sensitivity can also lead to unworthy celebration. As Welker observes: "A complete liberation from fears of contagion and problems of communication would ultimately result in self-service with shrink-wrapped bread and wine while seated in front of a screen showing a video of a holy communion service!"[27] In situations of conflict pastoral creativity and sensitivity are therefore of the utmost importance in order to celebrate communion in a way "which takes account of peoples' scruples, without destroying the biblically given forms".[28]

---

ahead of time" but can just mean "taking out". The reproach is then against people taking out their own food and eating it. Because the rich and the poor brought different kinds of food, this 'taking out' highlights social tensions and the poor are reminded of their oppressed condition. According to Welker, Hofius also argues that the phrase "wait for one another" (v 33) can also mean "welcome someone, show hospitality to someone". Paul is thus not making a plea for the separation of the normal and the ritual meal, but stating that the meal must not evince injustice and lack of consideration. Welker writes: "Instead of demonstrating mutual acceptance and justice in the celebration of the Supper, the perverted meal becomes a sign and demonstration of inequality and injustice ... The celebration of the meal happens 'for judgment' when egotistic, indifferent, and brutal forms of behavior not only injure fellow human beings, but at the same time pervert and make a laughing stock of Christ's intentions of instituting the meal. Under such conditions the community comes together 'for the worst' and 'for judgment'". Welker, *What Happens in Holy Communion?*, 78, 79.

25 Welker, *What Happens in Holy Communion?*, 73.
26 Welker, *What Happens in Holy Communion?*, 80.
27 Welker, *What Happens in Holy Communion?*, 81.
28 Welker, *What Happens in Holy Communion?*, 82.

The historic events leading to the 1857 synod decision of the Dutch Reformed Church in South Africa and its aftermath illustrate that it is not always easy to take into account peoples' scruples or 'weaknesses' without stepping over the thin line that results in the legitimisation of prejudice and the obstruction of justice. What is necessary is wise pastoral oversight by pastors, synods, presbyteries and above all by congregations as a whole that challenges self-interest and indifference, and protects the vulnerability of the socially weaker members,[29] a task that Welker describes as a "careful, loving, and creative labor".[30]

Welker rightly challenges the view of the Lord's Supper as an anxiety-producing means of moral gatekeeping and emphasises the need to affirm the importance of the Lord's Supper as a feast of unconditional acceptance and radical hospitality. The question can be asked, though, whether the problem for most churches and church members today is really one of guilt-ridden self-torment and harsh clerical control, or whether passive indifference, the lazy legitimisation of the status quo and the lack of commitment to communal pastoral oversight are not more prevalent. Welker rightly warns against Eucharistic malpractices. However, legitimate questions regarding church order and discipline also come to the fore when one reflects on the notion of the unconditional acceptance of all participants at the Lord's Supper. In many Christian traditions (also in Reformed traditions) one finds practices – often practices with long and complicated histories – that seek to protect the integrity of the meal, albeit through modes of 'exclusion'. How must one view the possible tensions between, on the one hand, the emphasis on the meal as a feast of radical hospitality and, on the other hand, the need to protect the integrity of the meal through disciplined practices? With this question in mind, let us turn to some aspects of the theology of John Calvin.

## 4. THE LORD'S SUPPER, CHURCH DISCIPLINE AND MUTUAL LOVE

In Book 4 of Calvin's *Institutes of the Christian Religion*, which considers "the external means or aids by which God invites us into the society of Christ and holds us therein," he comments: "I confess a great disgrace if pigs and dogs have a place among the children of God, and a still greater disgrace if the sacred body of Christ be prostituted by him. And indeed, if churches are well ordered, they will not bear the wicked in their bosom. Nor would they indiscriminately admit worthy and unworthy together to that sacred banquet".[31] Clearly church discipline is important for Calvin. Elsewhere in the *Institutes* he writes: "as the saving doctrine of Christ is the soul of the church, so does discipline serve as its sinews, through which the

---

29  It is important to note that Welker does not reduce the Supper to a ritual of mutual acceptance. Elsewhere in *What Happened in Holy Communion?* he writes: "Holy communion is by no means simply about the symbolisation of just, brotherly and sisterly relations. If we want to understand what happens in Holy Communion, thanksgiving to God, the glorification of God, and the breaking and distributing of the bread and wine must not be torn asunder and placed over against each other ... In the Supper the relation of humans to God and the intrahuman relations, the 'vertical' and 'horizontal' dimensions must remain closely and indissolubly bound together!" (62).

30  Welker, *What Happens in Holy Communion?*, 83,

31  Calvin, J, *Institutes of the Christian Religion*, Volume 2, McNeill, JT (ed.), Battles, FL (trans.) (Louisville: Westminster John Knox Press, 1960), 4: 1/ 15, 1029.

members of the body hold together, each in its own place".[32] For Calvin the removal or hindrance of discipline contributes to the ultimate dissolution of the church. His metaphors regarding discipline might not appeal to everyone today. For instance, when he writes that "discipline is like a bridle to restrain and tame those who rage against the doctrine of Christ; or like a spur to arouse those of little inclination; and also sometimes as a father's rod to chastise mildly and with the gentleness of Christ's Spirit those who have more seriously lapsed".[33]

One has to take care not to make a caricature of Calvin in this regard. While Calvin, for instance, admits that pastors are often more lenient towards the 'wicked in their bosom' than they should be, he also critiques those who think it a sacrilege to partake of the Supper with the wicked for being more rigid than Paul. Calvin argues that Paul "does not require that one examines another, or every one the whole church, but that each individual proves himself [1 Cor. 11:28]".[34] Here Calvin is making essentially the same point as Welker, albeit that Calvin adds that this "cognizance belongs to the church as a whole and cannot be exercised without lawful order".[35]

It is clear that Calvin sees the purpose of discipline to protect the honour of God and the integrity of the church as the body of Christ. This also relates to the Lord's Supper. He writes that "we must preserve the order of the Lord's Supper, that it may not be profaned by being administered indiscriminately. For it is very true that he to whom its distribution has been committed, if he knowingly and willingly admits an unworthy person whom he could rightfully turn away, is as guilty of sacrilege as if he had cast the Lord's body to dogs".[36] Having said this, one should also add that Calvin challenges a certain kind of misguided rigor and accordingly makes a plea for moderation and gentleness. He is even critical of the ancient church, which he often describes as the "ancient and better church," and argues that "we cannot at all excuse the excessive severity of the ancients … when they imposed solemn penance and deprivation from Holy Communion sometimes for seven, sometimes for three, sometimes for four years, and sometimes for life, what could be the result of either great hypocrisy or utter despair".[37] A careful reading of the *Institutes* reveals Calvin's plea for gentleness in both public and private censure. Without such restraint there

---

32   Calvin, *Institutes*, 4: 12/ 1, 1230. For a discussion of Calvin's views on church discipline see, for instance, Plomp, J, *De Kerkelijke Tucht bij Calvijn* (Kampen: Kok, 1969) and De Ridder, RR, "John Calvin's Views on Discipline: A Comparison of the Institution of 1536 and the Institutes of 1559" in Gamble, RC (ed.), *Articles on Calvin and Calvinism: Calvin's Ecclesiology: Sacraments and Deacons, Volume 10* (New York: Garland Publishing, 1992), 293-300; Haas, GH, "Ethics and Church Discipline" in Selderhuis, H J (ed.), *The Calvin Handbook* (Grand Rapids: Eerdmans, 2009), especially 342-344.
33   Calvin, *Institutes*, 4: 12/ 1, 1230.
34   Calvin, *Institutes*, 4: 1/ 15, 1029.
35   Calvin, *Institutes*, 4: 1/ 15, 1029.
36   Calvin, *Institutes*, 4: 12/ 5, 1232, 1233. Calvin refers in this regard to a quotation from a sermon by Chrysostom, in which Chrysostom attacks the priests who, fearing the power of great men, were afraid to exclude anybody. Calvin writes: "Let us not dread the fasces, the purple, the crowns; here we have a greater power" (4: 12/ 5, 1233). This example refers to fearing those with power. It is ironic, however, that the practices of exclusion are more often directed not at those in power, but at socially vulnerable members.
37   Calvin, *Institutes*, 4: 12/8, 1236.

is the danger of sliding "from discipline to butchery".[38] It would be a misreading of Calvin to say that his emphasis on church discipline lapses into one-sided moralism,[39] although one can certainly be critical of some aspects of his own application of these ideas. What is more, many Reformed churches have often mixed moralistic considerations into their practices of church discipline. In this regard the churches in the Dutch Reformed family of churches in South Africa have to a greater or lesser degree often been guilty of practising a moralising form of church discipline that has barred people from the Lord's Supper in a way that did not always protect the integrity of the meal. At times this understanding of discipline resulted in a reductive celebration that did not do justice to the Lord's Supper as the feast of unconditional acceptance, reconciliation and joy.

It is furthermore important not to separate Calvin's remarks on the necessity to preserve the order of the Lord's Supper through discipline from his emphasis that the Lord's Supper implies mutual love. Calvin argues that the Lord intended the Supper as a kind of exhortation that has the power to "quicken and inspire us both to purity and holiness of life, and to love, peace and concord". The Lord communicates his body to us in such a way that he is made completely one with us and we with him. And since we all participate in the one body, "it is necessary that all of us also be made one body by such participation".[40] Calvin also writes, and it is worth quoting him at length:

> We shall benefit very much from the sacrament if this thought is impressed and engraved upon our minds: that none of the brethren can be injured, despised, rejected, abused, or in any way offended by us, without at the same time, injuring, despising, and abusing Christ by the wrongs we do; that we cannot disagree with our brethren without

---

38 Calvin, *Institutes*, 4: 12/9, 1236.
39 As Wilhelm Niesel notes in his discussion of church discipline in Calvin's theology: "Thus church discipline does not exist in order to promote moral conduct of the church, or in order to attain purity in church life … The reality of the church depends not upon our standards, even though they may have been commanded by us, but solely upon the work of Christ accomplished towards us through Word and Sacrament". See Niesel, W, *The Theology of Calvin* (Philadelphia: The Westminster Press, 1956), 198, 199.
40 Calvin, *Institutes*, 4: 17/38, 1414, 1415. Calvin also refers to how the bread represents this unity: "As it is made of many grains so mixed together that one cannot be distinguished from one another, so it is fitting that in the same way we should be joined and bound together by such agreement of minds that no sort of disagreement or division may intrude" (1415). See also Calvin's "Treatise on the Lord's Supper" in Reid, J K S, *Calvin: Theological Treatises* (The Library of Christian Classics, Vol. XXII) (Philadelphia: Westminster Press, 1954), 151. For good discussions of the development of Calvin's views on the Lord's Supper see, for instance, Janse, W, "Calvin's Eucharistic Theology: Three Dogma-Historical Observations" in Selderhuis, H J (ed.), *Calvinus sacrarum literarum interpres* (Göttingen: Vandenhoeck &Ruprecht, 2008), 37-69 and Janse, W, "Sacraments" in Selderhuis, HJ (ed.), *The Calvin Handbook* (Grand Rapids: Eerdmans, 2009), 344-355. For reflections that bring Calvin's understanding of the Sacraments into conversation with questions concerning the unity of the church, see Brinkman, ME, "Calvin's Eucharistic vision and the unity of the Church", *Ned Geref Teologiese Tydskrif* 51, Supplementum (2010): 302-312, as well as Smit, DJ, "Calvin on the sacraments and church unity" in Smit, DJ, *Essays on Being Reformed* (Collected Essays 3), Vosloo, RR (ed.) (Stellenbosch: Sun Press, 2009), 165-188.

at the same time disagreeing with Christ; that we cannot love Christ, without loving him in the brethren; that we ought to take the same care of our brethren's bodies as we take of our own; for they are members of our body; and that, as no part of our body is touched by any feeling of pain which is not spread among all the rest, so we ought not to allow a brother to be affected by any evil, without being touched with compassion for him.[41]

This powerful passage from Calvin on the unity of the body of Christ has been quoted in full in a document written by the South African anti-apartheid theologian Allan Boesak entitled "God Made Us All, But … Racism and the World Alliance of Reformed Churches".[42] This document was sent by the Alliance of Black Reformed Churches in Southern Africa (ABRECSA) to delegates attending the meeting of the World Alliance of Reformed Churches in Ottawa, Canada in 1982 – an event that would become an important marker in the church's struggle against apartheid. This document, which was a plea for the World Alliance to play a more active role in the struggle against racism, described racism as structured sinfulness and also refers to the fact that racism in South Africa makes it virtually impossible to share in the natural expression of unity within the body of Christ, namely the Lord's Supper. These words gained special weight from the controversy that erupted when the delegations of the black Dutch Reformed Churches refused to share Holy Communion with the members of the white Dutch Reformed Church.[43] The events in Ottawa further prepared the ground for a process which resulted in the Dutch Reformed Mission Church calling a *status confessionis* with regard to apartheid and later adopting the famous Belhar Confession in which the notion of the unity of the body of Christ plays a pivotal role.[44]

It is thus not surprising that in the discussions on church reunification in South Africa the fact that the Lord's Supper implies mutual love has often been highlighted, also with reference to Calvin. For Calvin the Lord's Supper is sweet and delicate spiritual food for those who, in tasting it, are moved to thanksgiving and mutual love. But it is a deadly poison for those whom it does not arouse to thanksgiving and love. When people rush to the Lord's table without any spark of faith and zeal for love, they profane and pollute the sacrament by not discerning the Lord's body. They bring judgment on themselves by mixing the sacred symbol of Christ's body with their own discord. Calvin also makes it clear that it is faith and love that are required, not perfection. He writes:

> Therefore, this is the worthiness –the best and only kind we can bring to God – to offer our vileness and (so to speak) our unworthiness to him so that his mercy may make us worthy of him; to despair in ourselves

---

41  Calvin, *Institutes*, 4: 17/38, 1415.
42  Boesak, AA, *Black and Reformed: Apartheid, Liberation, and the Calvinist Tradition* (New York, 1984), 107.
43  For a discussion of these events, see Pauw, *Anti-apartheid theology in the Dutch Reformed Family of Churches*, 187-194.
44  For the draft confession of Belhar and the accompanying letter, as well as for some very informative essays on the confession, see Cloete, GD and Smit, DJ *A Moment of Truth: The Confession of the Dutch Reformed Mission Church* (Grand Rapids: Eerdmans, 1984).

> that we may be comforted in him; to abase ourselves that we may be lifted up by him; to accuse ourselves that we may be justified by him; to aspire to that unity which he commends to us in the Supper; and, as he makes all of us one in himself, to desire one soul, one heart, one tongue for us all.[45]

Calvin's eucharistic theology can thus rightly be described as a theology of grace and gratitude (to use the title of Brian Gerrish's study[46]).

## 5. GRACED PRACTICES

In the first part of this essay I referred to the decision of the 1857 synod in South Africa which opened the door for legitimising worship separated along racial lines.[47] In the light of this, and in the light of the discussion of aspects of the thinking of Welker and Calvin, a few theological trajectories can be highlighted concerning the celebration of the Lord's Supper by the church as the body of Christ.

First, it seems of paramount importance to affirm the view, as expressed by Welker and others, that Holy Communion is an event of unconditional acceptance or hospitality. The Lord's Supper, however, does not symbolise some kind of vague and abstract tolerance of an idealised or romanticised 'other', but must be viewed – as Calvin reminds us – as a concrete expression of, and call to, mutual love as a response to God's love for humanity in Christ. In this sense the one cup and the one bread symbolise the unity of the church and, at the same time, challenge sinful prejudices and unjust divisions within the one body of Christ.

Second, together with the focus on the Lord's Supper as an event of unconditional hospitality, we have to take care to celebrate the meal in accordance with its identity. This requires disciplined practices. Such a statement does not qualify the unconditional nature of the event, but radicalises it. While the emphasis on the protection of the integrity of the meal does challenge a *laissez-faire* approach to the Lord's Supper, it does not imply an opening for a moralistic form of church control that uses the sacrament as an instrument of 'moral gatekeeping' (to use Welker's

---

45 Calvin, *Institutes* 4: 17/42, 1419. Calvin also writes: "For it is a sacrament ordained not for the perfect, but for the weak and the feeble, to awaken, arouse, stimulate, and exercise the feeling of faith and love, indeed to correct the defect of both" (1420).

46 Gerrish, BA, *Grace and Gratitude: The Eucharistic Theology of John Calvin* (Eugene, Oregon: Wipf and Stock Publishers, 2002). Gerrish writes: "The holy banquet is simply the liturgical enactment of the theme of grace and gratitude that lies at the heart of Calvin's entire theology" (20).

47 It is, of course, also possible to talk about gender exclusion at the table. As Reformed feminist theologian Leanne van Dyk writes in her essay "The gifts of God for the people of God" in Pauw, AP and Jones, S (eds), *Feminist and Womanist Essays in Reformed Dogmatics* (Louisville: Westminster John Knox Press, 2006): "Ambiguity clusters around the wonderful Calvinian theme of feasting at the table of God's hospitality in the Lord's Supper. The Lord's Supper has long been undermined by the exclusion of women as ordained clergy ... A distinctively Reformed feminist approach might illuminate the issue of woman's ordination in a new way by stressing the implications of a Reformed sacramental theology for hospitality at the table" (218, 219); cf. also Smit, *Essays on Being Reformed*, 177.

phrase). On the contrary, it actually acts to counter such a focus by challenging us to see that it is exactly our prejudices against unconditional grace that are under judgement. As David Ford comments on the feast of the Kingdom in the light of Jesus' generosity and compassion: "There is a sharp note of exclusion, but it is one that follows from the inclusiveness. The excluded are those who cannot bear God's generosity and will not imitate it".[48]

Third, disciplined practices are not to be viewed as something over against grace and hospitality but, if done well, *as* acts of hospitality.[49] Both hospitality and discipline are graced practices.[50] Therefore the church's discipline must not mimic certain forms of the discipline of the state or the market. The uncritical juxtaposition of hospitality and church discipline, which equates hospitality with indifferent tolerance and church discipline with a reductive moralism, ought to be avoided. This requires a theology of wisdom that fosters a graced-tinted ethical optics that also takes the church's history of dehumanising exclusions into account. As Amy Plantinga Pauw writes: "As the body of Christ in the world, the church is a broken and diseased body, mirroring the ills and divisions of the larger society. Yet it remains a mysteriously powerful channel of God's grace to us".[51]

Lastly, while retaining the focus on the Lord's Supper as an event of unconditional acceptance of all participants, it is important to affirm that the integrity of the meal is protected when it is situated within a set of graced practices formed and transformed by the Word. These practices include lament, confession, forgiveness and truth-telling.[52] In Bonhoeffer's famous formulation he describes cheap grace as "preaching forgiveness without repentance," "baptism without the discipline of community," "the Lord's Supper without confession of sin" and "absolution without personal confession".[53] Bonhoeffer thus points to the interrelationship between the sacraments and other practices of the body of Christ.

## 6. CONCLUSION

The 1857 synod decision and its aftermath recalled in this essay serve as a reminder not to compromise the radical nature of the inclusivity of God's embrace. In reflecting on the events that led to the decision of the synod of 1857 one must also be mindful of the fact that the group of church members in the Eastern Cape who

---

48  Ford, DF, *Self and Salvation: Being Transformed* (Cambridge: Cambridge University Press, 1999), 269.
49  See Cavanaugh, WT, *Torture and Eucharist* (Oxford: Blackwell, 1998), 243.
50  On the notion of graced practices, see also Serene Jones's essay "Graced Practices: Excellence and Freedom in the Christian Life" in Volf, M and Bass, DC (eds), *Practicing Theology: Beliefs and Practices in Christian Life* (Eerdmans: Grand Rapids, 2002), 51-77.
51  See the essay by Pauw, AP, "The Graced Infirmity of the Church" in Pauw, AP and Jones, S (eds), *Feminist and Womanist Essays in Reformed Dogmatics* (Louisville: Westminster John Knox Press, 2006), 191.
52  For a theological engagement with some of these practices, see Volf and Bass, *Practicing Theology*; Buckley, JJ and Yeago, DS (eds.), *Knowing the Triune God: The Work of the Spirit in the Practices of the Church* and Ackermann, D M, *After the Locusts: Letters from a Landscape of Faith* (Grand Rapids: Eerdmans/ Cape Town: David Philip, 2003).
53  Bonhoeffer, D, *Discipleship (Dietrich Bonhoeffer Works*, Vol. 4) (Minneapolis: Fortress Press, 2001), 44.

wanted to have separate tables was a minority group in what they perceived to be a beleaguered situation. They were probably seeking for ways to affirm their identity and ensure their survival. In situations such as these, which are playing out with increasing frequency in various forms in our globalising and polarising world today, the temptation looms large to compromise the grace of God's embrace in the name of protecting identity, establishing security or ensuring survival. Amidst these temptations, the right administration of the Lord's Supper serves as a continual reminder to the church to embody visibly God's haunting hospitality.

The challenge remains, however, to emphasise the Lord's Supper as a feast of unconditional hospitality and to protect its integrity. How to give form and concrete manifestation to this challenge demands continuous theological reflection. Without doubt, Bram van de Beek's theological work (and more specifically his work on ecclesiology) will inform these important discussions by calling upon the church to remain faithful to its Christian identity.

# 20. ON THEOLOGICAL EDUCATION: CALVIN, THE ACADEMY OF GENEVA AND 150 YEARS OF THEOLOGY AT STELLENBOSCH[1]

## 1. 150 YEARS OF THEOLOGY

In 2009 the Faculty of Theology at Stellenbosch University celebrated 150 years of theological education theology at Stellenbosch. The official opening of the Theological Seminary took place on 1 November 1859. The festivities of that day are described in detail by one of the attendees ("een feestgenoot"), who recalls:

> The ceremony was to start at 10 a.m. in the church. But long before this hour the church was packed. Although the church seats only 600 people, on this day it accommodated 1 300. The congregation of Stellenbosch, as could be expected, attended in great numbers. Many also came from the congregations of Cape Town, Wijnberg, D'Urban, Somerset, Paarl and Wellington. Outside of the church stood a crowd of about 800 persons, mostly members of the local mission churches. They were dressed festively and seemed to compete with the members of the local congregation in showing their interest in this joyous occasion on this joyous day.[2]

The rest of this text also recalls the opening prayer by Rev. A Faure (who can rightly be called the father of the Theological Seminary[3]), the congregational singing, the sermon by Prof. NJ Hofmeyr, the closing prayer by Rev. JH Neethling of the local congregation, the ceremonial procession through the town and the opening address at the Seminary by Prof. John Murray. The author is clearly enthused and moved by these events and concludes with the conviction that God will make the Seminary a centre of light and life for the church in South Africa.

These recollections of the opening of the Theological Seminary in 1859 are included in a memorial book ("gedenkschrift"), dedicated to the members of the Dutch Reformed Church in South Africa "with the prayer that it may contribute to keep alive and operative their and their children's interest in the Theological Seminary".[4]

---

1 This essay was read at a meeting of the Church Historical Society of Southern Africa in June 2009 in Stellenbosch. The essay was originally published under the title "Calvin, the Academy of Geneva and 150 years of theology at Stellenbosch: Historical-theological contributions to the conversation on theological education" in *Studia Historiae Ecclesiasticae* 35 (Supplement), December 2009:1016.

2 *Gedenkschrift van de inwijding van het Theologisch Seminarium de Nederduitsch Gereformeerde Kerk in Zuid-Africa te Stellenbosch op den 1sten November, 1859, bevattende onder anderen de Redevoeringe bij die gelegenheid uitgesproken* (Cape Town: Van der Sandt de Villiers & Co., 1859), 27.

3 Faure had already pleaded for an institution for theological education 45 years before the opening of the Theological Seminary in 1814. See *Gedenkschrift*, 3.

4 *Gedenkschrift*, dedication page. This volume also contains a chapter on the pre-history of the Seminary by Abraham Faure, Prof. Hofmeyr's word to the congregation (with 1 Corinthians 3: 9 as text), the speech by the president curator Rev. Philip Faure and the opening address by Prof. John Murray.

These words testify to the close relationship between the Theological Seminary and the Dutch Reformed Church. In addition, one should consider the fact that the Theological Seminary played a key role in the establishment of Stellenbosch University (which was founded in 1918), pointing to a further significant relationship that continues to shape the identity of the Theological Seminary.[5] In 1963 the Seminary became a full faculty of Stellenbosch University. Another important milestone in the history of theology at Stellenbosch was the decision of the Uniting Reformed Church in Southern Africa to move its theological training to Stellenbosch, which meant that since 2000 the Faculty has had formal agreements with other churches than the Dutch Reformed Church as well. And in 2002 the first students of the Uniting Presbyterian Church of Southern Africa officially enrolled at the Faculty. Today the Faculty views itself as an ecumenical faculty, while it also acknowledges its Dutch Reformed roots.

In celebrating 150 years of theology at Stellenbosch one needs to be mindful of these historical beginnings and developments.[6] Although the Theological Faculty has strong Dutch Reformed roots, it is today not only a seminary of the Dutch Reformed Church. It is also not only a place that trains pastors for a variety of churches. Furthermore, the Faculty of Theology is placed within a specific university context with a particular vision on research, learning and teaching, and community interaction. Within such a setting one is faced with challenges regarding the optimal relationship between seminary and university, as well as the related questions regarding the interrelation between church, academy and society, to use David Tracy's well-known distinction of the three 'publics' of theology.[7] In addition to these challenging questions regarding the context of theological education at Stellenbosch today, one is challenged to grapple with the question of how to reconcile ecumenical and confessional commitments, as well as how to view the relationship between theology and the other sciences.

In addressing these seemingly perennial tensions, we are also reminded of the fact that the celebration of 150 years of theology at Stellenbosch coincides with the 500th anniversary of the birth of John Calvin, as well as with the 450th anniversary of the opening of the famous Academy of Geneva in 1559. For those who stand in the Reformed tradition, as well as for institutions with Reformed roots, these concurrent events offer the opportunity for some historical-theological reflections on the nature

---

5   Shortly after the opening of the Theological Seminary the two professors, Hofmeyr and Murray, together with the pastor of the Stellenbosch congregation, JH Neethling, became the driving force for the establishment of the Stellenbosch Gymnasium and other schools. In 1886 the section for higher education was renamed Victoria College and in 1918 it became the University of Stellenbosch. Cf. *Gedenkboek van het Victoria-Kollege* (Cape Town: Nasionale Pers Beperkt, 1918), and Coertzen, P (ed.), *Teologie Stellenbosch 150+* (Wellington: Bybel-Media, 2009).

6   For the most extensive history of the Theological Seminary at Stellenbosch, see Ferreira, IL, *Die Teologiese Seminarium van Stellenbosch 1858-1963* (Pretoria: Makro Boeke, 1979). See also *Gedenkboek van die Seminarie (N.G. Kerk) Stellenbosch: Driekwart Eeufees 1859-1934* (Stellenbosch: Pro Ecclesia-Drukkery, 1934); *Feesuitgawe van die Kweekskool Stellenbosch, 1859-1959* (Cape Town: N.G. Kerk-uitgewers, 1959), and Coertzen, *Teologie Stellenbosch 150+*.

7   Tracy, D, *The Analogical Imagination: Christian Theology and the Culture of Pluralism* (New York: Crossroads, 1991), 3-46.

and task of theological education from a Reformed perspective. In this process the danger arises of assuming too much of a continuity between ourselves and Calvin, or 16th-century education institutions and the seminaries or universities of today. Nevertheless, an engagement with the past, such as revisiting aspects of the history of the Genevan Academy or the history of theology at Stellenbosch, can contribute to the conversation on theological education – even if only to help us understand the complexity of the challenges or to hint at promising trajectories for consideration.

With this in mind, this essay revisits some aspects of the founding and early years of the Genevan Academy, highlighting three aspects. First, the architects of the Genevan Academy did not view theology as isolated from other sources of wisdom. Second, the Academy had as its goal the training of ministers for the Reformed churches. However, for Calvin this goal was also part of a larger vision to transform society. Third, the Genevan Academy was not immune to the tensions inherent in early modern Reformed higher education (tensions that are also familiar to us today). Karin Maag summarises this well in her book *Seminary or University? The Genevan Academy and Reformed Higher Education, 1560-1620*:

> On the one hand, especially in Reformed areas where sufficiently educated Reformed ministers were in short supply, ecclesiastical leaders in particular felt that centres of learning had to act primarily as training grounds in the doctrines and practices of the Reformed faith. On the other hand, more practical minded civic leaders felt that the strength and survival of their institutions lay in providing the best possible professors and education to students, irrespective of confessional constraints.[8]

Against the backdrop of these three brief observations, the rest of the essay offers some remarks on the challenges facing theological education in contexts such as the Faculty of Theology at Stellenbosch, reflecting also on the possible tension between confessional identity and ecumenism, as well as the tension between academic and ecclesiastical theology.

## 2. CALVIN, BEZA AND THE EARLY YEARS OF THE ACADEMY OF GENEVA

There is no doubt that theological education was high on John Calvin's agenda. When he came to Geneva in 1536, he was appointed as reader in Sacred Scripture and gave lectures on the New Testament, especially on the letters of Paul. The problem, however, was that these lectures were not backed by a comprehensive strategy for education in Geneva. Upon his return to Geneva from Strasbourg (where Calvin went after he was banned from Geneva in 1538), Calvin expressed his vision for a college different from the existing institutions. Calvin was influenced by his experiences in Strasbourg, where there was a well-established educational institution. In 1541 he writes in his *Ecclesiastical Ordinances*, within the context of a discussion of the office

---

8   Maag, K, *Seminary or University? The Genevan Academy and Reformed Higher Education, 1560-1620* (Aldershot: Scholar Press, 1995), 2.

of doctor, that a college should be instituted for instructing young people to prepare them "for the ministry as well as for civil government".[9]

Nothing came of Calvin's plans until the political situation changed in 1555, which led to the consolidation of Calvin's position of authority in the city. The 1550s saw a change in the power balance of Genevan politics, a process enhanced by the influx of French-speaking religious refugees. These developments contributed to Calvin's rise to power in Geneva.[10] Within such a context, the long-projected plans for the establishment of an academy could take shape once more. In 1556, when Calvin was on his way to Frankfurt, he visited Strasbourg to ask for advice from the head of the local academy, Jean Sturm.[11] Besides the strong influence of Strasbourg as a model, Calvin also had knowledge of the Academy of Melanchthon in Wittenberg. The fact that the buildings of the Collège de Rive, the Latin school started after the city accepted the Reformation in 1536, were in need of renovation offered further impetus to Calvin's plans for developing a new college.

Calvin and the other ministers submitted a plan to the Council, according to which the existing Collège de Rive was to become the *schola privata*, a lower-level Latin school. From there students could go on to the upper-level *schola publica*. When Calvin received the backing of the city authorities, he started searching for competent teachers, a process which initially met with some difficulties.[12] Calvin's search for professors was helped by the fact that a conflict arose between the professors in Lausanne and the Council of Bern (under whose jurisdiction they fell), resulting in the dismissal of the teaching staff of the Lausanne Academy. Theodore Beza (who taught Greek in Lausanne) left Lausanne for Geneva before the quarrel reached its peak and others would follow. The registers of the small council reported in March and May 1559 the acceptance of Antoine le Chevalier as professor of Hebrew, Francois Bérauld as professor of Greek and Jean Tagaut as professor of Philosophy, while Jean Randon, also from Lausanne, became the regent of the highest class of the *schola privata*.[13] Calvin and Beza became the professors of theology. It is clear that they saw their lecturing at the Academy as an extension of their role as ministers.[14] In addition, Calvin played an important role, bad health notwithstanding, in liaising between the Academy, the Company of Pastors and the City Council. Through his reputation and correspondence Calvin attracted many young men to come and study in Geneva.

---

9   Reid, JKS (ed.), *Calvin: Theological Treatises* (Philadelphia: Westminster, 1954), 63.
10  See, for instance, Naphy, WG, *Calvin and the Consolidation of the Genevan Reformation* (Louisville: Westminster John Knox Press, 1994).
11  See De Greeff, W, *The Writings of John Calvin: An Introductory Guide (Expanded Edition)* (Louisville: Westminster John Knox Press, 2008), 36; also Selderhuis, H J, *Calvijn een mens* Kampen: Kok, 2008), 206.
12  Calvin was especially interested in finding the right people to teach Hebrew and Greek. Attempts to attract Jean Mercier (who taught Hebrew at the Collège Royal in Paris) and Emmanuel Tremellius (who was rector at the new academy in Hornbach in Germany and had previously taught Hebrew at Oxford) failed.
13  See Maag, *Seminary or University?*, 14.
14  Cf. Maag, K, "Calvijn en de studenten", in Selderhuis, HJ (ed.), *Calvijn Handboek* (Kampen: Kok, 2008).

Calvin's vision of, and work at, the Genevan Academy must furthermore be seen within the context of the way he understood his calling as teacher and pastor, as well as in the light of his commitment to the church as a school. Zachman writes: "Calvin envisioned the church as a school in which Christians act as both students and teachers, under the instruction of the Holy Spirit, the author of Scripture".[15] Calvin described his own "sudden conversion to teachableness" in the Preface of his Psalms commentary and it was his life-long objective to teach people how to read Scripture. He did this through his *Institutes* and biblical commentaries, as well as through his work as pastor in Geneva. It is not surprising then that Calvin's passion for teaching found further concretisation in the Genevan Academy.

It is beyond the scope of this essay to go into the detail of the founding and early history of the Genevan Academy.[16] Suffice it to say that once sufficient funds and the personnel had been found, the official inauguration took place in the main church of Saint Pierre on 5 June 1559. After an opening prayer by Calvin, the secretary of the small council (Michel Roset) read aloud the Academy's statutes and ordinances and its confession of faith.[17] After that Theodore Beza, the first rector, gave the inaugural address. In this address Beza argues that scholars are endowed with intelligence and must make use of this gift of God, albeit that this requires training and hard work. Beza also saw continuities between the Academy of Geneva and the academies of antiquity:

> In our *respublica scholastica*, where doctors and students work together, it will be possible to acquire an education in good letters and in the rational disciplines, so that, as they used to say in antiquity, men of reason and intelligence will be metamorphosed out of wild and savage beasts. Wisdom comes down to us from Moses, but also from the Egyptians, passing from them to the Greeks … Among the *profana gentes*, especially among the Greeks, there was, by the grace of God, light in the darkness. Because of that we should regard ourselves as at one with the academies of antiquity".[18]

---

15  Zachman, RC, *John Calvin as Teacher, Pastor and Theologian: The Shape of his Writings and Thought* (Grand Rapids: Baker Academic, 2006), 7.

16  On this history see the standard work by Charles Borgeaud, *Historie de l'Universite de Geneve* (Geneva: Georg, 1900). See also the work by Marco Marcacci, *Historie de L'Universite de Geneve 1558-1986* (Geneva: University of Geneva, 1987). For a pre-history of the Genevan Academy, see also Naphy, WG, "The Reformation and the Evolution of Geneva's Schools" in Kumin, B (ed.), *Reformations Old and New* (London: Scholar Press, 1996). In this paper I will draw especially on Gillian Lewis's chapter "The Geneva Academy" in Pettegree, A, Duke, A and Lewis, G (eds), *Calvinism in Europe 1540-1620* (Cambridge: Cambridge University Press, 1994) and Karin Maag's study *Seminary or University?*

17  In 1559 Robert Estienne published the school's Statutes as *Promulgation Leges Academiae* for an international audience and as *L'Ordre du Collège* for Genevans and other French-speaking circles. For an interesting discussion of the subtle differences between these versions, see Lewis, "The Geneva Academy", 48-49. Cf. Coetzee, JCh, "Calvin and the School" in Hoogstra, JT (ed.), *John Calvin Contemporary Prophet: A Symposium* (Grand Rapids: Baker Book House, 1959), 206-211.

18  Lewis, "The Geneva Academy", 39.

In addition, Beza turned to the scholars and reminded them of Plato's famous saying rendered by Cicero: *Scientia quae est remota a iustitia, calliditas potius quam sapientia est appellanda* (That kind of knowledge which is remote from justice better deserves the name of ingenuity than of wisdom). Beza continues to give concrete content to this affirmation:

> Virtue is that which is subordinated to the will of the Almighty God. To this you must be obedient, and in that obedience, diligent in all your studies. To be idle and negligent is a perfidious rejection of the gift of God. You are not here to take part in frivolous games, but in order that you may become imbued with true religion and equipped with all good arts, the better to amplify God's glory and to be a credit to your native land. Never forget that you have enrolled under the sacred military discipline of the great Commander himself.[19]

Commenting on Beza's speech, Gillian Lewis notes that this inaugural speech displayed some characteristics of the ethos of the founders of the Genevan school. First, there is a note of warning against ingenuity or artificiality (*calliditas*), hence the emphasis "on the old Christian view that frivolity and 'curiosity' were a danger against which able men must guard".[20] A second characteristic that emerges is an emphasis on industriousness, since service to God is active service. A third aspect regards providence. Lewis writes: "The students are reminded to regard their obligations in the light of God's revealed purposes and never to forget that they are soldiers in an historic cause".[21] This emphasis on history is mirrored in the way Beza situated the circumstances leading to the establishment of the school in a local and European context of struggle and victory.

Lewis further emphasises the fact that the architects of the Genevan Academy did not share the view that Scripture offered a complete compendium of guidance relating to all aspects of human knowledge and that recourse to pagan writers is therefore unnecessary or blasphemous. On the contrary, pagan authors were regarded "not only as permissible, but indeed as indispensable in the early education of godly gentleman and citizens and of future ministers of the Word".[22] In our own discussion of theological education in institutions with a Reformed heritage, it is worthwhile remembering that the architects of the Genevan Academy were open to other sources of wisdom. This observation alerts one not to equate uncritically the Reformed tradition with an insular view of theology or a narrow orthodoxy.

Calvin's and Beza's openness to the wisdom found in antiquity must not obscure the fact that it was Calvin's intention that the Academy was to educate future ministers for the Reformed churches, including an increasing number of men from France. These would-be pastors were expected to hold public services on Saturdays in which they displayed their competence in biblical exposition. However, training

---

19  See Lewis, "The Geneva Academy", 39-40.
20  Lewis, "The Geneva Academy", 40.
21  Lewis, "The Geneva Academy", 40.
22  Lewis, "The Geneva Academy", 46. There was, however, also the provision that discretion must be exercised in the choice of authors and that the authority of the Word of God must be maintained. For Lewis this fact conceals an underlying dogmatism. See Lewis, "The Geneva Academy", 45.

for pastoral duties did not form part of the curriculum. The Geneva Academy was therefore not solely a seminary in the narrow sense of offering merely practical training for the ministry.[23] In another regard the *schola publica* was close to a seminary model. According to the founding statutes of the Academy, the schoolmasters, the professors and the students of the *schola publica* had to assent to a detailed confession of faith.[24] The close relationship between the Academy and the Reformed churches is also seen in the fact that the professors took part in the Friday meetings of the ministers (*congrégations*).

Moreover, it is important to take into account the fact that Calvin's vision for theological education was not only focused on the training of ministers, although this task was at the heart of the Academy's work. Already in the *Ecclesiastical Ordinances* of 1541 Calvin had expressed his vision of an educational institution for ministers and civil servants. We further ought to consider that Calvin's real aim was never education merely for the sake of education. Education – of ministers and civil servants – never formed an end in itself; it had a particular *telos*. As Lewis rightly remarks:

> For although he would not rest until he had secured formal backing from the city for the school in which teachers would be selected and put forward by the ministers, and recognised and paid by the magistrates, his real aim, as always, was to bring about a community-wide transformation of values. The institution of a school, as such, was to be only one means among many whereby ministers and magistrates could work together to make the city a single school of Christ.[25]

Calvin's focus was not merely on the church in Geneva, but also on the city itself, and in fact on the religious transformation of Europe. Indeed, for him Geneva became an important centre in the European religious landscape; this was also because of the many religious refugees who found refuge in the city and who would later contribute to Geneva's reputation as a centre of Reformed life. John Knox's well-known description of Geneva as "the most perfect school of Christ" shows something of the impact Geneva made on foreigners coming to the city, or at least on some of them.[26]

Given such remarks, one may be tempted to view the training of pastors and civil servants at the Academy in Calvin's Geneva as a type of 'golden age' not besieged by the problems, conflicts and challenges besetting theological education today.

---

23  Lewis also notes that the Academy cannot be regarded at its founding as a university either: "Unlike the ancient schools of Bologna, Padua, Paris, Oxford and Salamanca … it had not corporations of students, no 'faculties' of masters in arts, law, medicine or divinity, no chancellor, no dean and no proctors. It charged no fees (until 1584) and it awarded 'testimonia' instead of licenses or degrees". Lewis, "The Geneva Academy", 47.
24  See Lewis, "The Geneva Academy", 47-8 and Maag, *Seminary or University?*, 16-17. Maag comments: "Through this statement of belief, the Genevan company of pastors hoped to insure doctrinal conformity among its students, demonstrating again how close the *schola publica* was to a seminary model" (17). Over time the demand of the 1559 Rules for the students to declare in writing their assent to the confession of faith was weakened.
25  Lewis, "The Geneva Academy", 37.
26  See Van 't Spijker, W, *Calvin: A Brief Guide to His Life and Thought* (Louisville: Westminster John Knox Press, 2009), 108.

However, the early years of the Genevan Academy were not at all free of political strife. There were often conflicting views between the pastors and the magistrates on the direction of the Academy. Under the 1559 legislation the schools were placed under the authority of the Company of Pastors and the City Council. The former was responsible for overseeing the teaching and the latter for paying the staff and practical matters. The Academy therefore was under the joint direction of ministers and magistrates. While this joint leadership could conceivably be considered a healthy situation, over time tensions developed. Karin Maag observes that for many of the magistrates, and also a few of the pastors, the foundation of the Academy offered the opportunity to establish a prestige institution of higher education that could compete with other European universities. She comments:

> Thus, almost from the Academy's first years, the magistrates and ministers of the city embarked on a long-running conflict, rooted in their differing conceptions of the Academy's purpose and exacerbated by constant financial difficulties. While the ministers emphasized theology, the magistrates emphasized subjects such as civil law and medicine, among other strategies, to raise Geneva's profile in the sixteenth and early seventeenth century European education world, and thus to attract more wealthy and noble students to the Academy.[27]

What Maag's study confirms is that while the Academy's founding reflected the goal to train future ministers, the question soon arose whether Geneva's academy was to be a purely confessional institution. Recollecting this dispute reminds us not to harbour the nostalgic view that the Genevan Academy developed in a situation devoid of political strife and conflicting views about the nature and purpose of the educational institution.

Nevertheless, the first five years of the Academy of Geneva can be described as a resounding success. Student enrolment was high and students came from all over Europe. It is estimated that in the year of Calvin's death there were about 1 200 students at the *schola privata* and 300 students at the *schola publica*. Many scholars who later became well-known figures, including Thomas Bodley (the founder of the Bodleian library at Oxford) and Kasper Olevianus (co-author of the Heidelberg Catechism) attended the Academy. The Genevan Academy certainly contributed to Geneva's international reputation. Yet, as Alister McGrath has noted, even this illustrious Academy soon lost its appeal. With Calvinism becoming an international movement, the Universities of Leiden and Heidelberg "rapidly gained an international reputation both as centres of learning and as strongholds of Calvinism, eclipsing the more modest reputation of Calvin's personal foundation".[28] Nevertheless, the Academy of Geneva still occupies a privileged position in Reformed memory.

---

27  Maag, *Seminary or University?*, 3.
28  McGrath, A, *A Life of John Calvin* (Oxford: Blackwell, 1990), 201.

## 3. THE FACULTY OF THEOLOGY AT STELLENBOSCH, CALVIN AND 'THE REFORMED HABIT OF MIND'

It is to be expected that Calvin and the Genevan Academy played an important role in the memory of Reformed educational institutions. In 1959, for instance, the Vrije Universiteit in Amsterdam focused on Calvin and his Academy ("Calvijn en zijn Academie") as part of the Calvin memorial year.[29] In the same year the Theological Seminary at Stellenbosch celebrated its centenary but, surprisingly, not much is made in the centenary publications of the fact that this event coincided with the 400th anniversary of the founding of the Genevan Academy.[30] One also does not find reference to the Genevan Academy in the *Gedenkschrift*, which contained the proceedings and speeches at the opening of the Theological Seminary at Stellenbosch in 1859.

Notwithstanding this, Calvin and Calvinism are often closely associated with the Theological Seminary at Stellenbosch. For instance, in the aftermath of the infamous Du Plessis case (in which a Seminary professor, Johannes du Plessis, was accused of heresy and a drawn-out court case ensued), a form of confessional neo-Calvinism grew in strength from the 1930s onwards (although it was not uncontested). A detailed discussion of the reception of Calvin and Calvinism at the Theological Seminary at Stellenbosch during this period requires a fuller exposition than I am able to give here, but suffice it to say that Calvinism became equated with a certain type of confessional orthodoxy.[31] The editorials and many of the articles in a journal called *Die Gereformeerde Vaandel* (*The Reformed Banner*), started in 1933 with three Seminary professors (EE Van Rooyen, DG Malan and D Lategan) as editors, reflect something of the way in which Calvin and Calvinism were often used in an apologetic and antithetical way to counter perceived dangers and threats. In addition, this strand of Calvinism rather uncritically embraced the rising Afrikaner nationalism and patriotism. It is a question whether this form of Calvinism was really infused with an in-depth engagement with Calvin, yet Calvin and Calvinism were definitely used as identity markers and rhetorical devices. One should also note that Prof. BB Keet, a colleague of Van Rooyen, Malan and Lategan, did not share the narrow confessionalism of his colleagues and was more ecumenical in his approach to theology.

---

29   See Nauta, D, Smitskamp, H, Polman, ADR and Brillenburg Wurth, G, *Vier Redevoeringen over Calvijn* (Kampen: Kok, 1959). This publication includes the speeches by Nauta on "Calvijn en zijn Academie in 1559". and H. Smitskamp on "Calvijn's Akademie en die Nederlanden" at a public meeting of the senate of the Vrije Universiteit on 22 May 1959.

30   In *Die Kerkbode* of 8 July 1959, which celebrated the 450th anniversary of Calvin's birth, one does find a brief reference to the 400th anniversary of the Academy of Geneva in an article by André Hugo, which discusses lectures delivered at the Calvin celebrations at the University of Utrecht. See *Die Kerkbode* (8 July 1559): 8. One can note that the Preface to a volume in anticipation of the 125th anniversary of the Theological Seminary in 1984 does refer to the fact that the celebrations coincide with the founding of the Genevan Academy 425 years before. See Brown, E (ed.), *Calvyn Aktueel?* (Cape Town: N G Kerk-Uitgewers, 1982).

31   For a discussion of this strand of confessional (neo-)Calvinism in the aftermath of the Du Plessis case, see my essay "Konfessionele Calvinisme na die Du Plessis-saak", *NGTT* Vol. 51, Supplement 1 (January 2010): 275-288.

The Theological Seminary at Stellenbosch developed out of various concerns, one of them being an attempt to counter what was viewed as the prevailing liberalism at European educational institutions. Many saw this development as harmful to the church in South Africa. Within the context of such a perceived threat, it became important to find the right balance between 'the mind' and 'the heart'. That this was no easy feat is evident in the polarisation developing between, on the one hand, those who were accused of an over-optimistic acceptance of the Enlightenment ideals and, on the other hand, those who were suspected of an uncritical confessional orthodoxy. In the aftermath of the Du Plessis case it seemed that a narrow confessional understanding of theology won the day, rooted in a particular understanding of Calvin and Calvinism.

When we reflect on theological education at Stellenbosch we can indeed ask whether this strand of confessional Calvinism is the most authentic and responsible way of claiming the legacy of the 16th-century Reformer. There is also another strand of Calvin's reception in the Reformed tradition in South Africa that presents a more ecumenical, even radical, Calvin.[32] As the Faculty of Theology reflects on its Reformed roots, we need to consider the ways in which some of the former students, some of whom later became professors at Stellenbosch and other theological institutions, embodied this different understanding of Calvin in their writings and witness. The fact that other Reformed institutions became part of the faculty after 2000 adds to this list the names of influential theologians who did not, or could not, study at Stellenbosch, but whose work drew on the Reformed tradition and Calvin, often against the way the Reformed tradition and Calvin were portrayed by those who defended apartheid theologically. Regarding this 'other' strand of Reformed theology, one could mention, for instance, Bennie Keet, Ben Marais, Jaap Durand, Beyers Naudé, Willie Jonker, Dirkie Smit, Allan Boesak, Russel Botman and Douglas Bax, as well as the work of John de Gruchy. In my view, an engagement with this strand of Reformed theology offers valuable resources for the revitalisation of the Reformed tradition in South Africa, also within the context of institutions that explicitly claim their ecumenical identity.

The Faculty of Theology at Stellenbosch (like theological faculties and departments elsewhere) continues to be challenged by the fact that the Faculty is both part of a university setting *and* that it houses seminaries for the various churches. This reality raises a number of issues that correspond with the debate over whether seminaries or universities are the best setting for theological education. One often hears the comment that universities and seminaries seem to be drifting further apart, or that the gap between the church and the academy is widening. For some this is a reason for great concern, while others see no reason to bemoan this fact. In his essay "Tradition in the Modern World: The Reformed Habit of Mind", the Reformed scholar Brian

---

32  See in this regard Smit, DJ, "Views on Calvin's ethics: Reading Calvin in the South African context", *Reformed World* 57/4 (2007): 306-344, as well as Vosloo, RR, "Calvin and Anti-Apartheid Memory in the Dutch Reformed Family of Churches in South Africa" in De Niet, J, Paul, H and Wallet, B (eds), *Sober, Strict, and Scriptural: Collective Memories of John Calvin, 1800-2000* (Leiden: Brill, 2009): 217-244.

Gerrish highlights a double stereotype often at work in this conversation between proponents of academic and ecclesiastical theology:

> On the one side, the seminaries are suspicious of what they call the 'academic theology' of the university. They perceive it as addressed to the wrong audience and the wrong situation; namely, to supposedly enlightened colleagues in other departments of the university for whom theology has become a quaint anachronism ...
>
> On the other side, the universities, when they notice theology at all, gladly turn it over to the seminaries because it is not a serious intellectual discipline: it lacks rigorous norms of argument and inquiry, is helplessly captive to passing fads and fashions, and trades critical reflection for mere ideology.[33]

Although one certainly ought to respect the difference between Gerrish's North American context and the particularities of the South African theological landscape, many scholars in our interwoven global context may identify with Gerrish's remark that some theologians find themselves in a type of uncomfortable middle position in these debates "under fire from either side, depending on which of their friends they are eating their lunch with".[34]

Gerrish goes on to argue that the university and the seminary suffer from a similar educational malaise, namely disintegration. For Gerrish a remedy, or at least a partial remedy, for this condition "is education viewed as imparting not information or skills, but good habits".[35] With this remark in mind, Gerrish continues by discussing what he calls five notes on the Reformed habit of mind. The first is the habit of *respect for the past*, in the way that one shows deference to an elder. This habit implies that we realise that we stand in a tradition. Second, the Reformed habit of mind is *critical*. It is no easy task to show respect for the past and at the same time be critical, but without criticism of the tradition there will also be no renewal of the tradition. Third, the Reformed habit of mind is *open* to wisdom and insight wherever it is to be found. Theological education in the Reformed tradition cannot therefore become insular and ingrown. Fourth, the Reformed habit of mind is unabashedly *practical*. This implies that knowledge of God is assimilated for the sake of both personal and social change. For Calvin knowledge of God was linked to piety, and piety was directed at transforming society into a mirror of God's glory. The fifth note of the Reformed habit of mind regards *standing under the Word*; hence the idea of the Reformed church "reforming according to the Word of God".[36]

---

33  Gerrish, B, "Tradition in the Modern World: The Reformed Habit of Mind" in Welker, M and Willis, DW (eds), *Towards the Future of Reformed Theology: Tasks, Topics, Traditions* (Grand Rapids: Eerdmans, 1999), 3-4.
34  Gerrish, "Tradition in the Modern World", 3.
35  Gerrish, "Tradition in the Modern World", 5.
36  In the light of this fifth note, Gerrish concludes his article: "The end product of a seminary education in the twenty-first century may very well be *master* in divinity, or a *doctor* of ministry, or even a doctor of divinity *honoris causa*. Let us hope so. But as long as there are Reformed pastors and theologians, they will understand themselves first and foremost, whatever their degree, as *servants* of the Word of God". Gerrish, "Tradition

I briefly recall Gerrish's discussion of 'the Reformed habit of mind' here because it offers, in my view, important insights for institutions that want to claim or reclaim their Reformed roots in a way that is not opposed to theological education in an ecumenical and university context. In addition, Gerrish's remarks offer the implicit challenge to be critical in our thinking about the nature and purpose of ecumenism and the university. The tension between church and academy, and the concomitant stereotypes, will probably not be easily resolved. Perhaps the best that one can hope for is that this tension remains healthy and constructive, and that it does not result in a schism in which a choice is made for either an academic theology with a strong anti-church bias or for an insular ecclesiastical theology.

## 4. CONCLUSION

The concurrent celebrations of the 500th anniversary of Calvin's birth, the 450th anniversary of the opening of the Genevan Academy, and 150 years of theology at Stellenbosch invited reflection on theological education by drawing on the Reformed tradition. One certainly has to acknowledge that the Reformed tradition is filled with ambiguities and inherent tensions, but it also contains insights that can help to unmask a climate of anti-intellectualism and insular thinking. In the discussion of the Genevan Academy I have referred to its openness to other sources of wisdom. A reading of a document setting out a vision for a Reformed theological seminary in South Africa (at the synod of 1824) also indicates a broader intellectual vision.[37] In our day a similar spirit might be displayed in the willingness to engage in interdisciplinary modes of doing theology, while at the same time maintaining theological integrity.

Even a cursory overview of Calvin's vision of theological education, and its concretisation in the early years of the Genevan Academy, reveals that there was a very clear *telos* to train pastors and civil servants as part of the transformation of the church, the city and society – a goal linked to Calvin's theological stance. In our very different context, we are challenged to reflect on the question of what we view as the *telos* of theological education today. As in Calvin's day, we cannot address this question in a vacuum devoid of political strife, but we have to acknowledge that it is an environment characterised by budgetary constrains, and a culture of exclusion and conflicting views. Amidst these realities, the challenge remains to cultivate what Elna Mouton called in her reflection on the future of theological education at Stellenbosch "an ethos that is transformative, healing and hopeful for all".[38]

---

in the Modern World", 20. This remark, in my view, further implies the need for a responsible hermeneutic.

37 See the addendum "Ontwerp van een reglement voor het Theologisch Seminarium" in *De Handelingen der Eerste Vergadering van de Algemeene Synode der Nederduitsch Gereformeerde kerk van Zuid-Afrika* (1824) This document suggests that the church had more than just a theological seminary in mind, as is seen in the way the text envisaged faculties of arts and philosophy, natural science and theology. Cf. Ferreira, *Die Teologiese Seminarium van Stellenbosch 1858-1963*.

38 Coertzen, *Teologie Stellenbosch 150+*, 155.

# 21. ON THE HEIDELBERG CATECHISM: REMEMBERING A 16TH-CENTURY REFORMED CONFESSION IN SOUTH AFRICA TODAY[1]

## 1. INTRODUCTION

When the English delegates returned home from the famous synod of Dort (1618/1619), they reported back enthusiastically: "Our brothers on the continent have a booklet, of which the pages cannot be bought with tons of gold".[2] The booklet they referred to was the Heidelberg Catechism, a document that was first published in 1563. In 2013 we commemorated the 450th anniversary of this valuable Reformed confessional document. Several conferences and public celebrations were held worldwide to commemorate this event, including a conference in Heidelberg in Germany, where the document originated. In South Africa, too, churches and theological educational institutions hosted events that commemorated the Heidelberg Catechism. At Stellenbosch, for instance, the theological day at the beginning of the 2013 academic year had as its theme: "Alienation and Gift: The Relevance of the Heidelberg Catechism for today", and during the same year several other conferences aimed at pastors were held that specifically engaged with the history, theological meaning and relevance of the Heidelberg Catechism. Moreover, the Faculty of Theology at Stellenbosch University also hosted a conference (from 31 October – 1 November 2013), in collaboration with the University of Pretoria and the University of the Free State, as well as with several church partners.

In addition to these events, several South African publications marked the 450th anniversary. For example, a special edition of the theological journal *In die Skriflig/In Luce Verbi* was published that contains several academic articles on the Heidelberg Catechism,[3] and seven young theologians published a creative engagement with this 16th-century Reformed document under the title *Sewe stories en 'n stock cube: Die Heidelbergse Kategismus se troos vir vandag* ("Seven stories and a stock cube: The Heidelberg Catechism's comfort for today").[4]

In this essay I attend specifically to the theme of the 2013 Stellenbosch conference: "Remembering the Heidelberg Catechism in (South) Africa today". The essay is

---

1. A first draft of this essay was read as an opening paper at a conference held from 30 October to 1 November 2013 at the Faculty of Theology, Stellenbosch University. The theme of the conference, which commemorated the 450th anniversary of the Heidelberg Catechism, was "Remembering the Heidelberg Catechism in (South) Africa today?" My essay was published as "Remembering the Heidelberg Catechism in South Africa today? Some remarks on the commemoration of a 16th-century reformed confession" in *Remembering the Heidelberg Catechism in South Africa Today: Essays on the Occasion of the 450th Anniversary of a Reformed Confession* (Guest Editors: Van Tonder, H & Vosloo, R), *Acta Theologica* Supplementum 20, 2014, 1-15.
2. Cf. Plasger, G, *Glauben heute mit dem Heidelberger Katechismus* (Göttingen: Vandenhoeck & Ruprecht, 2012), 9.
3. *In die Skriflig* 47/2 (2013).
4. Van Tonder, H (ed.), with Du Toit, C, Müller-Van Velden, N, Pretorius, H, Van Velden, W, Van Wyngaard, C, and Williams, J, *Sewe stories en 'n stock cube: Die Heidelbergse Kategismus se troos vir vandag* (Wellington: Bybelkor, 2013).

structured by attending to the different words and phrases of this theme. First I will say something about the word *remembering*. Then I will turn to the fact that we are remembering *the Heidelberg Catechism*, a specific 16th-century document, in the process placing the emphasis on the fact that it is a document associated with *Heidelberg*, and that it is a *catechism*. Thirdly, I will pose some questions and offer some observations related to the reception or commemoration of the Heidelberg Catechism *in (South) Africa*. In the final section I will conclude with some remarks on the word *today*.

## 2. *REMEMBERING* THE HEIDELBERG CATECHISM?

Between 2009 and 2013 several conferences were held in Stellenbosch that commemorated important figures and events in the Reformed tradition. In 2009 a conference was held that remembered and reflected on the legacy of John Calvin, the influential 16th-century Reformer.[5] This coincided with the 150th anniversary of theological education at Stellenbosch. In 2011 a consultation was held that celebrated the 450th anniversary of the *Confessio Belgica*, another important Reformed confessional document that had an interesting reception in South Africa.[6] And in 2012 a conference was held which had as its theme "The Reformed Churches in South Africa and the Struggle for Justice: Remembering 1960-1990".[7] In the opening address to that conference I emphasised the importance of a responsible historical hermeneutic when engaging our shared but also divided (Reformed) past.[8] When we remember or commemorate the past, we should continually ask self-critical questions and be troubled by what the philosopher Paul Ricoeur refers to as "the unsettling spectacle offered by an excess of memory here, and an excess of forgetting elsewhere, to say nothing of the influence of commemorations and abuses of memory – and of forgetting".[9] Much can be said in this regard, but for the purposes of this essay let me make two brief remarks.

First, commemorations invite us to be conscious of the close link between memory and identity. On the one hand, we should be aware of the great distance between us and the past, between, for example, us and the 16th century. Therefore we should respect the strangeness of the past, also the mystery of the past,[10] mindful of the fact that our access to the past is possible only via vulnerable epistemological routes. On the other hand, we should also affirm that this strange, and in many ways unknowable, past is also *our* past.[11] The past has formed or malformed our

---

5   For some published articles resulting from this conference, see *NGTT* 51, Supplementum (2010): 289-437.
6   For the published articles resulting from this conference, see *NGTT* 53, 3&4 (2012).
7   For a selection of papers from this conference, see Plaatjies Van Huffel, M and Vosloo, RR, *Reformed Churches in South Africa and the Struggle for Justice: Remembering 1960-1990* (Stellenbosch: Sun Press, 2013).
8   See Plaatjies van Huffel and Vosloo, *Reformed Churches in South Africa and the Struggle for Justice*, 15-25.
9   Ricoeur, P, *Memory, History, Forgetting* (Chicago: University of Chicago Press, 2004), xv.
10  Moltmann, J (ed.), *Das Geheimnis der Vergangenheit: Erinnern –Vergessen –Entschuldigen –Vergeben – Loslassen – Anfangen* (Neukirchen-Vluyn: Neukirchener Theologie, 2012), 5.
11  Williams, R, *Why study the past? The quest for the historical church* (Grand Rapids: Eerdmans, 2005), 1.

identity in significant ways. Even if we don't have direct access to authoritative documents from the distant past (such as the Heidelberg Catechism) through our personal memory, these documents may form part of what scholars such as Jan and Aleida Assmann have described as cultural memory,[12] and as such they continue to exert an influence on our personal, communal and cultural existence. In the already mentioned publication *Sewe stories en 'n stock cube* the young theologians argue that even though one doesn't often hear about the Heidelberg Catechism in worship services and catechism classes, the document still influences, often unconsciously, the way people think and speak about God, since – in a way – it is in our blood.[13]

The close relationship between memory and identity also challenges us to reflect on the way in which our projects of identity construction, often over against others whom we experience as a threat, influence the way in which we remember and represent the past. Therefore we should be mindful that the ways in which we recollect, or our predecessors in previous centuries recollected, the Heidelberg Catechism are not to be abstracted from the identity projects and theological controversies from our time and theirs. Hence the importance of asking questions such as: Who are we who remember the Heidelberg Catechism? What are the power configurations that possibly influence our historical recollections? And with what future in mind are we remembering the Heidelberg Catechism?

A second remark that I would like to make regarding the word 'remembering' concerns the fact that the memory of the Heidelberg Catechism is also a contested memory. For many people from a Reformed background the Heidelberg Catechism is not remembered with joy and a sense of affinity, but is viewed as an oppressive document that formed part of a repressive tradition. For many the question is therefore not how we can remember the Heidelberg Catechism, but how we can forget it, or at least not bother to rekindle the memory of it. But there are also those people who feel that we should consciously reclaim the Heidelberg Catechism as a liberating document, albeit in a theologically responsible way, and who believe that this document, and the rich heritage associated with it, can still speak to us today.

## 3. REMEMBERING THE *HEIDELBERG CATECHISM*

The first edition of the Heidelberg Catechism appeared in Heidelberg in January 1563, with the preface dated 19 January, and the Heidelberg theologian Zacharias Ursinus is today generally acknowledged as the prime author.[14] The Heidelberg Catechism has a very interesting and complicated history of origin, and in order to also understand the theological meaning and relevance of the Heidelberg Catechism for today, it is important to attend with a responsible historical hermeneutic to the pre-history, birth and early reception of this document. It important to remain

---

12  See, for instance, Assmann, J, *Religion and Cultural Memory: Ten Studies* (Stanford: Stanford University Press, 2006), 1-30; and Assmann, A, *Der lange Schatten der Vergangenheit: Erinnerungskultur und Geschichtspolitik* (München: C.H. Beck, 2006), 51-54.
13  Van Tonder *et al.*, *Sewe stories en 'n stock cube*, 8.
14  See, for instance, Ehmann, J, "Von Breslau in die Pfalz – die Wege des Zacharias Ursinus", in: Heimbucher, M, Schneider-Harpprecht, C, and Siller, A (eds.), *Zugänge zum Heidelberger Katechismus: Geschichte – Themen – Unterricht* (Neukirchen-Vluyn: Neukirchener Theologie, 2012), 33.

mindful of the fact that the Heidelberg Catechism originated in a specific historical setting and era, albeit that it also in some way transcends its time and place of origin. It is, moreover, probably true to say that one reason why the Heidelberg Catechism transcended its time and place lies exactly in the pertinent and powerful way that it spoke to its own time and context.

In addition to the history of its origin – which is closely associated with the Kurpfalz region in Germany, and more specifically the town of Heidelberg[15] – the reception history of the Heidelberg Catechism also deserves to be known and studied. This reception history reveals contested responses to it, but it is nevertheless clear that there are strong strands that attest to the way in which this document was received with gratitude, affirming the statement of the English delegates referred to at the beginning of this article that the pages of this booklet cannot be bought with tons of gold. One could even argue that the Heidelberg Catechism has become a religious classic. In his influential book *The Analogical Imagination* the Chicago theologian David Tracy remarks as follow on the notion of the classic and its normative element:

> My thesis is that what we mean in naming certain texts, events, images, rituals, symbols and persons 'classics' is that here we recognize nothing less than the disclosure of a reality we cannot but name truth ... here we find something valuable, something 'important'; some disclosure of reality in a moment that must be called one of 'recognition' which surprises, provokes, challenges, shocks and eventually transforms us; indeed a realized experience of that which is essential, that which endures.[16]

This description rings true if we consider the reception history of the Heidelberg Catechism. Since its first publication in Heidelberg in 1563 people have testified to the fact that this 'classic' disclosed something to them that rang true, in which they recognise something valuable, essential and important.[17] And in the process this little booklet has exercised a great influence, and continues to do so, as is evident from the fact that it has been translated into more than 40 languages, ranging from Afrikaans to Vietnamese.[18]

---

15   The link between Heidelberg and the Heidelberg Catechism is of course not merely limited to the history of its origin. For a recent collection of sermons on the Heidelberg Catechism by theologians from Heidelberg, see Schwier, H and Ulrichs, HG, *Nötig zu wissen: Heidelberger Beiträge zum Heidelberger Katechismus* (Heidelberg: Universitätsverlag Winter, 2012).
16   Tracy, D, *The Analogical Imagination: Christian Theology and the Culture of Pluralism* (New York: Crossroad, 1991), 108.
17   A possible reason for the Heidelberg Catechism's influence is well captured by Doug Ottati: "it succeeds as a passionate and personally moving statement of life reordered and reconfigured by the strange logic of grace". Ottati, DF, *Theology for Liberal Presbyterians and Other Endangered Species* (Louisville: Geneva Press), 48.
18   For various translations of the Heidelberg Catechism, see the website of Refo500 at http://www.refo500.nl/en/pages/10/Heidelberg%20Catechism%20in%20Various%20 Languages.html (accessed 23 October 2013). There is even a Twitte-chismus in Dutch. For an article on the first Afrikaans translations of the Heidelberg Catechism, see Britz, D, "Die eerste vertalings van die Heidelbergse Kategismus in Afrikaans", *In die Skriflig* 47(2) (2013): 1-12. For an edition of the text in its original language, see Freudenberg,

For many members of the Reformed tradition (and for other Christians as well) the first thing that comes to mind when they hear a reference to the Heidelberg Catechism is the first question of the catechism: "What is your only comfort in life and death?", as well as the first part of the answer to this question: "That I am not my own, but belong – body and soul, in life and in death – to my faithful Saviour Jesus Christ.[19] At least part of the enduring power and influence of the Heidelberg Catechism is linked to the existential and pastoral tone of its first question and answer. In an essay for the anniversary publication *Power of Faith: 450 years of the Heidelberg Catechism*, Herman Selderhuis refers to Anna Maria van Schurman, the first woman to attend lectures at the University of Utrecht, who reported that when, as a four-year-old girl, she was picking flowers in the field, her family's maid asked her to recite question and answer one of the Heidelberg Catechism. As she recited the words "that I am not my own but belong to my faithful Saviour Jesus Christ", she experienced such joy that this event and her experience of it remained with her for the rest of her life.[20] The testimonies of many others since then, also in South Africa, confirm that hers was not an isolated experience.

In addition to its famous first question and answer, the Heidelberg Catechism is also well known for its three-fold structure, already announced in the second question of the catechism, which asks how many things are necessary to know concerning the comfort announced in answer one. The answer is simple and concise: "Three things: first, how great my sin and misery are; second, how I am set free from all my sins and misery; third, how I am to thank God for such deliverance".[21] The theological brilliance of this structure has often been praised. Karl Barth, for instance, said in a famous lecture on the Heidelberg Catechism in 1938: "The outline human misery–human redemption–human gratitude is in its simplicity an ingenious restatement of the essence of the whole Reformation".[22]

Many South African Reformed Christians will still recall that the structure of the Heidelberg Catechism was taught to them in catechism class as encapsulated in the notions of sin, redemption and gratitude, following Gerdener's *Handboek by die Katkisasie* (*Handbook for Catechism*),[23] and the later General Sunday School commission of the Dutch Reformed Church's *Die Katkisasieboek* (*The Catechism Book*).[24] The strong focus on sin as the main organising concept for the first part of the catechism is revealing, especially since the heading in the original version of the Heidelberg Catechism refers not to 'sin' but to 'human misery' ("von des Menschen Elend)". In an interesting article, a published version of a paper read in 2013 at the theological day of the Theology Faculty at Stellenbosch, Dirkie Smit addresses

---

    M and Siller, A, *Was ist dein einiger Trost? Der Heidelberger Katechismus in der Urfassung* (Neukirchen-Vluyn: Neukirchener Theologie, 2012).
19  *Heidelberg Catechism: 450th Anniversary Edition* (Grand Rapids: Faith Alive Christian Resources, 2013), 8.
20  Apperloo-Boersma, K and Selderhuis HJ (eds), *Power of Faith: 450 Years of the Heidelberg Catechism* (Göttingen: Vandenhoeck & Ruprecht, 2013), 24.
21  *Heidelberg Catechism*, 8.
22  Barth, K, *Learning Jesus Christ through the Heidelberg Catechism* (Grand Rapids: Eerdmans, 1964), 122.
23  Gerdener, GBA, *Handboek by die Katkisasie* (Kaapstad: Die N.G. Kerk-Uitgewers, 1927), 158.
24  *Die Katkisasieboek* (Bloemfontein: Die Sondagskool Boekhandel, 1950), 124.

the possible misinterpretations when the first part of the catechism is reduced to a certain understanding of sin that negates the wider meaning of misery.[25] In the article Smit also attends to some challenges arising out of the spirit of our times against the three-fold structure of the catechism,[26] including the way in which the catechism is understood as promoting a pessimistic anthropology and the charge that gratitude cannot serves as motivation for the Christian life (as is reflected, for instance, in the philosophical discourse on the question 'Can a gift be given?'). One can therefore speak of both appreciation for and critique of the three-fold structure of the Heidelberg Catechism, as well as the theological and ethical ideas underlying it.

In commemorating the Heidelberg Catechism the opportunity arises not only to reflect on the theological meaning and historical origins of the Heidelberg Catechism, but also on its genre and purpose, mindful of the fact that it is a catechism, intended for the teaching of the faith. The Heidelberg Catechism – which can be viewed in line with several other catechisms of the 16th century – was thus designed for teaching, as is also noted in the Preface by Frederick III to the original 1563 Catechism. The purpose was not merely the training of the youth, but also to provide a reliable teaching aid for the pastors and schoolmasters themselves.[27] Today the teaching of the faith is faced with huge challenges in secular or post-secular societies, and the question can be asked whether a renewed engagement with the Heidelberg Catechism can contribute in a meaningful and fruitful way to addressing contemporary concerns and realities regarding the transmission of the Christian tradition. Can we find a way between over-playing and under-playing the possible role of the Heidelberg Catechism in this regard? It falls beyond the scope of this essay , however, to address these important questions.

The Heidelberg Catechism, moreover, was not merely intended as a catechetical tool, but also as preaching guide and as a form of confessional unity among the different Protestant factions in the Palatinate.[28] There is no doubt that the impact of the Heidelberg Catechism can hardly be over-estimated, as its reception in the rest of Germany as well as further afield and especially in the Netherlands bears witness to, including through the tradition of catechism preaching.[29] The specific reception

---

25  Smit, DJ, "Vervreemding en gawe – sleutelmotiewe in die Heidelbergse Kategismus", *NGTT* 54 (1&2) (2013): 173-188.
26  Smit comments in this regard: "The spirit of our times no longer knows *this* kind of awareness of sin and feelings of guilt. The worldview of our day no longer needs *this* kind of forgiveness, redemption and justification. Contemporary people experience the call to show gratitude – which finds expression in commandment and prayer – as something legalistic and in conflict with their need for individual freedom". Smit, "Vervreemding en gawe", 174 (my translation).
27  Freudenberg and Siller, *Was ist dein einiger Trost?*, 15.
28  Cf. Bierma, L D, *An Introduction to the Heidelberg Catechism: Sources, History, and Theology* (Grand Rapids: Baker Academic, 2005), 51; and Barth, *Learning Jesus Christ through the Heidelberg Catechism*, 12.
29  On Catechism preaching in the Netherlands, see Baars, A, "The Simple Heidelberg Catechism … A brief history of the catechism sermon in the Netherlands" in Apperloo-Boersma, K and Selderhuis, HJ (eds), *Power of Faith: 450 Years of the Heidelberg Catechism* (Göttingen: Vandenhoeck & Ruprecht, 2013), 137-146.

For a more extensive discussion see his book Baars, A, *'De eenvoudige Heidelberger …!' Een korte geschiedenis van de Catechismuspreek in Nederland* (Apeldoorn: Theologische

history of the Heidelberg Catechism in the Netherlands is of special importance for South Africa, given the fact that when the Dutch came to the Cape in the mid-17$^{th}$ century they brought along their Reformed faith and tradition (which included the Heidelberg Catechism as part of their confessional heritage).

## 4. REMEMBERING THE HEIDELBERG CATECHISM IN (SOUTH) AFRICA

With this in mind, I now turn to some aspects of the reception of the Heidelberg Catechism *in (South) Africa*. We should also remember that through the mission work of the Dutch Reformed Church (DRC) the Heidelberg Catechism also had an impact on other countries in Africa, and the Catechism still forms part of the confessional base and church polity discourse of many of the churches that were born out of the DRC's mission work.[30]

From the time of the Dutch settlement at the Cape the Heidelberg Catechism played a role in teaching and preaching, as was the practice in the 'Nederlandse Hervormde Kerk', of which the early congregations formed a part. In a letter to the classis in Amsterdam (dated 20 April 1655), the sick comforter Willem Wylandt, for instance, reported that every second Sunday he read a commentary from the Catechism from Ursinus' *Het Schatboek der Verklaringen van de Heidelbergse Catechismus* or from Lansberghius. After the reading the children had to recite the questions, with some Scripture references.[31] Catechism sermons were also part of ecclesial practice from early on, although reports to Synod in 1773 and again in 1829 mentioned lukewarm attendance of these afternoon services. In time the Catechism was used less and less, in part replaced by the summary of the Catechism, the well-known *Korte Begrip*, as well as by new catechism books. The Catechism, however, retained its status as Reformed Confession.[32]

In reflecting on the reception history of the Heidelberg Catechism in South Africa, one should also take note of the fact that its reception history evinces conflict and contestation. In the 1860s, for instance, the Heidelberg Catechism – together with the other confessions that formed part of the Three Formulae of Unity – was at the heart of the so-called Liberal (or Modernistic) Controversy. Several ministers of the Dutch Reformed church, who were influenced by Modernism (among them JJ Kotze and TF Burgers), were challenged to defend their ideas. In his book *Vroom of*

---

Universiteit, 2012). This title of this book refers to the famous words of the 19$^{th}$-century Dutch theologian and preacher Hermann Friedrich Kohlbrugge on his deathbed: "De Heidelberger! De eenvoudige Heidelberger! Houdt daaraan vast, kinderen!" (The Heidelberger! The simple Heidelberger! Hold it fast, children!").

30   For a discussion of the reception and relevance of the Heidelberg Catechism with reference to the Nkhoma Synod of the Church of Central Africa, Presbyterian, see Zeze, WSD, *Christ, the Head of the Church? Authority, Leadership, and Organisational Structure within the Nkhoma Synod of the Church of Central Africa, Presbyterian* (Stellenbosch: Unpublished DTh dissertation, 2012).

31   See Spoelstra, C, *Bouwstoffen voor de Geschiedenis der Nederduitsch-Gereformeerde Kerken in Zuid-Afrika, Deel 1* (Amsterdam: Hollandisch-Afrikaansche Uitgevers-Maatschappij, 1906), 3. Cf. Oberholzer, JP, *Die Heidelbergse Kategismus, in vier teksuitgawes, met inleiding en teksvergelyking* (Pretoria: NHW-Pers, 1986), 7.

32   Oberholzer, *Die Heidelbergse Kategismus*, 7-8.

*Regsinnig? (Pious or Orthodox?)* Vincent Brümmer has argued that Andrew Murray,[33] who was then the moderator of the Cape Church, was conscious that the court could not charge these proponents of what is referred to as "the Modern Strand" ("die Moderne rigting") on grounds of their piety, but could challenge them on grounds of their commitment to the Reformed Confessions, which they signed upon their legitimation as ministers.[34] One of them, Rev. JJ Kotze of Darling, did not want to defend the view that the Confessions were always in line with ("in ooreenstemming met") the Bible. In this regard he referred to Sunday 23 (question 60), which described human beings as "still inclined toward all evil" ("nog gedurigdeur tot alle kwaad geneig is"). For him these words should not even come out of the mouth of a pagan and certainly not out of the mouth of a Christian. For him this statement was neither Reformed nor biblical. At a synod meeting both Kotze and Burgers were suspended, although their later appeal to the civil court was successful.

In the theological struggles of the late 19th and early 20th century, Modernism and Liberalism, understood in a certain way, continued to be viewed as a danger for the church. The Reformed confessions were often used in order to define the 'true' Calvinistic faith, over against the dangers of Modernism and Liberalism. In the process a form of neo-Calvinism developed that had a specific understanding of the Reformed Confessions, and if you read, for instance, the articles of these neo-Calvinist theologians of the 1930s and 1940s, you get the sense that the Confessions functioned in a rather abstract way to fight different '–isms', ranging from modernism, to liberalism, to communism, ecumenism, even to what is described as 'other-ism'.[35]

If one speaks of the reception of the Heidelberg Catechism, one can also consider the way in which the Catechism functioned in an alternative strand of Calvinism in South Africa, the strand that became associated with the critique of apartheid and the Belhar Confession (a new confession that arose out of the church and theological struggles in South Africa, and that was adopted as draft confession in 1982, and as official fourth confession of the then Dutch Reformed Mission Church in 1986). The early negative reception of this document in the white Dutch Reformed Church focused mainly on what was seen as the link between the Belhar confession and liberation theology, but this critique often failed to notice the way in which the Belhar Confession is deeply embedded in the Reformed confessional tradition, including the ecclesiology put forward in the *Confessio Belgica* (articles 28 and 29) and the Heidelberg Catechism (Sunday 21, question and answer 54 and 55). I have a copy of the first handwritten draft of the Belhar Confession (the original document is stored by the Uniting Reformed Church in Southern Africa in the church archive at Stellenbosch), and it is interesting to note that above the first article is written in the margins HK XX1, 54-55. The ecclesiology of articles 54 and 55 of the Heidelberg Catechism was therefore part of the theological imagination that produced this document.

---

33 One the volumes in Andrew Murray's collected works contains his meditations on the Heidelberg Catechism; see Murray, A, *Die Heidelbergse Kategismus (Versamelde Werke, Deel X)* (Kaapstad: Nasionale Pers Bpk., 1945).
34 Brümmer, V, *Vroom of Regsinning? Teologie in die NG Kerk* (Wellington: Bybel-Media, 2013), 107.
35 Cf. Vosloo, RR, "Konfessionele Neo-Calvinisme na die Du Plessis-saak", *NGTT* 51, Supplementum (2010): 275-288, here 281.

The influence of the Heidelberg Catechism is also more explicit. As Piet Naudé has highlighted in his award-winning book on the Belhar Confession, *Neither Calendar nor Clock*, the words in article 1 of the Belhar Confession that follow "We believe in the triune God, Father, Son and Holy Spirit", namely the words "… who gathers, protects and cares for his Church by his Word and his Spirit, as He has done since the beginning of the world and will do to the end", are an almost direct quotation from the Heidelberg Catechism, question and answer 54, which reads: "What do you believe of the holy catholic church? That the Son of God … from the beginning to the end of the world gathers, defends, and preserves for himself … by his Spirit and Word … a church chosen to everlasting life".[36] Much more can be said on the direct and indirect influence of the Heidelberg Catechism on the Belhar Confession, but suffice it to say that the issue of the underlying ecclesiology operative in the Reformed churches in South Africa is still a highly contested, but also extremely vital, conversation. When one speaks about the reception of the Heidelberg Catechism in South Africa, one cannot separate this discourse from the debates around the Belhar Confession (and its reception and non-reception in other churches in the Dutch Reformed church family). At the heart of these debates are questions related to our ecclesiology, as well as to what is understood by confessional theology[37] and what it means to be a confessional church.

Let me conclude this section on the reception of the Heidelberg Catechism in South Africa by saying that it is highly significant that the theologian who wrote probably the most influential work on Reformed Confessions in South Africa – I am speaking of Willie Jonker and the book is *Bevrydende Waarheid: Die karakter van die gereformeerde belydenis* (*Liberating Truth: the Character of Reformed Confession*)[38] – uses as one of the mottos for a later publication on his personal life journey within the Dutch Reformed Church, entitled *Selfs die kerk kan verander* (*Even the church can change*), question and answer 55 from the Heidelberg Catechism.[39] Clearly for Jonker the ecclesial vision of the Catechism is not that of a church divided or isolated along racial lines (a type of 'volkskerk'), but of a united church in which people (who share the treasures and gifts in Christ) joyfully share their gifts and lives with each other.

## 5. CONCLUSION: REMEMBERING THE HEIDELBERG CATECHISM *TODAY*

The conference held in Stellenbosch in 2013 that commemorated the 450th anniversary of the Heidelberg Catechism had as its theme "Remembering the Heidelberg Catechism in South Africa today". The word "today" in the theme suggests that it is also important to ask questions about the relevance of the Heidelberg Catechism for church and society, and not merely engage with the document out of intellectual curiosity or for antiquarian purposes. Much can be said on the relevance of the Heidelberg Catechism for today, but for the purposes of this essay

---

36 Naudé, P, *Neither Calendar nor Clock: Perspectives on the Belhar Confession* (Grand Rapids: Eerdmans, 2010), 6.
37 Tshaka, RS, *Confessional Theology? A Critical Analysis of the Theology of Karl Barth and its Significance for the Belhar Confession* (Newcastle: Cambridge Scholars Press, 2010).
38 Jonker, WD, *Bevrydende waarheid: Die karakter van die gereformeerde Belydenis* (Wellington: Hugenote-Uitgewers, 1994).
39 Jonker, WD, *Selfs die kerk kan verander* (Kaapstad: Tafelberg, 1998).

I want to emphasise in closing how important it is for the hermeneutical process of interpreting and embodying the Heidelberg Catechism to be guided by a sense of the Christian tradition (and also the Reformed tradition) as a *living tradition*, a tradition that always seeks, in deference and faithfulness to its history, fresh articulations of the faith we confess.[40] Karl Barth has expressed this poignantly:

> We no longer live in the sixteenth but in the twentieth century ... If we concern ourselves today with Christian doctrine, there is no point in staring spellbound at the sixteenth century and holding on to what was said then and there as immovably and unchangeably as possible. Such a procedure would be inconsistent with the Reformation. It is always a misunderstanding of the communion of saints and a misunderstanding also of the fathers when their confession is later understood as chains, so that Christian doctrine today could only be repetition of their confession. In the communion of the saints there should be reverence and thankfulness for the fathers of the church, those who have gone before us and in their time have reflected on the gospel. But there is also freedom in the communion of the saints ...[41]

This quotation challenges us not to see the Heidelberg Catechism as a chain that binds us (in the sense that we view it as a document that requires mere repetition), but as a gift that we can receive without regret as we seek to confess our faith *with* the Heidelberg Catechism,[42] in Christian freedom, and with joy.

---

40  For one fresh articulation, see Theissen, G, *Glaubenssätze: Ein kritischer Katechismus* (Gütherloh: Gütherloher Verlagshaus, 2012). This book is tellingly dedicated to Zacharius Ursinus, the author of the Heidelberg Catechism.
41  Barth, *Learning Jesus Christ through the Heidelberg Catechism*, 21.
42  On understanding "with the Heidelberg Catechism", see Busch, E, *Der Freiheit zugetan: Christlicher Glaube heute – im Gespräch mit dem Heidelberger Katechismus* (Neukirchen-Vluyn: Neukirchener Verlag, 1998), vi.

# 22. ON THE BELHAR CONFESSION: REMARKS ON THE RECEPTION OF A 20$^{TH}$ CENTURY CONFESSIONAL DOCUMENT IN THE DUTCH REFORMED CHURCH[1]

## 1. INTRODUCTION

The story of the reception of the Belhar Confession in the Dutch Reformed Church (DRC) is a long and complicated – and for many a frustrating and confusing – story (indeed a story of stories), about which much has already been written.[2] This is, furthermore, a story that could be told from different perspectives, and with different goals in mind. My aim in this essay is to share some information about more formal and official processes on synodical level within the DRC, but realising that the story of the reception of the Belhar Confession should not be reduced to synodical decisions and official statements.

---

1. This essay was presented at a consultation on the Belhar Confession with representatives of presbyteries of the Presbyterian Church in the United States (PCUSA) in October and November 2014 in Stellenbosch. Part of this essay draws on my article "The Reception of the Belhar Confession in the Dutch Reformed Church and Church Polity" Koffeman, LJ and Smit, J (eds), *Protestant Church Polity in Changing Contexts II* (Vienna and Berlin: LIT Verlag, 2014): 71-84.

2. See, for instance, Botha, J and Naudé, P, *Op pad met Belhar: Genie nuus vir gister, vandag en môre!* (Pretoria: J.L. van Schaik, 1998). For some literature on the Belhar Confession – on its pre-history; on the socio-political contexts in which it developed and was received; on the link to the Bible and the Reformed confessing tradition; on its continuity and discontinuity with the Barmen declaration of 1934; on its local and international reception; and on its promise for dealing on a theological level with some contemporary challenges – see for instance, Cloete, GD and Smit, DJ, *A moment of truth: The Confession of the Dutch Reformed Mission Church 1982* (Grand Rapids: Eerdmans, 1984); Botha & Naudé, *Op pad met Belhar*; Adonis, JC, "The History of Belhar", *NGTT* 47, 1&2 (2006): 234-239; Koopman, N, "Reconciliation and the Confession of Belhar 1986: Some challenges for the Uniting Reformed Church in Southern Africa", *NGTT* 48 (2007): 96-106. Koopman, N, "Belhar: A Transforming and Dignifying Tradition", *Journal of Theology for Southern Africa* 139 (2011): 32-41; Boesak, A, "To stand where God stands: Reflections on the Confession of Belhar after 25 years", *Studia Historiae Ecclesiastica* XXXIV/1 (2008): 143-172; Naudé, P J, *Neither Calendar nor Clock: Perspectives on the Belhar Confession* (Grand Rapids: Eerdmans, 2010); Botha, J and Naudé, P, *Good news to confess: The Belhar Confession and the road to acceptance* (Wellington: Bible Media, 2011); Smit, DJ, "Oor die Belydenis van Belhar: Oor die teologiese inhoud van die Belydenis van Belhar", in Remembering Theologians - Doing Theology: Collected Essays 5 (ed. Robert Vosloo) (Stellenbosch: Sun Press, 2013), 47-58. Plaatjies van Huffel, M, "Reading the *Belhar Confessions* as a historical text" in Plaatjies van Huffel, M and Vosloo, R (eds), *Reformed Churches in South Africa and the Struggle for Justice; Remembering 1960-1990* (Stellenbosch: Sun Media, 2013). For critical readings of the Belhar Confession, see Strauss, PJ, "Belydenis, kerkverband en Belhar", *NGTT* 46/3&4 (2005): 560-575 and Theron, P (ed.), *Belhar geweeg* (Pretoria: Kraal uitgewers, 2012).

The first strong synodical recommendation to make the Belhar Confession part of its confessional base came from the Western Cape Synod. On 10 May 2011[3] this regional Synod discussed the following motion put forward by the *Moderamen*:

> The Synod is convinced that the Biblical call for justice for all people, reconciliation between people, and the unity of the church are at the heart of the gospel. The Belhar Confession gives expression to the call of the gospel in a different way than the other confessions of the church. The Synod, as a church meeting, accepts the Belhar Confession and calls on the General Synod of the Dutch Reformed Church to make the Belhar Confession in a church-orderly way part of the confessional base of the Dutch Reformed Church.[4]

Given the long history of controversy surrounding the Belhar Confession, it came as quite a surprise when the Western Cape synod accepted this proposal with a large majority (around 80%). Although there were also some strong and passionate dissenting voices speaking against the proposal, this decision reflects an important development regarding the discourse on the Belhar Confession at synod meetings in the DRC. It should be noted, however, that since 1982 there has always also been a minor, but nevertheless theologically significant and influential, strand that unequivocally supports the acceptance of the Belhar Confession as a fourth confession. Even so, this meeting in 2011 was the first time that a synod actually voted in favour of a proposal regarding the acceptance of the Belhar Confession as part of the confessional base of the Dutch Reformed Church. This decision by the Western Cape Synod in May 2011 also meant that at its meeting in October 2011 the General Synod had to discuss the call by some of its regional synods to make the Belhar Confession part of the confessional base of the Dutch Reformed Church in a church-orderly (i.e. in accordance with the Church Order, "kerkordelike") way.

In October 2011 the 14th session of the General Synod of the Dutch Reformed Church took place in Boksburg. The proposal of the Western Cape Synod regarding the acceptance of the Belhar Confession was taken up and – again to the surprise of many – Synod decided with an overwhelming majority (of around 90%) to support the proposal. The official decision taken by the General Synod reads:

> The General Synod decides to make the Belhar Confession in a church-orderly manner part of the church's confessional base and commissions

---

3   10 May, incidentally, is also the day on which we commemorate the birthday of Karl Barth, the great Swiss Reformed theologian, who contributed much to the discourse in the 20th century on the nature and meaning of Reformed confessions. 10 May is, furthermore, also the birthday of Beyers Naudé, the controversial South African church leader who played such a prominent and decisive role in the struggle against apartheid and who, already in the mid-1960s, had made an influential plea for the need for a confessing church in South Africa.

4   Agenda, Dutch Reformed Church in South Africa (2011): 7. This proposal to synod resulted from an in-depth discussion of the Belhar Confession at a meeting of the Moderamen of the Western Cape Synod on 24 March 2009. See Hanekom, B (in conversation with Neels Jackson), "'n Bybelse weg uit die konflik", *Die Kerkbode*, (1 August 2014): 10. This proposal to synod stemmed from an in-depth discussion of the Belhar Confession at a meeting of the Moderamen of the Western Cape Synod on 24 March 2009.

the Moderamen to start the necessary church-order(ly) processes ("kerkorderlike prosesse") that are required in this regard.[5]

This decision represents a definite shift from earlier positions of the General Synod of the DRC regarding the Belhar Confession. But before saying something about the process after the General Synod of 2011, let's take a step back and look at a few important episodes in the reception of the Belhar Confession in the DRC after 1982.

## 2. THE OFFICIAL RESPONSE FROM THE DRC: 1982-1990

The first official response of the DRC after the declaration of a *status confessionis* and the acceptance of the draft Belhar confession by the Dutch Reformed Mission Church (DRMC) in 1982 had a strongly critical tone. The DRC General Synod in Pretoria in October 1982 stated: "Synod has with great sorrow taken note that, as a result of the status confessionis, a confession has come into being that stands in conflict with the DR Church and on the same footing as our other confessions".[6]

In the stormy years that followed the draft confession the relations between the DRC and the DRMC became more strained. In 1984 the Broad Moderature ("Bree moderatuur") of the DRC formulated a response to several important documents on church unity, including the draft confession, and this response was sent to the DRMC on 23 March 1984. Again the response to the draft confession was mostly negative. Although the Broad Moderature acknowledged the right in principle of a church to accept a confession under certain circumstance, it did state that "your envisaged confession does not do justice to the legitimate pluriformity ["regmatige pluriformiteit"] of the church".[7] In addition to some other points of critique, the report further suggested that the idea "that the church as property of God must stand ... by the oppressed" is too one-sided: "Your point of departure is, however, different from ours, since you seemingly reach this conclusion based on an unacceptable horizontal exegesis ["'n onaanvaarbare horisontalistiese eksegese"] typical of liberation theology".[8] The report of the Broad Moderature concluded that they want to declare emphatically that the DRMC must seriously consider whether they want to continue with this new confession, since it could lead to new polarisation. The report further expressed an openness to continuing the conversation in the light of the joint history of these churches.

The DRMC's response to this report also makes for interesting reading.[9] Suffice it to say for our purposes here that at this stage there was strong official antagonism from the side of the DRC against the draft confession. The official correspondence and discussions between the DRC and the DRMC also reveal underlying theological

---

5   Acts, Dutch Reformed Church General Synod (2011).
6   Acts, Dutch Reformed Church General Synod (1982): 1403.
7   Cf. Agenda, Dutch Reformed Church General Synod (1986): 26.
8   Agenda, Dutch Reformed Church General Synod (1986): 27.
9   Agenda, Dutch Reformed Church General Synod (1986): 27-29

tensions and conflicting paradigms. Jaap Durand, systematic theologian at the University of Western Cape, has made some telling comments in this regard:

> The DRC's first reaction – from its general synod of October 1982 in Pretoria – gives the impression that a parting of ways is inevitable. This reaction can be understood in more ways than one. On the face of it, the synod's reaction was an unmistakable attempt to render the urgent appeal of the DR Mission Church fruitless for all practical purposes by expressing the synod's 'sadness and dismay' over the 'unreasonable accusation of theological heresy' without, however, addressing the theological merit of the situation ... It would be a fair judgment to say that the DRC was not theologically strong enough to cope with the event. The sterility of the particular theology of creation orders with which the DRC equipped itself in the difficult area of race relations rendered it incapable of responding sensibly.[10]

In the years that followed these early reactions to the draft confession, voices critical of the church's official criticism of the Belhar confession (also from within the Dutch Reformed Church) became more vociferous and influential. These theological responses to the critique against the Belhar Confession (drawing also on insights from Reformed sources), together with important changes in the South African socio-political landscape, contributed – at least to some extent – to an important proposal brought before the General Synod of 1990 by the General Synodical Commission (the executive committee, "Algemene Sinodale Kommissie", or ASK). This proposal was accepted, with some minor changes, by Synod. Point 5 of this decision reads: "The General Synodical Commission (ASK) is of the opinion that the Belhar Confession, taken by itself, is not in contradiction to the Three Formulae of Unity, and that it need not bring separation between the churches". Moreover, the commission was also of the opinion (see point 8 of the decision) that "certain statements could have been formulated differently, such as paragraph 4 of the Belhar Confession, and that the description in *Church and Society* [an important reformist document for the DRC accepted in 1986 and further amended in 1990] regarding the Lord as God of the 'the poor and the oppressed' states the matter in a more sound biblical way".[11]

What is significant in the 1990 decision is that the DRC accepted that the Belhar Confession viewed on its own[12] (i.e. divorced from any possible ideological setting and motivation) is, in effect, in accordance with the other confessions, and thus by implication in accordance with Scripture. Nevertheless, some reservations were still emphasised (as seen in point 8). Some commentators on the reception of the Belhar Confession in the DRC have noted that the 1990 decision points to the need for the full acceptance of the Belhar Confession, as well as that point 8 of the decision reveals

---

10 Cloete and Smit, *A moment of truth*, 119,120.
11 Agenda, Dutch Reformed Church General Synod (1990).
12 It is, of course, an important question whether the Belhar Confession, and also other confessions, can in fact be viewed in isolation in this way. For an argument that makes the point that one should judge a confession in terms of its theological content, and – at the same time – should place it in its historical context, see Smit, "'n Blik op eenheid, versoening en geregtigheid 1986 en 2011".

a theological deficiency in the DRC.[13] Although the 1990 decision was viewed by many as an insufficient response to the Belhar Confession, it did mark an important milestone on the road to the decision of October 2011. The 1990 decision that Belhar, taken on its own, is not in contradiction to the Three Formulae of Unity, was again affirmed in 1998. In addition the executive committee ("Dagbestuur") was of the opinion that the church should look anew, in consultation with other conversation partners, to ways in which the Belhar Confession could be incorporated into the confessional base of the newly unified denomination.[14]

## 3. THE OFFICIAL RESPONSE FROM THE DRC: 1990-2011

Between 1998 and 2011 the general synod of the DRC met three times (in 2002, 2004 and 2007). The way in which Synod dealt with the important matter of church reunification and the Belhar Confession during this period, as well as with the broader processes in the church, deserves a fuller account than I am able to give in this essay.[15] Suffice it to say that it seemed to be the case that the process of reunification (including discussions on the acceptance of the Belhar Confession) was, as Piet Naudé has observed, "still continuing with strides of both hope and despair".[16] Before 2011 there were several attempts to test the views of church members and congregations on the Belhar confession. One such process produced varied results in 1998, but the received commentary was nevertheless mainly negative about the acceptance of the Belhar Confession.[17] Although there were some significant joint meetings between members of the DRC and URCSA, no new principles regarding the Belhar Confession and church unity were accepted at the meeting of the General Synod in 2002. At the synod of 2004 more than a quarter of the delegates expressed their commitment to church unity by signing the Belhar Confession in a symbolic gesture, even though this gesture had no legal status. The period between 2004 and 2011 can be seen as a road with many highs and lows regarding church unity and the reception of the Belhar confession, and this history certainly warrants further church historical and theological inquiry.

In essence the decision of 1998 was confirmed by the synods of 2002 and 2004. And in 2007 no specific decision was taken on the Belhar Confession. This meant that the decision still stood that accepted the content of the Belhar Confession, without actually accepting the Belhar Confession as a fourth confession. Even the above

---

13  Russel Botman, for instance, has stated in a comment on the 1990 decision: "Centrally, the DRC stands against the Confession of Belhar 1986, with specific reference to the fourth clause, because it lacks the universe of theological discourse that is required for a real understanding of the Confession of Belhar". See Botman, R, "Belhar and the white DRC: Changes in the DRC: 1974-1990", *Scriptura* 76/1 (2001): 33-42, here 39.
14  Acts, Dutch Reformed Church General Synod (1998): 305.
15  For such an account, see, for instance, Botha, J and Naudé, P, *Good news to confess: The Belhar Confession and the road to acceptance* (Wellington: Bible Media, 2011). For some thought-provoking statements in the light of this history, see Naudé, *Neither Calendar nor Clock*, 138-148.
16  Naudé, *Neither Calendar nor Clock*, 138.
17  Acts, Dutch Reformed Church General Synod (1998): 305. A later process of testing the congregations (that started after the 2007 General Synod) also had a negative impact on unity talks.

broad cursory overview of some important synod decisions reveals an important development from the initial official reactions in 1982. Although we should not equate the DRC with the sum total of decisions and discussions at official meetings, these developments nevertheless represent an important aspect of the reception of the Belhar Confession within the Dutch Reformed Church. It is furthermore clear that the decision of October 2011 marks an important new stage in the reception history of the Belhar Confession in the DRC, and prepared the way for the decisions that were taken at the meeting of the General Synod meeting in October 2013 in Port Elizabeth.

## 4. THE BELHAR CONFESSION, THE DRC CHURCH ORDER AND CHURCH POLITY DISCOURSE

The General Synod of 2011 decided to make the Belhar Confession in a church-orderly manner part of the church's confessional base. But what does this mean?

Article 43 of the Church Order of the Dutch Reformed Church deals with the tasks of the General Synod. Among these tasks are included "the stipulation of the confessions according to article 44" (Article 43.1.4.). But what does article 44 say? The first two parts of this article are of crucial importance for the process of accepting the Belhar Confession "in a church-orderly way".

> Article 44.1: The amendment of the confession can only take place after each synod separately decides with a two-thirds majority in favour thereof *and* two-thirds of all church councils each with a two-thirds majority decide in favour of it as well.

> Article 44.2: Articles 44.1. and 44.2 are amended after each synod separately decide in favour of this with a two-thirds majority and after that the General Synod decides in favour thereof with a two-thirds majority.[18]

The Church Order of the DRC therefore points towards an elaborate process when it comes to amending the confessions of the church. Two thirds of all church councils must approve such a decision with a two-thirds majority, as must all the regional synods, again with a two-thirds majority. It is important to note, furthermore, that this current formulation, as is found in the two most recent DRC Church Orders (2004, 2007), was the result of an amendment based on a decision at the Synod of 2004. In the 2002 Church Order, for instance, article 44.1 still states that the Confession can only be changed "after each synod decides separately with a two-thirds majority in favour thereof". Why was this article amended to include the provision that not only the regional synods but also two thirds of all congregations must approve the change with a two-thirds majority? Was this an attempt to put in place more hurdles in order to delay or stifle church reunification and the acceptance of the Belhar Confession?

---

18   Dutch Reformed Church, Church Order (2007).

In an article in *Die Kerkbode* in 2011, entitled "Tweederdebesluit hou kerk nie gevange" ("The two-thirds majority decision does not hold the church captive"),[19] Dr Johann Ernst, at that time the registrar (or actuarius, "aktuarius") of the Synod of the Dutch Reformed Church argues that some good and honest reasons can be given for these changes to article 44. For our purposes here, let me recall the first two, and in my view most important, reasons that he mentions. Ernst points, firstly, to the fact that URCSA has a similar church order article. This is indeed the case, since article 11 of the Church Order of URCSA states, among other things, that General Synod shall deal with all matters pertaining to "the doctrinal standards of the church, on condition that any change to the doctrinal standards of the church can only be made after two-thirds of all the congregations have decided in favour thereof". The Church Order of URCSA therefore also requires that two thirds of the congregations decide in favour of the change to the doctrinal standards (although this specific article does not mention that a further decision is required by the regional synods or specify the size of the majority needed within congregations for the change to come into effect). It should be added, though, that there is still a difference between the requirements of the DRC and URCSA (as seen in the relevant articles in their church orders). The second reason that Ernst mentions why changes were made to article 44 in the DRC Church Order is of special importance. He refers to a ruling by the Appeal Court in 1998 that suggested that each congregation (via its representation in the regional synod) should have a say in the possible change of the confession by the General Synod. General Synod does not have the authority to change a congregation's nature or identity. During this case Judge W Viviers then made an important side remark (*obiter dictum*): "That one remaining congregation member can form the congregation, must be taken into account in the current situation, given the stipulations of the Church Order according to which the Church Council is the authoritative body that acts on behalf of the congregation".[20] It the light of this remark by Judge Viviers the General Task Group for Legal Affairs ("Algemene Taakspan Regte", or ATR) obtained some legal advice that suggested that if the Church Order does not make provision for majority decisions, then unanimity ("eenstemmigheid") might be required for making changes. In order therefore to avoid a situation in which one remaining church member can have a right to the church's assets, the Church Order was changed in 2004 to read as it currently stands.

This decision has indeed made it harder to amend the confession of the church and has complicated the process for the DRC to accept the Belhar Confession as part of its confessional base. According to Ernst, this longer route is, however, not necessarily less desirable. As he argues in the conclusion of his article in *Die Kerkbode*: "It cannot be viewed as unfair that a large majority of church councils be in favour of weighty matters ... After the Dutch Reformed Church family is united, there must be only one church denomination with a legitimate common confessional base. In this regard the Church Order, with sensitivity to both sides, points towards the responsible path".[21] It needs to be said, as also pointed out by Ernst, that neither the majority nor the minority is necessarily right, hence the need for the majority and the minority to be open to the Word of God in a process of continual openness to reform in the light of

---

19  Ernst, J, "Tweederdebesluit hou kerk nie gevange", *Die Kerkbode* (2011).
20  Quoted by Ernst in "Tweederdebesluit hou kerk nie gevange", 19.
21  Ernst, "Tweederdebesluit hou kerk nie gevange", 19.

Scripture. This implies, at least, that there must always be an openness to the process of reflecting on the confession of the church, even after a decision-making process by the synods or congregations has been completed.

Article 44 of the DRC Church Order thus requires a specific process for amending the church's doctrinal standards and, at the meeting of the DRC General Synod in 2011, the decision was taken to follow this route. Moreover, the process to make the Belhar Confession part of the confessional base of the DRC in a church-orderly way requires some carefully crafted regulations regarding the process. Some important questions come to the fore in this context, such as: According to what process should concurrence and approbation be sought? In this regard Synod accepted a proposal to add the following footnote to article 44.1: "For the way in which church councils should handle the decision regarding the amendment of the confessional base of the DR Church in order to attain agreement and approbation from congregations, see Church Order Regulation 6:6". In addition, the new heading of Regulation 6 in the Church Order is changed to read "Regulation for the Multiplication, Combination, Unification and Amalgamation of Congregations, and for the Formation of a New Denomination". Under Regulation 6.6 on "The Formation of a New Denomination" the process of seeking agreement and approbation is described in detail.[22] Against the backdrop of these remarks, one can attend in more detail to the decision taken at the DRC General Synod meeting in October 2013.

## 5. WHAT HAPPENED AT THE GENERAL SYNOD OF 2013?

At the General Synod meeting of the DRC in Port Elizabeth the decision was taken to propose a process to change article 1 of the Church Order. The church orderly way to do this, as indicated already, requires that two thirds of all church councils and all the regional synods accept with a two-third majority the proposed change to the confession base (article 1).

The current article 1 reads:

> The Dutch Reformed Church is based on the Bible as the holy and infallible Word of God. The doctrine which the Church confesses in agreement with the Word of God, is expressed in the Forms of Unity as formulated at the Synod of Dort in 1618-19, namely the thirty-seven articles of the Belgic Confession, the Heidelberg Catechism and the five Canons of Dort.[23]

This article is short and has stood in this form since the constitution of the General Synod of the DRC in 1962. It is important that church order articles be precise and don't try to say too much. But is it not here the case that too little is said? If one compares article 1 of the current DRC Church Order with, for instance, the corresponding articles in the Church Order of the *Protestantse Kerk in Nederland* (PKN) or the URCSA Church Order, one is immediately struck by the fact that there is no explicit reference to the Ecumenical Symbols (The Apostles' Creed, The Nicene Creed, The Athanasian Creed). I would like to argue that a revision is needed in this

---

22  Agenda, Dutch Reformed Church General Synod (2011), ATR Report 2.5.2.
23  Dutch Reformed Church, Church Order (2007).

regard that makes it much more evident that the confession of the church stands in continuity with the "catholic" church ("die algemene Christelike kerk") of the ages. This seems of special importance, given, among other things, the way in which a certain mindset of ecumenical isolationism has haunted the DRC in the past. The current article 1 of the DRC Church order does not sufficiently safeguard, in my view, against the danger of atomising and absolutising the 16$^{th}$- and 17$^{th}$-century Reformed confessions. It order to challenge such a danger, it is important to affirm the link between the Three Formulae of Unity and the Ecumenical Symbols, as well as to affirm that – within the Reformed tradition – confessions are never fixed and that new confessions can always arise. In this regard article 2.3 in the URCSA Church Order highlights well the idea that the Reformed tradition is a living tradition and that Reformed churches are not simply communities that have confessions, but that they are *confessing* communities: "The Uniting Reformed Church in Southern Africa accepts that it has not completed its task of confessing the faith. Changed circumstances and a better understanding of God's Word in the future may lead to the acceptance of further articles of faith, or the revision of existing articles of faith". Therefore it is worthwhile, in my view, for the DRC to consider stating more explicitly the reference to the Ecumenical Symbols in article 1, as well as to emphasise the fact that the church is always open to the possibility of new confessions or revisions to existing confessions. The new proposed article does this, in some way at least, but also does something else that has evoked both strong approval and strong critique.

The proposed new article 1 reads (in an unofficial translation):

> 1. The Dutch Reformed Church is founded on ("gegrond op") the Bible as the holy and infallible Word of God.
>
> 2.1. The faith that the church confesses in accordance with the Word of God, is expressed in the ecumenical confessions, namely the Apostles' Creed, the Nicene Creed and the Athanasian Creed; as well as the Three Formulae of Unity, namely the Belgic Confession, the Heidelberg Catechism and the Canons of Dort.
>
> 2.2. The Belhar confession is part of the confessional base of the church, in such a manner that there is space for congregation members, office bearers, and church assemblies that confess the Belhar confession as in accordance with the Word of God, as well as for congregation members, office bearers, and church assemblies that do not want to underwrite the Belhar Confession as a confession.
>
> 3. The church accepts that her calling to confess her faith is a continuing task, and that the broadening of her confessional base should be done without compulsion ("sonder dwang").

This decision is viewed as a consensus decision, but I think it is safe to say that this decision was a pragmatic decision that was the result of a compromise in order to keep the process of making the Belhar confession part of the DRC's confessional base on track. It should also be said that the DRC leadership showed a commitment to the process, making clear statements and providing the necessary resources for the process. Nevertheless as the process unfolded after the 2013 General Synod meeting, the church-orderly requirements could not be met, resulting in the fact that even this proposal to change the church order to make some room for the Belhar Confession as part of the church's confessional base did not receive the required support.

## 6. SOME CONCLUDING REMARKS

Let me make three brief concluding remarks about what I see as important lessons to be learned from the history of the reception (or non-reception) of the Belhar Confession in the Dutch Reformed Church.

### a. *The need for the greater alignment of ecclesial, theological and church polity discourse.*

One should be careful not to oppose the need for carefully crafted church-order articles and regulations (that are also sensitive to juridical aspects) with the need for responsible theological speech. Theological speech (also on Reformed ecclesiology and the Reformed Confession) that does not impact on church polity remains abstract, while Reformed church polity discourse that is not informed by Reformed theological insights remains reductive. It is therefore important not to juxtapose uncritical church polity discourse and theological discourse, but to see church polity discourse in itself as deeply theological, albeit with its own particularity. In the process we should further be aware of the way power and institutional control function in our discourse. One way to ensure the theological integrity of church polity discourse is to continually seek the appropriate relationship between Scripture, Confession and church polity documents, such as church orders. In our compilation, revision and appropriation of church orders the question of an adequate theological hermeneutics remains of paramount importance.[24] Reformed Church orders should be the distillation or concentration of the best insights from a Reformed theological, and in particular ecclesiological, perspective. Church orders are our ecclesiology taking on concrete form; they mirror the confession and they are also instruments for the church to be a confessing church.[25]

### b. *The need not to settle for a compromise as a permanent solution, hence the need for the church as truth-seeking community to engage in continuous processes of discernment in the light of the Bible, guided by an adequate historical and theological hermeneutic.*

In my view the failure of the Dutch Reformed Church to receive unconditionally and with gratitude the Belhar Confession as a gift has done much harm to the integrity of this denomination, and has robbed it of an important theological resource for comfort and orientation. It is probably still true that the unconditional acceptance of the Belhar Confession and the uncompromising commitment to visible unity within the Dutch Reformed family of church remain the acid test for the Dutch Reformed Church to indicate the integrity and credibility of the way it is dealing

---

24 Cf. Van de Beek, A, "Hermeneutiek van het kerkrecht" in Van 't Spijker, W and Van Drimmelen, LC, *Inleiding tot de studie van het kerkrecht* (Kampen: Kok, 1991), 59.
25 Cf. Koffeman, L J, *Het goed recht van de kerk: Een theologische inleiding op het kerkrecht* (Kampen: Kok, 2009), 23.

with its own complex and ambivalent past. It can be argued that the attempt to accept the Belhar Confession by way of changing article 1 of the DRC Church Order is a step in the right direction, but it still does raise some ecclesiological questions. It might be possible to justify a compromise, but one should be careful to speak about an ethics of compromise. Compromise can only be viewed as part of a broader ethics of responsibility. This is in my view the only way forward with regard to the proposed change to article 1. It cannot be the end of the road, but should be viewed as a stop – and maybe even a detour – on the road towards theologically responsible ecclesiological statements on the church's confessional base.

### c. The need to challenge reductive concepts of unity, reconciliation and justice.

The Belhar Confession speaks in its three central articles about unity, reconciliation and justice. There is a danger that we can work with a reductive understanding of these concepts, and this is not merely a temptation for the Dutch Reformed Church. We can view unity as exclusively the unity within my cultural or language group, and in order to protect this unity we lose sight of the unity of the one body of Christ. In similar manner our commitment to reconciliation can be abstracted from a truthful engagement with the past and a hopeful search for a common future. Furthermore, our focus on (ecclesial) survival can blind us to injustices resulting from our will to survive. Thus maybe the value of the Belhar Confession (also for the Dutch Reformed Church) is not merely to challenge us to believe in the importance of unity, reconciliation and justice, but rather to help us unmask the false forms that these notions take on in our midst today.

www.ingramcontent.com/pod-product-compliance
Lightning Source LLC
Chambersburg PA
CBHW080222170426
43192CB00015B/2725